What is...
THE FARM HOLIDAY BUREAU?

In a nutshell, it's a national network of farming and country people offering a range of quality accommodation, plus a glimpse of life on a farm.

The Bureau is the result of a partnership between the Royal Agricultural Society of England, the English Tourist Board, the Ministry of Agriculture (ADAS) and Farmers Weekly, Britain's leading agricultural magazine.

In 1983, these organisations recognised that tourism in the countryside was becoming increasingly popular and formed the FARM HOLIDAY BUREAU to draw this scattered 'industry' under one umbrella.

With nearly 1,000 members, the Bureau has established itself as a sign of good value and quality the length and breadth of the country. Its now familiar symbol is being sought out by tourists, holidaymakers and business people looking for a reliable seal of approval, and one that is endorsed by the National Tourist Board's Inspection Scheme.

The Society's offices at the National Agricultural Centre house the Bureau's headquarters, where a permanent staff is involved in the day-to-day running of the Bureau.

CONTENTS	Page No.
Where to go at a glance (Index & Map)	2
How to use this Guide	4
ENGLAND	9
WALES	234
SCOTLAND	271
NORTHERN IRELAND	280
Index of ♿ DISABLED WELCOME Establishments	303

WHERE TO GO AT A GLANCE

Area		Page No.	Area		Page No.
	ENGLAND				
1	Cornwall	9	40	Cheshire	180
2	Upper Tamar	17	41	Ribble Valley	186
3	NW Devon	20	42	Vale of Lune	189
4	N Devon	23	43	S Pennines	192
5	Heart of Devon	28	44	Yorkshire Dales	195
6	W Devon	30	45	Herriot Country	198
7	Cream of Devon	32	46	Rydale	204
8	Dartmoor & S Devon	35	47	Yorks Coast	206
9	Moor to Shore	41	48	S Lakeland	211
10	E Devon	44	49	Eden Valley	217
11	Exmoor & Somerset	49	50	Hadrian's Wall	222
12	W & Mid Somerset	54	51	Teesdale	226
13	N Somerset	57	52	Northumberland	230
14	Bath & Wiltshire	61			
15	Dorset	64			
16	Heart of Dorset	68		**WALES**	
17	Isle of Wight	72			
18	Hampshire	77	53	Pembrokeshire	234
19	Sussex & Surrey	79	54	Dyfed	238
20	Kent	84	55	Ceredigion	241
21	Essex	89	56	Gwent	245
22	Suffolk & Norfolk	93	57	Brecon & Radnor	247
23	Cambridgeshire	98	58	Mid Wales	250
24	Hertfordshire	98	59	Heart of Wales	253
25	Bedfordshire	99	60	Tanat	257
26	Thames Valley	101	61	Clwyd	259
27	Cotswolds	106	62	Snowdonia	263
28	Herefordshire	114	63	Lleyn Peninsula	267
29	Worcestershire	120			
30	Warwickshire	127			
31	S Shropshire	134	64	**SCOTLAND**	271
32	N Shropshire	139			
33	Vale of Trent	145		**N IRELAND**	
34	Peak & Moorlands	152			
35	Dovedale	163	65	Down	280
36	Northamptonshire	168	66	Antrim	288
37	Leicestershire	171	67	Londonderry	294
38	Sherwood Forest	174	68	Tyrone	297
39	Lincolnshire	177	69	Fermanagh	300

2

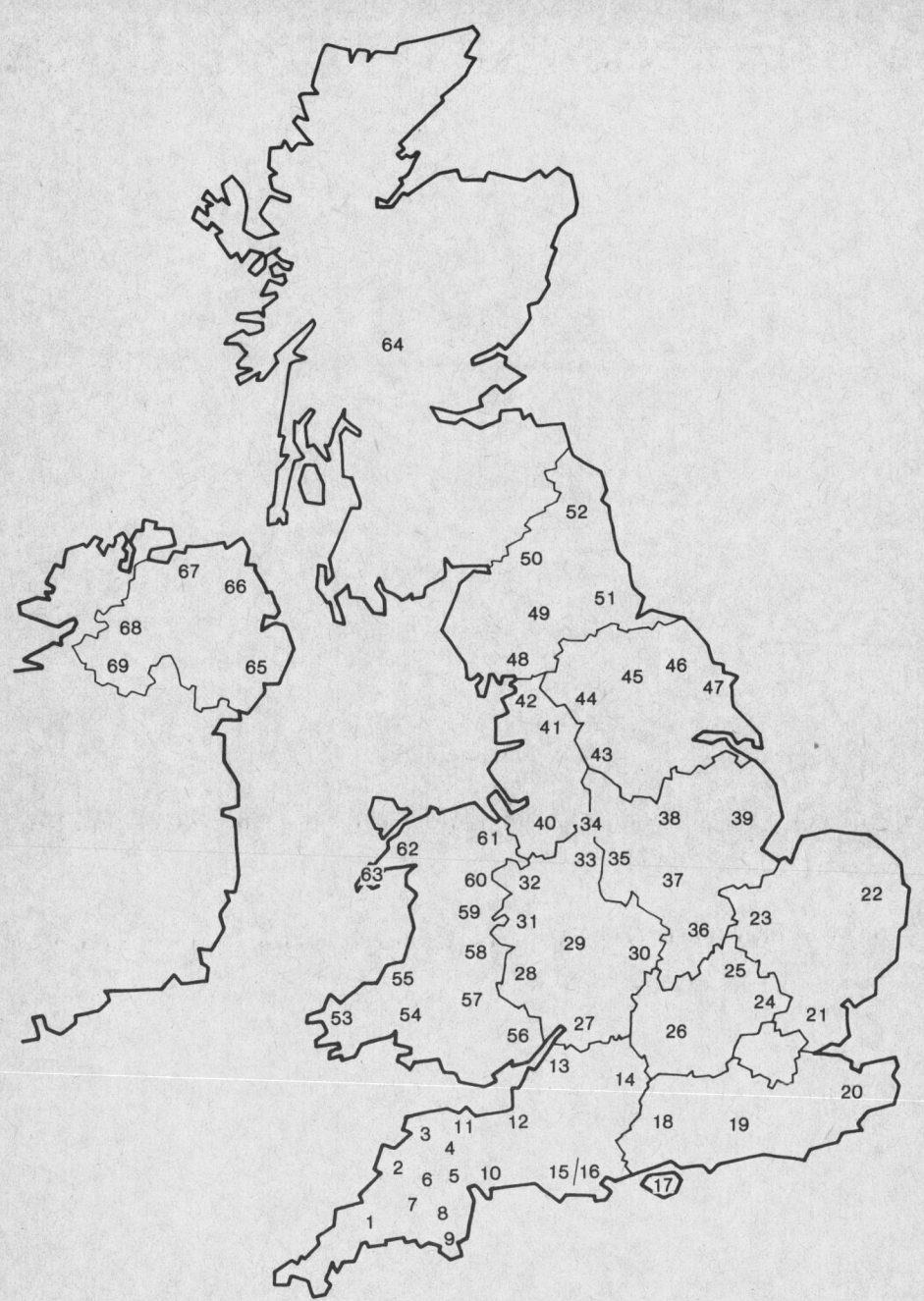

3

HOW TO USE THIS GUIDE

Staying on a Farm

The majority of holidays in this guide are located on working farms, estates, smallholdings and nurseries. A few are "country houses" (indicated by (CH) in the heart of the countryside, often adjacent to, but not on, a working farm.

On many farms, visitors can — after checking with the farmer — walk around the farm and even help with chores. A number of farms have special trails for visitors to follow. If you are taking children, ask whether livestock are kept and if it is possible for children to see them. Always check with the farmer before walking round and never allow children to play in the farmyard.

About the Farm Holiday Groups

The bureau is built up of over 70 Farm Holiday Groups — each chapter in the guide (except Scotland) represents a different local group. These groups are well organised, have tight admission criteria, are constantly exchanging ideas and comparing notes to improve the service they offer. Many groups have a Vacancy Secretary whose name is given at the beginning of each chapter and who can help you to find accommodation within the area. In other groups, there is a Contact Secretary who cannot help with bookings but can advise you on the most suitable accommodation for your needs.

The groups represent a national network. If you are touring, most hosts will be able to recommend you to stay with a bureau member in another area.

Types of accommodation

(FH) Farmhouse Bed and Breakfast (B&B) and sometimes Evening Meal (EM) on a working farm, estate, smallholding or nursery.

(CH) Country House Bed and Breakfast (B&B) and sometimes Evening Meal (EM) not on a working farm.

(SC) Self-catering in cottages, apartments or wings, chalets, static caravans.

(TV) Tents and/or Touring Caravans (T-tents, V-caravans). Some sites only take tents, some only five caravans (check: these may be restricted to Caravan Club members). Other sites are larger and offer a range of amenities.

Prices

Please check all prices at the time of booking and confirm what is included in the price, e.g. if self catering, does price include linen hire, is electricity metered? Change of circumstances since the information was printed may cause fluctuation in price.

Where a range of prices is given for B&B, the highest may apply to a single person staying one night, the lowest to a family staying a week in a family room. For self-catering the range usually indicates the low to high season variation.

B&B	Bed and Breakfast. Price per adult per night.
EM	Evening Meal. Price per adult.
SC	Self-catering. Price per unit per week.
TV	Tents/Caravans. Price per pitch per night.

Will they take children?

The symbol ⌘ indicates which establishments take children and the minimum age accepted, e.g. ⌘ (6) — children over 6 years old only. Some establishments have family rooms (a double plus two single beds) enabling the family to share the same room often at a reduced cost. Check whether there are reductions for children, give ages and any special requirements.

What about my pet 🐕 ?

Where livestock are kept many farms do not take dogs. If you wish to take your dog or other pets look for the 🐕 but check before you arrive — your Chihuahua may be welcome, but not your Great Dane!

Dogs are not usually allowed in the bedrooms and may need to sleep in your car or in specially provided kennels or stables. Make sure that your dog is fully vaccinated, well behaved and is kept on a lead when near livestock.

What happens if I am disabled ♿ ?

The establishments have let us know whether they can accommodate the disabled and the less physically able visitor. Please check before booking as **we have not limited the symbol to just those taking wheelchairs but have included establishments with ground floor bedrooms stair lifts and other aids to help you enjoy a holiday in the country.**

Standards and Inspections

Properties in this guide have been inspected by the National Tourist Board. As a basic requirement, all provide a high standard of cleanliness, courtesy and service and are well maintained. In addition, the properties have been classified according to the range of facilities and services provided, or graded according to the quality of the accommodation.

The only exception to this is self-catering in England which, as a rule, has been inspected by the local group.

Classifications:

Applied		Awaiting inspection at the time of going to print.
Listed	(B&B)	Good, comfortable accommodation which may also offer some of the facilities offered by crowned properties.
♛	(B&B)	Also: washbasins in bedrooms, guests' bathroom and lounge.
♛♛	(B&B)	Also: morning/evening tea or coffee facilities, lounge separate from dining room.
♛♛♛	(B&B)	Also: unlimited access to accommodation, one-third of bedrooms with private bathrooms, fixed/central heating.
♛♛♛♛	(B&B)	Also: bedrooms with radio, TV and telephone, threequarters with private bathrooms.
Listed	(SC)	Good, comfortable self-catering accommodation sufficiently furnished for the maximum advertised number of occupants.
♛	(SC)	Also: fridge, access to iron and board and cot if needed.
♛♛	(SC)	Also: three-ring cooker, availability of TV, at least one bedroom without bunk beds.
♛♛♛	(SC)	Also: colour TV, four-ring cooker, groceries provided for your arrival, linen and towels available for hire/free.
♛♛♛♛	(SC)	Also: washing machine and tumble dryer.
♛♛♛♛♛	(SC)	Also: shower and bath, freezer, dishwasher, food processor, hair dryer, garden furniture.
Approved		Accommodation is at least the minimum standard required by the Tourist Board.

Grading

When grading the accommodation, quality is the keynote. The grades represent an assessment of the standard of interior furnishing, furniture, decoration, equipment, exterior, grounds and — for B&B — friendly welcome and food.

1 Dragon   Standard
2 Dragons   Approved
3 Dragons   Good   Grades given to Self-catering in Wales
4 Dragons   Very Good

5 Dragons	Excellent	
Approved	Acceptable	Grades given to Bed & Breakfast
Commended	Good	and Self-catering
Highly Commended	Excellent	in Scotland
Grade B		Grading used in Northern Ireland. Grade A Guest Houses
Grade A		provide more facilities (washbasins in all rooms, additional bathrooms, full board) and are judged to be of a higher grade than Grade B Guest Houses.

Your arrival and departure

As most of the holidays listed are on busy working farms, please do not expect to arrive before **4.30 pm unless pre-arranged** with your host. If you turn up unexpectedly there may be no-one around to greet you. At the end of your stay you will usually be expected to depart by **10.30 am.**

Can I stay in the farmhouse during the day?

Some farms are happy for B&B visitors to remain in the house all day, **but check before booking** as this is not practical on many farms and often guests are asked to be out of the farmhouse between **10.30 am and 4.30 pm.**

Evening Meals

The time of the Evening Meal varies from farm to farm and sometimes a special high tea is served for the children. Make sure you give your host ample warning (12 hours) if you require an evening meal.

If you need a special diet, have an allergy or other special requirements, check **before you book** that this can be accommodated. Farms are not hotels — nor do they wish to be — and cannot fulfil special requirements without prior notice. Remember, you could be staying in someone's home.

Smoking

Many farms ask their guests to refrain from smoking in the bedrooms. Some farms are non-smoking establishments.

Fire Safety

A few of the establishments listed in this guide are subject to the requirements of the Fire Precautions Act of 1971 and have a valid fire certificate. As a general rule, this means that fire doors, smoke detectors, adequate means of escape are provided if the B&B accommodation sleeps more than six guests on the first floor, or where any guest sleeps on the second, or attic floor.

Making a booking

Simply write to or telephone the establishment of your choice. If you telephone, remember that the person may be milking or out in the fields so give them time to answer. Better still — and cheaper — make your call in the evening.

Use the check list on Page 7 when making your booking.

If the establishment is booked for the period you want, you will find that they will be able to suggest other accommodation within their group.

Confirming a booking

Confirm your booking in writing, specifying what you have booked and the price you expect to pay, enclosing a deposit if required. Either ask your host or travel agent about cancellation insurance and read the section in this guide on Cancellation and Insurance.

Cancellation

Once you have agreed a booking, whether by letter or telephone, you have made a legally binding contract with the proprietor. If you cancel a reservation, fail to take up the accommodation or leave prematurely, the proprietor may be entitled to compensation if the accommodation cannot be re-let for all or a good part of the booked period. If a deposit has been paid, it is likely to be forfeited and an additional payment demanded.

However, no such claim can be made by the proprietor until after the booked period, during which every effort should be made to re-let it. Any circumstances which might lead to a repudiation of a contract may also need to be taken into account and, in the case of a dispute, legal advice should be sought by both parties.

It is in your interest to advise the proprietors immediately if you have to change your travel plans, cancel a booking or leave prematurely, and to take out appropriate insurance.

Insurance

Travel and holiday insurance protection policies are available quite cheaply and safeguard you in the event of cancellation or curtailment of your stay. Your insurance company or travel agent can advise you further and most bureau members have details.

Insurance of personal property: check that valuables such as jewellery, video and other cameras are covered by your household insurance when you take them away on holiday. Some policies only extend limited cover and the proprietors cannot accept liability for any loss or damage to your property however caused.

BOOKING CHECK LIST

★ Mention the Farm Holiday Bureau.
★ Give arrival and departure dates.
★ Specify accommodation needed and any particular requirements (twin beds, child's cot, ground floor bedroom).
★ Check and confirm prices and other details, particularly if you are disabled or wish to take children or pets with you.
★ If needed, check that your special diet can be provided.
★ Arrange time of arrival.
★ If applicable, check whether access to B&B accommodation is restricted between 10.30 am and 4.30 pm.
★ Ask if, and when, a deposit is required and for how long a provisional booking will be held.
★ Check method and date of payment.
★ Give your host your name, address and telephone number.
★ Ask your host to send you details of holiday cancellation insurance AND directions to the farm.
★ CONFIRM YOUR BOOKING IN WRITING.

Finding your farm

Many proprietors have given their OS references, which can be used to locate the property on a road atlas using the OS Grid.

Proprietors will give you directions when you book and may send you a map. If you have problems finding the farm, STOP AND TELEPHONE. Don't keep driving around getting lost!

As you near the property, look for the Farm Holiday Bureau Member sign hanging outside.

Comments and Complaints

If a problem occurs, tell your host immediately, allowing the problem to be resolved there and then. It is usually very difficult to deal effectively with a complaint if it is reported at a later date. If your host has failed to resolve the problem, write to the Farm Holiday Bureau, National Agricultural Centre, Stoneleigh, Kenilworth, Warks CV8 2LZ.

Compliments

The bureau receives many complimentary letters from satisfied guests. If you have enjoyed a special something during your stay which makes you think "wouldn't it be nice if every place did this" — we would like to hear about it. Please write to the Farm Holiday Bureau at the address given above.

Enjoying the countryside

Ask you host about the best places to visit and for directions to those delightful country pubs. If you need a local guide, walk or nature trail, or want details or a guide to place of interest, visit or write to the nearest Tourist Information Centre. A free "Directory of TICs" is available from Department D, Bromells Road, Clapham, London SW4 0BJ.

Walk a Farm Trail

All over the country, the public can walk special farm trails and see how wildlife exists happily in the midst of commercial farming.

Many of these trails have come to light as a result of the National Farm Trails Competition run by Bayer UK (Agrochemicals Division) and the Farming and Wildlife Advisory Group to show how farmers carry out their business while caring for and conserving the countryside.

Ask you hosts if they, or any of the farms in the area, have a farm trail or ask the local TIC for a copy of the "Walk a Farm Trail" leaflet.

And lastly`...

Do take suitable clothes such as wellies, jumpers and jeans to allow you to enjoy your stay in the country. As one farmer jests: "cows are messy creatures, even in summer!"

Published November 1987 by the Farm Holiday Bureau,
National Agricultural Centre, Stoneleigh, Kenilworth,
Warwickshire CV8 2LZ

Type set by the Birmingham Post and Mail and printed by Cradley Print PLC,
P.O. Box 34, Chester Road, Cradley Heath, Warley, West Midlands B64 6AB.
Designed by New Enterprise Publications, 212 Broad Street, Birmingham B15 1AY.
New illustrations by Jeff Platten

* Farm Holiday Bureau 1987
ISBN 1-869952-01-4

The information contained in this guide has been published in good faith on the basis of the information submitted to the Farm Holiday Bureau by the proprietors of the premises listed. These proprietors are current members of the Farm Holiday Bureau, and have paid for their entries in this guide.

Whilst every effort has been made to ensure accuracy in this publication, the Farm Holiday Bureau cannot guarantee the accuracy of the information in this guide and accepts no responsibility for any error or misrepresentation.

All liability for loss, disappointment, negligence or other damage caused by reliance on the information contained in this guide, or in the event of bankruptcy, or liquidation, or cessation of trade of any company, individual or firm mentioned is hereby excluded.

CORNWALL

CORNWALL

Cornwall is a unique part of this country with a coastline of 326 miles. The north coast has wonderful stretches of firm golden sands and soaring cliffs. Many beaches afford surfing, and further north you can visit the Harbour at Boscastle and the cliff top castle Tintagel with its Arthurian connections.

Newquay with its beaches stretching for seven miles, sheltered coves, and shops make it a premier attraction in the north. St Ives is another surfing honeypot which has great charm, attracting artists for so long.

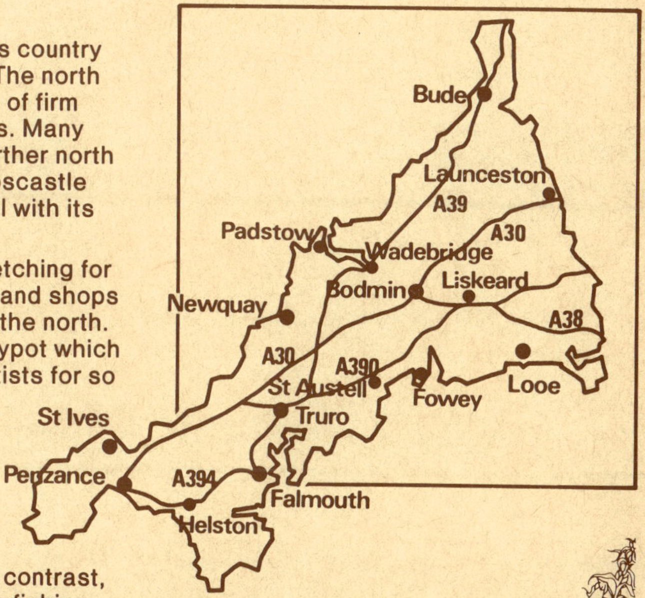

The south coast is a complete contrast, wooded estuaries, picturesque fishing ports and popular resorts. Penzance with its vivid colours, has wonderful views across the bay to St. Michaels Mount. Here are excellent facilities for sailing and deep-sea fishing, as there are at Fowey, overlooking its busy estuary harbour. St. Mawes is a charming, unspoilt village across the Fal from Falmouth, Mevagissey, Polperro and Looe are fine examples of traditional Cornish fishing villages.

Inland, Cornwall has its attractions. To the east of Bodmin, the county town, are the open uplands known as Bodmin Moor with the county's highest peaks at Rough Tor and Brown Willy. The historic market town of Launceston is dominated by its ruined castle.

All the properties within this section — including self-catering and camping/caravan sites — have been inspected and approved by the Cornwall Tourist Board.

VACANCY SECRETARIES:
B&B — Jean Pengelly
(0326) 72271
Self Catering — Pam Mount
(08403) 233

(FH) TREFFRY FARM Lanhydrock, Bodmin, Cornwall, PL30 5AF

Pat Smith
Tel:-(0208) 4405
Open Mar-Oct
B&B £9.50-£10.50
EM £5
Sleeps 6

Historic Georgian farmhouse on 170 acre dairy farm in beautiful countryside adjoining National Trust, Lanhydrock. Guests guaranteed a warm welcome with spacious well furnished, centrally heated accommodation, own lounge & separate dining room. Ideal location for touring Cornwall & only 7 miles from nearest beach. Visitors welcome to explore & help on the farm. Pony rides. One double/family room with ensuite shower, 1 twin & 1 single, all with washbasins. OS Ref SX 078637

(FH) POLSUE MANOR FARM Tresillian, Truro, Cornwall, TR2 4BP

Geraldine Holliday
Tel:-(087252) 234
Open Apr-Oct
B&B £8.50
EM £5
Sleeps 6

The farmhouse set in 160 acres of farmland lies above the village of Tresillian overlooking the tidal river. It commands views over one of the prettiest parts of Cornwall and is centrally situated between the Atlantic and Channel coasts, an ideal touring centre with delightful country walks. We offer good home prepared food and a comfortable and relaxed frendly atmosphere. OS Ref SW 858463

(FH) POLHORMON FARM Mullion, Helston, Cornwall, TR12 7JE

Mrs Alice Harry
Tel:-(0326) 240304
Open Easter-Sep
B&B £7-£8.50
Sleeps 6

A dairy farm by the sea offering old fashioned comfort with lovely coastal views. Sandy beaches, fishing, golf, superb cliff walks, birdwatching, sailing on the Helford River. Set in unspoilt countryside, Mullion has good pubs, a 14th Century church, harbour, shops, cafes & restaurants. 2 family rooms, 1 double & 1 twin. TV lounge, separate WC & access to rooms at all times. OS Ref SW 676 198

(FH) SHEPHERDS FARM Newlyn East, Newquay, Cornwall, TR8 5NW

Heather Jill Harvey
Tel:-(087254) 340
Open all year
B&B £8-£10
EM £4
5 bedrooms in both farmhouse & annexe

A warm welcome awaits you at Shepherds, a large working farm. Situated between Newquay and Perranporth close to the best sandy beaches of Cornwall. House pleasantly decorated and furnished. All rooms H/C, half en-suite. Large dining room, comfortable lounges. Pony to ride. Games room, with pool and snooker. Good home cooking with personal service. Tea making facilities. OS Ref SX 816545

(FH) LONGSTONE FARM Trenear, Helston, Cornwall, TR13 OHG

Gillian Lawrance
Tel:-(0326) 572483
Open Feb-Nov
B&B £8.50
EM £4
Sleeps 10

A warm welcome awaits you at Longstone Farm, a 62 acre dairy farm situated in the centre of peaceful countryside in West Cornwall - ideal for touring, beaches and visiting many holiday attractions including Poldark Mine, Cornwall Aero Park and Leisure Centre. Also horseriding nearby. Modernised farmhouse all bedrooms have H & C, good farmhouse fare served, separate tables in dining room and large sun lounge/playroom. OS Ref SW 661319

(FH) TRECOLLAS FARM Altarnun, Launceston, Cornwall, PL15 7SN

Gladys Baker
Tel:-(0566) 86283
Open Mar-Sep
B&B £8-£9
EM £5
Sleeps 6

Homely and comfortable accommodation, H/C in rooms, tea/coffee making facilities in Breakfast room. Near Bodmin Moor, lovely for walks or drives. About 10 miles from Tintagel, 2 miles from the picturesque village of Altarnun with its beautiful church known as the Cathedral of the Moor. Reasonably priced evening meals available within 1 mile. OS Ref SX 214837

Cornwall ENGLAND

(FH) TREWEN FARM   Budockwater, Falmouth, Cornwall, TR11 5DZ

Kathleen Hutchings
Tel:-(0326) 73369
Open Mar-Oct
B&B   £7-£9
Sleeps 6

Trewen Farm house on a 145 acre dairy farm with wooded walks and sea views. Two miles Falmouth a beach resort, boating/yatching centre. One mile golf course, 3½m Helford River famous for Frenchman's Creek, 4 beaches within 2 miles. Good, reasonably priced eating places within easy reach. OS Ref SW 778315

(FH) TREBAH FARM   Mawnan Smith, Falmouth, Cornwall, TR11 5JZ

Jean Kessell
Tel:-(0326) 250295
Open Mar-Nov
B&B   £8-£9
EM   £4
Sleeps 6

Guests receive a warm welcome at our comfortable & peaceful farmhouse set in 150 acres of beautiful countryside, adjoining Nat. Trust Gardens & the renowned Helford River where a variety of watersports are available. There are miles of scenic coastline to walk with numerous watering holes, or come back to good home produced & cooked food. OS Ref SW 768 276

(FH) MANUELS FARM   Newquay, Cornwall, TR8 4NY

Jean Wilson
Tel:-(0637) 873577
Closed Xmas-New Year
B&B   £6.50-£8
EM   £4.50-£6
Sleeps 12

Manuels is a 44 acre working farm situated in a sheltered valley, 2 miles inland from Newquay. We offer the peace of the countryside with the charm of a traditional 17th Century Cornish farmhouse. Emphasis is placed on comfort, good fresh food and a relaxed atmosphere. 3 families accommodated, children especially welcome to help on the farm. Pets galore, large gardens, games room and free babysitting. OS Ref SW 839601

(FH) TREGINEGAR FARMHOUSE   St. Merryn, Padstow, Cornwall, PL28 8PT

Wendy Pollard
Tel:-(0841) 520117
Open Easter, May-Oct
B&B   £8-£11
EM   £4
Sleeps 12

Victorian farmhouse with traditional slate fireplaces. Wash-hand basins, tea/coffee making facilities, heating to all bedrooms. Launderette, TV lounge, small swimming pool. Generous farmhouse food! Situated on a 200 acre working farm with sea and coastline views. Seven golden sandy bays only minutes away by car. Excellent amenities for golf, horseriding, watersports, fishing, birdwatching, coastal walking, sight seeing. OS Ref SX 883713

(FH) TREGONDALE FARM   Menheniot, Liskeard, Cornwall, PL14 3RG

Stephanie Rowe
Tel:-(0579) 42407
Closed Xmas
B&B   £9-£10
EM   £4.50
Sleeps 6

Tregondale, a mixed farm of 180 acres, ideally situated close to coast, Moors, National Trust properties, golf, fishing, Cornish pub, heated swimming pool, children's amusements. The characteristic farmhouse provides a high standard of comfort with home cooked produce. Three double bedrooms, H/C. Surrounded by a walled garden including picnic table, swing, see-saw, tarmac parking area. Picturesque walks and farm pony. OS Ref SX 293643

(FH) GOONHOSKYN   Summer Court, Newquay, Cornwall, TR8 4PP

Toyah Richards
Tel:-(0637) 510226
Open Mar-Dec
B&B   £8.50-£10.50
EM   £5-50
Sleeps 6

(6)

Comfortable farmhouse with rose garden, quiet & peaceful holiday. Centrally situated for visiting National Trust properties, touring & the beach. Traditionally prepared food with many Cornish flavours. The bedrooms have H/C, TVs, tea making facilities. Regret no facilities for children under 6yrs & regret no pets. OS Ref SW 871 573

(FH) ENNYS St Hilary, Penzance, Cornwall, TR20 9BZ

Susan White
Tel:-(0736) 740262
Open Mar-Nov
B&B   £10-£12.50
EM   £8
Sleeps 6

Beautiful 16th Century manor on a 50 acre arable/beef farm in idyllically peaceful surroundings. Excellent food from our own produce, comfort guaranteed. Within easy reach of many lovely beaches. Log fires, bread baked daily. 3 double bedrooms, 2 en-suite facilities, 1 with romantic 4-poster bed. 2 bathrooms. Special weekly rates. OS Ref SW 555328

(FH) TREWORGIE BARTON Crackington Haven, Bude, Cornwall, EX23 ONL

Pam Mount
Tel:-(08403) 233
Open May-Sep
B&B   £8.50-£10
EM   £6
Sleeps 6

A warm welcome awaits you at Treworgie Barton, our 221 acre beef & sheep farm situated at the end of a secluded lane. The farm has 50 acres of natural woodland, through which trails have been laid & is 2 miles from the sandy surfing cove of Crackington Haven & 10 miles from Bude. The 16th Century farmhouse has 2 bedrooms & 2 bathrooms. Excellent farmhouse food is our speciality. OS Ref SX 178969

(FH) TREVIGUE FARM Crackington Haven, Bude, Cornwall, EX23 OLQ

Janet Crocker
Tel:-(08403) 418
Open Easter-Sep
B&B   £11-£12
EM   £7.50
Sleeps 6

A 500 acre dairy and mixed farm with emphasis on imaginative cuisine. The farm is mentioned in the Domesday Book and the present house is early 16th Century built round a cobbled courtyard just a few hundred yards from spectacular National Trust cliffs and the footpath to an unspoilt beach. Flagstones, beams and huge fireplaces combine with comfort and en suite bathrooms. OS Ref SX 136952

(FH) TREWELLARD MANOR FARM Pendeen, Penzance, Cornwall, TR19 7SU

Marion Bailey
Tel:-(0736) 788526
Closed Xmas
B&B   £8.50
EM   £5.50
Sleeps 6
SC   £65-£135
Sleeps 4

The 270 acre mainly dairy farm situated in a superb coastal position twixt Lands End and St. Ives, offers a friendly relaxed atmosphere with seasonal log fires (& central heating). Use of solar heated swimming pool with many good beaches within easy reach, also horse riding available nearby. This is an outstanding area for walking either inland or the coast path. Also available SC cottage. OS Ref 374 338

(FH) DEGEMBRIS FARMHOUSE St. Newley East, Newquay, Cornwall, TR8 5HY

Kathy Woodley
Tel:-(0872) 510555
Open Easter-Oct
B&B   £8.50-£10   Listed
EM   From £4.50
Sleeps 12

A character farmhouse with recorded history as far back as 11th Century. The house is set on 165 acre farm overlooking beautiful wooded valley where pleasant walks may be enjoyed. All rooms with H&C & tea/coffee making facilities. We will provide you with comfort, home cooking & a taste of country life. Fire Certificate. OS Ref SW 852568

(FH) TREVORRIAN Trelill, Bodmin, Cornwall, PL30 3HZ

Margaret Kingdon
Tel:-(0208) 850434
Open Easter-Oct
B&B   £8-£9
EM   £5
Sleeps 2

(3)

Traditional farmhouse hospitality in this Victorian farmhouse on a 145 acre mixed farm - 4 miles from picturesque Port Isaac. Good home cooking assured using home produced food - soups, pates, rolls & clotted cream all freshly made. Separate lounge & dining rooms - colour TV. H/C in bedroom, also tea making facilities. Brian & Margaret Kingdon welcome you into their home OS Ref SX 043 792

Cornwall ENGLAND

(FH) WHEATLEY FARM   Maxworthy, Launceston, Cornwall, PL15 8LY

Valerie Griffin
Tel:-(056681) 232
Open Easter-Nov
B&B   £8-£11
EM   £5
Sleeps 12

Informal & relaxing family holidays are the speciality of our 160 acre dairy/mixed farm at Wheatley. Spacious Georgian styled farmhouse set in rolling Cornish countryside, near many beaches. We offer high standard of accommodation with family & ensuite rooms. Emphasis is placed on traditional farmhouse cooking, homemade rolls, soups, delicious desserts, served with our own clotted cream. OS Ref SX 245 929

(FH) CADUSCOTT   East Taphouse, Liskeard, Cornwall, PL14 4NG

Mrs Lindsay Pendray
Tel:-(0579) 20262
Open Easter-Sep
B&B   £9-£11.50
EM   £5
Sleeps 6

17th Century listed farmhouse, double room en-suite, adjoining twin-bedded room, comfortable accommodation, personal attention, facilities for children. 500 acre mixed dairy farm. Come in Spring to see the lambs, in Autumn to see the calves. 10m coast, 3m Moors. Visit National Trust properties/gardens, Thorburn's paintings, miniature railway, steam organs or Woolly Monkey Sanctuary. OS Ref SX 208639

(FH) LOWER CROAN   Sladesbridge, Wadebridge, Cornwall, PL27 6JH

Ruth Derryman
Tel:-(020884) 237
Closed Xmas-New Year
B&B   £10
EM   £5
Sleeps 10

Lower Croan, a mixed farm with 300 year old farmhouse set in rolling countryside with outstanding natural views offers a warm welcome and real country cooking. Large garden for children to play. Walking on Bodmin Moor, sailing at Rock and surfing at Polzeath & north coast beaches. Horse stabling for guests bringing their own horses. Pony rides for children. OS Ref SX 024715

(FH) HIGHER KERGILLIACK FARM   Budock, Falmouth, Cornwall, TR11 5PB

Jean Pengelly
Tel:-(0326) 72271
Open all year
B&B   £9-£10
EM   £6.50
Sleeps 6

18th Century granite built Georgian farmhouse. Former residence of Bishop of Exeter. 130 acre family farm with very friendly dog, ducks & calves. Rooms with washbasins & shaver points - 1 with en-suite shower - there are also 2 bathrooms, central heating, tea/coffee making facilities. Evening meals by prior arrangement. Farm walks. Coarse & trout fishing, sea angling. Baby sitting. OS Ref SW 780330

(FH) SKEWES FARM   Cury Cross Lanes, Helston, Cornwall, TR12 7BD

Sandra Boaden
Tel:-(0326) 240374
Open Easter-Sep
B&B   £8.50   Listed
      BB&EM
      £84/week
Sleeps 11

The Boaden Family welcome guests to their 100 acre mixed farm situated between Helston and the Lizard, ideal for touring the Lizard Peninsula and surrounding areas. Poldhu Cove with its sandy beach and adjacent golf course, 2 miles away. Picturesque Helford River 5 miles distance with boating available, also close by riding stables. English breakfast and 4 course evening meal. OS Ref SW 682214

(FH) TREZARE FARM   Fowey, Cornwall, PL22 1JZ

Mrs Rosemary Dunn
Tel:-(072683) 3485
Open Easter-Oct
B&B   £9
EM   £5
Sleeps 6

This part 14th Century farmhouse on 220 acres, 1½m from Fowey has panoramic views over farmland to the sea beyond. An ideal base for touring, sandy beaches, National Trust properties, golf course, sports and leisure facilities, moors, all in close proximity. One family room, two double rooms, attractively furnished, cot available. BB, evening meal optional, excellent farmhouse food. OS Ref SX 112538

ⓢⓒ GRANARY STEPS AND THE HAYLOFT   Treffry Farm, Lanhydrock, Bodmin, Cornwall, PL30 5AF

Pat Smith
Tel:-(0208) 4405
Open Mar-New Year
SC   £50-£250
          sleeps 4/6

Delightful stone cottages converted from range of granite farm buildings retaining much olde worlde character and charm. Furnished to high standard in traditional country style set in the heart of beautiful countryside adjoining National Trust park at Lanhydrock, 7 miles from sea. Visitors welcome to explore farm and watch milking. Evening meals available. Pony rides, fishing, rambling, sailing, windsurfing nearby. OS Ref SX 078637

ⓢⓒ TREVALGAN FARM   St. Ives, Cornwall, TR26 3BJ

Jean Osborne
Tel:-(0736) 796433
Closed Feb
SC   £60-£210
          sleeps 2/7

Trevalgan is a coastal stock-rearing farm 2 miles from St. Ives. Enjoy magnificent scenery by walking the coastal footpath running through our farm or visit Land's End, St Michael's Mount or Lamorna, all within easy reach by car. We have converted granite barns into 7 lovely holiday homes situated around an attractive courtyard. OS Ref SW 490402

ⓢⓒ LOWER TRENGALE FARM   Liskeard, Cornwall, PL14 6HF

Louise Kidd
Tel:-(0579) 21019
Open all year
SC   £60-£245
          sleeps 2/6

A small farm where visitors are very welcome to participate. We have cows, sheep, lambs, calves, pigs and hens. There are ponies to ride, a playground, games room, & space for children to play in safety. Our four comfortable cottages, carefully converted from a stone barn, are well equipped, fully carpeted & heated. Linen supplied and home cooked food available. OS Ref SX 211672

ⓢⓒ MORLAND COTTAGES   Shepherds Farm, Newlyn East, Newquay, Cornwall, TR8 5NW

Heather Jill Harvey
Tel:-(087254) 340
Open all year
SC   £75-£250
          sleeps 6/8

Morland Cottages recently modernised. Both have 3 bedrooms, bath, large lounge, dining room, fitted kitchen all electric, high standard of fittings, colour TV, automatic washing machine, large lawns, tarmac parking area. Games room. Pony. Situated in heart of Shepherds Farm, mainly dairy. Easy reach of large sandy beaches. Ideal surfing and swimming. A30 1 mile. Good touring and long walks. Meals can be provided. OS Ref SX 816545

ⓢⓒ TREGLASTA COTTAGE   Treglasta Farm, St Clether, Launceston, Cornwall, PL15 8PY

Molly Hooper
Tel:-(08406) 536
Open all year
SC   £80-£160
          sleeps 5

Early 17th Century cottage, quietly situated in an area of outstanding natural beauty. Comprising fitted kitchen, auto-washing machine, fridge-freezer, lounge with studio couch, colour TV, 2 bedrooms with H/C, centrally heated, sleeps 5 plus cot. Separate WC & bathroom with shower. Large lawn, barn games room. Enjoy the animals & river walks, near sandy beaches, stables, golf. OS Ref SX 181 862

ⓢⓒ NANCOLLETH FARM CARAVAN PARK   Newquay, Cornwall, TR8 4PN

Joan Luckraft
Tel:-(0872) 510236
Open May-Oct
SC   £70-£135
          Sleeps 6

Nancolleth is 250 acre farm, situated mid-Cornwall, 5 miles inland from Newquay, with its beaches stretching for 7 miles. An ideal centre for touring Cornwall. Secluded caravan park, with 4 modern 6 berth caravans, in garden setting, well spaced, hard standing, parking. Laundry. Each caravan has two bedrooms, colour TV, shower, toilet, fridge, spacious lounge, dining & kitchen areas. Families & couples welcomed. No pets. Tel: Mitchell (0872)510236. OS Ref SW 860570

Cornwall ENGLAND

(sc) NANCOLLETH COTTAGE c/o Nancolleth Farm, Newquay, Cornwall, TR8 4PN

Joan Luckraft
Tel:-(0872) 510236
Open Easter-Oct
SC   £80-£215
       Sleeps 6
       + cot

Nancolleth Cottage, one of a pair of cottages, situated adjoining the private farm drive, in peaceful rolling countryside. The farm of some 250 acres is within 5m of Cornwall's finest beaches & Newquay, central for touring Cornwall. Comfortable, fully furnished, fitted carpets, storage heaters. 3 bedrooms, bathroom, large lounge/diner, colour TV. Fully fitted kitchen, washing machine. Parking. Picnic table. Walks. No pets. Tel Mitchell (0872) 510236. OS Ref SW 860570

(sc) PENNANCE MILL FARM   Maenporth, Falmouth, Cornwall, TR11 5HJ

James & Angela Jewell
Tel:-(0326) 312616
Open Mar-Nov
SC   £50-£180
Tent   £3-£4
Van   £3-£4
       SC 4/7
       T/V 50

Pennance Mill Farm chalets, situated on a dairy farm in a sheltered valley facing south. The 4 detached chalets comprise 2 bedrooms, bathroom, kitchen, lounge, TV and are fully equipped. Farm is 2m from Falmouth, ½m from Maenporth beach which is safe for bathing and close to the Helford River which is National Trust. Falmouth Golf Course ½m. Caravanning and camping available. OS Ref SW 791306

(sc) POLTARROW FARM COTTAGE   Poltarrow Farm, St Mewan, St Austell, Cornwall, PL26 7DR

Judith Nancarrow
Tel:-(0726) 67111
Open all year
SC   £50-£200
       sleeps 6

Situated close to the market town of St Austell, the cottage nestles in the midst of a working farm. Offering modernised facilities, retaining "Olde Worlde" features & sleeps up to 6. It is difficult to imagine a better spot from which to explore the real charm of Cornwall with its fishing villages, sandy beaches, golf courses, sailing, riding & much more. OS Ref SW 982 992

(sc) WOODGATE AND TREVIGUE COTTAGE   Trevigue Farm, Crackington Haven, Bude, Cornwall, EX23 0LQ

Janet Crocker
Tel:-(08403) 418
Open all year
SC   £50-£260
       sleeps 6/9

Woodgate is a delightful stone farmhouse about 100 years old overlooking a deeply wooded valley. A charming garden leads into the woods. A few hundred yards from spectacular National Trust cliffs. It sleeps 9, has all amenities including washing machine and colour TV. Trevigue Cottage next to but separate from farmhouse, sleeps 6. Charming with all amenities. OS Ref SX 136952

(sc) BOKIDDICK FARM   Lanivet, Bodmin, Cornwall, PL30 5HP

Gill Hugo
Tel:-(0208) 831481
Open Easter-Oct
SC   £80-£185
       sleeps 5

Attractive well furnished 2 bedroomed country bungalow in own garden, enjoys views of picturesque Helman Tors. Situated on 170 acre dairy farm where we specialise in making real Cornish Clotted Cream. A real cream tea awaits all our guests. Visitors are welcome to watch the milking, see the donkeys & pigs. Situated central Cornwall ideal for either coast. Excellent walking country. National Trust Lanhydrock House close-by. OS Ref SX 052 622

(sc) SOUTH VIEW   Wheatley Farm, Maxworthy, Launceston, Cornwall, PL15 8LY

Valerie Griffin
Tel:-(056681) 232
Open all year
SC   £60-£220
       Sleeps 7

South View is a smart detached stone built cottage set in beautiful Cornish Countryside. Ideally situated for touring, within easy reach of many coves & sandy beaches. Furnished to a high standard, all amenities including washing machine, colour TV, CH, modern kitchen. Sleeps 7. Visitors welcome to watch milking, explore 160 acre farm. Evening meals by arrangement. OS Ref SX 245 929

(SC) KEEPERS COTTAGE Trewen Farm, Bodock Water, Nr. Falmouth, Cornwall, TR11 5DZ

Joan Hutchings
Tel: (0326) 73369
Open Easter-Xmas
SC   £90-£200
sleeps 6

Keepers Cottage sleeps 2/8 plus cot. Modern, detached, private setting on a farm with wooded walks, 2m Falmouth, a beach resort, boat/yatching centre. One mile golf course, 3½m Helford River famous for Frenchman's Creek, 4 beaches within 2 miles. Lounge/diner, colour TV, coal fire, 2 bedrooms, oil radiators, kitchen, automatic washing machine, bathroom. OS Ref SW 778315

(SC) THE ROOST Higher Kergilliack Farm, Budock, Falmouth, TR11 5PB

Jean Pengelly
Tel:-(0326) 72271
Open Easter-Oct
SC   £55-£195
sleep 4

The Roost - converted from granite farm building with tasteful pine cladding in hall & living room. It is situated on a working farm 2 miles from Falmouth with its lovely beaches. The Helford river is near with its lovely wooded valleys. There is a lounge diner with electric cooker & fridge, spin drier & colour TV. Immersion heater meter 50p. 1 bedroom with double & single bed, cot available. OS Ref SW 780330

(SC) TREGELLAST BARTON St. Keverne, Helston, Cornwall, TR12 6NX

Rachel Roskilly
Tel:-(0326) 280479
Open Apr-Oct
SC   £115-£235
sleeps 5/6

Tregellast Barton is a listed Tudor farmstead with attractive gardens and farm buildings, some converted into separate cottages. We have 135 acres and 80 Channel Island cows, pigs, 2 donkeys, hens and bees. We make clottedcream. Visitors are welcome to watch milking, feed calves and hens, collect eggs, etc but please bring boots! Cows are messy creatures even in the driest weather! OS Ref SW 794206

(SC) LOWER CROAN COTTAGE Sladesbridge, Wadebridge, Cornwall, PL27 6JH

Ruth Derryman
Tel:-(020884) 237
Open all year
SC   £60-£160
Sleeps 6

Lower Croan Cottage is set in 2 acres of gardens, ½m off the main road. Sleeps 6 people comfortably, all amenities provided including use of washing machine & tumble drier. Colour TV. Animals to feed if you wish. Pony rides. Meals can be provided. OS Ref SX 024 715

(TV) SEAGULL TOURIST PARK Treginegar Farm, St.Merryn, Padstow, Cornwall, PL28 8PT

Wendy Pollard
Tel:-(0841) 520117
Open Easter-Oct
Tent   £1.80-£2.30
Van   £2.30-£3.30
75 caravans

A family site situated on a farm with field and coastline views only minutes from 7 golden sandy bays, ideal for families. Amenities: flush toilets, showers, launderette, play area, small swimming pool, T.V., games room. In high season barn dances and Bar-B-Qs. Takeaway meals, small farm shop. Two letting caravans also available. Good internal roads for children, biking, country walks. Watch the cows being milked. OS Ref SX 883713

Dairy Land

Milking on a Merry-go-round
FARM PARK, PLAYGROUND, NATURE TRAIL & COUNTRY LIFE MUSEUM
On A3058 4 miles from Newquay
Tel: Mitchell (0872) 510246

OPEN EVERY DAY — April & October — 1.30-5.30 p.m.
Easter and May to September 10-6 p.m.
Last admission 1 hour before closing
Milking: 3-4.30 p.m. (approx.)
Schools and other parties welcome by appointment
Facilities for the disabled — **FREE PARKING**

Upper Tamar ENGLAND

UPPER TAMAR
N. Devon/Cornwall

UPPER TAMAR, NORTH WEST DEVON

This area covers the North Cornwall/Devon border area with glorious coastline and miles of sandy beaches, sheltered coves and rugged cliffs, friendly resorts and quiet villages, country market towns and wide open spaces peacefully set in undulating countryside.

The coastline from Hartland to Crackington Haven is as dramatic as it is beautiful. Bude, once described by the late Sir John Betjeman 'as the least

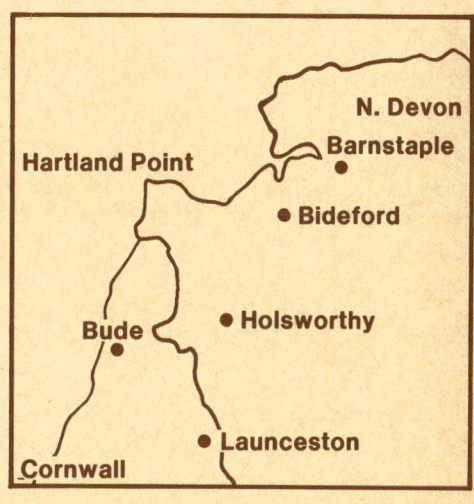

rowdy resort in the country' has retained its atmosphere of easy going charm whilst catering for the most discerning of modern day tourists. Another resort which tourists are advised to visit is Clovelly with its steeply cobbled streets.

Holsworthy and Launceston have weekly cattle and pannier markets. Both have a golf course and sports hall with Launceston having a heated swimming pool. There are several pony trekking centres in the area and facilities for fishing either at sea, on the lake or by the river.

This area has been recommended as a restful, comfortable base for touring the whole of Devon and Cornwall. There are many tourist attractions including the moors, National Trust properties, steam railways, leisure parks, museums and the cities of Exeter, Plymouth and Truro all within easy driving distance.

GROUP CONTACT
Rosemary Risdon (040927) 238

(FH) **PINSLOW FARM** St Giles-on-the-Heath, Launceston, Cornwall, PL15 9SU

Mary Tucker
Tel:-(0566) 2140
Open Apr-Oct
B&B   £8
EM   £4
Sleeps 6

260 acre mixed working farm with trout fishing on River Tamar. Quiet situation with lovely walks. The house was built by the Duke of Bedford in 1863 and sleeps 6 with H/C in bedrooms and tea making facilities. The market town of Launceston is 5m with golf course, leisure centre and pony trekking. OS Ref SX 348901

(FH) **WESTCOTT FARM** North Tamerton, Holsworthy, Devon, EX226SF

Carol Denning
Tel:-(040927) 260
Closed Xmas and New Year
B&B   £7.50-£8.50
EM   £4
Sleeps 11
W'kly b'kings prefered

Wescott is a working dairy farm, there is a large garden with a tree house also hens and goats to feed, good accommodation with central heating, washbasins with H/C, shaver points and tea making facilities in all bedrooms, cot and highchair available, bathroom with shower and WC, separate WC. Lounge with colour TV, dining room, laundry room, fire certificate. Good home cooking. OS Ref SX 307 993

(FH) **THORNE PARK** Holsworthy, Devon, EX22 7BL

Marlene Heard
Tel:-0409 253339
Open Mar-Nov
B&B   £7.50   Applied
EM   £3.50
       Redn children
SC   £60-£150
Sleeps 7/10

A warm welcome awaits everyone including children at Thorne Park, a 96 acres working farm set in pleasant countryside. Guests are welcome to wander around & watch the milking & farm activities. Pony for children to ride. Comfortable accommodation with plenty of good farmhouse cooking. Also self contained wing of farmhouse. Holsworthy market town, with golf course & sports hall 1½m. Coast 10mls. BB&EM £75/week. OS Ref 062 345

(FH) **THE BARTON** Pancrasweek, Holsworthy, Devon, EX22 7JT

Linda Cole
Tel:-(028881) 315
Open May-Sept
B&B   £7.50-£8.50   Listed
EM   £5 redn for children
Sleeps 12

140 acre dairy farm on N Devon/Cornwall border. Conveniently placed for N Cornwall coast with fine beaches and famous fishing villages. Good home cooking, ample portions, home produced vegetables. 5 bedrooms with H/C and shaver points. Guests' bathroom, shower room, lounge with TV, dining room, games room, babysitting available. Family atmosphere. OS Ref SS 293056

(FH) **BLAKES** Bulkworthy, Holsworthy, Devon, EX22 7UP

Mrs K Peggy Hockridge
Tel:-(040926) 249
Open May-Sep
B&B   £9-£10
EM   £5
Sleeps 4

(14)

Blakes Farmhouse AA listed, well recommended accommodation midway Bideford/Holsworthy. Ideal touring centre for day trips Devon, Cornwall, local beaches. Many guests return yearly to enjoy relaxed informal atmosphere, personal attention, high standard of cleanliness & excellent farmhouse fare. Large lounge with colour TV, electric organ. Cool dining room. 1 double, 1 family bedrooms, H/C washbasins, shower points, divan beds.

(SC) **THORNE MANOR** Pancrasweek, Holsworthy, Devon, EX22 7JD

Charles & Pat Clarke
Tel:-(0409) 253342
Open Mar-Oct
SC   £57.50-£200
Sleeps 4-5

Thorne Manor is a large working dairy farm with 10 self-catering flats with own Nature Reserve and Trail. Licensed bar, shop, children's games room and play area, tennis court, 2 squash courts. Watch the cows being milked and farm ice cream being made. S.A.E. for brochure. Dogs by arrangement only.

Upper Tamar ENGLAND

 **EAST VENTON** North Tamerton, Holsworthy, Devon, EX22 6SF

Rosemary Risdon
Tel:-(040927) 238
Open all year
SC   £117-£234
     Sleeps 9
     + 2 cots

On Devon/Cornwall border in peaceful rural surroundings, well equipped, self contained, homely accommodation in part of listed farmhouse. Microwave, dishwasher etc. 4 bedrooms, sleep 9 + 2 cots. Electric heat throughout, two lounges. Large enclosed garden with swing and sandpit. Visitors welcome to watch milking & wander around farm. Babysitting and pets by arrangement. Linen, fuel, electricity inclusive. OS Ref SX 315992

HOLIDAY GUIDE TO DEVON

The handy pocket guide which makes more of your holiday

£3.95

from bookshops and newsagents, or in case of difficulty from the address below

NICHOLSON 16 Golden Square, London W1R 4BN

VISIT PHILIP AND JEANNE WAYRE'S
Tamar Otter Park & Wild Wood
at North Petherwin, Near Launceston, Cornwall

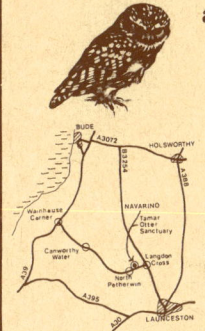

A branch of the famous Otter Trust where young British Otters are being bred for release into the wild. Enjoy a wonderland of wildlife deep in the wood where four species of deer and other animals roam free.
See the aviaries for breeding British and European Owls. Wander round the waterfowl lake while Peacocks and Golden Pheasants strut nearby. Watch the Otters playing and swimming.
A fascinating Nature Trail for younger visitors.
The Park is a must for every family interested in wildlife and conservation.
ATTRACTIVE TEA ROOM, GIFT SHOP AND FREE CAR PARK
OPEN DAILY — 10.30 am to 6.00 pm
Good Friday until 31st October

Regret no dogs allowed

3 NORTH WEST DEVON

NORTH DEVON COAST AND COUNTRY

North Devon is a warm, friendly and still largely unspoilt area of Britain. It is an area of tremendous contrast with dramatic cliffs, small coves and miles of golden, sandy, surf-washed beaches

The coast offers miles of sand and surf at Westward Ho, Saunton, Croyde, Putsborough and Woolacombe. Typical seaside towns and villages at Instow, Illfracombe, Combe Martin and the twin villages of Lynton and Lynmouth where Exmoor reaches the sea and the famous cliff railway runs between the two.

The countryside of inland north Devon still preserves the rural life of England which many people think has disappeared. The rolling hills and patchwork of small fields and family farms is a predominantly livestock area. In the spring and early summer the hedgerows are massed with wild flowers. There is an abundance of wildlife with red deer, badgers, foxes, hares, rabbits, buzzards and many more species commonplace.

Nearby Exmoor offers magnificent scenery with rolling heather clad hills and steeply wooded combes. Whatever sort of holiday you prefer you can find it

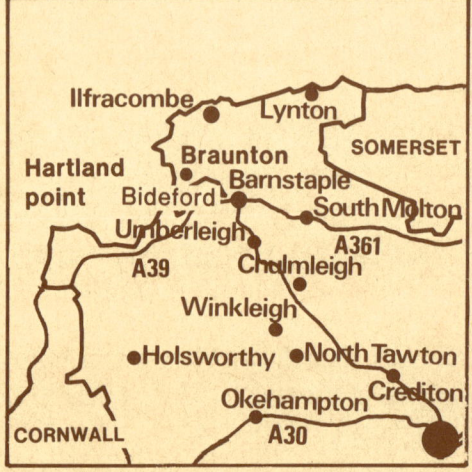

here. A wonderful place for a quiet touring holiday or perfect for a family seaside holiday with, many tourist attractions should the weather be less than perfect. The sportsman is well catered for with windsurfing, golfing, sailing, riding and much more available. Short breaks out of season are particularly rewarding with the area almost to yourself.

VACANCY SECRETARY:
Jean Barnes (0271) 890297

North West Devon ENGLAND

(FH) HIGHER CLIFTON FARM   East Down, Nr Barnstaple, N Devon, EX31 4LX

Elizabeth Smyth
Tel:-(027182) 372
Open May-Sep
B&B   £8-£9   Listed
EM   £4
Sleeps 6

Everyone is made welcome on this 340 acre family run, working farm with beef, cattle, sheep, lambs, cats & dog! 17th Century farmhouse, lovely views, peaceful, few minutes walk to village pub. Close to Barnstaple, Exmoor & beaches. Riding, golf, fishing, sports. Good home cooking. Home produce when possible. Lounge with tea/coffee making facilities. 1 double, 1 family, 1 twin. OS Ref SS 598415

(FH) HIGHER CHURCHILL FARM   East Down, Nr Barnstaple, Nth Devon, EX31 4LT

Mrs Andrea Cook
Tel:-(027182) 543
Closed Xmas and New Year
B&B   £7-£9   Listed
EM   £5
Sleeps 6

Higher Churchill Farm is a working farm of 220 acres, owned by the National Trust. We have a dairy herd, sheep, ponies, goat, hens, geese, collies and cats. The 300 year old farmhouse is full of character, good traditional farmhouse food is served, mostly our own or fresh local produce. Beautiful countryside, central for coast and Exmoor. Children Welcome at reduced rates. OS Ref 407 595

(FH) HALSINGER FARM   Braunton, N Devon, EX33 2NL

Vi Burge
Tel:-(0271) 812415
Open Mar-Nov
B&B   £10   Applied
EM   £3.50-£4.50
Sleeps 8/10

Clean comfortable family accommodation on small farm. Peaceful area pleasant garden. Few restrictions for children. Exmoor, Ilfracombe and Woolacombe near. Shops at Braunton or Barnstaple. Many guests return year after year, centrally heated 5 bedrooms (2 family) with basins, two bathrooms, 4 toilets. Cot, highchair, babysitting & reduced rates for children. Car essential. Games room and private fishing on farm. OS Ref SS 388513

(FH) DENHAM FARM   North Buckland, Braunton, N Devon, EX33 1HY

Jean Barnes
Tel:-0271 890297
Open Mar-New Year
B&B   £8.50-£9.50
EM   £5.50
Sleeps 15

Denham is 160 acre beef farm in the centre of a small hamlet 1 mile from the village of Georgeham. It is only 10 minutes ride from the golden sands of Croyde, Braunton, Woolacombe & Putsborough. An ideal touring base for all local amenities & the beautiful scenery of Exmoor. Good home cooking, desserts a speciality with lots of farm cream, Residential Licence. OS Ref SS 480 404

(FH) WAYTOWN FARM   Shirwell, Barnstaple, N Devon, EX31 4JN

Hazel Kingdon
Tel:-(0271) 82396
Open Easter-Nov
B&B   £8.50-£9.50
EM   £4.00
Sleeps 6

Waytown Farm is a mixed beef and sheep farm where a warm welcome greets you. Guests can enjoy comfort and privacy in this traditional farmhouse situated 3 miles from Barnstaple. Plenty of good home cooked food. 1 twin, 2 family bedrooms all with H/C, lounge with colour TV, dining room, bathroom with toilet, separate toilet, ample parking. Riding, fishing and lovely walks nearby. Leisure centre 3 miles. OS Ref SS 586 365

(FH) CASTLE HILL BARTON   Filleigh, Nr Barnstaple, N Devon, EX32 0RX

Angela Sexon
Tel:-05986 242
Open Easter-Oct
B&B   £7-£8   Listed
EM   From £3
       Redcn child
       under 12

A 330 acre dairy & beef farm, situated 500 yds off the A361 on the Fortescue Estate, between Barnstaple & South Molton. Good farmhouse cooking with fresh garden produce & home-made cream. Family/double rooms with washbasins, large lounge, colour TV & dining room. Ideal touring centre for Exmoor & the North Devon Coast.

(FH) COMBAS FARM   Croyde, Braunton, N Devon, EX33 1PH

Gwen Adams
Tel: (0271) 890398
Open Mar-Nov
B&B   £8.50-£10.50   Listed
EM   £4
Sleeps 10

Combas Farm is a mixed stock farm set in a secluded valley where wildlife abounds, yet only ¼m to superb sandy beach, safe surfing/windsurfing. A 17th Century farmhouse which has attractive gardens and large orchard. We offer guests a relaxed happy atmosphere and an abundance of home produce carefully prepared and presented. Skittle evening at "local" numbers permitting. Golf, squash, tennis, riding available locally. OS Ref SS 396449

(FH) SLOLEY BARTON   Shirwell, Barnstaple, N Devon, EX31 4LF

Angela Worth
Tel:-(027 182) 250
Open Jun-Oct
B&B   £7-£8   Applied
EM   £5
Sleeps 6

Peacefully situated on a 300 acre beef & sheep farm, 4m from Barnstaple. Ideal base for Exmoor and 10m from lots of local beaches. Spacious large farmhouse with 3 bedrooms, dining room, sitting room and own bathroom.

(FH) NORWOOD FARM   Hiscott, Barnstaple, N Devon, EX31 3JS

Linda Richards
Tel:-(027185) 260
Closed Xmas and New Year
B&B   £12.50
EM   £7
Sleeps 6

Norwood Farm is 104 acre dairy farm with a lovely old farmhouse which has been tastefully renovated to a comfortable country house, maintaining inglenook fireplaces and log fires. The ensuite bedrooms have brass beds, antique furniture and Laura Ashley decor. There is a guest lounge with colour TV/video. The large garden at rear of house has barbeque and safe children's play area. OS Ref 547 262

(FH) METTAFORD FARM   Hartland, Bideford, N Devon, EX39 6AL

Pat England
Tel:-(02374) 249
Closed Xmas and New Year
B&B   £10-£11   Applied
EM   £6.50
Sleeps 10

A very quiet setting for this Georgian farmhouse situated in 18½ acres of its own unspoilt woodlands. Nicely furnished with many antiques. Six Laura Ashley decorated bedrooms, one with ensuite facilities. 3 bathrooms. Large sitting room with wood burning fireplace. Separate TV lounge on request. Children eat at 6.00pm, adults at 7.00pm Cordon Bleu. OS Ref SS 284 244

(SC) PICKWELL BARTON HOLIDAY COTTAGES   Georgeham, Braunton, N Devon, EX33 1LA

Sheila Cook
Tel:-(0271) 870387
Open all year
SC   £70-£170
Sleeps 7/8
plus cot

Sunnyside and Pickwell Barton Cottages are two comfortable, spacious farm holiday cottages on a beef, sheep and corn farm. Pickwell Barton is situated between Putsborough and Woolacombe. 5 minutes walk across our fields for beautiful views of 3 miles of golden sands between Baggy and Morte Point. Each cottage has 3 bedrooms plus cot. Solid fuel Rayburn available out of season.

(SC) KNOWLE FARM   Holmacott, Instow, Bideford, N Devon, EX39 4LR

John & Patsy Ford
Tel:-(0271) 860482
Open all year
SC   £100-£300
Sleeps 5/7

A traditional Devon Holiday, Knowle Farm provides a superb rural setting for our 2 cottages, ideal family holidays located 3 miles from Bideford, yet minutes from Instow beach. Converted from stone barns both cottages offer luxury accommodation with all modern amenities, linen and towels provided. Sleeps 5/7. Fishing, riding, golf available. Brochure available. OS Ref SS 503288

N. Devon ENGLAND

NORTH DEVON

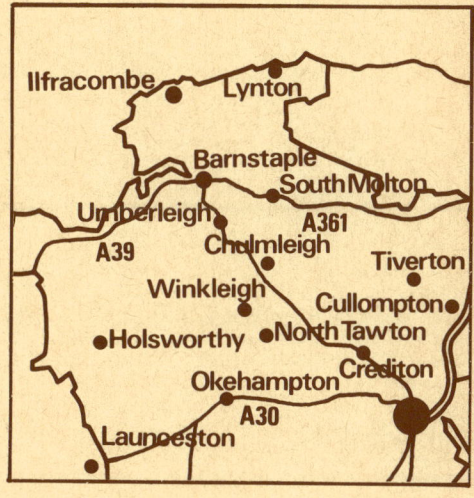

NORTH DEVON

North Devon offers you the chance to escape from routine to some of the most beautiful rolling countryside surrounded by a coastline of varying mood and beauty. From the majestic and awesome cliffs of Hartland, to the estuaries of the Taw and Torridge converging as they reach the sea, the miles of sandy beaches and the host of rocky coves on the north coast — there is everything for the visitor.

Devon is famous for its clotted cream and cider, but it should also be remembered for its ancient hedgerows, small fields and the high banks which line every lane. Farming has not changed the face of the countryside in North Devon, and you can still see the ancient farms with a variety of livestock in the fields, old water mills, and cottages in the deep coombes or high up on the moor. Craftsmen and painters are at work in many towns and villages.

Lovers of R. D. Blackmore's novel "Lorna Doone" can explore the many scenes he so vividly described.

Woolacombe, Saunton and Croyde offer miles of sandy beaches, and surfing is a popular sport in this area. Braunton Burrows is a nature reserve famous for its wild flowers and Lundy Island is an interesting day trip by steamer.

VACANCY SECRETARIES:
B&B: Carol Webber (0884) 860308.
Self Catering:
Ruth Woollacott (0884) 860300.

(FH) HUXTABLE FARM West Buckland, Barnstaple, N Devon, EX32 0SR

Barbara Payne
Tel:-(05986) 254
Closed Xmas
B&B £8-£10
EM   £6
Sleeps 8

A mediaeval longhouse carefully restored, furnished with antiques, Huxtable Farm is 80 acre mixed farm (mainly sheep) situated ½ hour drive from Exmoor, N. Devon coasts. Excellent meals of garden, farm, local produce (including home-made bread, clotted cream) are served. Home-made wine with 4 course, candlelit dinner. Private bath/shower, reductions for children and short/long breaks. Children's high teas £1.50 - £2.00. OS Ref SS 665308

(FH) WOODHOUSE FARM South Molton, North Devon, EX36 4JH

Marjorie Radford
Tel:-(07695) 2321
Open Apr-Oct
B&B £8-£9
EM   £4.50
Sleeps 6

We offer relaxation, comfort, hospitality and plenty of good fresh farmhouse food. Mixed stock and arable farm. 2m from the market town of South Molton. Nestling in peaceful, secluded & unspoilt countryside. The farmhouse has been carefully restored & modernised whilst retaining its original character. Washbasins in all bedrooms, guests own bathroom, separate toilet, colour TV, tea/coffee facilities. Weekly terms available. OS Ref SS 714221

(FH) STOCKHAM FARM Thelbridge, Crediton, Devon, EX17 4SJ

Carol Webber
Tel:-(0884) 860308
Open Mar-Nov
B&B £8-£9.50   Listed
EM   £4.50
Sleeps 8

Stockham Farm is a mixed farm of 150 acres set in the heart of the Devon countryside approximately 2½ miles off the A373 Tiverton - South Molton road near Witheridge. 14th century farmhouse, separate lounge TV dining room, games room with information area, double, family, twin and single rooms, tea/coffee making facilities. Children especially welcome. Lots of animals, lovely walks, woodlands, fishing. OS Ref SS 780133

(FH) NORTH NEWTON FARM Chittlehampton, Umberleigh, N Devon, EX37 9QS

Margaret Thomas
Tel:-(07694) 544
Open all year
B&B £8.50-£9.50   Listed
EM   From £4.50
Sleeps 6

A 52 acre dairy working farm. Large traditional farmhouse set in beautiful countryside with extensive views offering personal attention. Traditional farmhouse food and homely atmosphere. Family/double rooms with washbasins, lounge, colour TV, dining room, central heating. Four miles from South Molton.Ideally situated for touring Exmoor and north Devon coast. Leisure centre 10 miles. Tennis, swimming, riding and fishing locally. OS Ref SS 660252

(CH) WEST TRAYNE Georgenympton, South Molton, N Devon, EX36 4JE

Phyl Rawle
Tel:-(07695) 2534
Closed Xmas-New Year
B&B £9-£10
EM   £4
CH   Sleeps 10

A 16th Century house with a large garden in a quiet village close to Exmoor. We provide all the ingredients for a peaceful, relaxing holiday in a warm friendly atmosphere, combined with plenty of good home-cooked food. Dining room, lounge, 5 double rooms with washbasins, 2 baths, showers and toilets. Facilities locally for golf, riding, fishing, tennis and swimming. OS Ref SS 701229

(FH) ROMANSLEIGH BARTON Romansleigh, South Molton, N Devon, EX36 4JP

Jennifer Webber
Tel:-(07697) 233
Open Easter-Oct
B&B £8-£8.50   Listed
EM   From £4
Sleeps 6

Romansleigh Barton, surrounded by beautiful countryside with views to Exmoor. Relax in a comfortable 16th century longhouse on a 300 acre mixed working farm in peaceful hamlet 4m from South Molton. Traditional farmhouse cooking; private sitting room and dining room; 2 large family bedrooms; children welcome. Easy reach of North Devon coast, golf, riding and fishing available in the area. Dogs by arrangement. OS Ref SS 728206

24

N. Devon ENGLAND

(FH) CRANGS HEASLEIGH FARM Heasley Mill, North Molton, South Molton, N Devon, EX36 3LE

Mary Yendell
Tel:-(05984) 268
Closed Xmas-New Year
B&B £8.50-£9.50 Applied
Sleeps 6

Crangs Heasleigh is a traditional 13th Century, Devon long-house which forms the hub of a busy farm. Situated in Exmoor's National Park, Crangs is ideally placed for walkers, riders and lovers of other country pursuits, while market towns and beaches are within easy reach. Tea/coffee making facilities. OS Ref SS 737322

(SC) WILLESLEIGH FARM COTTAGE Willesleigh Farm, Goodleigh, Barnstaple, N. Devon, EX32 7NA

Charles & Anne Esmond-Cole
Tel:-(0271) 43763
Open all year
SC £94-£217
Sleeps 9
+ 2cot

Spend happy peaceful holidays in the cheerful, comfortable, well equipped cottage wing of our farmhouse. 3 bedrooms. All electric (included in price) Large lawn, picnic table, portable barbecue. Unlimited summer use of our swimming pool. Our Jersey cows & calves are great favourites, also spring lambs, on our 86 acre, all grass, family run farm. Lovely countryside, excellent touring centre. Illustrated brochure. OS Ref SS 600333

(SC) WELCOMBE FARM Charles, Nr Barnstaple, N Devon, EX32 7PU

Margaret & Malcolm Faulkner
Tel:-(05988) 440
Open Easter-Oct
SC £50-£90
Sleeps 6

For a restful holiday away from it all but near enough to sandy beaches and moors, try our modern, comfortable caravan on our dairy/sheep farm. Imaginative private setting with panoramic views to Exmoor. Fully equipped for 6. Facilities include shower, flush toilet, fridge, spin dryer, hot water. Safe, enclosed garden with picnic table. Lots of animals. Ideal for walking and touring. OS Ref SS 684337

(SC) HOLLACOMBE BARTON Hollacombe, Chulmleigh, Devon, EX18 7QG

Christine Stevens
Tel:-(083783) 385
Open all year
SC £40-£210
Sleeps 2/8
plus cot

Friendly family run dairy farm with Domesday links offers very comfortable accomodation overlooking peaceful meadows. Luxury kitchen, includes microwave, fridge/freezer and washer/dryer. Colour TV & video. Phone. CH throughout. Log fire. All linen and electric blankets provided. Pets corner and games room. Baby alarm listening service. Golf riding and fishing close by. Handy for sea/moors. Please phone for brochure. OS Ref SS 628113

(SC) NORTHCOTT BARTON FARM Northcott Barton, Ashreighney, Chulmleigh, Devon, EX18 7PR

Sandra Gay
Tel:-(07693) 259
Open all year
SC From £70
Sleeps 9
+ cot

Comfortable, self contained wing of lovely old farmhouse on a working farm, where guests can explore and see the animals. Accommodation comprises three bedrooms, bathroom, kitchen/diner, cosy oak beamed lounge, Colour TV and log fire, central heating, bed linen provided. Large garden, swing, slide and barbeque. Riding, fishing, golf, gliding close by. Forty minutes drive to glorious beaches. Warm welcome assured. OS Ref SS 598146

(SC) BEECH GROVE East Westacott, Riddlecombe, Ashreigney, Chumleigh, Devon EX18 7PF

Joyce Middleton
Tel:-(076 93) 210
Open all year
SC £76-£176
Sleeps 8
+ cot

This delightful bungalow offers relaxation and comfort, in peaceful, pleasant surroundings on our friendly, family run, mixed farm. Attractive lawned gardens, with sun-patio and barbeque. Lovely views. Glorious beaches only half-hour's drive. Golf, riding and fishing nearby. Central heating and log fires. Exceptionally well equipped, including snooker, table-tennis etc. Sleeps 5 - 8 plus cot. OS Ref SS 601139

ⓢ WEST YEO FARM West Yeo, Witheridge, Tiverton, Devon, EX16 8PY

Ruth Woollacott
Tel:-(0884) 860300
Open all year
SC   £70-£125
Sleeps 6

Self-contained wing of large farmhouse 1m from Witheridge with churches, shops, and tennis courts. Ideal touring centre for North and South Devon coast & moors. Guests are welcome to take an active interest in the working of the 140 acre mixed farm. Spacious living room with wood burner. Kitchen, modern shower and WC. Upstairs, 2 large bedrooms with double & single beds & WC. OS Ref SS 788149

ⓢ MANOR FARM Riddlecombe, Chulmleigh, N. Devon, EX18 7NX

Eveline Gay
Tel:-(07693) 335
Open all year
SC   £58
Sleeps 9

A charming old farmhouse which has a completely self-contained wing, with lovely views of the surrounding valley and overlooks a large lawn. Variety of animals for guests to see on this family run dairy farm. Extensive games room catering for all ages. Accommodates 9 plus cot, well equipped kitchen, lounge, bathroom, 3 bedrooms, colour TV. Bed linen provided. Heating throughout. Dogs by arrangement only. OS Ref SS 612142

ⓢ SANDICK COTTAGE Sandick Farm, Swimbridge, Barnstaple, Nrth Devon, EX32 0QZ

Margaret Bartlett
Tel:-(0271) 830243
Open Easter-Oct
SC   £80-£130
Sleeps 6

Spacious cottage in peaceful situation 200yds from dairy farm, own yard, large lawn providing safe playing area for children. Colour TV, electric cooker, spin dryer, fridge, optional oil-fired Rayburn. 2 large carpeted bedrooms each with double, single beds, bathroom upstairs. Lounge with open fire, kitchen/dining area, pantry downstairs. 5m from Barnstaple with leisure centre, swimming, squash etc. Central for beaches, Exmoor OS Ref SS 629322

ⓢ DREWSTONE FARM South Molton, N Devon, EX36 3EF

Ruth Ley
Tel:-(07695) 2337
Open Easter-Sept
SC   £90-£145
Sleeps 8
+ cot

Drewstone is a 16th Century traditional Devon Longhouse on 215 acre family run farm on edge of Exmoor, with views, walks of outstanding beauty. Accommodation has been converted into cottage style dwelling adjoining farmhouse. Sleeps 8 + cot, 3½ bedrooms, bathroom, fully equipped kitchen/diner. TV, fitted carpets throughout. Enclosed garden, pony. Linen & pets by arrangement. OS Ref SS 274745

ⓢ NETHERCOTT MANOR FARM Rose Ash, South Molton, N Devon, EX36 4RE

Carol Woollacott
Tel:-(07697) 483
Open all year
SC   £65-£125
Sleeps 4/9

Denis and Carol assure a friendly welcome at Nethercott, a 17th Century thatched house on a 200 acre working farm. There are 2 comfortable self contained wings sleeping 4/9. Trout pond for fishing. Ponies for riding, games room, barbecue facilities. Six miles from South Molton. Excellent for touring Exmoor and coast. OS Ref SS 795209

ⓢ THE OLD COACH HOUSE Densham, Ashreigney, Chulmleigh, Devon, EX18 7NF

Mrs Mary Cole
Tel:-(07697) 273
Open all year
SC   £65-£135
Sleeps 5

Delightful, 2 bedroomed coach-house on large farm. Peace and comfort guaranteed. A former coach house having lost none of its original character or charm, tastefully converted with luxury furnishings. Fully equipped kitchen, central heating, electric blankets, colour TV, barbeque facilities. Beautiful country walks starting at the front door. Immediate area golf, riding, fishing, gliding. Rough shooting and fishing on farm by arrangement. OS Ref SS 639126

North Devon ENGLAND

(SC) DOWN COTTAGE   Kingsnympton, Umberleigh, N Devon, EX37 9TF

Norma Latham
Tel:-(07695) 2463
Open all year
SC   £60-£150
      Sleeps 8

A warm welcome awaits you at Down Farm amidst the unspoilt countryside. 4m from the market town of South Molton. Comfortable, semi-detached cottage. Carpeted throughout. Large garden swing. Wonderful views of Exmoor, Dartmoor, easy reach of coastline. Guests welcome to wander over 400 acre working farm. Plenty of animals & harvesting to watch. Three bedrooms, colour TV, Log fire, night storage heaters. OS Ref SS 684211

(SC) MILLBROOK FARM   Twitchen, South Molton, Devon, EX36 3LP

Annette Bray
Tel:-(05984) 275
Closed Xmas-New Year
SC   £75-£145
      Sleeps 6

Millbrook is family run sheep/cattle farm on the edge of Exmoor National Park. Minutes away from the peace and serenity of Exmoor yet within easy reach of North Devon's popular resorts, sandy beaches. Self contained part of farmhouse which is a 300 year old traditional longhouse comfortably accommodates 4-6 people. Centrally heated for out of season. Snooker room. Childrens play area. OS Ref SS 759304

5 HEART OF DEVON

HEART OF DEVON

If you're undecided as to which part of Devon to take your holiday, why not opt for the heart of the county . . . you can then tour and explore in all directions to get a taste of all that's best.

The Heart of Devon itself is all thatched cottages, lush meadows, steeply wooded valleys, rivers and streams, high banked lanes studded with wild flowers — unspoilt and rather special.

This is also an area of traditional sheep and cattle farming — and a visit to one of the local towns on market day will give you the chance to get the full flavour of the occasion, plus the opportunity to sample the produce itself . . . cheese, smoked trout, clotted cream and farmhouse cider.

As always in Devon there's much to see and do, and here it tends to offer a hint of nostalgia as well. Take Tiverton for example; the town's museum is one of the best folk museums in the West Country with its large railway galley complete with restored GWR loco — and the restored Grand Western canal, eleven miles long, offers trips by horse-drawn barge.

There is, of course, much more — and all within easy reach of Exmoor, Dartmoor the south coast resorts and dramatic seascapes of the north.

GROUP CONTACT:
Anne Boldry (03985) 347

Heart of Devon ENGLAND

(FH) BRINDIWELL FARM Cheriton Fitzpaine, Nr Crediton, Devon, EX17 4HR

Doreen Lock
Tel:-(03636) 357
Open all Year
B&B   £8.50-£10   Listed
EM   £5-£6
      Sleeps 6
SC   £50-£100
      Sleeps 4

Delightful old farmhouse with oak beams and panelling. Colour TV, tea facilities in all rooms. Situated midway between north and south coasts and moors. Outstanding views to Dartmoor. 120 acre working sheep farm. Two double rooms, 1 single bedroom. AA listed. Also self-catering wing of farmhouse - 1 double + extra bed, 1 single, colour TV. OS Ref SY 896079

(FH) NEWHOUSE FARM Oakford, Tiverton, Devon, EX16 9JE

Anne Boldry
Tel:-(03985) 347
Closed Xmas
B&B   £9.50   Listed
EM   £5.50
      All Prices less 10%
      over 3 days
      Sleeps 6

"Newhouse" is an "old house" built around 1600, featuring oak beams and inglenook fireplace. Comfortably furnished, all bedrooms have central heating, wash-basins and tea/coffee making facilities. Home-baked bread and own and local produce used for tastier meals. This 40 acre farm is set in a peaceful valley close to Exmoor, 25 miles from Exeter, Barnstaple and Taunton. AA listed. OS Ref SS 892227

(FH) HARTON FARM Oakford, Nr Tiverton, Devon, EX16 9HH

Lindy Head
Tel:-(03985) 209
Closed Xmas
B&B   £8-£9   Listed
EM   £4
      Redn for
      children
      Sleeps 6

1 double, 2 twin rooms. A stone built farmhouse dating from the 17thC, situated in a secluded position near Exmoor, yet within ½ mile of the A361. We serve traditional food using our own dairy produce, eggs, pork, lamb and organically grown vegetables. Home baking a speciality. Vegetarian menu on request. Colour TV, home-spun wool available. OS Ref SS 905225

(FH) LOWER COLLIPRIEST FARM Tiverton, Devon, EX16 4PT

Linda Olive
Tel:-(0884) 252321
Open Easter-Oct
B&B   £12-£13
EM   £6
      Sleeps 4

220 acre dairy farm with 17th Century thatched farmhouse offering luxurious accommodation, central heating, colour TV, in comfortable lounge with inglenook fireplace. Twin bedded rooms with bathroom en-suite. Tea making facilities. Traditional, speciality cooking using own/local produce. Beautiful walks over farm. Private fishing, golf, swimming nearby. Coasts, moors easy reach. Weekly terms available. Fire certificate. Children over 14 welcome. OS Ref SS 955115

(SC) CIDER COTTAGE Great Bradley Farm, Withleigh, Tiverton, Devon, EX16 8JL

Mrs Sylvia Hann
Tel:-(0884) 256946
Open all Year
SC   £75-£180
      Sleeps 5

Charming cottage - originally a 17th Century cider barn on 155 acre dairy farm. Beautiful views & spacious accommodation for 5. Three bedrooms, 2 double, 1 single. Excellent lounge, kitchen & dining area. Furnished & equipped to high standard. Bed linen inclusive. Lovely local walks. Ideal situation for touring moors and coasts - or stay & enjoy the farm. Winter breaks a speciality - with a warm welcome. OS Ref SS 908135

(SC) LONGHAM COTTAGE Longham Farm, Cove, Tiverton, Devon, EX16 7RU

Sue Haigh
Tel:-(0398) 31496
Open all year
SC   £70-£95
      Sleeps 2
      + baby

Enjoy the delights of rural Devon. Stay in our cosy well-equipped cottage, adjoining the farmhouse - one double bedroom plus cots (baby-sitting available). Longham is a small farm near the delightful market town of Bampton. Central base for exploration of the beautiful Exe valley, Exmoor, coasts; walking, riding, fishing. Guests welcome to roam the farm. Stables & kennelling available. Non-smokers only. OS Ref SS 965195

WEST DEVON

WEST DEVON

West Devon, a quiet land of sheltered valleys, rugged hills and villages centred on the ancient towns of Tavistock and Okehampton. The heart of Devon that brings together all that's best in a holiday.

The area covers a large slice of Dartmoor's famous rugged landscape, providing a unique contrast to the lush valleys, towns, villages and ancient hamlets.

If you like to spend some of your holiday on foot, this is the part of Devon to go for; whatever changes the years bring to other parts, Dartmoor remains untouched with its pools, streams, huge granite out-crops and inquisitive ponies,

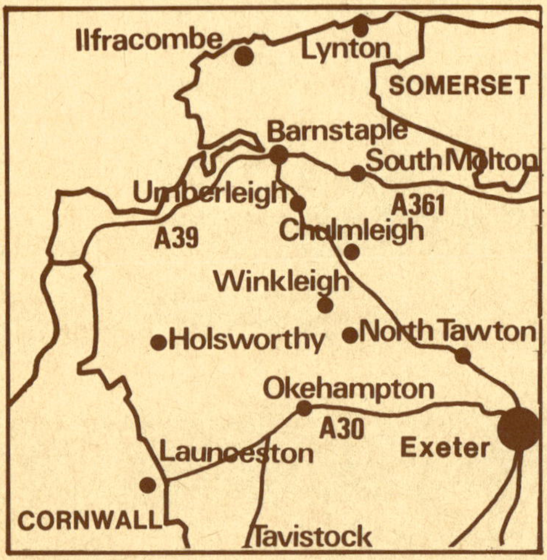

Just one word of caution — stout shoes and a compass are good companions on the moors

You can round off your days with a visit to a friendly inn or cosy country pub — and you'll find plenty to choose from.

The "Friendly Farm Holiday" group offers a special type of holiday which appeals to all the family. The group is made up of traditional Devon farms and the children will find the animals and the running of the farms both fascinating and educational. Looking further afield, your farm will make an ideal base for exploring the many places of interest in this beautiful and unspoilt part of Devon.

GROUP CONTACT:
Jenny King (083785) 647.

W. Devon ENGLAND

FH HIGHER TOWN FARM Sampford Courtenay, Okehampton, Devon, EX20 2SX

Marion Pratt
Tel:-(083782) 285
Open Easter-Sep
B&B £7-£10   Listed
EM   £5
Sleeps 6

Comfortable 16thC farmhouse accommodation offering family, double or twin rooms & guests' TV lounge featuring authentic oak beams, cupboards & fireplaces. Situated in centre of picturesque Sampford Courtenay. "Britain in Bloom" winners and international "Entente Florale" winners. Steeped in history back to 1545 prayer book rebellion & earlier. Central for moorland & coastal attractions. Plentiful home cooking guaranteed. OS Ref FS 633012

FH LOWER OAK FARM Inwardleigh, Okehampton, Devon, EX20 3AS

Rosemary Banbury
Tel:-(0837) 810412
Open Apr-Sept
B&B £8-£8.50   Listed
EM   £4
B&B Weekly £50
B&B + EM weekly £77
Sleeps 8

16thC farmhouse on 172 acre mixed farm, near Okehampton. Home comforts, friendly atmosphere, good cooking - cream a speciality. Ideal for touring coast & Dartmoor, pleasant walks, spinning and weaving crafts next farm, short distance reservoir for fishing & sailing, golf course. Fire Certificate. Accommodation 4 rooms with H/C. 1 family, 1 single, 1 double, 1 twin. Reduced rates for children. OS Ref SX 537992

FH HIGHER CADHAM FARM Jacobstowe, Okehampton, Devon, EX20 3RB

Jenny & John King
Tel:-(083785) 647
Open Mar-Nov
B&B £8
EM   £4.50
Sleeps 7/10

A period farmhouse with oak beams & log fires offers traditional farm holidays on 139 acre working farm. The 4 bedrooms are comfortable, all have sinks, locks & heating. The premises have a residential licence and are AA listed. Fishing, shooting, a games room & play area are just a few of the facilities offered for the inclusive price of £80 pw. OS Ref SS 584027

FH MIDDLECOTT FARM Broadwood Kelly, Winkleigh, Devon, EX19 8DZ

June Western
Tel:-(083783) 381
Closed Xmas-New Year
B&B £7-£8
EM   From £5
Sleeps 6

A traditional mixed 180 acre family-run farm, offering good farm fayre, set in peaceful surroundings with views of Dartmoor. Ideal touring centre for sea and moors, within easy reach of Inch's cider factory & local potteries. I offer a cooked breakfast & 4 course evening meal. 1 double room, 2 family, 1 single. Children under 12 ½ price. Weekly terms BB & EM £80 OS Ref SS 612063

FH FORDE FARM Sticklepath, Nr Okehampton, Devon, EX20 2NS

Rosie Young
Tel:-(0837) 840346
Open Easter-Oct
B&B £8.50-£11   Applied
EM   £6.50-£7.50
Sleeps 6

A really "olde worlde" mediaeval farmhouse. In a convenient position. All modern comforts. Ideal for walking, riding, golf, windsurfing, touring, relaxing. Home cooking. In Dartmoor National Park. Our fields adjoin the moor. Our guests return again and again, come and be spoilt. My aim is to give you a happy and enjoyable holiday. Caravan available for self-catering, also camping. OS Ref SX 641938

FH FAIRHAVEN FARM Gooseford, Whiddon Down, Okehampton, Devon, EX20 2QH

April Scott
Tel:-(064723) 261
Open Apr-Oct
B&B £8-£8.50   Listed
EM   From £4
Sleeps 6

Fairhaven is situated amid the National Park with panoramic views of Dartmoor 200 acres mixed farming, always animals for children to see, within easy reach of North and South coasts, Castle Drogo. Plentiful home cooking guaranteed. Two doubles, one twin, bathroom and showers. We are 1m through Whiddon Down on A30 signposted Gooseford on your left. OS Ref SX 683917

31

7 CREAM OF DEVON

CREAM OF DEVON

Sheltered valleys, rugged hillsides, picturesque villages . . . there's a wealth of contrast awaiting you in West Devon — an area renowned for its welcome and good farmhouse fare.

Okehampton and Tavistock are the major towns in this most rural of Devon's boroughs, both of them well worth spending some time in. Okehampton, a busy market town, boasts a castle — once the seat of the Courtenay family, Earls of Devon — and is dominated by the imposing tors of "High Willhays" and "Yes Tor".

Tavistock, an ancient stannary town on the western side of Dartmoor, is another market town with an interesting industrial past revived at Morwellham Quay.

There are many places of great historical interest such as Buckland Abbey, Cotehele House and Brentnor Church within a few miles of each other.

The coastal area of North and South Devon are within easy reach, as are the shopping centres of Plymouth and Exeter.

Within this area of Dartmoor there is outstanding scenery viewable from every farm. There are many spots of natural and man-mde beauty, such as the lakes of Burrator Reservoir and Meldon Dam and the National Trust property of Lydford Gorge. In addition, there are ample opportunities for a leisurely stroll or, for the experienced rambler, longer walks where you can get away from the bustle of life and enjoy the peace of Dartmoor National Park.

VACANCY SECRETARY:
Valerie Hill (0822) 4319

Cream of Devon ENGLAND

(FH) RUBBYTOWN FARM Gulworthy, Tavistock, Devon

Mary Steer
Tel:-(0822) 832493
Open Mar-Dec
B&B   £8-£8.50
EM   £4.50
       Sleeps 7

Well appointed character farmhouse on working dairy farm (180 acres) on Devon/Cornwall border overlooking Tamar Valley. Children are welcome & can help collect eggs. Places of interest locally; beaches, Dartmoor, woodland walks & old tin mines. Guests are assured every comfort, fresh produce & own clotted cream. Separate bathroom & shower room for guests. 2 doubles, 1 family, 1 twin. Tea/coffee, H/C facilities in all rooms. OS Ref SX 446727

(FH) NEW COURT FARM Lamerton, Tavistock, Devon, PL19 8RR

Valerie Hill
Tel:-(0822) 4319
Open all year
B&B   £7.50-£8.50   Listed
EM   From £5
       Sleeps 6

New Court was originally a barn, recently restored and converted to a farm house situated in a small rural village. Set in its own peaceful, well kept grounds with extensive views. Ideal centre for touring. Picnic area and swing for children, central heating, tastefully and comfortably furnished. 1 double/family, 1 twin-bedded and 1 single room and separate bathroom. OS Ref SX 450770

(FH) SOUTHCOMBE FARM Milton Abbot, Tavistock, Devon, PL19 8PL

Vera Dawe
Tel:-(082287) 221
Open all year
B&B   £7.50-£8   Listed
EM   £4
       Sleeps 6

Situated in the Tamar Valley with lovely views over Cornish hills and River Tamar. Southcombe, built in 1846 on 195 acre mixed farm, formerly part of the Duke of Bedford's Estate. Two miles Endsleigh House (now a fishing club). 7 miles Tavistock, 4m Callington, 8m Launceston. Dining room, TV lounge, 2 doubles, 1 twin with tea/coffee facilities. OS Ref SX 394765

(FH) THE KNOLE Bridestowe, Nr Okehampton, Devon, EX20 4HA

Mavis Bickle
Tel:-(083786) 241
Closed Xmas
B&B   £9.50-£10
EM   £5
       Sleeps 11

A family farm with a homely atmosphere. Situated 1m from the A30, central for Dartmoor and coast. Visitors are free to come and go, and are welcome to view the farm where safety permits. Traditional farmhouse breakfast, 4 course dinner with ample portions. 1 family, 2 doubles, 1 set bunks. Washbasins, razor points and teamaking facilities in rooms. Fire Certificate. OS Ref SX 512878

(FH) WEEK FARM Bridestowe, Okehampton, Devon, EX20 4HZ

Margaret Hockridge
Tel:-(083786) 221
Open all year
B&B   £9.50-£10
EM   £6 (Redn for
       weekly
       booking)
       Sleeps 14

A warm welcome awaits you at Week, set in peaceful countryside, ¾ mile from A30, central for Dartmoor & coasts, 8 miles from Cornish border. Good home cooking assured, traditional English breakfast & 4 course evening meal. Log fires in lounge when cold. 1 double, 1 single, 4 family rooms (1 with shower) all with washbasins & razor points, night storage heaters, tea making facilities. AA listed. Fire certificate. OS Ref SX 518913

(FH) HELE FARM Gulworthy, Tavistock, Devon, PL19 8PA

Rosemary Steer
Tel:-(0822) 833084
Open Mar-Dec
B&B   £7.50   Listed
EM   £5
       Sleeps 6

Hele is an "off the beaten track" working dairy farm. The farmhouse, dated 1780 is an architecturally listed building set in the Tamar Valley beside a forest. It has a large well kept garden with home grown produce. 2 double/family rooms with wash basins, tea making facilities. 1 twin. Central base for Moors, beaches and historic places of interest. OS Ref SX 446727

(FH) **LOWER WOODLEY FARM** Lamerton, Tavistock, Devon, PL19 8QU

Anita Stock
Tel: (0822) 832456
Closed Dec, Xmas-New Year
B&B £8.50   Listed
EM £4
Reductions for children.
Sleeps 6

Lower Woodley is situated at the end of its own ¼ mile lane with views over beautiful countryside. The area has much to provide of historical interest. 6 people can be accommodated in 2 twin and 1 double room with 2 bathrooms. Separate dining and sitting room. Farmhouse cooking. E.M. optional. Children very welcome, with babysitting provided. OS Ref SX 421751

(FH) **SLEEKERS FARM** Sourton, Okehampton, Devon, EX20 4HN

Helen Alford
Tel:-(083786) 381
Open Easter-Oct
B&B £9-£10
EM From £4.50
Sleeps 5

A working beef/sheep farm situated in a small village with church and inn. Ideal base for walking on Dartmoor which is just 2 minutes away. Recreational facilities are within easy reach. 1 double/family, 1 twin, H/C in both rooms. OS Ref SX 905535

(FH) **VENN MILL FARM** Lewdown, Okehampton, Devon, EX20 4EB

Monica Horn
Tel:-(083786) 288
Open Mar-Oct
B&B £9-£10   Listed
EM £5.50
Sleeps 8

160 acre working farm with modern farmhouse situated midway betwixt the attractive historic towns of Launceston, Okehampton and Tavistock. Just off the A30 trunk road. Good home cooking our speciality. Trout fishing available on the farm. Good facilities for pony trekking and coarse fishing nearby. AA approved. OS Ref SX 485885

Friendly Farm Animals in a traditional farmyard setting
OPEN MAY - SEPTEMBER
1 p.m.-6 p.m. every day (except Tuesdays)
Admission 70p (under 2's free)
Pony & Cart rides. Craft & Home Produce Shop. Farm ice-cream.
Traditional Cream Teas.
SMITHALEIGH
(Nr. Lee Mill), Plympton, Devon
TEL: PLYMOUTH (0752) 893772

BOOKING TIPS

FARM HOLIDAY BUREAU

NO VACANCIES? If you have any difficulty finding a vacancy in this area, contact the Vacancy Secretary or Group Contact whose name appears at the beginning of this section.

34

Dartmoor & S. Devon ENGLAND

DARTMOOR & SOUTH DEVON

DARTMOOR & SOUTH DEVON

If you enjoy the outdoor life, this area offers unlimited opportunities in the 365 square miles of Dartmoor National Park, with its contrasting open moorland, wooded valleys, and the coast. Walking, horseriding, climbing, bird-watching and golf, or alternatively coarse, game and sea-fishing, sailing and wind-surfing, are all within approximately half-an-hours drive.

Also easily accessible are many places of interest. Dartington Hall, centre of culture and the arts, Buckfast Abbey, the Dart Valley Steam Railway and the Shire Horse Centre. You may also visit historical sites from the bronze age onwards, country mansions, busy markets, antique and craft shops, country parks, National Trust properties, museums and resorts of all kinds from bustling Torquay to tranquil villages.

Food and drink can be a special delight in this part of the world — no visit would be complete without sampling a traditional cream tea . . . and the best of this delicacy should come with a yellow crust and be thick enough to stand your spoon in. Then there's the local cider!

And for appetites of a different kind you can spend your evenings enjoying the theatre, concert and show life on offer in Torquay, Paignton, Plymouth and Exeter.

VACANCY SECRETARIES:
B&B — Noreen Atkinson (0626) 852352
Self Catering — Linda Harvey (0626) 833266

(FH) WELPRITTON FARM Holne, Ashburton, S Devon, TQ13 7RX

Sue Townsend
Tel:-(03643) 273
Closed Xmas
B&B £10-£11
EM £6
£91-£98/week
Sleeps 12

♛ ♛

🐴 (5) 🐎

A warm welcome awaits you at Welpritton, a working farm with a beautiful farmhouse in panoramic countryside on the edge of Dartmoor ½ hour's drive from Exeter, Plymouth, Torbay. Riding, fishing, walking, sailing, golf nearby. Modernised to a very high standard, most rooms have ensuite facilities. Caring personal attention, plenty of mouth-watering farm produced food. Games room, swimming pool. Rabbits, donkeys & goats for children. OS Ref SX 716704

(FH) VENN FARM Ugborough, Nr Ivybridge, Devon, PL21 0PE

Pat Stephens
Tel:-(03647) 3240
Open Easter-Sep
B&B £9.50   Listed
EM £4.50
Sleeps 6

🐴

Working farm amid peaceful scenery in the 'South Hams' on the edge of Dartmoor. Easy access to Plymouth, Exeter and beaches. Children encouraged to take an interest in farm life. Accommodation comprises 2 family bedrooms each with washbasin, 1 twin bedroom. Bathroom. The speciality of the house is 'carve your own roast' and the majority of the food is home produced and plentiful. OS Ref SX 686565

(FH) HIGHER VENTON FARM Widecombe-in-the-Moor, Newton Abbot, South Devon, TR13 7TF

Betty Hicks
Tel:-(03642) 235
Closed Xmas
B&B £8.50-£9   Listed
EM £4-£5.50
Sleeps 6

🐴 🐎

A 17th Century thatched farmhouse, ½m from the pretty village of Widecombe-in-the-Moor. Ideal for touring Dartmoor and 16 miles from the coast. Riding stables nearby. Colour TV Two double rooms and 1 twin, 2 double rooms with wash basins. Bathroom upstairs, H/C. Good home cooking, local produce. Homely atmosphere. Car space. OS Ref SX 723761

(FH) NARRACOMBE FARM Narracombe, Ilsington, Newton Abbot, Devon, TQ13 9RD

Sue Wills
Tel:-(03646) 243
Closed Xmas and New Year
B&B £9   Listed
Sleeps 6

🐴 🐎

Set within Dartmoor National Park, this lovely 16th Century listed farmhouse is surrounded by attractive gardens with panoramic views to the coast. The bedrooms are spacious, pretty and the atmosphere is relaxed and peaceful. Guests are welcomed into the family lounge with colour TV and have the exclusive use of dining room to enjoy their farmhouse breakfast. Reductions for children. OS Ref SX 788768

(FH) NEW COTT FARM Poundsgate, Newton Abbot, Devon, TQ13 7PD

Margaret Phipps
Tel:-(03643) 421
Open Apr-Dec
B&B £9-£10   Listed
EM £5
Sleeps 8

🐴 (3) ♿

Working farm in Dartmoor National Park with sheep/cattle overlooking lovely Devon countryside. Private fishing for trout in own ponds. Good area for birdwatching, walking, riding. Friendly relaxed atmosphere in well-appointed accommodation 1 twin, 3 doubles, with handbasins, tea/coffee facilities, electric heating, large lounge/diner, colour TV. Plenty of good food, fresh local produce including cream, free range eggs. Weekly rates from £80 BB & EM. OS Ref SX 701729

(FH) THE OLD FARMHOUSE Fore Stoke, Holne, Ashburton, Devon, TQ13 7SS

Candida Ker
Tel:-(03643) 361
Closed Xmas
B&B £9   Applied
EM £6.50
Sleeps 6

🐴 🐎

A small working farm, adjoining the moor, with sheep and ponies. Quiet position with magnificent views over fields, woods and moorland. The extensively modernised old stone longhouse provides double and twin bedded rooms, family room with own bathroom. Friendly atmosphere, good food, walking, fishing and ponies to ride. Pets by arrangement only. OS Ref SX 698701

Dartmoor & S. Devon ENGLAND

(FH) GREENWELL FARM Nr Meavy, Yelverton, Devon, PL20 6PY

Mrs Bridget Cole
Tel:-(0822) 853563
Closed Xmas-New Year
B&B   £8.50-£9.50   Listed
EM   From £5.50
      Sleeps 6

16th Century listed farmhouse within Dartmoor National Park. Spacious guest rooms look on to the Moors. A busy family farm we encourage our guests to look around & even participate. Local riding, swimming & walks. 8m from Plymouth & the coast. Good home cooking to high standards using fresh local produce.

(FH) SHARPHAM BARTON Ashprington, Totnes, Devon, TQ9 7DX

Claire Grimshaw
Tel:-(080423) 278
Open all year
B&B   From £9.50   Listed
EM   From £6
      Sleeps 6

Sharpham Barton is situated close to Totnes in a peaceful valley overlooking the River Dart. Accommodation comprises en suite bedrooms, TV in sitting room, tea/coffee making facilities. Our charges include use of outdoor heated swimming pool, grass tennis court, full size croquet lawn, ponies for riding, sailing dingies and a rowing boat kept on the river. OS Ref SX 813582

(FH) ADAMS HELE FARM Ashburton, South Devon, TQ13 7NW

Dorothy Dent
Tel:-(0364) 52525
Open Jan-Nov
B&B   £9-£10.50
EM   £5.50
      Sleep 6

This 16th Century listed farmhouse nestles on a south facing hill overlooking the Dart Valley and moors. It is a comfortable base from which to explore the beauties of Dartmoor. 90 acres are stocked with cattle, sheep and ponies. The south Devon coast is within 12 miles. There are 3 double rooms all with wash hand basins. OS Ref SX 743 703

(FH) HEADBOROUGH FARM Ashburton, Devon, TQ13 7QR

Brenda Tuckett
Tel:-(0364) 52360
Closed Xmas and New Year
B&B   £8-£9
EM   £4
      Sleeps 6

Headborough Farm is mixed working farm, ½m from ancient stanary town of Ashburton with sea & moor all within easy reach. 12th Century farmhouse with traditional beamed lounge/dining room has 3 double rooms with H/C. Toilet upstairs and bathroom/toilet downstairs. Guests are provided with home-produced fare such as clotted cream and free-range eggs. Ample parking space. OS Ref SX 765 710

(FH) DODBROOKE FARM Michelcombe, Holne, Newton Abbot, Devon, TQ13 7SP

Judy Henderson
Tel:-(03643) 461
Open Mar-Nov (not Easter)
B&B   £8.50-£9.50   Applied
EM   £5
      Red'n for
      children
      Sleeps 4

Dodbrooke Farm is a listed 17 Century former longhouse in an idyllic valley at the foot of Dartmoor. Food is mostly home produced on the farm. There are sheep, goats and poultry and guests are welcome to explore the fields and bordering Holy Brook. Local attractions include walking on Dartmoor, fishing in the River Dart and carriage driving. OS Ref SX 697588

(FH) LYNEHAM FARMHOUSE Chudleigh, Newton Abbot, Devon, TQ13 0EH

Noreen Atkinson
Tel:-(0626) 852352
Open Easter-Sep
B&B   £10-£12
EM   £5
      Sleeps 5

Enjoy the atmosphere of this 16th Century farmhouse, beautifully renovated. Oak beams and open fireplaces. Guests' own bathroom, dining and sitting room. All furnished to a high standard. Breakfast and evening meal freshly cooked using Devon produce. Walk in 7 acres orchard and woodland with pond, wild flowers, sheep and hens. We are a non smoking family and ask guests not to smoke. OS Ref SX 856794

FH KNOWLE FARM   Rattery, South Brent, Devon, TQ10 9JY

Shirley and Stephen Bradley
Tel:-(03647) 2143
Closed Xmas
B&B   £8.50   Listed
EM   £5.50
Sleeps 6

Mixed farm with 17th Century Listed farmhouse, set in Lush River Valley, conveniently situated for Dartmoor, Totnes, South Hams coast and A38. Informal atmosphere, generous portions of fresh food, river to paddle & fish for brook trout. Children's splasher pool, garden, Shetland pony, pets, babysitting. Excellent village inn, beer garden, 1 double, 1 family room with brass beds, guests bathroom, TV lounge. OS Ref SX 722 610

FH LOWER SOUTHWAY FARM   Widecombe in the Moor, Newton Abbot, South Devon, TQ13 7TE

Dawn Nosworthy
Tel:-(03642) 277
Closed Xmas and New Year
B&B   £8.50-£9.50   Listed
EM   From £5
Sleeps 6

Situated close to the lovely village of Widecombe in the Moor in the Dartmoor National Park. Ideal for walking, riding (stables nearby) and only 30 minutes from coast. 1 family, 1 twin each with hand basins, tea and coffee facilities and heating. Bathroom, toilet, lounge with colour TV. Good home cooking. OS Ref SX 725771

FH GREAT SLONCOMBE FARM   Moreton Hampstead, Newton Abbot, Devon, TQ13 8QF

Trudie M. Merchant
Tel:-(0647) 40595
Open all year
B&B   £8.50-£9.50   Listed
EM   £5-£5.50
Sleeps 6

Dairy Farm in the National Park, central for exploring Devon and Cornwall. The farmhouse dates from the 13th Century. Farm walk, guests can watch milking etc. Only six guests at a time. All bedrooms have tea/coffee making facilities, electric blankets and heating. Dining room, separate tables, sitting room, colour TV. Children welcome - reduced rates. Crafts made on the farm. OS Ref 862 738

FH WOOSTON FARM   Moreton Hampstead, Newton Abbot, Devon, TQ13 8QA

Mary Cuming
Tel:-(0647) 40367
Open Mar-Oct
B&B   £8-£9
EM   From £5
Sleeps 6

Situated in the Dartmoor National Park, Wooston Farm is a mixed farm of 280 acres, with a friendly atmosphere, comfortable accommodation & good food. It is ideally situated for exploring Dartmoor the Teign Valley & the Cathedral City of Exeter with many interesting aspects also easy reach of the Devon coastline. OS Ref SX 904 761

FH NEWHOUSE BARTON   Ipplepen, Newton Abbot, Devon, TQ12 5UN

(Mrs) Sue Stafford
Tel:-(0803) 812539
Open all year
B&B   £11-£12.50
EM   £6.50
Sleeps 8

A lovely old farmhouse set in 115 acres of Devon's rolling countryside yet only a short drive to the coast or Dartmoor. All bedrooms have private bathrooms, tea/coffee making facilities & colour TV, oak beamed lounge with stone fireplace & dining room with separate tables. Table tennis & ¼ size snooker table in games room. Plenty of good food & friendly atmosphere. OS Ref 823 650

CH GLEN COTTAGE   Rock Road, Chudleigh, S. Devon, TQ13 0JJ

Jill Shears
Tel:-(0626) 852209
Open all year
B&B   £9
EM   From £4.50

Situated in a beautiful glen at Chudleigh, once chosen by Bishop Lacey for his summer palace in the XI Century; 20 mins from Dartmoor and coast. Basins in all rooms, residents lounge, colour T.V., swimming pool, 4 acre garden and woodlands, with lake and river. Adjoining beauty spot with rocks, caves and waterfall. Good home cooking. Reductions for children and for weekly bookings. OS Ref SX 8679

Dartmoor & S. Devon **ENGLAND**

(sc) **WOODER FARM** Widecome in the Moor, Newton Abbot, Devon, TQ13 7TR

Angela Bell
Tel:-(03642) 391
Open all year
SC £50-£190
Sleeps 2/8

Granite cottages and converted coachhouse on 108 acre friendly family farm, nestled in picturesque valley of Widecombe surrounded by unspoilt woodland, moors and granite tors. Excellent centre for touring Devon and exploring Dartmoor by foot or on horseback. Inn with good food ¾m. Clean and fully equipped including TV, laundry room, central heating. Large gardens, courtyard for easy parking. OS Ref SX 720778

(sc) **SHIPPEN AND DAIRY COTTAGES** Look Weep Farm, Liverton, Newton Abbot, Devon, TQ12 6HT

Marion Harbinson
Tel:-(0626) 833277
Open Mar-Oct
SC £68-£245
Sleeps 4

Within the Dartmoor National Park set in peaceful farmland with wooded valleys and spectacular moorland just beyond. Close to south coast. Golf, riding, fishing locally. The 2 delightful cottages were converted from a traditional barn across former farmyard from the farmhouse. Sleeping 4/5, equipped luxuriously and in keeping, own gardens with beautiful views. Heated swimming pool. High chairs, cots, linen available. OS Ref SX 808957

(sc) **HOCKMOOR LODGE** Hockmoor House, Buckfast, Nr. Buckfastleigh, South Devon, TQ11 0HN

Julia Cross
Tel:-(0364) 42819
Open all year
SC £70-£205
Sleeps 6

Chauffeur's Lodge set in the delightful surroundings of the Dartmoor National Park, adjacent to National Trust woodland and the River Dart. Walking, riding, fishing, birdwatching close by. Seaside ½hr drive. Comfortably furnished to a high standard for 6. The Lodge comprises 3 bedrooms, sitting room with TV, log burning fire. Fully fitted kitchen/dining room, bathroom, games room, CH, garden. Linen and electricity included. OS Ref SX 731676

(sc) **CROWNLEY** Mill Coombe, Ilsington, Newton Abbot, Devon, TQ13 9RT

Sue Retallick
Tel:-(03646) 430
Open all year
SC £65-£135
Sleeps 7

Crownley, bungalow sleeping 5/7. Fully furnished. Three bedrooms, sitting/cum bedroom; sitting room, kitchen/diner. Set in lovely valley with woods and fields, with the moor just over the hill. Ideal for touring Dartmoor and South Devon. Plymouth, Exeter and Torquay being not too far away, sea approximately 14 miles away. Children and pets welcome. OS Ref SX 768755

(sc) **ROVERLEE** Mill Coombe, Ilsington, Newton Abbot, Devon, TQ13 9RT

Sue Retallick
Tel:-(03646) 430
Open all year
SC £95-£185
Sleeps 8

Roverlee is a house sleeping 8. Fully furnished, six bedrooms; large kitchen/diner; large sitting room, with lovely views of Dartmoor and countryside. Ideal for touring Dartmoor and South Devon. Plymouth, Exeter and Torquay being not too far away, sea approximately 14 miles away. Children and pets welcome. OS Ref SX 772764

FARM HOLIDAY BUREAU

(sc) **STICKWICK HOUSE** Frost Farm, Bovey Tracey, Newton Abbot, S Devon, TQ13 9PP

Linda Harvey
Tel:-(0626) 833266
Open all year
SC £110
Sleeps 5-12

A delightful period house, farmhouse & cottage furnished to a high standard, open fires, colour TV. Just outside Hennock, a typical Devon village in the foothills of Dartmoor National Park. Childrens farmyard, games barn, play area. Barbecue. 2m from Bovey Tracey, the gateway town to Dartmoor and A38. Market town of Newton Abbot 6m. Beaches at Teignmouth & Dawlish. AA listed. OS Ref SX 837795

39

SC THE LOFT The Old Farmhouse, Fore Stoke, Holne, Ashburton, Devon TQ13 7SS

Candida Ker
Tel:-(03643) 361
Open all year
SC £80-£150
Sleeps 4/6

Self contained family unit in spacious loft of stone farmhouse, separate access leading from stable yard. Entrance lobby/boot room with airing cupboard, living room/kitchenette, double bedroom, twin bedded room, bathroom, WC, Colour TV, CH, linen, iron & board. Completely modernised to provide high standard of accommodation. Own pony welcome. Pets by arrangement. Electricity included. Evening meals usually available in farmhouse on request. OS Ref SX 698601

SC SEALE STOKE BARN Holne, Newton Abbot, Devon, TQ13 7SS

Charles Hill-Smith
Tel:-(03643) 408
Open Feb-Nov
SC £100-£180
Sleeps 6

Traditional stone built organic stock farm, situated high above the River Dart on the edge of Dartmoor, with magnificent views, and at the end of a quiet lane 1m from the village of Holne. Converted to the highest standards. The Barn is fully equipped for 6, with an open plan kitchen/sitting room, 3 bedrooms and bathroom. Linen, towels and TV provided. OS Ref SX 695708

SC LYNEHAM FARM Chudleigh, Newton Abbot, Devon, TQ13 0EH

Noreen Atkinson
Tel:-(0626) 852352
Open all year
SC £70-£170
Sleeps 5

Feel at home in this beautifully converted barn. Accommodation includes kitchen, lounge/diner, with exposed beams, 2 bedrooms and bathroom. Full central heating, fitted carpets and a high standard of furnishings. Walk in 7 acres of orchard and woodland with pond, wild flowers, sheep and hens. Easy access to coast and Dartmoor. We ask our guests not to smoke. OS Ref SX 856 794

BECKY FALLS

A MUST FOR ALL VISITORS to DARTMOOR

A truly delightful beauty spot set in 50 acres of woodland.
Newly opened Nature Trails and excellent 'SPOTTER PACK' to accompany walks.

Open daily Easter to late Autumn
Becky Falls is on the B3344 Bovey Tracey to Manaton Road.

BECKY FALLS DARTMOOR

Manaton
Nr. Bovey Tracey
Tel: Manaton 259

ALL INCLUSIVE PRICE
£1.00
per vehicle including all occupants

Gift & Craft Shop
Riverside & Nature Walks
Restaurant . Picnic Area
1988 Season

MOOR TO SHORE
South Devon

9

MOOR TO SHORE

The South Hams, in South Devon, is a unique part of the West Country, catering for a wide variety of tastes. The area lies between Plymouth and Torbay, is easily accessible from the A38 and is renowned for its beauty and variety of countryside. Not just the countryside either, it has such towns as Elizabethan Totnes with its castle, or the historic seaport of Dartmouth scattered around the Dart Estuary and plenty of attractive villages.

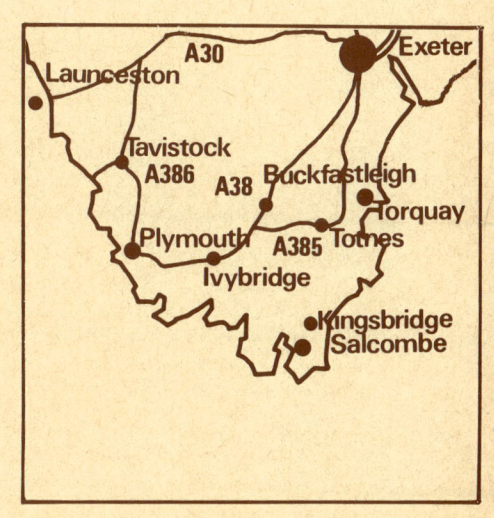

The coastline, which is truly spectacular, has sheltered harbours and estuaries at Yealm, Salcombe and Dartmouth. Fishing, riding and golf can be enjoyed in many places, and if you could ever possibly tire of the area, turn north and the Dartmoor National Park is just a stone's throw away. The mild climate of the area makes it particularly attractive for out-of-season visits.

The area also includes wildlife and country parks, a Shire horse centre at Dunstone near Yealhampton and a wide variety of interesting museums. For those fans of steam, the area boasts two steam railways on the Dart Valley Railway, one of which connects with Totnes mainline.

VACANCY SECRETARY:
Jill Balkwill (0548) 550312

(FH) SOUTH ALLINGTON HOUSE Chivelstone, Kingsbridge, South Devon, TQ7 2NB

Edward & Barbara Baker
Tel:-(054851) 272
Closed Xmas
B&B £9-£10   Listed
EM   £6
Sleeps 16

Country residence set in 4 acres of grounds, now a working farm on the south Devon coast. Cider and home grown produce served with the evening meal. We have family, double and twin bedded rooms. H & C and tea making facilities in all bedrooms. Spend your evenings on our lawns, with a game of bowls, or just stroll amongst the trees. OS Ref SW 793387

(FH) BURTON FARM Galmpton, Kingsbridge, South Devon, TQ7 3EY

David & Anne Rossiter
Tel:-(0548) 561210
Closed Xmas-New Year
B&B £8.75   Listed
EM   £5.50
Sleeps 6
SC   £80-£200
Sleeps 5

Large working unit situated in South Huish Valley, 1m village of Hope Cove, 3m famous sailing haunt of Salcombe. Walking, beaches, sailing, windsurfing, bathing, diving, fishing. Farm has dairy herd and 2 flocks pedigree sheep. Guests welcome to take part in farm activities when appropriate. Traditional farmhouse cooking, home produce (clotted cream, eggs etc) 4 course dinner. S/C also available. Warm welcome assured. OS Ref SX 6840

(FH) COURT BARTON FARMHOUSE Aveton Gifford, Kingsbridge, Devon, TQ7 4LE

John & Jill Balkwill
Tel:-(0548) 550312
Closed Xmas-New Year
B&B £8-£10.50
Sleeps 16

Lovely 16th Century farmhouse in peaceful setting. Rooms have comfortable quilted beds & washbasins. There is access at all times to bedrooms and to a TV lounge with tea-making facilities and a plentiful supply of holiday reading. Use our games rooms, playroom, swimming pool or walk across our 300 acre farm down to the estuary. This is a beautiful area - come and share it with us. OS Ref SX 696479

(SC) SOUTH ALLINGTON HOUSE Chivelstone, Kingsbridge, S Devon, TQ7 2NB

Edward & Barbara Baker
Tel:-(054851) 272
Open all year
SC   £100-£225
Sleeps 5
+ cot

South Allington House East Wing. Set in 4 acres of mature gardens. Close to many safe beaches & coastal walks. The accommodation has been designed & furnished to give you home comforts in relaxing surroundings. Equipped to a high standard. All rooms are centrally heated & close carpeted. Send SAE to Barbara Baker for details. OS Ref SW 793387

(SC) FLEAR FARM COTTAGES East Allington, (nr Kingsbridge), Devon, TQ9 7RF

Di Scott
Tel:-054 852 227
Open Mar-New Year
SC   £140-£560
Sleeps 2-8

Exclusively for non smokers. Converted stone barns offering great comfort & style. Fitted kitchens with microwaves, full central heating, telephones, unique paintings. Set in a wooded valley with flowers, birds, trout fishing, peace, covered swimming pool & more. Phone for a brochure. OS Ref SX 766 465

(SC) REVETON FARM Loddiswell, Kingsbridge, South Devon, TQ7 4RY

Jaap & Anneke Starrenburg
Tel:-(054 8550) 265
Open all year
SC   £100-£160
Sleeps 8

Modern bungalow with all possible comforts. Sleeps 6 in beds, 2 more possible in folding beds. Well equipped kitchen and dining room. Colour television. Outside a most beautiful view of Avon valley and rail road bridge. Hunting and fishing on the farm is possible. OS Ref SX 722 498

Moor to Shore ENGLAND

(sc) WIDLAND FARM Modbury, Ivybridge, South Devon, PL21 OSA

Ian & Bridgette Anthony
Tel:-(0548) 830719
Open all year
SC £54-£170
Max guests 20

Widland is a small sheep and grass farm in a peaceful sheltered position between Dartmoor and Bigbury Bay. A stone barn, converted to immaculate 2 bedroomed flats, faces south over the farm. Each sleeping ¾. An ideal family holiday all year. Cotton bed linen and colour television included. Short breaks off season. Personal attention and high standards of maintenance assured. OS Ref SX 674516

(sc) HOPE BARTON FARM COTTAGES Hope Cove, Kingsbridge, Devon, TQ7 3HT

Anita Ling
Tel:-(0548) 561393
Open Mar-New Year
SC £110-£330
Sleeps 4-8

Hope Barton is a working farm standing amidst National Trust property with its cliff walks and wildlife, and adjoining the friendly village of Hope Cove with its safe beaches. The old farm buildings have been tastefully converted into luxury cottages offering comfort and tranquillity. Bed linen supplied. Come once and become like many others - a "regular" we hope! OS Ref SX 684396

(sc) STONE BARTON Court Barton Farmhouse, Aveton Gifford, Kingsbridge, Devon, TQ7 4LE

John & Jill Balkwill
Tel:-(0548) 550312
Open all year
SC £110-£320
Sleeps 8/10

Stone Barton is a modern house adjoining the main farmhouse. Sleeping 8/10 people in 4 bedrooms with comfortable quilted beds. The fully-fitted kitchen (with freezer & washing machine) leads into an L-shaped sitting room with steps taking you to the large garden & patio with furniture & barbeque. Use our games rooms, playroom, swimming pool or walk across our 300 acre farm down to the estuary OS Ref SX 696479

10 EAST DEVON

EAST DEVON

East Devon has picturesque villages and miles of sandy and pebble beaches. This is the country of the old sea dogs of Elizabethan times, such as Sir Francis Drake and Sir Walter Raleigh, the latter having been born in one of the farmhouses!

East Devon Farm and Country Holidays offer a choice of Farmhouse Bed and Breakfast and Self Catering Accommodation all of a high standard.

Wherever you stay you are not far from the coast where you can enjoy peaceful cliff-top walks and spectacular seascapes; inland a little way you can wander over moors and common land or down winding country lanes. For the more active there's swimming, riding, sailing, fishing and windsurfing.

If it's places of interest you want, East Devon won't let you down — there are craft centres, churches, markets and museums. Exeter alone boasts a cathedral with a 300ft nave — the longest span of unbroken Gothic vaulting in the world, plus priceless manuscripts; a maritime museum with more than 100 crafts from all over the world, and the Royal Albert Memorial collection of lace, china and glass.

If all that leaves you hungry, you can choose to take meals in village inns, thatched cottage cafes or seaside restaurants — whatever your choice you will find excellent fare . . . at very fair prices.

VACANCY SECRETARY:
Marion Down (03954) 3372

E. Devon ENGLAND

(CH) HEATHLANDS   Higher Metcombe, Ottery St Mary, Devon, EX11 1SH

Michael Dickens
Tel:-(040 481) 4065
Open Apr-Oct
CH   Sleeps 6
B&B   £9.50

Set in 9½ acres of gardens, woodlands, orchards, pastures, this country house offers spacious accommodation in beautiful surroundings. Bedrooms have washbasins and tea-making facilities. Comfortable sitting room with log fire. Full English breakfast. This smallholding produces organic fruit & vegetables, with free range eggs from our ducks & chickens. Well situated for exploring E Devon & particularly suited to nature lovers & walkers. OS Ref SY 066926

(FH) LOWER PINN FARM   Peak Hill, Sidmouth, Devon, EX10 0NN

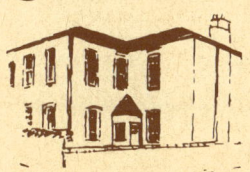

Elizabeth Tancock
Tel:-039 55 3733
Open Easter-Sep
Sleeps 6
B&B   £9-£10

A friendly welcome awaits you at this family run working farm of 200 acres. 2 miles from Sidmouth in a scenic area. 1 family, 1 double bedroom, H/C, colour TV, tea/coffee facilities in bedrooms. Access at all times, lounge, separate dining room. Full English Breakfast served. OS Ref SY 096865

(CH) THE BULSTONE   Higher Bulstone, Branscombe, Nr Seaton, Devon, EX12 3BL

Peter & Barbara Freeman
Tel:-(029780) 446
Open Feb-Nov
B&B   £10-£13
EM   £8.45
CH   Sleeps 12

Catering especially for young families, we have everything for mother and child. Children under 2 free (under 5 out of season), reductions for other age groups. We have a reputation for good food and can cater for special diets. Licenced Bar. OS Ref SY 178897

(FH) PINN BARTON   Pinn Lane, Peak Hill, Sidmouth, S Devon, EX10 0NN

Betty Sage
Tel:-(03955) 4004
Open Mar-Nov
B&B   £9-£11

A warm welcome awaits you on 330 acre farm by the coast, 2m Sidmouth seafront, lovely walks along cliff paths, around farm. Bedrooms have H/C, colour TV, hot drink facilities, electric blankets, heating, access at all times. Family room has ensuite bathroom. Guests have TV lounge, dining room has separate tables, full English breakfast is served. Restaurants, inns, places to visit nearby. OS Ref SY 100868

(FH) HILL FARM   East Budleigh, Nr Budleigh Salterton, Devon, EX9 7DA

Betty Quick
Tel:-(03954) 2761
Opens Feb-Nov
B&B   £8-£9   Listed
EM   £5
Sleeps 4

A fully modernised working dairy farm. Perfectly situated between coast and countryside. Ideally suitable for family holidays. High standard of home cooking using locally grown produce. The bedrooms are equipped with washbasins and hot drink facilities. Heating and electric blankets are provided for early and late season. Colour TV available in lounge/dining room. Reductions for children. OS Ref SY 090310

(FH) RYDON FARM   Woodbury, Nr Exeter, Devon, EX5 1LB

Sally Glanvill
Tel:-(0395) 32341
Open all year exc Xmas
B&B   £8.50-£10   Listed
Sleeps 6

A warm welcome awaits you at our 16th C Devon Longhouse. Ideal for exploring the coast, moors and the historic city of Exeter. A working dairy farm where guests are welcome to watch the milking, calf feeding etc. Bedrooms have heating, washbasins and tea/coffee making facilities. Lounge with colour TV. Full English Breakfast is served. Several excellent local pubs and restaurants. OS Ref SX 207085

FH PITT FARM Ottery St Mary, Devon, EX11 1NL

Susan Hansford
Tel:-(04081) 2439
Closed Xmas and New Year
B&B £9-£10.50 Listed
EM From £5
Sleeps 16

A warm family atmosphere awaits you at this 16th century thatched farmhouse which nestles in the picturesque Otter Valley. ½m off A30 on B3176. Within easy reach of all East Devon resorts and pleasure facilities. Good home cooking using fresh local/own produce. A working beef-arable farm surrounded by lovely countryside and rural walks. Family, double and twin rooms. Lounge with TV, dining room. OS Ref SY 089966

FH MARIANNE POOL Clyst St George, Exeter, Devon, EX3 0NZ

Janet Bragg
Tel:-(039287) 4939
Open Easter-Oct
B&B £8-£9 Listed
Sleeps 4 + 2-3 children

Welcome to our thatched Devon Longhouse on a working farm, rurally situated betwixt the historic city of Exeter and the beaches of Exmouth & Budleigh Salterton, within easy reach of a variety of eating places. We offer one family room and one double room with tea-making facilities, separate dining and sitting room with TV, and a large garden suitable for children. Car essential. OS Ref SX 888987

FH HAYES BARTON East Budleigh, Budleigh Salterton, Devon, EX9 7BS

Marion Down
Tel:-(03954) 3372
Closed Xmas-New Year
B&B £10-£16 Listed
Sleeps 6

A charming thatched farmhouse, famous as the birthplace of Sir Walter Raleigh. The 200 acre dairy and cereal farm is 1m from the picturesque village of East Budleigh. 1 bedroom with a 4 poster bed with en suite bathroom and 1 family suite with private bathroom. All rooms have tea/coffee making facilities. A hearty breakfast served. Lovely walks nearby and a peaceful garden to relax in. Grass tennis court. OS Ref SX 051851

FH CREALY BARTON Clyst St Mary, Exeter, Devon, EX5 1DR

Marion Down
Tel:-0395 32567
Closed Xmas
B&B £9-£15
Sleeps 6

A lovely farmhouse overlooking the 250 acre dairy & cereal farm, 2m from M5 (exit 30) 1½ miles from Clyst St Mary village. Ideally placed for exploring Devon. Spacious rooms - 2 family rooms, 1 double room, all with ensuite bathrooms. Tea/coffee making facilities & access at all times. Lounge with colour TV. Full English breakfast. A warm welcome assured. OS Ref SX 002905

FH HIGHER COOMBE FARM Tipton St John, Sidmouth, Devon, EX10 0AX

Kerstin Farmer
Tel:-(040481) 3385
Open Easter-Oct
B&B £8-£9.50 Listed
EM £5
Sleeps 5

A warm welcome awaits you at this 160 acres beef/sheep farm. Peacefully situated in the beautiful Otter Valley, only 4m from Sidmouth seafront. Ideal for touring the whole of E Devon and beyond. Family, twin and single rooms, dining room and lounge with colour TV. Good mainly home produced farmhouse food and full English breakfast. OS Ref SY 101920

FH HIGHER BAGMORES FARM Woodbury, Exeter, Devon, EX5 1LA

Myrtle Glanvill
Tel:-(0395) 32261
Open Easter-Oct
B&B £8.50-£9.50 Listed
Sleeps 6

A red brick farmhouse set in delightful East Devon countryside. A working beef, sheep and arable farm situated 7 miles from Exeter, 5 miles from Exmouth and Budleigh Salterton. Bedrooms are equipped with tea and coffeemaking facilities. Lounge with colour TV Transport is essential. Ample free parking. Horse riding is available locally. OS Ref SY 996877

E. Devon ENGLAND

(FH) CLAYPITTS FARM East Hill, Ottery St Mary, Devon, EX11 1QD

Jayne Burrow
Tel:-(040481) 4599
Open Easter-Sep
B&B £8-£9.50   Listed
EM   £5
Sleeps 6

Jayne Burrow & family welcome you to their 70 acre dairy farm situated in an area of outstanding beauty, about 450ft above sea level. With picturesque views of the surrounding Otter Valley, yet only 15mins from the seaside town of Sidmouth. We offer farmhouse cooking using local/own produce. Comfortable accommodation, guests own bathroom, 2 WC, lounge with colour TV, dining room, parking. OS Ref SY 109924

(FH) CADHAY BRIDGE FARM Ottery St Mary, Devon, EX11 1QS

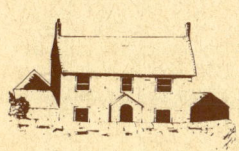

Joan Burrow
Tel:-(040481) 2761
Open Easter-Oct
B&B £8.50-£10   Listed
EM   £5
Sleeps 6

Joan Burrow and family welcome you to their dairy farm, lying beside the River Otter, only 15 minutes walk from Ottery town centre. We offer mostly home produced farmhouse cooking, and the comfortable accommodation in the mid-Victorian farmhouse consists of 1 double room and 2 single beds in adjoining room and 1 double room, bathroom and WC upstairs. OS Ref SY 095962

(FH) HOME FARM Escot, Ottery St Mary, Devon, EX11 1LU

Doreen Turl
Tel:-(0404) 850241
Open Easter-Sep
B&B £8.50-£10   Listed
EM   From £4.50
Sleeps 6

16th century Home Farm is a 300 acre mixed working farm situated in beautiful parkland near the historic town of Ottery St Mary & Sidmouth, approx ½ mile A30. Many places of architectural interest & pleasure facilities nearby. Double family with H/C & twin rooms, tea/coffee making facilities, lounge with colour TV. Dining room where good mainly home produced food is served. Parking. OS Ref SY 082982

(FH) GULLIFORD FARM Lympstone, Nr Exmouth, Devon, EX8 5AQ

June Hallett
Tel:-(039287) 3067
Closed Xmas
B&B £11-£15   Listed
Sleeps 6

You are assured of a warm welcome to our 16th Century farmhouse with its beautiful garden, tennis court, swimming pool, lounge with inglenook fireplace. All bedrooms have washbasins and tea making facilities. Full English breakfast served. This 236 acre dairy/arable farm stands in the beautiful Exe Valley near beaches and moors. Facilities for fishing, sailing, golf, riding, birdwatching nearby. OS Ref SY 997852

(FH) MAER FARM Maer Lane, Exmouth, Devon, EX8 5DD

Avril Skinner
Tel:-(0395) 263651
Closed Xmas
B&B £9-£11   Listed
Sleeps 6

Welcome to this dairy/arable farm on edge sea/town. Spacious bed/sitting rooms. Tea/coffee facilities. Quiet rural setting with splendid views of the Exe Estuary and Haldon Hills. Welcome to return during day. Reductions for children. AA Listed. Brochure on request. OS Ref SX 018808

(FH) FORD FARM Woodbury, Exeter, Devon, EX5 1NJ

Linda Brown
Tel:-(0395) 32355
Open Jan-Nov
B&B £8-£9   Listed
Sleeps 6

For an overnight stop or long stay, a friendly family welcome awaits you on this working farm near Woodbury Common and handy for East Devon coastal resorts. Children are always welcome as we have youngsters of our own. There is a family room, 1 double, 1 twin, also lounge with TV. Ample parking space and garden. Ideal touring centre. OS Ref SY 016867

47

(SC) 1 COOMBELAKE COTTAGE Pitt Farm, Ottery St Mary, Devon, EX11 1NL

Susan Hansford
Tel:-(040481) 2439
Open all year
SC   £30-£130
Sleeps 5

This bright end of terrace cottage sleeping 5, is 1¼m from Ottery St. Mary, in the picturesque Otter Valley with golf, squash, pony trekking, swimming, river walks, country inns and all East Devon resorts within 6-10 miles. Fully modernised and furnished except linen, with colour TV. Small garden. Parking nearby. Electricity by meter extra. Car essential. Accommodation is 1 double, 1 twin, 1 single. OS Ref SY 089966

(SC) PARKFIELD COTTAGES Gulliford Farm, Lympstone, Nr Exmouth, Devon, EX8 5AQ

June Hallett
Tel:-(039287) 3067
Open all year
SC   £69-£230
Sleeps 5-6

These 2 delightful country cottages are situated in the beautiful Exe valley, in sunny positions overlooking fields on our 236 acre dairy/arable farm. Both fully modernised and comfortably furnished to a high standard. Both have 3 bedrooms, lounge, TV, kitchen/diners, bathroom, large gardens and parking. Within easy reach of sea, moors. Sailing, fishing, golf, riding, walking, birdwatching all nearby. OS Ref SY 997852

(SC) MEADOWHAYES COTTAGE Courtneys Farm, Clyst Hydon, Nr Cullompton, Devon, EX15 2NH

Mary Mitchem
Tel:-(0404) 822446
Open Mar-Oct
SC   £130-£180
Sleeps 6

Character cottage set in walled rose garden, overlooking orchard on 300 acre dairy farm - watch cows being milked or calves fed, children love it! Spacious comfortable accommodation, all modern conveniences, colour TV, sleeps 2/6, plus cot. Nine miles cathedral city Exeter, 9 miles coast. Five miles M5 (junction 28). Lovely countryside, rural walks. A warm welcome awaits you. OS Ref ST 045002

(SC) DRUPE FARM Colaton Raleigh, Sidmouth, Devon, EX10 OLE

Jean Daniels
Tel:-(0395) 68838
Open all year
SC   £50-£265
Sleeps 4/9

Drupe Farm is in the beautiful Otter Valley approx. 3 miles from the East Devon Coast. Farm buildings tastefully converted to form high quality self-catering cottages around landscaped courtyard. Cottages sleep 4/9, colour TV, linen and electricity included. Central heating available. Resident warden, laundry room, games room and play area and a warm welcome! AA listed. OS Ref SY 077872

EXMOOR, SOMERSET North Devon

EXMOOR, SOMERSET/NORTH DEVON

This area is dominated by the Exmoor National Park which is situated on the North Coast of Devon and Somerset. The Park has miles of moorland which are ideal for country pursuits such as walking and riding but also has many beautiful villages in the folds of the countryside.

On a journey of 10 miles, you could pass through narrow valleys dominated by beech woods, then suddenly, you're onto the bleak moor, a mile or so on, you are surrounded by rich, green farmland and then suddenly you hit the coast — with some of England's highest cliffs towering over the sea. Exmoor is famous for its wild herds of ponies and red deer. The rivers Exe and Barle rise high on the moors creating attractive moorland valleys. This is also the country that Blackmore made famous with "Lorna Doone," and you can still find places described in the book.

Apart from excellent inland attractions like the famous Tarr Steps — an ancient clapper bridge — there are bustling and delightful resorts like Minehead, Porlock, Lynmouth and Lynton — dotted along its glorious coastline, with rocky coves and small sandy beaches.

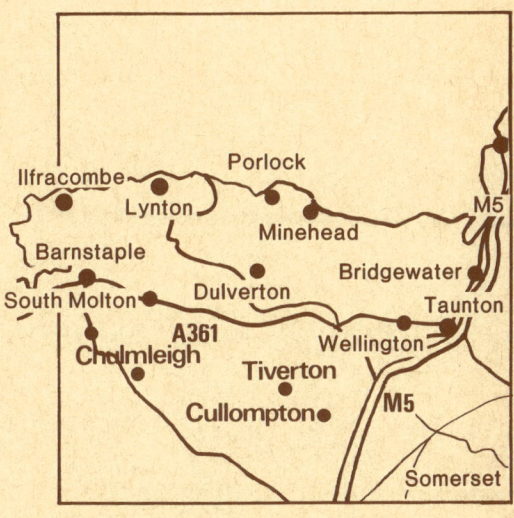

VACANCY SECRETARIES:
B&B — Julia Brown
(064383) 282
Self Catering — Joan Bindon
(064383) 347

(FH) COOMBE FARM Countisbury, Lynton, Devon, EX35 6NF

Rosemary Pile
Tel: (05987) 236
Open Apr-Oct
B&B £10.50-£17.00
EM £7.50
Sleeps 13

A 365 acre hill stock farm ideally situated for touring, walking coast and moorland, Doone Valley and Exmoor beauty spots. Riding, fishing nearby. 17th Century stone farmhouse offers comfortable accommodation, excellent home cooked breakfast & 4 course dinner. 1 twin, 2 family with washbasins, 2 double en-suite all with hot drink facilities. Centrally heated. Residential licence. Dogs by arrangement. Reductions for weekly bookings. OS Ref SS 766489

(FH) SHEEPWASH FARM Molland, South Molton, Devon, EX36 3NN

Rosalind Hayes
Tel: (07697) 276
Open Easter, May-Sep
B&B £9-£10
EM £5
Sleeps 6

Situated in a peaceful valley on outskirts of Exmoor National Park amidst rolling countryside with walks and riding close by. A mixed stock farm with many animals. A delightful character farmhouse, large oak beams, partly modernised, but keeping its large rooms. Ideal setting for a relaxing holiday with personal service in friendly company and good farmhouse cooking. Ideal for a family holiday. OS Ref SS 789266

(FH) EMMETTS GRANGE FARM Simonsbath, Minehead, Somerset, TA24 7LD

Julia Brown
Tel: (064383) 282
Open Mar-Oct
B&B £12-£14.50
EM £10.50
£140-£155/week
Redn child 12yr
Sleeps 6

Comfortable, centrally heated farmhouse standing in a lovely quiet position with beautiful moorland views on a 1,200 acre stock farm. Residents' lounge with log fire. Attractive dining room with seperate tables. Two en-suite bedrooms. two with H/C, sharing bathroom. All bedrooms with col. TV Renowned for our delicious large breakfast & four course dinner. An ideal situation for exploring Exmoor. OS Ref SS 753369

(FH) HOLDSTONE FARM Hunters Inn Road, Combe Martin, Ilfracombe, Devon, EX34 0PE

Jayne Lerwill
Tel: (027 188) 3423
Open all year
B&B £8.50-£10 Listed
EM £8
Sleeps 6

This 12th Century farmhouse is on a working farm set in a secluded moorland valley and has been comfortably modernised. Central heating and log fire. Two well furnished bedrooms sleeping four and two with guests' bathroom. Comfortable lounge with colour TV, separate dining room. The best of home cooking. Within reach of the famous north Devon beaches and adjoining the coastal footpath. OS Ref 104519

(CH) FOLLY Winsford Hill, Winsford, Nr. Minehead, Somerset, TA24 7JL

Mrs C Sharman-Courtney
Tel: 064 385 253
Closed Xmas-New Year
B&B £9-£19 Listed
EM £5
CH Sleeps 6

Folly is a comfortable house almost surrounded by open moorland in Exmoor National Park. We offer a homely, friendly atmosphere with good country style cooking. An open log fire burns whenever necessary & there is full central heating & a colour TV. It is ideally situated for walking or touring Exmoor & North Devon. The view is breathtaking! OS Ref SS 889 338

(CH) EDGCOTT HOUSE Exford, Nr Minehead, Somerset, TA24 7QG

Gillian Lamble
Tel: (064383) 495
Open all year
B&B £10-£11
EM £7
CH Sleeps 6

Country house of great charm and character, in a sheltered garden amidst beautiful countryside in the heart of Exmoor. Peaceful & quiet, ¼ mile from the village of Exford. All bedrooms have washbasins & private bathrooms are available. Excellent home cooking is served in the elegant "longroom" with its unique murals. A comfortable centre for walking, riding, fishing and exploring. OS Ref SS 846487

Exmoor, Somerset/N. Devon ENGLAND

(FH) **CUTTHORNE FARM** Luckwell Bridge, Wheddon Cross, Minehead, Somerset, TA24 7EW

Ann Durbin
Tel:-(064383) 255
Open Mar-Nov
B&B £9.50-£10.50   Listed
EM £6.50
Sleeps 6

18th Century farmhouse, totally secluded in 25 acres of glorious countryside 1,000 feet above sea level close to Dunkery. A working farm where children can help with small animals. Spacious and comfortable accommodation, 2 luxury bathrooms, one with shower. 4 poster bed. Candle-lit dinners, high teas for children. Ideal for families, beautifully appointed barn conversion on side of farm with private facilities. Stabling. Dogs welcome. OS Ref 887388

(FH) **GALLON HOUSE** Simonsbath, Minehead, Somerset, TA24 7JY

Trudy & Andrew Hawkins
Tel:-(064383) 283
Open Mar-Nov
B&B £9.20-£11.20
EM £4.60
Sleeps 6

Gallon House is a large family run working moorland farm, ideally situated for exploring Exmoor. We offer comfortable centrally heated accomodation with excellent home cooking with local fresh produce. Hot drink making facilities and H/C in all rooms. Drying room and ironing facilities. Colour TV, visitors welcome to see farm activities. Stabling available. OS Ref ST 811344

(FH) **SPRINGFIELD FARM** Dulverton, Somerset, TA22 9QD

Tricia Vellacott
Tel:-(0398) 23722
Open May-Oct
B&B £7.50-£9.50   Listed
EM £5
Sleeps 6

A 270 acre working hill stock farm, peacefully situated with magnificent views, between Dulverton and Tarr Steps. Carpeted bedrooms overlook the River Barle. Separate toilet and bathroom for guests; also dining room and sitting room with TV. A warm welcome and plentiful good home cooked food. Garage. Horse riding nearby. Children welcome.

(SC) **WEST ILKERTON FARM** Lynton, North Devon, EX35 6QA

Chris & Victoria Eveleigh
Tel:-(0598) 52310
Open all year
SC £80-£170
Sleeps 6

Spacious, well-equipped, semi-detached cottage on a secluded hill livestock farm bordering open moorland. 2 double rooms, 1 twin, 2 bathrooms, living room, kitchen. Oil fired Rayburn, CH, colour TV, cot & high chair. Linen available. Coast 3m, riding stable ½m. Children, dogs & horses welcome. Ideal for walking, riding, fishing, or a relaxed family farm holiday. OS Ref SS 704467

(SC) **EMMETTS GRANGE FARMHOUSE** Simonsbath, Minehead, Somerset, TA24 7LD

Julia Brown
Tel:-(064383) 282
Open Mar-Nov
SC 72.45-218.50
Sleeps 8

2 farm cottages sleeping 6 and 7. 1 large modern bungalow for 8 and a self-contained flat for 4. All on a 1,200 acre hill stock farm in a lovely position. All well equipped with CH, colour TV, Calor gas cookers and fridges. Milk from farm included in price. Dinners available from farm guest house with 24 hours notice please. Facilities for disabled guests in bungalow. OS Ref SS 753369

(SC) **WESTERMILL FARM** Exford, Nr Minehead, Somerset, TA24 7NJ

Jackie Edwards
Tel:-(064383) 238
Open Mar-Nov
SC £95-£290
Sleeps 4-8

Scandinavian log cottages of superior quality in small paddocks and a bright comfortable cottage adjoining farmhouse for self catering on a beef/sheep farm in centre of Exmoor National Park. 4 fascinating waymarked walks over 500 acres and 2½m of river for fishing & bathing. Payphone, small shop, information centre, dog exercising field. 6 cottages with 2, 3 or 4 bedrooms. AA listed. OS Ref SS 825398

51

(SC) RUGGS FARM HOUSE AND BUNGALOW Higher Holworthy Farm, Brompton Regis, Dulverton, Somerset, TA22 9NY

Jill Scott
Tel:-(03987) 236
Open all year
SC   £90-£265
Sleeps 5/9

17th Century farmhouse with many period features. Recently restored and comfortably furnished, fitted carpets, colour TV, washing machine. The bungalow is spacious and comfortably furnished and well equipped. Both are on a 360 acre dairy and stock farm and look across Wimbleball Lake. Beautiful walks, sailing, fishing and birdwatching. OS Ref ST 977307

(SC) CUTTHORNE FARM Luckwell Bridge, Wheddon Cross, Minehead, Somerset, TA24 7EW

Ann Durbin
Tel:-(064383) 255
Closed Jan-Feb
SC   £150-£250
Sleeps 6

Situated in the heart of glorious Exmoor. A luxuriously appointed barn conversion on side of Georgian farmhouse. Overlooking pond and farm yard with private patio and sunbathing area. Lounge with log fire, TV, kitchen/dining hall, two double bedrooms, bathroom with shower. Evening meals available in farmhouse. Baby listening. Pets and horses welcome. Inclusive of linen, towels, heating and electricity. OS Ref 887388

(SC) WHITES FARM Elworthy, Lydeard St Lawrence, Taunton, Somerset

Roger & Kitty Paul
Tel:-(0984) 56283
Open all year
SC   £100-£150
Sleeps 6

Nestling on the edge of the Exmoor National Park, within easy reach of moorland, coast and centres of historic interest (Montacute, Dunster, Sedgemoor). This property comprises a farmhouse sleeping 6 and cider house sleeping 4. Both comfortably and imaginatively renovated. Whites Farm is in the centre of a small hamlet with farmland and animals-ideal for a family holiday. OS Ref ST 084350

(SC) HILL FARM Great Champson, Molland, South Molton, North Devon, EX36 3ND

Paula Dart
Tel:-(07697) 263
Open all year
SC   £80-£150
Sleeps 8

Spacious Exmoor type farmhouse in heart of beef and sheep farm. Peace and tranquility. Mile from village. Four bedrooms, sleeping 8. Comfortable and equipped to high standard. Open log fire, colour TV, tiled dining room with Rayburn. Kitchen, electric cooker and fridge. Lovely walking area. Horse riding nearby. Free to roam on the farm. Dogs by arrangement only. OS Ref SS 709208

(SC) THE COTTAGES Honeymead, Simonsbath, Minehead, Somerset, TA24 7JX

Lorna Vigars
Tel:-(064383) 450
Open Easter-Oct
SC   £85-£165
Sleeps 5

Two cottages on a farm in the heart of the Exmoor National Park. Each has: sitting room, dining/kitchen with Rayburn for cooking and water heating and alternative electric cooker and immersion heater. Bathroom and separate WC. Two twin-bedded rooms and one single. Close-carpeting. Good parking. Guests should provide their own linen. Evening meal can be prepared by prior arrangement and brought to cottage. Telephone and colour television. OS Ref SS 393798

(SC) CROFT COTTAGE Higher Burrow Farm, Timberscombe, Minehead, Somerset, TA24 7UD

Diana Rusher
Tel:-(064384) 427
Open all year
SC   £80-£160
Sleeps 7

Attractive stone built cottage has been converted into one. Situated 200 yds from farm, with own garden, and lovely views. Croft is spacious with one double room, 2 twin, 1 single, cot available. Large bathroom upstairs, second bath and WC downstairs. Colour TV, log fire and small library. Horses or other animals accommodated by arrangement at farm. Electricity extra. FRIDAY CHANGE OVER.

Exmoor, Somerset/N. Devon ENGLAND

(TV) **WESTERMILL FARM** Exford, Nr Minehead, Somerset, TA24 7NJ

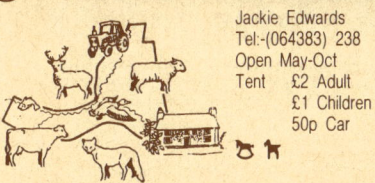

Jackie Edwards
Tel:-(064383) 238
Open May-Oct
Tent   £2 Adult
       £1 Children
       50p Car

Beautiful site for tents & dormobiles beside upper reaches of River Exe. Centre of Exmoor National Park. 4 waymarked walks over 500 acre working farm. 2 ½m of shallow river for fishing or bathing. Information centre. Small shop. Hot showers. Flush lavatories. Payphone. A site & farm to enjoy in the most natural way. Children's paradise. £2 adult, 50p vehicle. No caravans. AA listed. OS Ref SS 825398

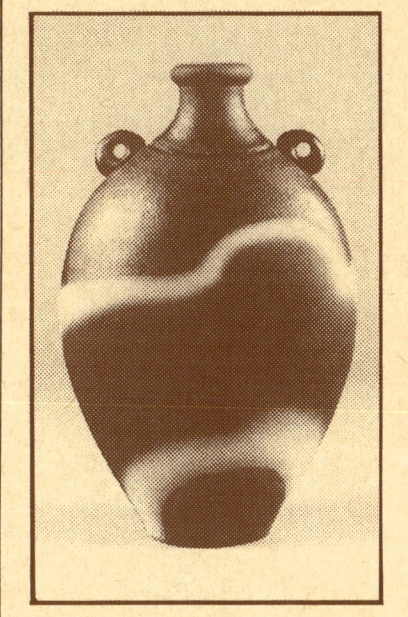

JOHN LEACH

works in his thatched workshop 1 mile south of ancient Muchelney.

A selection of unique hand thrown pots, including signed individual pieces, is always available in the shop

OPEN:
Monday to Friday 9-1, 2-6
Saturday 9-1

MUCHELNEY POTTERY
Nr. Langport, Somerset TA10 0DW
Tel: (0458) 250324

Individual "Black Pot"

53

12 WEST & MID SOMERSET

WEST & MID SOMERSET

Cheddar Cheese and Scrumpy are not the only things Somerset has to offer. Sandy beaches on the coast combine with the moorlands of the Exmoor National Park and the Quantocks, the plains of Sedgemoor and the fertile farmland of Taunton Vale to form a varied countryside. Taunton itself was the scene of Judge Jeffries Bloody Assizes in 1685 and the County Museum in the Castle traces the town's history. Golf, riding, tennis and swimming are available locally. Somerset Cricket Team play regularly at the County Ground.

For those who wish to explore further, Somerset offers a tremendous range of things to do and see from National Trust properties, such as Dunster Castle and Barrington Court; Muchelney with its thatched 14th Century Priest House and 7th Century Abbey ruins; the gardens of Montacute House and Clapton Court, to the delights of Cheddar Caves. Bath and Wells are but an hour away. Neroche Forest and the Blackdown Hills offer nature trails and waymarked walks. For steam enthusiasts the West Somerset Railway runs from Taunton to Minehead and and for those interested in aeroplanes the Fleet Air Arm Museum is open daily.

Watch pots thrown, trout farmed, cheese made or the cider makers art — there is something for everyone.

Properties marked ✱ are members of Rural Sommerset and accommodate only one family at one time
GROUP CONTACT:
Mary Neale (0823) 42260
Properties marked ● are members of West Somerset
GROUP CONTACT:
Moira Garner-Richards (0984) 23725

W. & Mid-Somerset ENGLAND

(CH) ORCHARD HAVEN Langford Budville, Wellington, Somerset, TA21 0QZ *

Jenny Perry-Jones
Tel:-(0823) 672116
Open Mar-Nov
CH   Sleeps 4
       adults
       plus child
B&B   £9-£10
EM   £6

(5)

A warm welcome awaits guests to Orchard Haven. Set in a large garden flanked by the River Tone, all rooms have lovely views of surrounding farmland. The house is comfortably furnished, with stone fireplace and beamed ceiling in the lounge. Ideal for touring the region's attractions. Nature reserve ½ mile, olde worlde inns ¾ mile and 2 miles. Good food. EM by arrangement. OS Ref ST 099221

(FH) HOWLEIGH FARM Blagdon Hill, Taunton, Somerset, TA3 7SS *

Mary Neale
Tel:-(0823) 42260
Closed Xmas-New Year
B&B   £8.50-£10   Listed
EM   £6
       Sleeps 4

Guests are welcome to our dairy/arable farm at the foot of the Blackdown Hills; join in the farming activities, explore the local footpaths or visit the county's varied attractions. Accommodation is a suite (2 twin rooms) with private bathroom, tea/coffe facilities, suitable for one couple or a family, dining room & lounge. Cot available. Colour TV & games room. Good farmhouse cooking. OS Ref ST 206 191

(FH) PINKSMOOR MILLHOUSE Pinksmoor Farm, Wellington, Somerset, TA21 0HD *

Nancy Ash
Tel:-(0823) 672361
Open all year
B&B   £11-£12.50
EM   £6
       Sleeps 6

Period millhouse offering farmhouse hospitality and cooking with personal service. Spacious rooms, central heating, log fires in winter. Bedrooms with tea making facilities, some ensuite. Sited adjacent to the old mill and stream. A family run dairy farm with an abundance of wildlife and scenic walks. Conservation area. Ten minutes M5 Junction 26. Close to coasts and moors. AA listed. OS Ref ST 108197

(FH) WHITTLES FARM Beercrocombe, Taunton, Somerset, TA3 6AH *

Mrs Claire Mitchem
Tel:-(0823) 480301
Open Mar-Oct
B&B   £14.50-£15.50
EM   £8.50
       Sleeps 6

(10)

Superior 16th Century farmhouse set in 200 acres of dairyland and situated at the end of a 'no through road'. 1 mile from the village of Beercrocombe, and 7 miles from Taunton. Lovely, well appointed rooms with ensuite bathrooms, colour TV, tea/coffee making facilities. Ideal touring centre. Good English cooking and personal service. Licensed. AA National Award.

(CH) SLAPES COTTAGE Staplegrove, Taunton, Somerset, TA2 6SL *

Mrs Marcelle Webb-Whish
Tel:-(0823) 45250
Open May-Oct
CH   Sleeps 4   Listed
B&B   £9-£10
EM   £6

Excellent accommodation is offered in this beautifully furnished 16th Century cottage of great charm and historical interest. Surrounded by farmland, it offers peace, at the foot of the Quantocks, 2½m from Taunton. Home grown produce is used in the "high standard" cooking. 1 family or couple at a time for privacy - coloured TV, lounge, private bathroom, dining room, tea facilities are offered. OS Ref ST 325120

(CH) WATERCOMBE HOUSE Huish Champflower, Wiveliscombe, Nr Taunton, Somerset, TA4 2EE ●

Moira Garner-Richards
Tel:-(0984) 23725
Open Easter-Oct, Xmas-NY
CH   Sleeps 4
B&B   £11-£12
EM   From £6.50

A warm welcome awaits you at our smallholding for an enjoyable happy holiday, relax from the pressures of everyday life. Easy access to Exmoor, Quantocks, Blackdown & north coast with Minehead, Porlock and Doone Valley & its historic associations. Fishing at Clatworthy ½m, sailing and surfing at Wimbleball lake 2m. Log fires, home cooking. Riding by arrangement. Deep freeze facilities for fishermen. SAE for brochure. OS Ref ST 048303

55

(CH) DEEPLEIGH FARM HOTEL Langley Marsh, Wiveliscombe, Somerset, TA4 2UU ●

Linda & Lester Featherstone
Tel:-(0984) 23379
Open Mar-Nov
B&B £13.50-£17.50
EM £8.50
CH Sleeps 10 plus 11 children

The hotel is a charming 16th Century country house situated in Brendon Hills, surrounded by beautiful pastureland. Sitting room with oak beams and panelling, log fire. Well stocked bar. In the dining room, emphasis on "good food" prepared from Linda's own recipes. All bedrooms en-suite, colour TV, tea making facilities. Central heating. Riding stables, BHS & POB approved, close by. OS Ref ST 085295

(FH) HALSDOWN FARM Waterrow, Wiveliscombe, Taunton, Somerset, TA4 2QU

Ann James
Tel:-(0984) 23493
Open Apr-Sep
B&B From £9
EM From £4
Sleeps 6

Listed

Halsdown is a working, family farm on the edge of the Brendon Hills with a dairy herd and a variety of small animals. The 15th Century farmhouse is set in spacious gardens in which visitors are welcome to relax. We only cater for a small number of guests and offer a friendly and relaxing atmosphere in a truly rural setting. Self-catering also available. Non group member. OS Ref ST 046257

(SC) BROOK COTTAGE Glebe Farm, Tolland, Lydeard St Lawrence, Nr Taunton, Somerset TA4 3PR ●

Elisabeth Cookson
Tel:-(09847) 268
Closed Nov
SC £70-£145
Sleeps 4/5

Come and have a peaceful holiday, enjoy West Somerset. Ideal area for walking, touring, fishing and riding. A charming former farm cottage nestles in the middle of the hamlet alongside a bubbling brook. Accommodation 2 bedrooms, lounge/diner, kitchen, bathroom. Car space. 50p slot meter. Linen included. Use of private swimming pool, alternatively have a look round a working farm. Children must be supervised. OS Ref SS 102322

(SC) TONE VALLEY FARM LODGES Waterrow, Nr Wiveliscombe, W Somerset, TA4 2AU ●

Cliff & Vanessa Rance
Tel:-(0984) 23322
Closed February
SC £78-£195
Sleeps 6

18 acre smallholding with farm shop and restaurant, set amidst delightful scenery. The 5 "Scandinavian Pine" lodges nestle in a wooded valley, each with balcony and lovely views. Built and furnished to a very high standard, exceeding ETB category 3 requirements. Each lodge is fully equipped for 6, fitted carpets throughout, TV, fitted kitchen, dining area and luxury bathroom. Prices include VAT, bed linen. OS Ref 055258

(FH) HIGHER DIPFORD FARM Trull, Taunton, Somerset, TA3 7NU

Maureen & Chris Fewings
Tel:-(0823) 275770
Closed Jan-Feb
B&B £18
EM £10
Sleeps 6

Dairy farm situated 2½ miles Taunton, accommodation in 600 year old farmhouse, formerly original Somerset Longhouse, exposed beams, inglenook fireplaces. Bedrooms have en-suite bathrooms, colour TV. Visitors welcome to see daily workings on farm, 4 course evening meal consists of our own fresh produce, cheese, cream, home cured hams, lamb, beef, pork, salmon, all helped down by jug of cider-licensed.

(FH) HURSTONE FARMHOUSE HOTEL Waterrow, Wiveliscombe, Somerset TA4 2AT

John Bone
Tel:-(0984) 23441
Open all year
B&B From £17.50
EM From £9.50
Sleeps 12

Small family run hotel in Brendon Hills, close to Exmoor National Park, Quantock Hills, north coast. Family suite & 4 double bedrooms, all ensuite with central heating, colour TV, telephone & tea/coffee making facilities. All rooms face south with glorious views over River Tone valley. Good home cooking with own produce. Licenced. Winter Weekends & mid week breaks. Discount for weekly bookings. Pets by arrangement. OS ST 056252

NORTH SOMERSET & AVON

13

NORTH SOMERSET & AVON

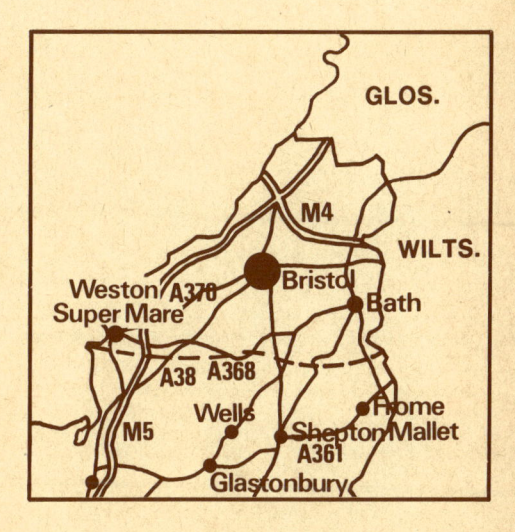

This area has a wealth of history going back to prehistoric times. The Druid Stones near Pensford are 600 years older than Stonehenge and there's always been a touch of magic and mystery in the air around Glastonbury the ancient town and lengendary Isle of Avalon, where it is rumoured King Arthur and his queen were buried.

The visitor is within easy striking distance of the beautiful city of Bath, with its Regency architecture, and older vestiges of civilisation like Roman Baths. The whole town is alive with shops and pavement cafes.

Another city within easy reach is Bristol, renowned as one of the world's leading ports. With Clifton Zoo, museums, theatres and marvellous shops, it's a visitor's delight.

At the famous Wookey Hole Caves you can see the Witch of Wookey and visit a cave chamber in which the acoustics are said to be near perfection.

Looking from Ebbor Gorge you will see what must be one of the grandest views in the world.

Interested in wine? There are two vineyards; at Pilton and North Wootton where you can taste the local brew. And, of course, if you fancy something stronger, there is always the famous Somerset cider.

With Cheddar Caves, the Quantock Hills, Stately Homes, and sea on both coasts you'll be spoilt for choice.

GROUP CONTACT:
Josie Pullin (07612 1) 280

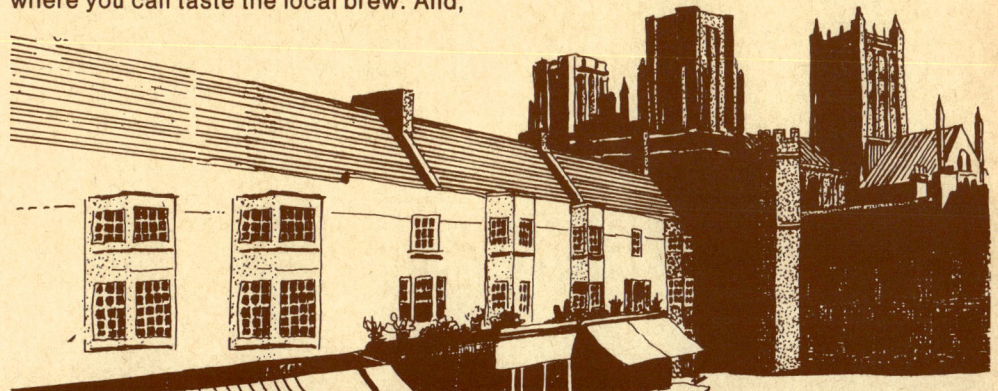

(FH) LEIGH FARM Pensford, Nr Bristol, Avon, BS18 4BA

Colin & Jo Smart
Tel:-(07618) 281
Open Mar-Nov
B&B   £11.50-£14   Listed
Sleeps 6

A beautiful natural stone built farmhouse in a quiet position between Bath and Bristol - both approx. 20 mins. Mixed farm, mainly beef and sheep. Family, double, single rooms with hot and cold. Tea/coffee making facilities. Guest lounge, with log fires in cold weather. Bathroom, dining room. Evening meal by arrangement. Some bedrooms with private facilities. OS Ref ST 304180

(FH) HERONS GREEN FARM Compton Martin, Bristol, Avon, BS18 6NL

Sandra Hasell
Tel:-(0272) 333372
Closed Xmas-New Year
B&B   £8.50-£10.00   Listed
Sleeps 6

Comfortable family farmhouse, peacefully situated by the side of Chew Valley Lake. Ideal for fly fishing, birdwatching, horseriding, walking Mendip Hills or touring Bath, Wells, Cheddar etc. South facing patio in pretty garden. Oak beamed dining room, featuring the original water well. One double and one family room with wash basins & razor points. Tea/coffee making facilities. Homely atmosphere, large breakfasts. OS Ref ST 551596

(CH) THE PANTILES Bathway, Chewton Mendip, Nr Bath, Somerset, BA3 4ND

Pat Hellard
Tel:-(076121) 519
Closed Xmas-New Year
CH   Sleeps 6
B&B   £8.50-£11.50

You are assured of a warm welcome from family and pets at the Pantiles. An attractive home, set in 2 acres of garden and paddock. Accomodation comprising of 2 twin or family rooms, 1 double room, all with H/C, TV, tea/coffee making facilities. Guests' private bathroom. Central heating. Ideal centre for touring West Country beauty spots. OS Ref ST 305104

(FH) REDHILL FARM Emborough, Nr Bath, Somerset, BA3 4SH

Mrs. Jane Rowe
Tel:-(076121) 294
Closed Xmas-New Year
B&B   £9.50-£12   Listed
Sleeps 5

Our listed farmhouse, built in Cromwellian times is situated high on the Mendips between Bath and Wells. It is the perfect centre for outdoor activities and sightseeing. We are a working small-holding with a variety of animals to delight the children. Sleeps 5. Centrally heated with private bathroom. Fresh home produce. OS Ref ST 605509

(FH) BARROW VALE FARM Farmborough, Nr Bath, Avon, BA3 1BL

Cherilyn Mary Langley
Tel:-(0761) 70300
Closed Xmas-New Year
B&B   £9
Sleeps 6
(3)

A modern working dairy farm of 200 acres. The large farmhouse has been tastefully modernised. It has central heating throughout and washbasins in each room. Farmborough is equidistant from Bristol, Bath and the city of Wells, with the Mendip Hills and Cheddar Gorge within easy reach. Several recommended pubs and restaurants close by. OS Ref ST 649603

(CH) WAYSIDE BUNGALOW Old Down, Emborough, Nr Bath, BA3 4RY

Mrs Rena Mills
Tel:-(0761) 232449
Closed Dec-Xmas
CH   Sleeps 5   Listed
B&B   £10-£12
EM   £6-£8
(5)

A quiet bungalow with an attractive garden set amidst the beautiful surroundings of the Mendip Hills. Ideal location for visiting the lovely cities of Bristol, Bath and Wells. Cheddar, Longleat, Downside and Wookey Hole are nearby. We offer own garden produce in season, residents' lounge with colour TV, open fire and parking. Tea and coffee available at all times. OS Ref ST 633513

58

N. Somerset & Avon ENGLAND

(FH) CLIFF FARM   Farrington Gurney, nr Bristol, BS18 5TS

Judy & Tim Candy
Tel:-(076121) 274
Closed Xmas
B&B   £10-£13
Sleeps 5

(10)

A traditional family farm set ¾ mile from the A37/39 under the Mendip Hills. Share peaceful country surroundings where we cater for your every comfort, all bedrooms have lavatory and shower or bath en-suite, tea and coffee making facilities. Residents own lounge/dining room with log fire and colour TV. Approximately 10 miles from Wells, Bath and Cheddar. Non Smokers preferred. OS Ref ST 632547

(CH) MIDWAY HOUSE   Ston Easton, Nr Bath, Somerset, BA3 4DQ

Mrs Jose Pullin
Tel:-(076121) 280
Closed Xmas-New Year
B&B   Prices on Application
CH   Sleeps 6

An 18th Century listed country house offering excellent B&B accomodation in beautifully furnished bedrooms with every amenity, some with private bathroom. Set in the lovely Mendip countryside, we are an ideal base from which to explore local places of interest, Bath, Wells, Cheddar and Glastonbury. There is central heating and ample parking space. OS Ref ST 615533

(FH) WOODBARN FARM   Denny Lane, Chew Magna, Bristol, Avon, BS18 8SZ

Judi Hasell
Tel:-(0272) 332599
Open Mar-Oct
B&B   £8.50-£10   Listed
Sleeps 6

Woodbarn is a working beef/arable farm, only 5 minutes walk from the beautiful Chew Valley Lake - trout fishing, birdwatching etc. Chew Magna has fine Georgian houses, a Norman Church and 16th century church house and is central for touring. There are 2 family/double with washbasins and tea/coffee making facilities. Guests' lounge and dining room. Cream teas by arrangement. OS Ref ST 575619

(FH) THE MODEL FARM   Norton Hawkfield, Pensford, Bristol, Avon, BS18 4HA

Margaret Hasell
Tel:-0272 832144
Open Easter-Oct
B&B   £8-£9   Applied
Sleeps 6

The farmhouse is a listed building situated 2 miles off the A37 in a peaceful hamlet, nestling under the Dundry Hills. A working arable & beef farm which is in easy reach of Bristol, Bath, Cheddar & many other interesting places. The accommodation consists of 1 family room & 1 double room. Guests' lounge & dining room. OS Ref ST 592 651

(FH) GLEBE HOUSE FARM   Chelwood, Nr Pensford, Bristol, BS18 4NW

Ann Sherborne
Tel:-(07618) 586
Open Easter-Nov
B&B   £8.50-£9   Listed
Sleeps 5

Small family working dairy farm situated on A368 Bath road at Chelwood and ideally situated for visiting the Cities of Bath, Wells and Bristol and many other places of interest. The farmhouse offers bed and breakfast accommodation with washbasins and tea/coffee making facilities in each room. Good pubs and restaurants in the local area. OS Ref ST 636619

(FH) MELLS GREEN FARM   Mells, Nr. Frome, Somerset, BA11 3QF

Judy Turner
Tel:-(0373) 812259
Open Easter-Oct
B&B   £8.50-£9.50   Listed
Sleeps 6

Attractive stone-built comfortable farmhouse, containing original oak beams and open fireplaces. Situated in the historical village of Mell's where Little Jack Horner's rhyme originated. Within easy reach of Longleat, Wells, Bath and Cheddar. Two double rooms and 1 family bedroom, spacious dining room and lounge. Generous home cooked farmhouse breakfast. OS Ref ST 120360

(SC) **LEIGH FARM** Pensford, Nr Bristol, Avon, BS18 4BA

Colin & Jo Smart
Tel:-(07618) 281
Open all year
SC   £60-£225
Sleeps 2-8

An attractive mixed farm near Bath & Bristol. Picturesque & beautifully quiet. Large lawns from which you can watch the animals. 3 bedroomed character cottage sleeping 6-8, bungalow type accomodation sleeping 2-5. Full size cookers & fridges, shower rooms with washbasin & WC. Cots available. Linen hire, payphone, TV, milk delivery. Split weeks & week-ends, at short notice. AA listed. Enquiries SAE. OS Ref ST 304180

'I made them myself'

The most comfortable shoes you'll ever wear!

Simple Way shoe kits are an ideal gift, hobby or home business and are in kit form or ready made.
Visit our workshop and see our Simple Way kits being made - try a pair on - see our range of foot comfort products as well. We're well worth a visit. We're open every weekday and on Saturday mornings. Write or phone for a free catalogue.

'SIMPLE WAY' ™

Unit 5 The Tanyard, Leigh Road, STREET
tel **(0458) 47275**

BATH ẞ WILTSHIRE   14

BATH & WILTSHIRE

The saying "as different as chalk from cheese" is believed to have been inspired by the marked contrasts in Wiltshire's glorious landscape. Rolling chalk uplands, guarded by seven giant white horses, give way to lush and fertile lowlands, the source of Wiltshire's famed dairy products.

The wide peaceful downland is rich in historic interest; Stonehenge, Avebury, Silbury Hill stand out on the rolling green plain, with the picturesque villages hidden away along the chalk stream valleys.

Castle Coombe (setting for Dr. Dolittle) and the National Trust village of Lacock are well known to many of us, but there are scores more in the north west of the county waiting to be discovered. Historic houses and landscaped gardens range from Longleat, Bowood House and Corsham Court to smaller manor houses such as Sheldon Manor which have the atmosphere of a family home.

The Bristol Avon river sails through this region of small market towns and picture postcard villages before turning west, north and west again into Bath.

To many people Bath is THE Roman City and there is a special thrill in walking down the steps the Romans used and finding the warm spring water still flowing. Bath continues to be one of the most popular attractions for visitors from home and abroad.

GROUP CONTACTS:
Cynthia Fletcher (03808) 2254
Shirley Mackintosh (03808) 28295

FH SEVINGTON FARM Yatton Keynell, Chippenham, Wilts, SN14 7LD

Mrs J Pope
Tel:-(0249) 782408
Open Feb-Nov
B&B Single £10-£11 Listed
       Double &
       family
       £18-£29
Sleeps 6

Beautiful 18th Century farmhouse in lovely peaceful village just 1½m from Castle Combe. Ideal for touring Bath, Bristol, Longleat, Bowood and many other places of interest. Horse riding available nearby, golfing enthusiasts well catered for at Chippenham and Kingsdown. A comfortable bed and a hearty English breakfast served.

FH FRYING PAN FARM Broughton Gifford Rd, Melksham, Wilts, SN12 8LL

Barbara Pullen
Tel:-(0225) 702343
Open Easter-Nov
B&B £9 Listed
Sleeps 5

(2)

Comfortable stone built farmhouse in rural position. 1m from Melksham, Bath 12m. Many National Trust properties nearby. Ideal for touring, 1 family room, 1 twin bedded. Both with Tea/coffee facilities. Guests' own lounge with TV. OS Ref ST 634891

FH GREAT THORNHAM FARM Trowbridge Rd, Seend, Melksham, Wilts, SN12 6PN

Shirley & Bob Mackintosh
Tel:-(0380) 828295
Open Easter-Oct
B&B £9-£10.50 Applied
Sleeps 4
TV £1.80

(2)

Great Thornham is a 120 acre working farm run with conservation in mind. Ideally situated for touring Wiltshire and Bath. The lovely old farmhouse has exposed beams, inglenook fireplace and beautiful views all adding to its character. Lounge for guests, with TV, separate dining room. Family bedroom, shower ensuite. Double room H/C. Also caravans, camping & fishing in season.

FH LONG WATER Lower Rd, Erlestoke, Devizes, Wilts, SN10 5UE

Mrs Pam Hampton
Tel:-(0380) 830095
Closed Xmas-New Year
B&B £10.50
EM £5.50
Sleeps 6

A peaceful country retreat overlooking our own lakes and parkland. Longwater offers the comfort of a young house and atmosphere of a family home. Within 20m is a wealth of places of ancient, historic & general interest. Double, twin bedded & family room all en suite & TV. Tea/coffee facilities. (2 ground floor bedrooms). Our menu is traditional farmhouse fare. Special diets by arrangement. Coarse and trout fishing available. OS Ref ST 965537

FH PICKWICK LODGE FARM Corsham, Wilts, SN13 0PS

Gill Stafford
Tel:-(0249) 712207
Open Mar-Nov
B&B £8-£10 Listed
EM £5
Sleeps 6

The Stafford family welcome guests to their 275 acre mixed farm, situated ½m off the A4 between Corsham & Bath. 10 mins Junction 17 M4. 2 large double rooms (could be family) colour TV, shaver points, tea/coffee facilities. Guests' own bathroom. One room downstairs with log fire when required. Spacious peaceful garden, ample parking, swimming, golf, riding nearby.

FH SALTBOX FARM Drewetts Mill, Box, Corsham, Wilts, SN14 9PT

Mary & Tony Gregory
Tel:-(0225) 742608
Open Easter-Oct
B&B £10-£12 Listed
Sleeps 5

Mary Gregory and her family welcome you to stay in their 18th Century farmhouse, set in the quiet unspoilt countryside of the Box Valley. The 166 acre dairy and stock farm is conveniently situated between Bath and Chippenham, about 1m off the A4, offering guests easy access to numerous places of interest, country walks - village pubs/restaurants. OS Ref ST 84 69

Bath & Wiltshire ENGLAND

(FH) STOWFORD MILL HOUSE Wingfield, Trowbridge, Wilts, BA14 9LH

Elinor Bryant
Tel:-(02214) 2253
Open all year
B&B £10
       Sleeps 6
Applied

Stowford is a peaceful hamlet comprising a medieval manor, 17th Century mill house and mill on the river Frome. The farm is 250 acres with 50 Jersey cows, cereals, sheep and free range hens. Fishing, craft workshops, cream teas on site. Good pub food ½m. On A366 between Trowbridge and Farleigh Castle only 15 minutes from Bath. OS Ref ST 381158

(FH) LOWER FOXHANGERS FARM Rowde, Devizes, Wilts, SN10 1SS

Colin & Cynthia Fletcher
Tel:-(038082) 254
Open Easter-Oct
B&B £9-£12
       Sleeps 6
SC   £75-£115
TV   £2.25
Applied

A 90 acre beef farm lying in a quiet hollow by the Kennet and Avon Canal in central Wiltshire. Walking, fishing, canoe and boat hire. 18th Century spacious farmhouse offers double family and twin-bedded rooms, all with washbasins, tea/coffee making facilities. 3 self-catering mobile homes with lounge, kitchen, bathroom, sleeping 4/5 situated in orchard. Small certificated caravan and camp site. OS Ref ST 968 617

Visit Lackham Gardens & Agricultural Museum

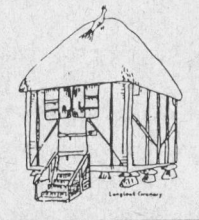

Open 11 a.m. to 4 p.m. £1.50, children 50p. Every day 5th April to 2nd Oct. Light refreshments. Childrens Corner.
3 miles south of Chippenham in Wiltshire on A350, signposted Lackham College of Agriculture, Lacock, Chippenham, Wiltshire.
Chippenham 656111 (for all course details).

63

15 DORSET

DORSET

Come and explore Dorset, with its delightful villages in the west of the county, the dairy pastureland of Blackmore Vale in the north, scenic Cranborne Chase in the east and the Purbeck Hills around Corfe Castle in the south. The unspoilt countryside so vividly described by the famous author, Thomas Hardy is still unchanged in places — rolling downland and fertile valleys with picturesque villages of mellow stone and thatch cottages.

For a day out, travel to Wells, Salisbury and Winchester Cathedrals, or the theatres and other attractions of major resorts like Bournemouth and Poole. Dartmoor lies to the west and the New Forest to the east, both within easy reach. Sea trips for fishing or pleasure can be made from many of the ports along the coast.

Summer is not the only season in which to savour this delightful area. Winters are mild on the South Coast and spring and autumn are particularly good times for a Dorset holiday. The footpath network is unsurpassed, both inland and along the coast. The Coastal Way in particular offers dramatic and exciting scenery, as safe and sandy beaches give way to shifting banks of shingle and rugged cliffs, teeming with birds.

Historic houses, famous gardens, exciting coastline — you name it, Dorset has it!

GROUP CONTACT:
Gill Espley (0258) 820412

Dorset ENGLAND

(FH) LOWER FARM   Chedington, Beaminster, Dorset, DT8 3JA

Ian & Jean Stanford
Tel:-(093589) 371
Closed Xmas
B&B £11.50-£12.50
Sleeps 6

16th Century thatched farmhouse in picturesque village. 120 acre farm with rare breeds cattle, sheep, pigs, working Suffolk Punch horses. Fully modernised accommodation, 2 double, 1 twin bedrooms, CH, H/C, shaver points, 2 bathrooms, dining room, sitting room. CTV, AA listed. Farm trail, trout fishing. Area of interest to naturalists, historians, holidaymakers. Near sea, golf courses. Chedington 40 minutes from M5 at Taunton. OS Ref ST 487054

(FH) HALE FARM   Cucklington, Wincanton, Somerset, BA9 9PN

Pat & Jim David
Tel:-(0963) 33342
Open Easter-Oct
B&B £9-£10
EM £5
Sleeps 6
SC £30-£110

Lovely 17th Century farmhouse full of beams, inglenook, where a warm welcome and good food awaits you. 55 acre mixed farm on edge of quiet village, only 2 miles from A303. 1 family, 1 double room. Children very welcome. Also lovely converted character cottages fully equipped, sleeping 2/4. Linen supplied. One suitable for disabled. OS Ref ST 706208

(FH) HOLEBROOK FARM   Lydlinch, Sturminster Newton, Dorset, DT10 2JB

Sally Wingate-Saul
Tel:-(02586) 348
Closed Xmas and New Year
B&B £10-£13   Listed
EM £5.50
Sleeps 12
SC £95-£200

Situated in heart of Blackmore Vale and ideal as a central base for exploring Dorset, this is a family farm of 125 acres. Accommodation in Georgian farmhouse. Also delightfully converted stables. with own sitting room, and shower, WC, ensuite. Swimming pool, clay pigeon shooting, fishing on farm. Golf, tennis locally. Very comfortable, friendly, family atmosphere. Good home cooking. Also self catering bungalow. OS Ref ST 743118

(FH) PRIORY FARM   East Holme, Wareham, Dorset, BH20 6AG

Mrs Venn Goldsack
Tel:-092 95 2972
Closed Xmas-New Year
B&B £9-£9.50   Applied
Sleeps 4

16th Century thatched farmhouse on 400 acre dairy farm with pick-your-own fruit & vegetables enterprise. Ideally situated for both coast & countryside. Bird watching, National Trust, Tank Museum, Hardy country, Lawrence of Arabia, beautiful houses & gardens open to the public within easy reach. We like having visitors & only wish to make their holidays enjoyable.

(FH) MANOR FARMHOUSE   Yetminster, Sherborne, Dorset, DT9 6LF

Ann & Jack Partridge
Tel:-(0935) 872247
Closed Xmas and New Year
Sleeps 6   Listed
B&B £10-£15
EM £8-10

The modernised 17th Century farmhouse has 1 double, 2 twin & 1 single rooms all with ensuite facilities. The lounge and dining room have picturesque inglenook fireplaces giving an atmosphere of old world charm with every comfort. Local produce is cooked to traditional recipes, roast sirloin, roast lamb and roast pork specialities. Ann offers an intimate knowledge of Dorset both historical and geographical. Weekly terms available. OS Ref ST 596108

(FH) LOWER CHURCH FARM   Rectory Lane, Charlton Musgrove, Wincanton, Somerset, BA9 8ES

Alicia Teague
Tel:-(0963) 32307
Open Apr-Oct
B&B From £8.50
EM £5
Sleeps 6

60 acre working dairy farm situated 2 miles from A303 bordering on Wiltshire and Dorset, ideal for touring. 18th Century farmhouse has beams, inglenooks, bread oven, pleasant homely atmosphere, garden, patio, surrounded by lovely countryside. Two doubles, 1 double/family room, washbasins, guest bathroom with shower. Dining room/lounge with colour TV. Tea/coffee making facilities. Good home cooking. AA listed. OS Ref ST 721902

FH DOWNWOOD VINEYARD Wimbourne Road, Blandford Forum, Dorset, DT11 9HN

David and Jacky Hall
Tel:-(0258) 54228
Closed Xmas and New Year
B&B £12-£14 Listed
EM £6-£8
Redn for children
Sleeps 6

Country house set in 28 acres of woodland with vineyards and winery in converted stables, tennis court and swimming pool. 4 miles from Kingston, Lacy Estate and Badbury Rings and within easy reach of beautiful Dorset coast. 2 twin/double rooms with bathrooms, 2 singles with bathroom. Separate sitting/games room, TV & dining room. Children welcome, pets by arrangement.

FH KNITSON FARM Corfe Castle, Wareham, Dorset, BH20 5JB

Rachel Helfer
Tel:-(0929) 422836
Closed Xmas and New Year
B&B £9.50-£11 Listed
EM £5
Sleeps 5

15th Century Purbeck stone farmhouse (very modern; log fires) on 200 acre Jersey cattle and sheep farm. 2 miles from Swanage, 4 miles from Studland. Superb walking - downland, heathland, cliffs, beaches. 2 bedrooms: 1 twin, 1 family. Open all year round. Children April, July, August only. Licensed camping and caravaning site. OS Ref SZ 005808

FH TOOMER FARM Henstridge, Templecombe, Somerset, BA8 0PH

Ethelend Doggrell
Tel:-(0963) 250237
Open all year
B&B £8.50-£9.50 Applied
Sleeps 6

250 year old stone built house with charming walled in garden surrounded by 380 acres of dairy/arable land. Splendid rural setting in the Blackmore Vale 6 miles east of Sherborne. One family room, double bed and bunk beds with wash basin and TV, 1 twin bedroom with H/C and TV, 1 twin room. Lounge and dining room. OS Ref ST 708191

FH CHURCH GROUND FARM Salway Ash, Bridport, Dorset, DT6 5JD

Judy Lockyer
Tel:-(030888) 282
Closed Xmas and Jan
B&B £10
EM £6.50
Sleeps 6
SC £100-£150
Sleeps 4

Our friendly thatched farmhouse is situated on the edge of Marshwood Vale, ideal for exploring Hardy country & unspoilt West Dorset. Wildlife is frequently seen on the farm. We offer fresh farmhouse meals in dining room with separate tables. Guests lounge with colour TV. Bedrooms with H/C, 1 ensuite. Sea 3m, much of the coast being owned by the National Trust.

FH MANOR FARM West Orchard, Shaftesbury, Dorset, SP7 0LJ

Rita Stranger
Tel:-(0258) 72331
Open Easter-Oct
B&B £9-£10 Listed
EM From £3
Sleeps 6

A friendly family dairy farm, in a quiet hamlet between Shaftesbury and Sturminster Newton. This modern farmhouse on 140 acres offers accommodation for families who would enjoy the hospitality of the hosts and 4 sons. Ideal for touring surrounding counties, coast 25 miles. Two rooms, 1 with 3 single beds, 1 with double and single, own shower room and lounge/diner. Reductions for children. OS Ref ST 823169

FH PINETREES FARM Haycrafts Lane, Swanage, Dorset BH19 3EE

Doreen & Bunny Farr
Tel:-(0929) 480837
Open Mar-Oct
B&B £9-£10
EM £5.50
Reductions for Children
Sleeps 4

Recently built centrally heated farm bungalow situated in lovely countryside. Ideal for touring, walking, riding, sailing. Nearby sandy beaches, coastal paths. Horses and dogs welcome. One family room and one double room, both with en suite facilities. Comfortable spacious lounge with colour TV, children's games. Good home cooking using own and local produce. Tea/coffee facilities. Four course evening meal.

Dorset ENGLAND

(sc) MANOR FARM COTTAGE   Manor Farm, Bowden, Henstridge, Templecombe, Somerset, BA8 0PQ

Iris Pickford
Tel:-(0963) 70213
Open all year
SC   £50-£130
Sleeps 6

Semi-detached cottage on working arable/dairy farm near 16th Century farmhouse. Quiet location in the Blackmore Vale only 1½ miles from main A30 road. Ideal for walking and good base for touring Dorset, Somerset and Wiltshire. Three bedrooms (1 twin, 2 double), bathroom/shower, toilet, sitting room with colour TV. Fully equipped kitchen/dining room. Linen hire. Electricity meter. OS Ref ST 306101

(sc) YEW HOUSE COTTAGES   Yew House Farm, Marnhull, Sturminster Newton, Dorset, DT10 1NP

Gil & Mike Espley
Tel:-(0258) 820412
Open Jan-Dec
SC   £50-£180
Sleeps 4/5

Two delightful timber cottages equipped to high standard of comfort for summer or winter holidays. Situated on small family farm in secluded rural setting overlooking Blackmore Vale. Colour TV, woodburning stove. Linen supplied. Swimming pool. Excellent holiday centre for visiting many places of interest. Coarse fishing in River Stour. Many good pubs for local beer and food. OS Ref ST 773184

(sc) CAREFREE COTTAGE   c/o Creech Barrow Cottage, East Creech, Wareham, BH20 5AP

Simon and Billa Edwards
Tel:-(0929) 480548
Open all year
SC   £100-£340
Sleeps 6
Tent   £3
Van   £4

Relax in the Isle of Purbeck. Charming 17th Century thatched cottage set in an acre of garden/orchard, beamed living/dining room with original fireplace, kitchen with oil fired rayburn & electric cooker, fridge, washing machine, 3 double bedrooms, bathroom. Rent includes fuel, electricity, TV, bedlinen. Nearby 3 golf courses, 3 riding stables, Dorset coast path, 2 Bird Sanctuaries. Excellent sailing, aqua & sub-aqua sports.

(sc) MANOR FARM COTTAGE   Milborne Wick, Sherborne, Dorset, DT9 4PW

Robert & Jenny Mackintosh
Tel:-(0963) 250389
Open all year
SC   £100-£230

Delightful cottage in picturesque hamlet 3m from ancient abbey town of Sherborne, convenient centre for touring Dorset/Somerset's unspoilt countryside. Golf, riding available locally. 2 twin bedded rooms, 1 smaller room with double bunk, bathroom and toilet. Sitting and dining rooms with log fires, kitchen and garage. Phone and night storage heaters, linen not supplied. Electricity extra. Colour TV, washing machine. OS Ref ST 669206

(sc) GORE COTTAGE (W Milton Bridport)   c/o Wingham Well Farm, Wingham, Canterbury, Kent, CT3 1NW

Georgina Maude
Tel:-(0227) 720253
Open all year
SC   £80-£175
Sleeps 5

Listed, detached, stonebuilt, thatched cottage in its own secluded garden on the edge of the village. 2 doubles, 1 single, sitting room, kitchen large enough to eat in, bathroom, separate W.C. & washbasin, garage. The sea is about 5 miles away. Among other attractions are the Swannery at Abbotsbury, Maiden Castle, Cerne Abbas (the Giant), Montacute & RAF Yeovilton. Dogs by arrangement only. (Member of Kent Group). OS Ref SY 5096

16 HEART OF DORSET

HEART OF DORSET

The Heart of Dorset offers you a range of holiday accommodation in the countryside around Dorchester. It is an area of outstanding natural beauty renowned for its beautiful villages, magnificent hills and lovely valleys. Wherever you stay, the coast is but a short distance away with excellent swimming, sailing and fishing. For the country lover, the area has a wide choice of forest trails, coastal and inland walks, ancient monuments, historical houses and gardens.

Dorset's most famous son, Thomas Hardy was born within three miles of Dorchester; his rambling cottage, Higher Bockhampton is open to the public. Most of his books were based on villages and towns in the area, many of which still retain the rural atmosphere of Hardy's Wessex. Dorchester was the setting for "The Mayor of Casterbridge" and Puddletown was Hardy's Weatherby in "Far from the Madding Crowd."

A romantic figure of more modern times is Lawrence of Arabia, who spent a number of reclusive years in his remote and rather bleak cottage, Clouds Hill near Bovington Camp.

Corfe Castle, Brownsea Island, Lulworth Cove, Durdle Door . . . even the Tolpuddle Martyrs' Museum are all here — you'll need more than a few days to discover Dorset!

GROUP CONTACT:
Mildred Cox (030584) 232

Heart of Dorset ENGLAND

(FH) **LOWER LEWELL FARMHOUSE** West Stafford, Dorchester, Dorset, DT2 8AP

Marian Tomblin
Tel:-(0305) 67169
Closed Easter, Xmas & NY
B&B   £11
Sleeps 6

Situated in the Frome Valley, four miles from Dorchester, this old, historic farmhouse is reputed to be the Talbothays Dairy of Hardy's novel 'Tess of the D'Urbervilles'. Ideally situated for exploring the beautiful countryside and coast. Three bedrooms, washbasins, tea/coffee making facilities. Guests' sitting room. Central heating. Ample parking. A warm welcome awaits you at Lower Lewell. OS Ref SY 743897

(FH) **TROYTOWN FARMHOUSE** Troytown Farm, Puddletown, Nr Dorchester, Dorset, DT2 8QF

Deirdre Cox
Tel:-(030584) 241
Open Apr-Sep
B&B   £8-£10   Listed
Sleeps 6

Troytown Farm is a 275 acre mixed farm situated 3m east of Dorchester. Farm borders Puddletown forest near Thomas Hardy's cottage. Built in the early 1800s with a spacious garden & ample parking. The accommodation consists of 2 family rooms with tea/coffee making facilities & with guests own bathroom. There is a pleasant dining room where a traditional English breakfast is served. Dogs by arrangement. OS Ref SY 940737

(SC) **DAIRY COTTAGE** Trigon House, Wareham, Dorset, BH20 7PD

Sandra Sturdy (Mrs G)
Tel:-(09295) 2097
Open Easter-Oct
SC   £100-£185
Sleeps 7

An attractive, recently modernised 3 bedroomed cottage in a picturesque terraced row of farm cottages on a 1,400 acre working farm/estate. The estate is situated 3 miles NW of Wareham and comprises farmland, heathland, forestry and the River Piddle. Studland, Corfe Castle, Swanage, Bournemouth, Dorchester and Wimborne are all within ½ hour's drive. Sleeps 7. CH, Colour TV, dogs by arrangement only. OS Ref SY 893907

(SC) **GLEBE COTTAGE** Glebe House, Moreton, Dorchester, Dorset, DT2 8RQ

Carol Gibbens
Tel:-(0929) 462468
Open all year
SC   £70-£150
Sleeps 4

Glebe Cottage is set in an old rectory garden in the peaceful village of Moreton, noted for its church windows, engraved by Laurence Whistler and the grave of Lawrence of Arabia in the churchyard. The cottage is detached, on one floor and consists of 2 double bedrooms, sitting room, kitchen and bathroom. There are night storage heaters. OS Ref SY 803894

(SC) **LILAC COTTAGE** The Ramblers, Bradford Peverell, Dorchester, Dorset, DT2 9SG

Lorna McMillan
Tel:-(0305) 64523
Closed Jan-Feb
SC   £60-£110
Sleeps 4

A semi-detached thatched cottage built in 1832, with an L-shaped garden. The cottage has sitting room with TV, kitchen/diner (electric cooker & fridge), bathroom and WC. 1 double room and 1 with bunk beds. Night storage heaters and a parkray fire keep it cosy throughout the year. Linen available. Children and pets welcome. OS Ref SY 662928

(SC) **HIGHER COTTAGE** Higher Herringston, Dorchester, Dorset, DT2 9PV

Pollyann Williams
Tel:-(0305) 64330
Open all year
SC   £110-£190
Sleeps 6

Higher Cottage is warm, comfortable and well appointed set on a hill in a 450 acre arable and dairy farm it is reached by a private farm road and has fine views all round. Three bedrooms plenty of room for 6 people. Fenced in garden, enclosed patio, open fire. Children and dogs welcome. Bed linen provided. Automatic washing machine and TV. OS Ref SY 680880

THE OLD DAIRY COTTAGE Eweleaze Farm, Tincleton, Dorchester, Dorset, DT2 8QR

Rosemary Coleman
Tel:-0305 848391
Open Feb-Nov
SC   £60-£185
      Sleeps 6
      + cot

The Old Dairy Cottage has been modernized & comfortably furnished, still retaining original beams & inglenook fireplace. Sleeps 6 + cot. Eweleaze is a working dairy/arable/beef farm in a quiet village boardering the River Frome. Beautiful woodland and meadow walks, ideal birdwatching & fishing. All weather tennis court. Within easy reach of coast, golf, trekking & 'Hardy' country. OS Ref SY 774918

MEADOW VIEW BUNGALOW Eweleaze Farm, Tincleton, Dorchester, Dorset, DT2 8QR

Rosemary Coleman
Tel:-(030584) 391
Open all year
SC   £60-£185
      Sleeps 5/6
      plus cot

Meadow View is comfortable & cosy, fully carpeted sleeping 5 + cot. The farm has dairy & beef stock as well as horses, ducks etc. Tincleton is a quiet village situated on the River Frome but within easy reach of coast, towns, 'Hardy' country. Ideal for walking, birdwatching & fishing. All weather tennis court available on site & golf & trekking locally. Low season encouraged.

NEWMANS DROVE East Farm, Hammoon, Sturminster Newton, Dorset, DT10 2DB

Angela Hughes
Tel:-(0258) 860339
Open all year
SC   £65-£165
      Sleeps 6

Consisting of 3 self-contained bungalows, 1 specifically designed for wheelchair users. They represent a tasteful conversion of an old farm building within a farming complex, easily accessible. Delightfully situated in the Blackmore vale close to the River Stour with commanding views of the surrounding countryside. Carpeting throughout, colour TV, sleeps 4-6. Electricity 50p meter. Birdwatching, walking and coarse fishing. Regret no pets. AA inspected. Also (0258) 860284. OS Ref ST 821 125

TUMBLEDOWN 15 The Moor, Puddletown, Dorchester, Dorset, DT2 8TE

Mrs C Bowden
Tel:-(030584) 8695
Closed Xmas-New Year
SC   £60-£120
      Sleeps 2 plus
      2 children

Semi-detached thatched cottage standing on edge of village of Puddletown. Close all local amenities, shops, public houses, church. Village is on main bus routes Salisbury, Bournemouth and coast 12m, also numerous forest, country walks locally. Compact, comfortable accommodation suits max. 2 adults, 2 small children. Large lounge, kitchenette, colour TV large family bedroom, 1 double - 2 bunk beds, ensuite shower, toilet, bidet.

WINDWHISTLE COTTAGE Windwhistle Farm, Winterborne Kingston, Blandford, Dorset, DT11 0AP

Jill Batchelor
Tel:-(0929) 471789
Open Easter-Nov
SC   £90-£125
      Sleeps 6

Situated almost in centre of Dorset in the small sleepy village of Winterborne Kingston. Good facilities for pony trekking, fishing, rambling, birdwatching, golf and swimming. The spacious wing of a very old farmhouse, comfortably furnished with its own walled garden. Sleeps 6. Ample parking. OS Ref SY 862976

1. LONG LANE & 2. NORTHBROOK Stafford Park, Puddletown, Dorchester, Dorset, DT2 8TF

Mildred Cox
Tel:-(0305848) 232
Open all year
SC   £85-£155
      Sleeps 4/5

Formerly farm workers' cottages situated on a 500 acre mixed farm on the outskirts of Puddletown. Each cottage has undergone extensive alterations and is decorated & furnished to a high standard. The cottages are within easy walking distance of the village which has ample facilities. Guests are welcome to walk around the farm providing children are accompanied by their parents. Pets by arrangement. OS Ref SY 757947

Heart of Dorset ENGLAND

ⓈⒸ KENNEL COTTAGE Manor Farm House, Moreton, Dorchester, Dorset, DT2 8RF

Sue Hosford
Tel:-(0929) 462464
Open all year
SC   £80-£170
        Sleeps 5

Semi-detatched cottage in quiet setting on 500 acre mixed farm just outside unspoilt village of Moreton. Recently modernised. Suitable for active family holiday or restful break. 1 double, 1 twin, 1 bunk bedrooms (duvets and linen provided). Colour TV, night store heaters, open fire. Safe garden, sandpit, activity playground, children welcome. OS Ref SY 806894

ⓈⒸ WEST END COTTAGE East Farm, Martinstown, Dorchester, Dorset, DT2 9LF

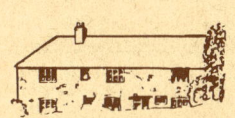

Gerald & Rosemary Duke
Tel:-(030588) 555
Open Easter-Oct
SC   £100-£180
        Sleeps 6

West End Cottage is situated in a peaceful country setting away from the road, well placed on the farm. The cottage is handy for the coast and many places of interest in the county. Guided farm tours are encouraged. The cottage sleeps up to 6 in comfort, and a cot & high chair are available if needed. All bed linen is provided. [Also (030588) 480].

ⓈⒸ THE OLD COACH HOUSE Manor Farm, Martinstown, Dorchester, Dorset, DT2 9JN

Patricia Marsh
Tel:-(030588) 279
Open Easter-Oct
SC   £90-£145

The Coach House has been modernised for comfort. It has central heating throughout, but the traditional character of the house is retained with its natural stone walls and windows. There is a small garden area in which to relax, making it an ideal choice for a leisurely country holiday. The house is in a secluded position yet in the centre of Martinstown. OS Ref SY 608808

ALL BED AND BREAKFAST PROPERTIES IN THIS GUIDE HAVE BEEN PERSONALLY INSPECTED.

ENGLISH TOURIST BOARD

WALES TOURIST BOARD

In England and Wales, the properties have been inspected and classified as 'Listed,' or '1, 2, 3 or 4 Crowns' by the English or Wales Tourist Boards. (See Introduction for details). The higher classification does not indicate that one property is better than another, but that it provides a greater range of facilities.

71

17 ISLE OF WIGHT

ISLE OF WIGHT

The Isle of Wight with its sandy beaches and small secluded coves with the sea never more than 15 minutes from wherever you may be, has a wide variety of holiday activities.

With Cowes and the Royal Yacht Squadron, an international symbol of all that is finest in yachting, the Island is famous for its seafaring activities with something for everyone who enjoys messing about in boats.

For the rambler, the birdwatcher, the angler and for those who merely wish to relax beside the splendours of ancient lighthouses or towering chalk cliffs, the Isle of Wight is the ideal holiday retreat with an internationally acclaimed network of well marked footpaths.

For those more adventurous, the Island is a haven for hang-gliders, windsurfers, water skiers, canoe enthusiasts and deep sea fishermen. The more leisurely sports such as tennis, golf or squash can be enjoyed in most parts of the Island.

Attractions for both children and adults include beautiful country parks, botanical gardens, bird and animal parks, nature reserves, Butterfly World, Blackgang Chine with its history of smuggling and shipwrecks, a steam railway featuring some of the earliest steam engines, Roman remains and vineyards open for guided tours and wine tasting. Above all, the Island boasts a climate that is regularly top of the Sunshine League in the British Isles.

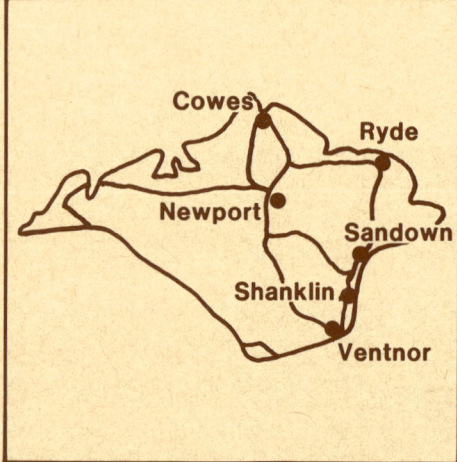

VACANCY SECRETARIES:
B&B — Diane Morris (0983) 407371
Self-Catering: Anne Kennerley (0983) 883993

Isle of Wight ENGLAND

(FH) BOBBERSTONE FARM Sandford, Godshill, Ventnor, I of W, PO38 3AT

Ann Russel
Tel:-(0983) 840660
Open Easter-Oct
B&B   £9-£11   Listed
Sleeps 6
🐕 (10) 🐎

A warm welcome awaits you at Bobberstone Farm, a 73 acre livestock farm tucked away in the heart of the island countryside. Magnificent views and peaceful surroundings give it that "we've got away from it all" atmosphere. Ideally situated for walking. Excellent pub and restaurant food in nearby villages. 2 double, 2 single rooms. Dogs by arrangement. OS Ref SZ 824551

(FH) YOUNGWOODS FARM Whitehouse Road, Porchfield, Newport, I of W, PO30 4LJ

Judith Shanks
Tel:-(0983) 522170
Closed Xmas-New Year
B&B   £8.50-£11   Applied
EM   £5 by prior
       arrangement
Sleeps 5
🐕 (8) 🐎

A grassland farm set in open countryside. The eighteenth Century stone farmhouse has been completely modernised retaining much of its character. The guest rooms are spacious and enjoy magnificent views of the West Wight (H/C in each room). Close to Newtown nature reserve, an ideal base for the naturalist. Good riding country, stabling available. Cowes sailing centre 4 miles. OS Ref SZ 456912

(FH) NEW FARM Coach Lane, Brading, (nr Sandown), I of W, PO36 0JG

Diane Morris
Tel:-(0983) 407371
Open Mar-Dec
B&B   £10-£12   Listed
EM   £4.50-£6
Sleeps 8
🐕

806 acres dairy and arable farm with many animals including pet peacock "Henry". Situated in the centre of beautiful parkland with magnificent views. Farm 5 mins walk to village or 5 mins drive to beach. House and converted stables make up accommodation. 1 family, 2 double, 1 twin. Showers en suite. Relaxed atmosphere. Home cooking, EM by arrangement. Dogs welcome. OS Ref SZ 598879

(FH) MOTTISTONE MANOR FARM Mottistone, Newport, I of W, PO30 4ED

Anne Humphrey
Tel:-(0983) 740232
Open all year
B&B   £8.50-£10   Listed
EM   £5
Sleeps 6
🐕

A warm greeting is extended to you at this 460 acre dairy and arable farm, in the lovely village of Mottistone on the South coast of the island, with superb views. The accommodation contains three spacious bedrooms lounge/dining room with colour TV, which overlooks a large garden and sea views. The sea is 20 minutes walk or 3 minutes drive. OS Ref 270c c5 05

(CH) BARWICK Rookley Farm Lane, Niton Road, Rookley, Newport, I of W, PO30 4ED

Pamela Wickham
Tel:-(0983) 840787
Open all year
B&B   £10.50-£11   👑👑
EM   £5
       Reductions for
       children
CH   Sleeps 12
🐕 ♿

Barwick is a large centrally heated family house, with good home cooking and friendly atmosphere, quietly situated in rural countryside, with easy access to all parts. There is ample garden and 6 acres with hand fed animals, pigs, lambs, cows, calves, ducks, chickens, geese etc., which children are welcome to feed. Horse riding, local Inn five minutes walk. Dogs by arrangement. OS Ref SZ 508830

(FH) HAZELGROVE FARM Ashey, Ryde, I of W, PO33 4BD

Sharon Curtis
Tel:-(0983) 63100
Closed Xmas
B&B   £8-£10   Applied
Sleeps 8
🐕

Modern semi-bungalow farmhouse situated on the main Ashey Down Road approximately 2 miles from beach and short walking distance to the Tennyson Trail, giving panoramic views of the Island. Beef cattle and prize winning Dorset Horn sheep graze the 40 acres of farmland. Also 10 rare breeds of sheep are situated adjacent to the farmhouse.

(FH) BRIDDLESFORD LODGE FARM   Wootton Bridge, Ryde, I of W, PO33 4RY

Mrs Judi Griffin
Tel:-(0983) 882239
Open Easter-Oct
B&B   £8.50-£11   Listed
Sleeps 6

A 250 acre working dairy/mixed farm with a Guernsey herd, lying in the heart of the Islands's lovely farming countryside, on the road ½ mile south of Wootton Common crossroads, the homely old family farmhouse is ideally situated for any kind of holiday. All kinds of eating places within easy reach. Tea/coffee making facilities in all rooms. OS Ref 533902

(FH) ASHENGROVE FARM   Calbourne, Newport, I of W, PO30 4HU

Jane Ball
Tel:-(0983) 78209
Closed Xmas
B&B   £8.50-£10   Applied
Sleeps 6

18th Century stone farmhouse, centre of a working family dairy farm on an old English estate with extensive woodlands. Full of wildlife and flowers. Fascinating walks can start from the door of this conservation award winning farm. Being centrally based it is ideal for touring the island. Numerous eating places are within easy reach. Self catering cottage also available. OS Ref SZ 444876

(FH) DURRANTS FARM   Porchfield, Nr Newport, I of W, PO30 4PE

Janet Attrill
Tel:-(0983) 523981
Open Apr-Oct
B&B   £9-£10   Listed
EM   £4
Sleeps 6

Durrants Farm is a working livestock farm situated in quiet unspoilt countryside two miles from Newtown Nature Reserve and approximately 5 miles from Newport, Cowes, Yarmouth. B & B, evening meal optional. Good home cooking, using own and local fresh produce, friendly, relaxed atmosphere with no restrictions. Car advisable. Pets by arrangement. OS Ref 445090

(CH) NORTHCOURT   Shorwell, Newport, Isle of Wight, PO30 3JG

Christine Harrison
Tel:-(0983) 740415
Open all year
B&B   £9-£12.50   Applied
CH   Sleeps 6

Large Jacobean Manor house set in private landscaped grounds of 10 acres. The house is on the edge of this small village in the middle of the island and is surrounded by woodland and the Downs. The bed and breakfast accommodation is on two floors, with that on the second particularly suited as a family suite with sitting room and TV OS Ref 4584

(FH) GREAT PARK FARM   Betty Haunt Lane, Newport, Isle of Wight, PO30 4HR

Sheila Brownrigg
Tel:-(0983) 522945
Open Easter-Oct
B&B   £8.50-£10   Listed
EM   £5
Sleeps 6
(10)

Centrally situated old Georgian Farmhouse set in 1300 acres of arable, woodland with beautiful views, is within easy reach of all main resorts. Accommodation is 1 double, 1 twin bedded room with H/C in each room, 2 attractive single attic rooms. Bathroom, dining room and sitting room, with colour TV, are for sole use of guests. Central heating, razor points, tea making facilities, car parking. OS Ref 4988

(FH) LISLE COMBE   St. Lawrence, Ventnor, Isle of Wight, PO38 1UW

Judy & Hugh Noyes
Tel:-(0983) 852582
Closed Xmas-New Year
B&B   £8.50-£11   Listed
Sleeps 6

Listed Elizabethan style farmhouse overlooking English Channel, home of the late Alfred Noyes (poet and author) and his family. Five acre coastal garden with rare waterfowl and pheasant collection (over 100 species). Surrounded by farmlands for owner's herd of pedigree Friesians. Superb sea views, coves and small beaches in area of outstanding natural beauty, adjoining Botanic Gardens and Tropical Bird Park. OS Ref SZ 545768

Isle of Wight ENGLAND

(SC) THE BREWHOUSE   Knighton Farm, Newchurch, Sandown, I of W, PO36 ONT

Anne Corbin
Tel:-(0983) 865349
Open Easter-Oct
SC   £70-£180
Sleeps 5

The self-contained wing of a 17th Century listed farmhouse with spacious accommodation for 4/5. Large beamed lounge/dining room opening on to a sunny courtyard, kitchen, and upstairs, two inter connecting bedrooms and bathroom. Well equipped and with colour TV. Situated south of the Downs on a small sheep farm in ideal walking country with many footpaths. Sunday bookings. Electricity included. OS Ref SZ 565867

(SC) LISLE COMBE COTTAGE   Lisle Combe, St. Lawrence, Ventnor, I of W, PO38 1UW

Judy & Hugh Noyes
Tel:-(0983) 852582
Open Easter-Nov
SC   £80-£180
Sleeps 4/5

Listed cottage overlooking English Channel. Own garden within 5 acre grounds of Lisle Combe farmhouse. Large pheasant and waterfowl collection. Adjoining glass works, Tropical Bird Park, Botanic Gardens. Many small beaches and coves for swimming or sunbathing. Colour TV. Everything provided except linen. Fine coastal walks in area of outstanding natural beauty. Surrounded by 180 acre family farm with pedigree Friesian herd. OS Ref SZ 545768

(SC) CHEVERTON FARM   Shorwell, Newport, Isle of Wight, PO30 3JE

Sheila Hodgson
Tel:-(0983) 741017
Closed Xmas-New Year
SC   £50-£160
Sleeps 4/6
B&B   £8.50-£10   Applied
Sleeps 4/5

This 550 acre sheep & arable farm lies in an area of outstanding natural beauty. The self contained accomodation is attached to the listed farmhouse, with 2 bedrooms, bathroom, sitting/dining room, kitchen. Exceptional walking and riding on Downland. Horses welcome, excellent stabling available. Also BB. OS Ref IW 845459

(SC) 2 MOUNT COTTAGES   Barton Manor Farm, Whippingham, East Cowes, I of W, PO32 6LB

Mrs Anne Orlik
Tel:-(0983) 293661
Open all year
SC   £80-£160
Sleeps 4

450 acre arable farm 1m from Osborne House on the outskirts of East Cowes. 1 semi-detached fully modernised stone built cottage to let. This cottage is in a rural setting away from the working farm. 2 bedrooms & bathroom upstairs, kitchen/diner & separate sitting room downstairs. Small conservatory at rear off the kitchen. Small garden laid down to grass. Children and pets welcome.

(SC) DUKES FARM   Rew Street, Nr Cowes, I of W, PO31 8NW

Mrs Peggy Jolliffe
Tel:-(0983) 296703
Open Apr-Sep
SC   £80-£180
Sleeps 6/8

This 165 acre stock farm has access to the beach which is situated in the north of the island, 3m from Cowes famous for yachting. The farm house has 3 bedrooms, dining room, sitting room, large kitchen. Linen not provided.

(SC) MOTTISTONE MANOR FARM   Mottistone, Newport, I of W, PO30 4ED

Mrs Anne Humphrey
Tel:-(0983) 740232
Closed Xmas and New Year
SC   £80-£180
Sleeps 6

This 460 acre dairy and arable farm is situated between Brighstone and Brook and has magnificent sea views. The accommodation comprises of three spacious bedrooms, sleeping 6, with bathroom, kitchen/diner and separate lounge; set in a large garden. Three minutes drive from the sea, and also lovely forest, downland, and farm walks around.

(sc) **LILAC & CHERRY COTTAGES**   Duxmore Farm, Down End, Newport, I of W, PO30 2NZ

Anne Kennerley
Tel:-(0983) 883993
Open all year
SC   £85-£160
      Sleeps 6/7

This 300 acre mixed farm is set in the heart of an area of outstanding beauty, with horses, calves, lambs and hens for children to see. A pair of attractive stone-built cottages with large gardens, spacious interiors and fitted carpets throughout. Each has three bedrooms. Children and well-behaved pets are welcome. Linen not provided. Horse riding nearby. OS Ref SZ 554880

(sc) **NORTH APPLEFORD FARM COTTAGES**   Barwick, Rookley Fm Ln, Niton Rd, Rookley, I of W, PO30 3PA

Pamela Wickham
Tel:-(0983) 840787
Open Easter-Oct
SC   £90-£185
      Sleeps 8

A pair of remote country cottages, reached by a gravel track and are both quiet and peaceful, enjoy excellent views. Located in the heart of the South Wight countryside, they provide a good base for touring and exploring the island. Built around 1890 mostly of local stone, each has 3 bedrooms, sitting room, kitchen and bathroom. Gardens and car space. Illustrated brochure available. OS Ref SZ 503 817

BOOKING TIPS

FARM HOLIDAY BUREAU

PLEASE REMEMBER . . .   Telephone or write to check prices and other details
— and confirm your booking in writing.

HAMPSHIRE

HAMPSHIRE

Hampshire is a beautiful county of contrasts — of creeks, harbours and beaches, and lush farmland with sleepy villages.

The main centres of the county, Winchester, Southampton and Portsmouth have all played their role in history. The Saxons made Winchester their capital, Southampton has traces of Norman invasion, Portsmouth of course, famous for its naval history — Nelson's victory and the Mary Rose.

Hampshire is also famous for it's people, you can visit Jane Austin's house at Chawton and Charles Dicken's birthplace in Portsmouth, both open to the public. For others, rich treasures lie in the museums in the county's towns and cities.

In the New Forest there are plenty of quiet picnic spots — and ponies. Hampshire is uniquely served by many Country Parks with long distance walks, plus all year round programmes of guided walks taking you right along the Solent Coastline, or inland if you wish, along the Test Valley with the inclusion of Stockbridge and Romsey.

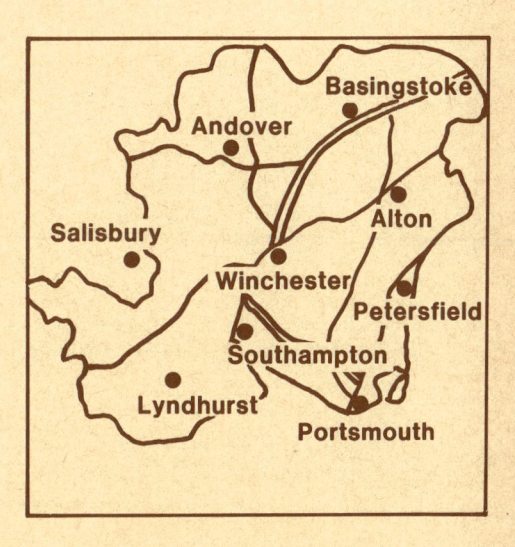

The country mansions of Broadlands, Breaumore House and Streitfield Sayre are amongst the many Hampshire homes open to the public.

Enjoy your holiday in this true English county.

(FH) ACRES DOWN FARM Minstead, Nr Lyndhurst, Hampshire, SO43 7GE

Mrs Anne Cooper
Tel:-0703 813693
Open Easter-Oct
B&B £9   Applied
SC   £90-£110
Van   £2

A homely New Foarest farm, keeping cattle, sheep, pigs & ponies according to the ancient laws of the Forest. Situated to the west of Minstead village, opening directly on to the Forest with its heathlands & wooded dales. Ideal for walkers, making a good centre for a touring holiday, farmhouse cream teas. Also a 2 unit self-catering cottage sleeping 4/5 open all year. OS Ref SU 271 098

(FH) BROCKLANDS FARM West Meon, Petersfield, Hampshire, GU32 1JN

Sue Wilson
Tel:-(073086) 228
Closed Xmas
B&B From £12.50   Listed
Sleeps 7

Brocklands Farm is situated on a hill in the famed Meon Valley with panoramic views of the countryside. Within easy reach of the coast & the ancient towns of Winchester, Petersfield & Chichester. The light & airy farmhouse has every modern convenience & a homely atmosphere. Day sailing in the Solent & afternoon tea available. Wheelchairs accepted. OS Ref SU 236638

(FH) CADNAM LODGE Cadnam, Southampton, Hampshire, SO4 2NS

Mrs Irene Banks
Tel:-0703 812007
Open Apr-Sep
B&B £12   Listed
EM   From £8
Sleeps 5

Only 1½ hours drive from London, this fine 18th Century house, originally a hunting lodge is superbly situated for riding, sailing, golfing or simply exploring the historic New Forest & beaches. Excellent stabling for guests own horses. Children especially welcome with high tea provided & a safe walled garden for play. Small animals kept besides home produced beef & lamb. OS Ref SU 135 295

(FH) VALE VIEW FARM Slab Lane, Woodfalls, Salisbury, Wilts, SP5 2NE

Sheila Barker
Tel:-(0725) 22116
Open Easter-Oct
B&B £8.50   Applied
Sleeps 4

Modern farmhouse accommodation situated close to the New Forest. Ideal for exploring the South. Plenty of good eating places in the village. Early tea/coffee laid on in all bedrooms.

FARM HOLIDAY BUREAU

(SC) SUNNYSIDE FARM Vernham Dean, Andover, Hants, SP11 0II

Barbara Whatley
Tel:-0264 89 281
Open Easter-Sep
SC   £45-£55
Sleeps 4-6

Set in deep countryside amongst the quiet lanes & woods of North Hampshire is Sunnyside Farm, & two spacious holiday caravans each comfortably accommodating 4-6 people. Both contain H/C water & electricity. Sited amongst trees in a sheltered corner of the farm they command 13 miles of uninterrupted views across the peaceful rural landscape. OS Ref SU 592 335

(SC) WOODSIDE FARM Privett, Nr Alton, Hants, GU34 3NJ

Mrs Peggy Newman
Tel:-(073088) 359
Open Easter-Sept
SC   £69-£138
Sleeps 4

Annexe to Georgian farmhouse. Under personal supervision. 2 Bedrooms, sleeps 4 plus zedbed. Colour TV. Part central heating. Electric fires in all rooms. Fridge-freezer. Well-furnished, comfortable, antiques. ETB highest category applied for. Groceries delivered daily. Quiet, overlooks garden, woodland, paddocks sloping down to A32. 6 miles south of Alton, 40 mins to coast. Clay shooting, riding near. Brochure on application. OS Ref SV 683299

SUSSEX ß SURREY

19

Further north busy towns such as Horsham, Crawley, East Grinstead and Reigate are surrounded by lush green countryside.

There is also a rich history here — Chichester with its famous Roman cross; nearby Fishbourne with the remains of a palace once ruled by a King Cogidubnus ... really; and Hastings — 1066 and all that.

In Surrey, the North Downs provide a dramatic wooded hillside and small, attractive towns and villages nestling in the valleys.

Here you can walk along the track claiming to be the Pilgrim's Way connecting Winchester to Canterbury; clamber up famous heights like Leith Hill — just short of 1,000ft — or its neighbour Box Hill, coming down via the intriguingly named Zig Zag Hill.

Yet nowhere in these counties are you ever more than a couple of hours from Central London should you wish to make a day trip there.

SUSSEX & SURREY

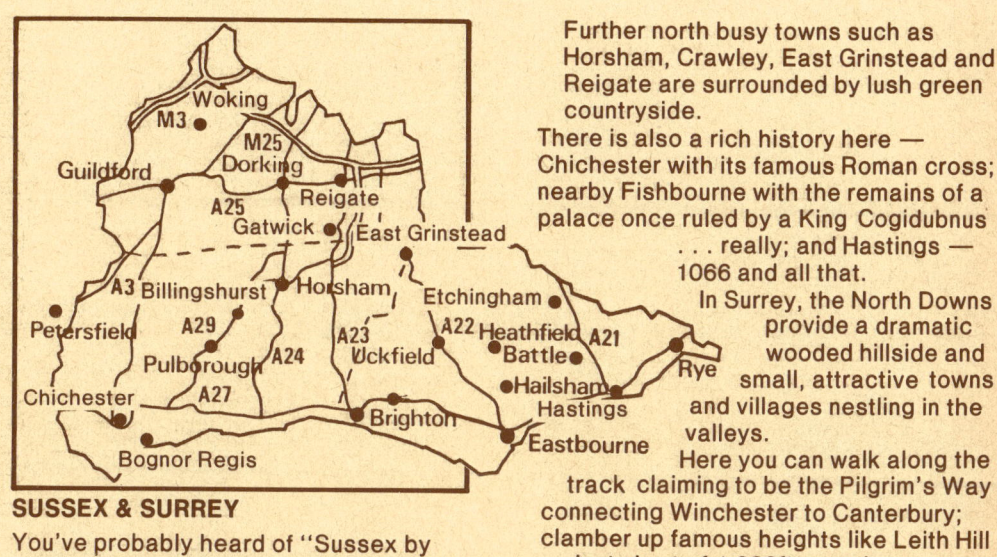

You've probably heard of "Sussex by the Sea" so perhaps to you Sussex means the traditional attractions of the popular seaside resorts such as Brighton, Eastbourne, Hastings, Bognor Regis, Littlehampton and Worthing. What you may not know, is that just inland there is a vast area of lovely downland punctuated with tiny villages and the occasional old market town.

GROUP CONTACTS
Surrey: Gill Hill (0306) 730210
Sussex: Philippa Gentry (0323) 833201

(FH) BULMER FARM — Holmbury St Mary, Dorking, Surrey, RH5 6LG

Gill Hill
Tel:-(0306) 730210
Open all year
B&B £10
Sleeps 6
Van £2

Beamed 17th century farmhouse with inglenook fireplace on a 30 acre beef farm in a picturesque quiet village amid the Surrey hills area of natural beauty. Three twin bedded rooms with washbasins and tea/coffee making facilities. Ideal walking country within easy reach of Gatwick, Heathrow, London and the coast. Own eggs and marmalade. Warm welcome assured. Good pub meals nearby. OS Ref TQ 114441

(FH) LITTLE GRANDTURZEL — Fontridge Lane, Etchingham, East Sussex, TN19 7DE

Norma Hawke
Tel:-(0435) 882279
Open Feb-Oct
B&B £9-£12   Listed
EM From £5.50
Sleeps 5

Beautiful spot in the heart of Kipling country. Many walks and centres of interest. Easy reach of sea and historic towns of Rye and Battle. Downstairs is a visitors' lounge with colour TV and radio. Upstairs are 1 double, 1 twin bedded, rooms with H/C and tea/coffee making facilities, 1 room fitted with bunk beds (children), separate guests' bathroom. Good home cooking. OS Ref TQ 695255

(FH) ST. MARY FARMHOUSE — Ridge Road, Falmer, Brighton, E. Sussex, BN1 9PL

Roland & Brenda Gough
Tel:-(0273) 692445
Closed Xmas
B&B £11-£12
EM £7
Sleeps 6

St. Mary Farmhouse - ideally situated, peaceful, scenic countryside but only 4 miles from Brighton. Country cooking with some home produce used. Sussex style house with central heating and open log fire in lounge. Family run home offering warm welcome to all guests. Evening meal by arrangement. 750 acre arable and dairy farm. 2 double, 1 family bedrooms. OS Ref PT 6774

(FH) DAIRY FARMHOUSE — Firle, Nr Lewes, E. Sussex, BN8 6NB

Kathy Hole
Tel:-079 159 280
Closed Dec-New Year
B&B £11
EM £5
Sleeps 6

A charming farmhouse quietly situated on a 1400 acre estate between Brighton & Eastbourne. 1 single, 1 double & 1 family room. Guests have their own bathroom, sitting room & dining room. Large garden backing onto parkland & South Downs Way. Firle Place Glyndebourne & Charleston farmhouse are all on the doorstep. Come & be spoilt in a relaxed, friendly & informal atmosphere! OS Ref TQ 080 474

FARM HOLIDAY BUREAU

(FH) THE STUD FARM — Bodle Street Green, Nr Hailsham, East Sussex, BN27 4RJ

Philippa & Richard Gentry
Tel:-(0323) 833201
Closed Xmas
B&B £9-£11   Listed
EM £6
Sleeps 6

Situated in peaceful surroundings. Beautiful countryside, ideal for walking. Only 8 miles from sea. Eastbourne, Hasting & S Downs within easy reach by car. Upstairs, family unit, consisting of double bedded room with hand basin, twin bedded room and bathroom. Downstairs, twin bedded room with shower, toilet, handbasin en suite. Guests' own sitting room, colour TV, spacious sunroom. Well behaved children welcome. OS Ref TQ 658163

(FH) SWALLOWS FARM — Dial Post, Horsham, West Sussex, RH13 8NN

Bette & Dick Sawyer
Tel:-(0403) 710385
Open Mar-Sep
B&B £11-£12.50
EM From £5.50
Sleeps 6

A Georgian farmhouse on Swallows Farm, a mixed beef, corn and sheep farm, in the quiet Sussex countryside, ½m from the A24 within easy reach of the coast and Downs, also historic houses and gardens. Golf and racecourses within 20 miles. Gatwick Airport is 16 miles. Special attraction see our Shire horses or our hand spun, hand made sweaters from our own sheep.

Sussex & Surrey ENGLAND

(FH) NEW HOUSE FARM — Broadford Bridge Road, West Chiltington, Nr Pulborough, Sussex, RH20 2LA

Alma Steele
Tel:-(07983) 2215
Closed Dec-Xmas
B&B   £12.50-£16
Sleeps 6
(10)

Listed 15th Century farmhouse with oak beams and inglenooks in picturesque village with 12th Century church. Bedrooms have tea/coffee facilities, colour TV washbasins, shaver points. 2 en-suite. In the area are Parham House, Petworth House, Goodwood House, Fontwell, Amberley Wildbrooks, Chalkpits Museum, Arundel Castle. Worthing 12m - Brighton 20m. Gatwick 45 mins. Good food at local pubs - few minutes walk! AA listed. OS Ref TQ 090185

(FH) SPARRIGHT FARM — Rackham, Pulborough, Sussex, RH20 2EY

Mrs Edith West
Tel:-(079 82) 2132
Open all year
B&B   £9-£10   Applied
EM   £5
       Sleeps 5
Tent   £1
Van   £1-£2

A listed farmhouse in a woodland setting. Ideal centre for touring, walking or birdwatching in the Amberley Wild Brooks. Swimming pool available during the summer months.

(FH) CROSSWAYS FARM — Raikes Lane, Abinger Hammer, Nr Dorking, Surrey, RH5 6PZ

Sheila Hughes
Tel:-(0306) 730173
Open Mar-Nov
B&B   £8.50-£12   Listed
EM   £5
       Sleeps 6

17th Century listed farmhouse, setting for George Meredith's "Diana of the Crossways". Situated in Surrey hills (just off A25) an area of outstanding natural beauty. Good centre for London and the south east, Gatwick and Heathrow. Large comfortable rooms with oak beams. Inglenook fireplaces. Cot and high chair available. OS Ref TQ 108473

(FH) MOONSHILL FARM — The Green, Ninfield, Battle, E Sussex, TN33 9JL

Mrs. June Ive
Tel:-(0424) 892645
Open Jan-Nov
B&B   £9-£12
EM   £6
       Sleeps 6
(5)

Farmhouse set in 10 acres, orchard, stables. In the heart of "1066 country" at centre of village opposite local pub, 4m Sussex coast, nice walks, riding/golf arranged. 4 bedrooms (3 ensuite), central heating, electric fires, tea/coffee making, car park. Family run assuring guests of every comfort with good country fresh cooking in a safe, quiet & peaceful home. Reduced rates for week bookings. OS Ref TQ 705125

(FH) CLANDON MANOR FARM — Back Lane, East Clandon, Nr Guildford, Surrey, GU4 7SA

Sally Grahame
Tel:-(0483) 222357
Closed Xmas
B&B   £9.50-£12   Applied
       Sleeps 8

An 18th Century timbered cottage next to the village pub. Breakfast cooked by the farmer's wife. Lots of horses, cattle, hens and ducks. Ideal for tourists and holiday makers looking for friendly overnight accommodation. Near to Guildford. Centrally heated, colour TV, comfortable clean beds. Set in miles of glorious countryside in an unspoilt village. Two treble and 1 double. OS Ref TQ 517061

(FH) MIZZARDS FARM — Rogate, Petersfield, Hants, GU31 5HS

Julian & Harriet Francis
Tel:-(073080) 656
Open all year
B&B   £13-£18
       Sleeps 6
(4)

1986 AA Award Winner, attractive 17th Century farmhouse in landscaped garden with a lake and covered swimming pool for guests. Superb guest suite with four poster bed and marble bathroom. All bedrooms have colour TV and ensuite bathrooms. Vaulted dining room. Easy reach of Arundel, Petworth, Uppark, Goodwood and coast. Children over 4 welcome.

(FH) LANNARDS Okehurst Lane, Billinghurst, W Sussex, RH1H 9HR

Betty & Derek Sims
Tel:-(040 381) 2692
Open Feb-Dec
B&B £12.50-£16   Listed
Sleeps 5

Comfortable bungalow with views & walks in Sussex Weald. Attached is a pottery workshop & gallery with quality work by British artists & craftsmen. Within easy reach of London, Chichester, Arundel, Goodwood, Brighton, Gatwick & there are many historical gardens & theatres to visit. There are polo, racing & riding schools and golf clubs in the area. A small licensed restaurant is attached for lunches & evening meals. OS Ref TQ 087279

(FH) MILL HOUSE FARM Broad Oak, Heathfield, E Sussex, TN21 8XB

Mr Mrs Don Knight
Tel:-(0435) 883316
Closed Xmas-New Year
B&B £10   Listed
EM   £4
Sleeps 6
Van £2

A comfortable 18th Century farmhouse with outstanding views of Sussex countryside. Set close to Kipling country and with easy access to many places of interest. A family run farm of 23 acres. 2 double, 1 twin room with use of lounge with colour TV, lovely gardens and swimming pool. All rooms are centrally heated. OS Ref TQ 631 233

(SC) BROWNINGS FARM HOLIDAY COTTAGES Blackboys, Uckfield, East Sussex, TN22 5HG

Alison Wright
Tel:-(082 582) 338
Closed Xmas-new year
SC   £110-£210
Sleeps 4-6
TV   £3-£5

5 comfortable, well equipped cottages, including 2 oast houses & a converted stable building, on 350 acre farm, situated in beautiful wooded countryside within easy reach of Ashdown Forest, South Downs, Sussex Coast and many local places of interest. Guests are welcome to follow the farm trails use the swimming pool and visit the craft workshops. Village nearby with shops and inns with restaurants. OS Ref TQ 530209

(SC) THE BLACK COTTAGE Newells Farm House, Lower Beeding, Horsham, Sussex, RH13 6LN

Vicky Storey
Tel:-(0403) 76326
Closed Xmas & New Year
SC   £65-£110
Sleeps 4

A charming secluded cottage, in the centre of a working sheep and arable farm with views to the South Downs, surrounded by fields, woods and lovely walks. Sleeps 4 people in comfort, recently modernised, it is 30 minutes from Brighton, 20 minutes from Gatwick, with fishing and golf and numerous lovely Sussex and Surrey gardens within easy reach. A delightful, small Sussex cottage. OS Ref TQ 206267

(SC) HOLLY & HONEYSUCKLE COTTAGES St. Mary Farm, Ridge Road, Falmer, Brighton, E Sussex BN1 9PL

Roland & Brenda Gough
Tel:-(0273) 692445
Open all year
SC   £84-£155
Sleeps 6
TV   £1-£3
Caravan Club
5 Van site

St. Mary Farm holiday cottages, Holly and Honeysuckle are situated in the heart of the South Downs. 4 miles Brighton, but away from it all in the peaceful, scenic countryside. Ideal for walking. Well equipped cottages including bed linen and TV. Farm is 750 acres, dairy and cereals. OS Ref PT 6774

(SC) THE COTTAGE The Stud Farm, Bodle Street Green, Nr Hailsham, East Sussex, BN27 4RJ

Philippa & Richard Gentry
Tel:-(0323) 833201
Open all year
SC   £60-£130
Sleeps 4

Peacefully situated close to farmhouse on 70 acre farm, 8 miles from sea. Attractions nearby; South Downs, children's zoo, adventure playgrounds, vintage steam railways, country trails, nature parks and many historic buildings. Also seaside resorts, Eastbourne, Hastings and Brighton. Downstairs, kitchen, sitting/dining room, colour TV. Bedroom with twin beds. Upstairs, twin bedded room, bathroom. Some rooms have low ceilings. OS Ref TQ 658163

Sussex & Surrey ENGLAND

JACKSBRIDGE FARM COTTAGE Lingfield House, East Grinstead Road, Lingfield, Surrey, RH7 6ES

Mrs Ann Barnes
Tel:-(0342) 832743
Open all year
SC   £85-£130
      Sleeps 4

A somewhat austere exterior conceals comfortable and very well equipped accommodation for four people. Renovated in 1986, this comprises 2 twin-bedded rooms, spacious living room, kitchen/diner and bathroom. Central heating, colour TV. Linen included. The cottage enjoys a rural aspect on our 150 acre farm which guests are welcome to explore. The village is close by. Easy access London, coast, Stately homes. OS Ref TQ834225

---

2 HIGH WEALD COTTAGES Sheffield Park Farm, Nr Uckfield, E Sussex, TN22 3QR

Mrs. Nicky Howe
Tel:-(0825) 790235
Open all year
SC   £120-£195
      Sleeps 5

An attractive, semi detached traditional farm cottage located on the edge of Chelwood Farm, Nutley, a working dairy farm close to Ashdown Forest. Sleeps 5 and baby. Accommodation comprises 3 bedrooms (1 double, 1 twin, 1 single) bathroom and separate WC, sitting room and colour TV, Electric cooker, fridge freezer and washing machine. Beds made up, no towels or cot linen. OS Ref TQ 424286

BORING HOUSE FARM Vines Cross, Heathfield, Sussex, TN21 9HB

Anne Reed (Mrs)
Tel:-(04353) 2285
Open Easter-Sep
SC   £90-£120
      Sleeps 7
      + cot

Boring House Farm Holiday Cottage is a fully self-contained portion of the 1950's style farmhouse. Consisting of utility room, hall, WC, kitchen, dining room, sitting room, 3 bedrooms, one with wash hand basin, one with shower, bathroom with WC, large garden. Lovely views and farm walks, fishing in trout stream and pond.

---

2 VICTORIA COTTAGES Hole & Alchorne Farm, Bell Lane, Nutley, Uckfield, Sussex, TN22 3PD

Pauline & Peter Graves
Tel:-(082 571) 2475
Open all year
SC   £110-£185
      sleeps 5

A charming comfortable semi-detached cottage, with a large, well kept garden. situated near the Ashdown Forest. Accommodation comprises 3 bedrooms (1 double, 1 twin, 1 single), bathroom & separate WC, sitting room with TV & telephone, dining room, kitchen with electric cooker, fridge. Ideal base for visiting South Downs, Castles, Gardens & Coast. OS Ref TQ 275 432

'The Erskine Collection'
of Aran Handknitwear
Cottage industry based in Surrey.

Traditional Aran designs as well as modern asymmetrical designs, handknitted in pure British wools in natural shades as well as a variety of dyes to choose from, also Jacob, Herdwick, Grey Welsh, Swaledale etc.
Quality garments produced by experienced knitters in Surrey, Hampshire and Berkshire.
Extensive range - Jackets, sweaters, waistcoats, hats, scarves, shawls, children's wear etc. Ready to wear or made to order, any size, any colour.
On sale at selected Craft and Trade Shows, telephone for dates and venues. Mail order - home and abroad.
Wool samples and prices on request, please telephone Camberley, Surrey 0276-62577.

Visitors by appointment only.

20 KENT

KENT

Kent is very much farming country, but the distinctive features are the many orchards, hop gardens, and oast houses to be found in the aptly named "Garden of England".

The hilly areas, like the North Downs and the High Weald, contrast with more low- lying parts such as the Low Weald and Romney Marsh. Each area has a distinct character, which makes the Kent countryside very varied and attractive.

Complementing the countryside are many historic towns and villages, among them: the mediaeval port of Sandwich, Tenterden in the Weald and its wide, tree-lined High Street, the traditional Kentish market town of West Malling, Cranbrook dominated by its splendid windmill, Rochester with its castle and cathedral, and the hilltop village of Chilham built around a square and dominated by its castle.

Kent has a wealth of attractions for the visitor. Some of these, such as Dover Castle and Canterbury Cathedral, are well known. But there is much more — Roman remains, castles such as Leeds, Walmer and Deal, fortifications like the series of coastal Martello Towers built as a defence against Napoleon, historic houses like Hever Castle, where Henry VIII courted Ann Boleyn, Churchill's home at Chartwell, Penshurst Place and Knole set in a deer park on the outskirts of Sevenoaks.

There are several vineyards open to the public, wildlife parks, like Howletts and Port Lympne, the Whitbread Hop Farm, a working farm museum numerous gardens, various country parks and picnic sites throughout the county, ideal for walks or family picnics, and three steam railways.

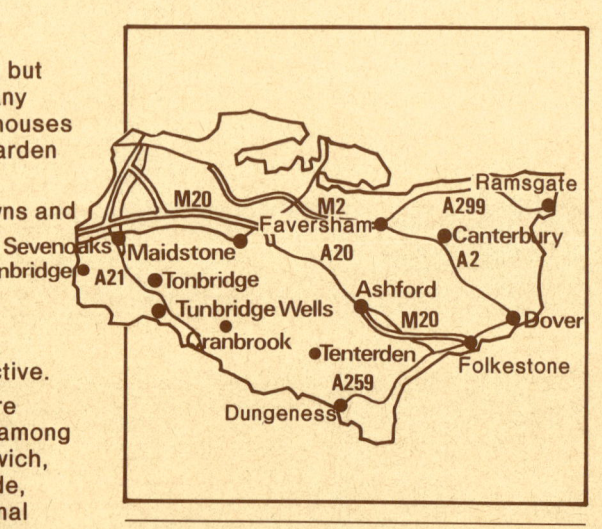

VACANCY SECRETARY:
Diana Day (0622) 831207

Kent ENGLAND

(FH) COURT LODGE FARM The Street, Teston, Maidstone, Kent, ME18 5AQ

Freddie & Rosemarie Bannock
Tel:-(0622) 812570
Xmas and New Year
B&B   £10-£18   Listed
EM   £7-£8
Sleeps 6

In centre of Kent, 4m from Maidstone & M20 (exits 4, 5, 6) less than 1 hour from London, Dover, Gatwick & Sheerness. This is a 16th Century oak beamed farmhouse with inglenook fireplaces, beautiful views over Medway Valley. Ideal for walking, touring or visiting many places of historical interest. We offer excellent home cooking using fresh local produce. Payphone for guests' use No. 0622 814200. OS Ref TQ 705535

(FH) GREAT CHEVENEY FARM Goudhurst Road, Marden, Tonbridge, Kent, TN12 9LX

Diana Day
Tel:-(0622) 831207
Open Apr-Sep
B&B   £11.50-£13.50   Listed
Sleeps 4

300 acre fruit and arable farm in Kent Weald, situated midway between Marden and Goudhurst. The 16th Century timber-framed farmhouse, has a wealth of exposed beams throughout, offers all modern facilities. Large garden. Within easy reach of Maidstone/Tunbridge Wells and ideal touring base for visiting the many castles, houses, gardens and other places of interest. Own transport essential. OS Ref TQ 738423

(FH) SISSINGHURST CASTLE FARM Sissinghurst, Cranbrook, Kent, TN17 2AB

James and Pat Stearns
Tel:-(0580) 712885
Closed Xmas
B&B   £11-£13   Listed
EM   From £6.50
Sleeps 6

Victorian Farmhouse with spacious rooms and beautiful views, set within the grounds of the famous Sissinghurst Castle Gardens. 1 bathroom and 1 shower ensuite. The surrounding farm is mainly arable. Beef animals, sheep and horses are kept. Guests are assured of every comfort with good farmhouse food. Guests' lounge. Reductions for longer stays. Lovely garden with croquet set. OS Ref TQ 807383

(CH) BEACHBOROUGH PARK Newington, Nr Folkestone, Kent, CT18 8BW

Gordon and Jan Wallis
Tel:-(0303) 75432
Open all year
B&B   £12.50-£15
EM   From £9
CH   Sleeps 10

Located just off M20 (junction 12). Listed grade II Regency Country House. Ideally situated for sight-seeing and shopping at Dover, Canterbury, Romney Marsh, the Continent, etc. Beach 4m, golf 1m, coarse fishing in our own lake. Heated swimming pool available in the season. Lovely grounds. Rare farm animals. 5 ensuite double rooms with CH, TV, tea/coffee making facilities. Dining room Licenced (Residential). OS Ref TR 169 382

(FH) HOMESTALL FARMHOUSE Homestall Farm, Nr Faversham, Kent, ME13 8UT

Sue Bones
Tel:-(0795) 532152
Open all year
B&B   £10-£12   Listed
Sleeps 6

Listed Georgian farmhouse, in a large beautiful garden close to ancient town of Faversham. Situated on a working 220 acre Hop, Fruit & Pick Your Own Farm, which also includes a collection of small, rare farm animals. Friendly atmosphere. Peaceful location ¾m from M2 intersection & all main routes. Ideal for Canterbury - 8m, coastal ports 25m & convenient for all routes to London. OS Ref TR 039 606

(FH) HALLWOOD FARM Cranbrook, Kent, TN17 2SP

David & Ann Wickham
Tel:-(0580) 713204
Open May-Oct
B&B   £12   Listed
EM   £6
Sleeps 6

Hallwood Farm is 15th Century yeoman's farmhouse situated in heart of Weald of Kent. Nearby is Cranbrook, a typical Wealden town with its architecture of local timber, brick. Centre of an area rich in mediaeval churches, cathedrals, castles, manor houses, offering the visitor a wide range of interesting sightseeing. Sitting room, TV, 3 doubles, 2 twins, 3 course EM, by arrangement, spacious garden, ample parking space. OS Ref 345 753

85

(FH) PULLENS FARM — Lamberhurst Road, Horsmonden, Tonbridge, Kent, TN12 8ED

Sally & John Russell
Tel:-(089 272) 2241
Open Mar-Nov
B&B £11-£12
EM From £7
No meals Wed
Sleeps 6

Comfortable 14th Century farmhouse has oak beams throughout and is found on B2162, half way between Lamberhurst & Horsmonden. Both double and family room have washbasins. Large streamed garden provides swing, slide, bikes for children. Visitors welcome to explore 200 acre farm which produces hops and cereals. Bewl Bridge Reservoir, Lamberhurst vineyard & Scotney Castle are close by. Reductions for children under 14. OS Ref TQ 690389.

(FH) OWENS COURT FARM — Selling, Faversham, Kent, ME13 9QN

Elizabeth Higgs
Tel:-0227 752 247
Closed Sept & Xmas
B&B £9-£10 Listed
12yrs & under
— ½ Price
Sleeps 6

Owens Court is a pleasant and peaceful Georgian farmhouse. It is situated 1 mile off the A2, 3 miles from Faversham, 9 from Canterbury and surrounded by orchards and hop gardens. The bedrooms are large and comfortably furnished with TV and tea/coffee making facilities. Guests are welcome to walk on the farm and use the large pretty garden. (Non group member) OS Ref TQ 027579.

(SC) TANNER FARM COTTAGES — Goudhurst Road, Marden, Tonbridge, Kent, TN12 9ND

Mrs. Lesley Mannington
Tel:-(0622) 831214
Closed Xmas and New Year
SC £60-£130
Sleeps 4/6
2 wks for price of 1
Spring & Autumn

Pretty 210 acre mixed farm. Once a hop and fruit farm, retains a 5-kiln Oast. Attractive woodlands walks, Shire horses bred & worked on farm. Coarse & game fishing available. 5 cottages comfortably furnished & equipped. Units are all electric; nightstore heating, open fires, w/machine, TV, fridge, gardens & parking areas. Linen & bicycle hire available. Mainline station (London/Dover) in Marden village. On B2079 between Marden & Goudhurst. Car essential. OS Ref TQ 734414.

(SC) THE COTTAGE, COURT LODGE FARM — The Street, Teston, Maidstone, Kent, ME18 5AQ

Rosemarie Bannock
Tel:-(0622) 812570
Open Easter-Nov
SC £80-£140
Sleeps 4 plus
2 children

This attractive period cottage, recently modernised, overlooks country park & Medway Valley in centre of Kent near Maidstone on A26, less than 1 hour from London, Dover, Sheerness, Gatwick. Close to village shop & restaurant. Sleeps 4/5. Ample parking. Ideal walking & touring base for exploring beautiful countryside. Nearby, Leeds castle, Great Comp gardens & Whitbread Hop Farm. Payphone for guests' use No. 0622 814200. OS Ref TQ 705535.

(SC) GREAT CHEVENEY COTTAGE — Goudhurst Road, Marden, Tonbridge, Kent, TN12 9LX

Diana Day
Tel:-(0622) 831207
Open all year
SC £60-£120
Sleeps 2/6

Comfortably furnished, semi-detached farm cottage situated in pleasant fruit growing countryside in Kent Weald. It has accommodation for up to 6 people and is well equipped. A colour television, well kept garden and garage. Ideal touring base for visiting castles, houses and gardens in the area. Main line station (London/Ashford/Dover) in Marden village. Own transport essential. Dogs by arrangement. OS Ref TQ 738423.

(SC) THE CLYDESDALE/SUFFOLK PUNCH — Manor Farm, West Malling, Maidstone, Kent, ME19 5NA

Mrs R Lambert
Tel:-(0732) 842091
Open all year
SC £85-£160
Sleeps 4/6

Situated on a 20 acre farm, 5 minutes walk from the Saxon town of West Malling. Within easy reach of Kent's historic castles & gardens & country houses. The Clydesdale & The Suffolk Punch converted from stables 4 years ago, sleep 5/6 and 4 respectively. The Clydesdale has upstairs sitting room, colour TV, carpeted throughout. Gravelled parking area. Small farm implement museum. Tennis court & table tennis available. OS Ref TQ 687577.

Kent ENGLAND

(SC) HOPE COTTAGE/OAST COTTAGE   Runhams Farm, Harrietsham, Maidstone, Kent, ME17 1NJ

Lady Monckton
Tel:-(0622) 850313
Open all year
SC   £80-£130
     Sleeps 4/5

2 cottages of character in mid-Kent. Excellent access to London and the continent and many other places of outstanding interest. Both cottages sleep 4/5 people. Fully equipped including colour TV, swimming pool available for guests by arrangement. The farm is 300 acres of grass and arable land. Hope Cottage is 14th century. The Oast is a genuine conversion. OS Ref TQ 873515

(SC) GOLDING HOP FARM COTTAGE   Bewley Lane, Plaxtol, Sevenoaks, Kent, TN15 OPS

Jacqueline Vincent
Tel:-(0732) 885432
Open all year
SC   £65-£135
     Sleeps 5
     + cot

26 acre farm producing Kent cobnuts for London markets. Surrounded by orchards and close to attractive village of Plaxtol. Secluded cottage, but not isolated. Sleeps 5, 2 double and 1 single. Central heating, colour television, automatic washing machine, dryer and fridge freezer. Horse riding, golf nearby. Car essential. Ample parking. Local station 2 miles with frequent trains to London. Motorway 4 miles. Dogs by arrangement only. OS Ref TQ 547 599

(SC) BRATTLE FARM   Staplehurst, Tonbridge, Kent, TN12 OHE

Anita Thompson
Tel:-(0580) 891222
Open all year
SC   £70-£115
     Sleeps 5

100 acre pig and arable farm in the centre of the Weald. Accommodation is part of an attractive moated 16th Century farmhouse with many exposed timbers. Coarse fishing in moat. Close to farm Museum run by owners. Car essential. Shops at Staplehurst 1 mile. Maidstone 10 miles. Tonbridge 17 miles. Hastings 25 miles. Ideal touring area. OS Ref TQ 7843

(SC) LITTLE SWALLOWS   Paddocks Farm, Cranbrook, Kent, NT16 3NW

Dereen Bartlett
Tel:-(0580) 712626
Open Easter-Sep
SC   £75-£140
     Sleeps 6

Little Swallows forms half of a large picturesque cottage on a farm near the old Wealden town of Cranbrook, a good centre for touring Kent and East Sussex, with the sea only 15m away. 3 twin bedded rooms, lounge, TV, dining room, kitchen, refrigerator, bathroom, phone (incoming calls only), CH, linen, towels available. OS Ref TQ 788 359

(SC) MOATENDEN COTTAGE   Moatenden Farm, Headcorn, Nr Ashford, Kent, TN27 9NU

Bridget Dungey
Tel:-(0622) 890505
Open all year
SC   £55-£100
     Sleeps 4

225 acre arable and livestock farm. Ground floor flat forming part of attractive cottage on farm. Adjoins 2 acre orchard which visitors can use. Lounge with colour TV, kitchen (electric cooker, fridge) bathroom, 1 double, 2 single bedrooms, solid fuel or electric heating. On A274 2m from Headcorn village with mainline BR connections to London and the coast. OS Ref TQ 819 464

(SC) BRAMLEY COTTAGE   Huggins Farm, Staplehurst, Tonbridge, Kent, TN12 OHS

Daphne Tipples
Tel:-(0622) 831269
Open all year
SC   £80-£145
     Sleeps 8

Modern 3 bedroomed detached house on a 300 acre farm, hops, fruit, corn, sheep and cattle. Pleasant wooded area in the Kentish Weald, many interesting places to visit, Bedgebury, Sissinghurst and Scotney Castle, Romney Marsh and the coast. Good train service to London - 1 hour. Own transport essential. Situated between Staplehurst, Marden and Goudhurst. OS Ref TQ 414 753

(SC) 1 & 2 WINGHAM WELL COTTAGES   Wingham Well Farm, Wingham, Canterbury, Kent, CT3 1NW

Georgina Maude
Tel:-(0227) 720253
Open all year
SC   £90-£120
      Sleeps 4/5

Situated in the small hamlet of Wingham Well, the Victorian terrace cottages have a pleasant view over the farm. Furnished simply and attractively, No 1 has 2 double & 1 single rooms, a sitting room, dining room, kitchen & bathroom. No 2 has 1 double & 2 single rooms, a sitting room, a kitchen-diner & bathroom. Canterbury (Cathedral), Sandwich (golf) 5-6 miles away, Channel ports 30 mins drive. Ideal for families holidaying together. OS Ref TR 230566

(SC) SPRING GROVE OAST   Wye, Ashford, Kent, TN25 5EY

Liz & Charles Amos
Tel:-(0233) 812425
Open all year
SC   £162-£477
      sleeps 5/7

A converted Oast house in the countryside, 10 minute walk from village of Wye. Situated in centre of Kent, 10 miles from Canterbury & Folkstone & 4m from Ashford for fast rail link to London. 6 spacious & well appointed flats with 1½ acres of grounds & a tennis court, fishing on the farm & riding locally.

(SC) MAYWOOD FARMHOUSE   R Sternberg Farms, Estate Office, Frenchay Farm, Tenterden, Kent TN30 7DJ

Estate Secretary
Tel:-(05806) 4988
Open all year
SC   £100-£240
      Sleeps 7

Small beef and arable farm forming part of estate based in the Weald. Delightful, recently renovated beamed farmhouse with inglenook, large garden and orchard in secluded rural position. Excellent access to Woodchurch, Tenterden and mainline station (London 60 minutes). Golf course, riding and coast nearby. Many local places of interest include Bodiam and Leeds Castles, Great Dixter, Rye and Canterbury. OS Ref TQ 926359

(SC) MARKBEECH COUNTRY COTTAGES   Falconhurst, Markbeech, Edenbridge, Kent, TN8 5NR

The Hon Mrs Cynthia Talbot
Tel:-(0342 86) 641
Open all year
SC   £60-£200
      Sleeps 2/6

Picturesque hamlet with church & pub in High Weald, (Tunbridge Wells 9m) with fine views north & south. Nearby Hever, Penshurst, Chartwell, Knole; bird sanctuaries, vineyards. 5 well-equipped Victorian cottages with tall chimneys and open fires adjacent to 600 acre dairy farm with lovely walks over fields. 17th Century farmhouse outside village, washing machines, storage heating. Holidays & longer lets. Dogs by arrangement only. OS Ref TQ 470426

BOOKING TIPS

FARM HOLIDAY BUREAU

A WARM WELCOME

Some farm and country houses in this guide only take six guests — others take more; but wherever you stay, you'll be sure of a warm welcome.

ESSEX

21

ESSEX

Essex surprises — it is still a rural county yet just a short trip from London. Rolling countryside and river valleys, creeks and estuaries with a scattering of villages and country towns.

While you are here take the opportunity to see for yourself all that Essex has to offer. Local farm produce, Essex wines and seafood, oak beamed country pubs serving real ale and traditionally cosy tea shops.

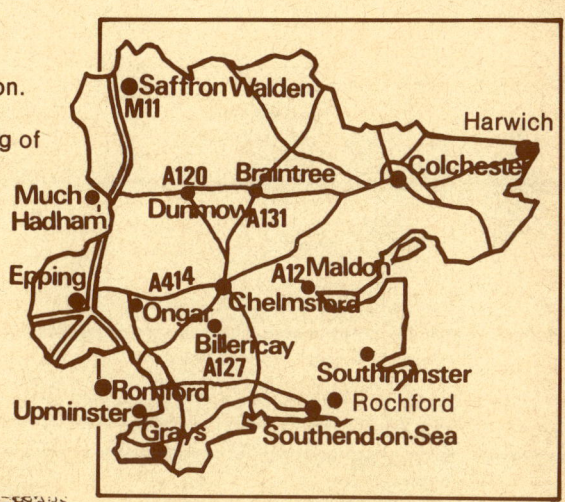

Explore the past — Colchester, the oldest recorded town in England, with a Norman castle built on the foundations of what was the largest Roman Temple in Northern Europe.

Lose yourself in the 6,000 acres of Epping Forest or wander through Hatfield Forest with its woodland, pasture, lake and nature reserve.

The Essex coastline is one of contrasts, from remote marshes to lively seaside resorts.

Burnham-on-Crouch, Brightlingsea Mersea and Tollesbury are established yachting centres. Seaside fun and safe beaches can be found in the resorts of Clacton, Walton, Frinton and Southend.

SPECIAL FACILITIES

Activity holidays for disabled people are available at Newhouse Farm; Weekend Breaks are run at Greensted Rectory, Newhouse Farm and Stanford Rivers Hall. Details from these addresses.

VACANCY SECRETARY
Inge Tweed (0206) 240377

(FH) ELMDON LEE Littlebury Green, Saffron Walden, Essex, CB11 4XB

Diana Duke
Tel:-(0763) 838237
Closed Xmas
B&B £13-£16
EM £10
Sleeps 4

This large farmhouse is situated on the village outskirts in pleasant countryside. The farm is arable, but a flock of sheep is also kept. Cambridge and Saffron Walden are within easy reach and London is only 1 hour away. Audley End House and the aircraft museum at Duxford are close by. OS Ref TL 482581

(FH) ROCKELLS FARM Duddenhoe End, Saffron Walden, Essex, CB11 4UY

Tineke Westerhuis
Tel:-(0763) 838053
Open all year
B&B £10-£12
EM £5
Sleeps 7

Rockells Farm is an arable farm in a beautiful corner of Essex. It has a large garden with a 3 acre lake for coarse fishing. There are opportunities for watching wildlife and sightseeing including Audley End House, Duxford Air Museum and the University town of Cambridge. The city of London is about 1½ hours by car or train. OS Ref TL 365467

(CH) KINGS VINEYARD Fossetts Lane, Fordham, Colchester, Essex, CO6 3NY

Inge Tweed
Tel:-(0206) 240377
Closed Xmas & New Year
B&B £9.50-£10
EM From £5
CH Sleeps 5
Tent £1-£1.25 (Max 7)
Van £1.75-£2 (Max 7)
(1)

Comfortable, centrally heated farmhouse close Essex/Suffolk border, once part of working farm, with large 3½ acre garden supporting flock of rare St. Kilda sheep. Short distance to picturesque Vale of Dedham, Colchester, Essex coast - Harwich, Felixstowe. The farm is adjacent to "Essex Way", ideal for walking/cycling/touring, relaxing. Home cooked E.M. available, also camping site & s/c caravan. OS Ref TL 940281

(FH) REDCROFT FARM Paglesham, Rochford, Essex, SS4 2EF

Rosemary Roberts
Tel:-(03706) 348
Open Apr-Oct
B&B £10
Sleeps 6

Built for an oyster merchant, Redcroft, a small farm with a large garden, a variety of farm animals and crafts. Set in marshland of smuggling fame, it is handy for Southend and London. The Roach and Crouch provide excellent sailing, and the sea walls give interesting walks. Single, twin & family rooms available, tea making facilities, TV lounge, log fires. OS Ref TQ 940922

(FH) NEWHOUSE FARM Mutton Row, Stanford Rivers, Nr Ongar, Essex, CM5 9QH

Beryl Martin
Tel:-(0277) 362132
Closed Xmas-New Year
B&B From £10   Listed
EM From £3.50
Sleeps 6

Tudor farmhouse with beams and inglenook fireplaces. Set in unspoilt countryside, 10 acres of grass surround the house and a lake for coarse fishing. Working arable farm within easy reach of Central Line (tube) to London. Cambridge & Colchester easy motoring distance. Oldest wooden church close by. 15th Century barn and stable block converted for Registered disabled accommodation, with recreational facilities sleeping maximum of 12. OS Ref TL 021531

(FH) NEWHOUSE FARM Radwinter, Saffron Walden, Essex, CB10 2SP

Mrs Caireen Ridsdill Smith
Tel:-079987 211
Closed Xmas-New Year
B&B From £10
(3)

This Georgian & Tudor farmhouse is set in 3 acres of gardens with a lake and moat. The farm is mostly arable but with some sheep and cattle. Cambridge, Saffron Walden, Audley End Mansion and the Imperial War Museum Aircraft Collection are close by. Ely, Lavenham and Long Melford are within easy distance. Bedrooms: 2 twin rooms, 1 with private bathroom.

Essex ENGLAND

(FH) DUDDENHOE END FARM Duddenhoe End, Saffron Walden, Essex, CB11 4UU

Peggy Foster
Tel:-(0763) 838258
Open all year
B&B £10-£12   Listed
Sleeps 4
SC £100-£130
🐴 (5)

Duddenhoe End Farm is situated on the outskirts of the peaceful hamlet of Duddenhoe End. The house is 17th Century with beams and inglenook fireplaces. Accommodation is 2 double rooms with washbasins central heating, tea/coffee making facilities, visitors own bathroom, Sitting/dining room with colour TV. Situated within easy reach of Cambridge, Saffron Walden, London 1 hour away. Also self catering cottage sleeps 4. OS Ref TL 560920

(FH) BONNYDOWNS FARM Doesgate Lane, Bulphan, Upminster, Essex, RM14 3TB

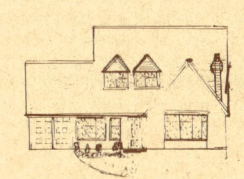

Rose Newman
Tel:-(0268) 42129
Closed Xmas and New Year
B&B From £12   Listed
EM £4
Sleeps 6
🐴 &

Bonnydowns Farmhouse, CH, double glazed, large, comfortably furnished. Situated on edge of Basildon Nature Park, Landon Hills. Conveniently placed for all road links (A13, M25, A127), London, Southend and South East England. Many local attractions short distances. Farm has large flock of sheep, cattle, ponies, goats, some arable. Large garden. 1 bath with shower, 1 shower room, sleeps 6. OS Ref TL 561866

(FH) GREYS Ongar Road, Margaret Roding, Nr. Gt. Dunmow, Essex, CM6 1QR

Joyce Matthews
Tel:-(024531) 509
Open Apr-Oct
B&B £10   Listed
Sleeps 6
🐴 (10)

"Greys", formerly two farm cottages. Pleasantly situated on the family farm - arable and sheep - just off the A1060. Easy journeying M11, London, Cambridge, coast etc. Ideal breaks, exploring. Beamed throughout, large garden. Dining and sitting rooms, CH, bathroom. Tea, coffees etc always available. (Regret no young children or pets). Two double bedrooms, one with H/C. One twin bedroom with H/C. OS Ref TL 604112

(FH) BLACKBUSH FARM Hook Lane, Lambourne End, Romford, Essex, RM4 1NR

Pamela Holloway
Tel:-(01) 500 6313
Closed Xmas
B&B £12-£14   Listed
EM £6
Sleeps 6
🐴

Listed timber frame farmhouse circa 1550 refurbished to modern standards without spoiling the original charm. 2 double bedrooms for guests sharing bathroom and dining lounge. 5 acres of ground include paddocks, flowers, fruit, vegetable gardens and lawns. Swimming pool with underwater lighting. Nearby golf courses and horse riding facilities at Hainault and Epping Forest. Easy access M25 and M11 and 50 mins London by underground. OS Ref TQ 488952

(SC) THE HOLIDAY COTTAGES Lorkins Farm, Orsett, Grays, Essex, RM163EL

Marilyn Wordley
Tel:-(0375) 891439
Open all year
SC £110-£225
Sleeps 2/6
Van £55-£159 /week
Sleeps 6
🐴 🐕 &

Orsett is delightful village just 22m from central London. Two adjoining cottages provide luxury accommodation having 2 and 3 bedrooms each, modern kitchens, bathrooms, spacious lounges, both superbly equipped. Ideal base for visiting London (35 minutes train), Cambridge, Canterbury or Southend-on-Sea. Local facilities include horseriding, golf, sailing, windsurfing, sports centre. A holiday for all the family. Also SC caravan at the farm. OS Ref TQ 646817

(SC) 1-2 RED LION COTTAGES Ashes Farm, Cressing, Braintree, Essex, CM7 8DW

Moran Ratcliffe
Tel:-(0376) 83236
Open all year
SC £85-£115
Sleeps 4
🐴 (7)

Two cottages dating back to 17th Century, set in a large grassed garden on fringe of a small village. Both have electric storage heating, 2 double bedrooms, sitting room, dining room, kitchen & downstairs bathroom & toilet. Excellent base for exploring East Anglia. Tourist information is in the cottages, which are Tourist Board Category 1. Children over 7 welcome. OS Ref TL 793211

(SC) **KEPPOLSMORE**   Ashes Farm, Cressing, Braintree, Essex, CM7 8DW

Moran Ratcliffe
Tel:-(0376) 83236
Open all year
SC   £95-£125
Sleeps 4

A modern retirement bungalow set in quiet secluded spot in small market town of Coggeshall. Only 2 minutes from shops & centre. Ideally suited to mature tenants. Coggeshall is renowned as a centre for antique shops and for its links with the wool trade, as demonstrated by Paycocke's House, a National Trust property. Keppolsmore is an excellent touring base. Category 3. OS Ref TL 852227

(SC) **HONEYSUCKLE COTTAGE**   Mistletoe Cottage, Great Wigborough, Colchester, Essex, CO5 7RH

Kevin Benner
Tel:-(0206) 35282
Open May-Oct
SC   £100-£135
Sleeps 4

Honeysuckle Cottage is a recently renovated 2 bedroomed beamed cottage with all modern amenities. It is well equipped, has full central heating, an open fire place in the lounge and is carpeted throughout. It is situated in rural open countryside with beautiful unrestricted views over the Blackwater Estuary. Pleasant coastal walks are 4 miles away whilst good sandy beaches can be reached in 30 minutes. OS Ref TL 97 14

(SC) **BLACKBUSH FARM**   Hook Lane, Lambourne End, Romford, Essex, RM4 1NR

Pamela Holloway
Tel:-(01) 500 6313
Open all year
SC   £100-£175
Sleeps 5

Bungalow behind the Tudor farmhouse is partly believed to have been built at about the same period. Refurbished to modern standards with CH from log room heater in lounge. 2 double, 1 single all with washbasins. Kitchen/diner equipped with new furniture and fittings. New shower room. Grounds include swimming pool with underwater lighting. Lawns, flower, fruit and vegetable gardens. Easy access M25, M11 and London. OS Ref TQ 488952

(FH) **STANFORD RIVERS HALL**   Stanford Rivers, Ongar, Essex

Jenny Sloan
Tel:-(0277) 362997
Open all year
exc Xmas
B&B   From £12   Applied
Max guests 10

Georgian farmhouse set in pleasant rural location yet within easy reach of London (tube or road), Cambridge, Stansted, Dartford Tunnel, M25 and M11. Centrally heated, comfortable accommodation comprises of characterful rooms with ensuite facilities. Friendly, atmospheric lounge with oak beams and wood burning stove, adjoining spacious dining room. Children and dogs by arrangement only.

NEW HALL VINEYARD   Chelmsford Rd, Purleigh, nr Maldon, **Essex**

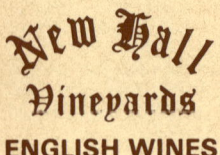

New Hall Vineyards
ENGLISH WINES

Piers Greenwood
Tel:-(0621) 828343
Cellar/shop open daily
Booked tours of
20 or more
Adults £3.50
May-Sept

Vineyard established in 1969, with over 35 acres, is one of the largest producing vineyards in England. Light red/white wine. Guided group tour includes film, winery, press-house, bottling room, vineyard, cellars, followed by wine tastings. Special English Wine Festival at New Hall during last weekend in September: crafts / food / tours & tastings and many other attractions for the whole family - £3/adult, 30p children.

SUFFOLK & NORFOLK

22

SUFFOLK & NORFOLK

Where better to spend your holiday than in this part of East Anglia, one of the driest and sunniest parts of England, within easy reach of the north, the Midlands, London ... and Europe.

In the north of the area is Norwich "Capital" of East Anglia, with its beautiful Norman cathedral. The coastline around Norfolk and North Suffolk is very beautiful and parts have been designated as Heritage Coast and an Area of Outstanding Natural Beauty. The holiday resorts, including Cromer and Great Yarmouth, provide all the entertainment one could wish for, and it is difficult to imagine them as formerly quiet fishing villages.

The coast and Broads are a haven for wildlife and there are many sanctuaries in the area, such as the Minsmere Nature Reserve and Bird Sanctuary, the Earsham Otter Trust and several farm and wildlife parks and museums.

Alternatively, you may prefer to spend your time enjoying the countryside, visiting the churches (and pubs!) of the villages, exploring the small market towns and discovering their history — often closely linked with the wool trade. There are many places to spend a day, a few examples being Somerleyton Hall and maze near Lowestoft; 14th century Wingfield College, a centre for music and the arts; Bressingham Steam Museum and Gardens and, of course, Lavenham with its beautifully timbered houses and inns.

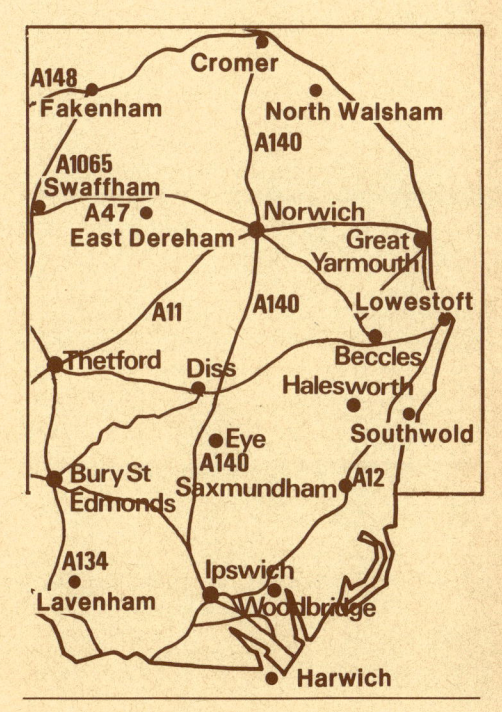

GROUP CONTACT:
Rose Tomson (037986) 443

(FH) MALTING FARM Blo Norton Road, South Lopham, Diss, Norfolk, IP22 2HT

Cynthia Huggins
Tel:-(037988) 201
Open all year
B&B £10-£11
EM £6
Sleeps 6

Malting Farm is situated on the Norfolk/Suffolk border and is a working dairy farm, with cows and farmyard pets. Elizabethan timber framed farm house with inglenooks and 4 poster beds. Six people can be accommodated in 2 family and 1 twin bedroom. Farmhouse cooking. Evening meal optional. Craft classes can be arranged i.e., embroidery, patchwork, quilting and spinning. OS Ref TM 035808

(FH) WOODLANDS FARM, FARMHOUSE Brundish, Nr Woodbridge, Suffolk, IP13 8BP

Jill Graham
Tel:-(037984) 444
Closed Xmas-New Year
B&B £10-£11
EM £4.50-£5.50
Sleeps 6

Small friendly family farm in rural Suffolk adjoining orchards. Close to historic town of Framlingham & within easy reach of coast and wildlife parks. Accommodation for 6 available all year in family room with private shower, toilet and washbasin and double room with en suite bathroom. Separate sitting and dining room for guests, both beamed with inglenook fireplaces. With full CH. OS Ref TM 272709

(FH) MANOR FARM Quidenham, Norwich, Norfolk, NR16 2NY

Jenny Leeder
Tel:-(095387) 540
Closed Xmas-New Year
B&B £10   Listed
EM £5
Sleeps 6

Large farmhouse in peaceful secluded setting on a 950 acre farm. Separate bathroom, dining room and lounge for guests. Reduced rates for children, use of large garden. Tea/coffee facilities in rooms. Home produced eggs, pork, poultry and vegetables used in breakfast & evening meal cooking. Vegetarians catered for if advance notice is given. Convenient to A11 & A1066. (Sorry no pets.) OS Ref TM 025888

(CH) STRENNETH FARMHOUSE Old Airfield Road, Fersfield, Nr Diss, Norfolk, IP22 2BP

Brenda Webb
Tel:-(0379 88) 8182
Open all Year
B&B £8.50-£14
EM £6
CH Sleeps 8

16th century former farmhouse, in quiet countryside. Central for many holiday attractions. Comfortable accommodation most rooms ensuite, H/C. Children catered for at reduced rates. Tea/coffee facilities in rooms. Wine & Spirits licence. 3 course evening meal with coffee. Separate lounge for non-smokers, log fires, CH. Pets welcome, ample parking. OS Ref TM 072841

(FH) HILLVIEW FARM Fressingfield, Nr Eye, Suffolk, IP21 5PY

Mrs Rose Tomson
Tel:-(037986) 443
Closed Xmas-New Year
B&B £10
EM £5
Sleeps 6

A working farm situated on the edge of an attractive village. The spacious modern farmhouse is delightfully furnished using antiques and traditional fabrics. Comfort is assured with full central heating and a wood burning fire for the cooler evenings. Separate lounge, dining room and bathroom. 2 double, 1 twin bedded rooms, with washbasins. Excellent food, friendly and relaxed atmosphere, ground floor accomodation. OS Ref TM 265773

FARM HOLIDAY BUREAU

(FH) LODGE FARM Algar Road, Bressingham, Diss, Norfolk, IP22 2BQ

David & Pat Bateson
Tel:-(037988) 629
Closed Xmas
B&B £9.50-£11   Listed
EM £5.50
Sleeps 12

We can't offer "en-suite" bathrooms but we can offer complete privacy with own bathroom and sitting room in a rambling 16th Century beamed farmhouse furnished in period and set in 10 acres of gardens, woodland and pasture. Read by the ponds, watch animals graze, spot birds, bats and amphibians, enjoy the peace, and see historic East Anglia from this central location. Brochure available. OS Ref TM 077827

Suffolk & Norfolk ENGLAND

(FH) GREEN FARM Cookley, Halesworth, Suffolk, IP19 0LH

Eileen Veasy
Tel:-(098685) 209
Open Easter-Nov
B&B From £10   Listed
EM   £5.50
     Sleeps 6
(8)

Guests are welcomed to the peace and quiet of this 45 acre working farm, 17th Century oak beamed farmhouse. Two twin bedded rooms, 1 double with 4 poster bed, all with H/C water and shaver points. Log fires on chilly evenings. Excellent 4 course dinner served. Good touring area with plenty of interesting places to visit. Children over 8 welcome. OS Ref TM 335764

(FH) ELM LODGE Fressingfield, Eye, Suffolk, IP21 5SL

Sheila Webster
Tel:-(037 986) 249
Open Easter-Oct
B&B £9-£10.50   Listed
EM   £5
     Sleeps 6

Elm Lodge is a working farm with large Victorian farmhouse peacefully situated overlooking a 40 acre common where cattle and horses graze in summer. Within easy reach Suffolk coast and places of interest throughout E Anglia. Accommodation comprises 1 family, 1 double, 1 twin bedded room with washbasins. Separate dining and sitting rooms with log fires or convector heaters. Excellent food and a warm welcome. OS Ref TM 288756

(FH) OLD HALL FARM South Walsham, Norwich, NR13 6DS

Veronica Dewing
Tel:-(060549) 271
Closed Xmas and New Year
B&B £9-£12
EM   £4.50
     Sleeps 6
Tent £1
Van £2

Thatched 17th Century Farmhouse, well situated for Norwich, the Broads and the coast. Fresh milk, vegetables and free-range eggs. Ground floor suite reserved for non-smokers. Special diets catered for if full details given in advance. OS Ref TG 362125

FARM HOLIDAY BUREAU

(FH) MANOR FARM Colby, Nr Aylsham, Norwich, NR11 7EE

Jane van Poortvliet
Tel:-(0263) 761233
Open Easter-Oct
B&B From £12.50   Applied
     £6.50 under 12s
     Under 4's free
     Sleeps 6

Attractive Georgian farmhouse set in secluded North Norfolk countryside offering 3 comfortable bedrooms (each with bathroom ensuite), guest dining room, and lounge. We are ideally based for leisurely or active pursuits, being in a National Trust Area and near the historic Weavers Way, beach and Norfolk Broads. Brochure on request. OS Ref TG 227 314

(FH) SALAMANCA FARM Stoke Holy Cross, Norwich, Norfolk, NR14 8QJ

Roy & Barbara Harrold
Tel:-(05086) 2322
Closed Easter,Xmas-NY
B&B £9.50-£12
EM   £5.50
     Sleeps 6
(6)

Situated in picturesque Tas Valley, our 165 acre dairy farm provides a lovely holiday setting, 4m from Cathedral City of Norwich. The house, named by a former owner who fought with Wellington in the Battle of Salamanca, is Victorian in character, although some parts are much older. Dinner includes home made soup, traditional farmhouse meat course, homemade sweets and a choice of cheeses and coffee. OS Ref TG 235623

(CH) MONK SOHAM HALL Nr Framlingham, Woodbridge, Suffolk, IP13 7EN

Gay Clarke
Tel:-(072882) 358
Open Mar-Dec
B&B £11-£12.50
EM   £6
CH   Sleeps 5
Tent £2   Van   £3
(10)

Delightfully situated listed 16th Century Tudor Hall with a wealth of beams, inglenooks and Tudor Rose ceilings, enjoying some of the finest views in Suffolk. The grounds include lawn tennis court, ponds and games room. Bedrooms are spacious with private bathroom facilities and guests have exclusive use of lounge and dining room. Ground floor suite for those with special needs. OS Ref TM 215867

SC YEW TREE COTTAGE Micklehaugh Farm, Banham, Norwich, Norfolk, NR16 2DJ

Bridget Clarke
Tel:-(037988) 351
Open all year
SC   £60-£150
        Sleeps 5

A 17th Century oakbeamed cottage in a friendly village on Norfolk/Suffolk border. Well modernised and equipped with central heating. Garden suitable for children and dogs. Sleeps 5. In rural countryside and central for forest, coast and many places of interest. Near to Bressingham Gardens and wildlife/tourist parks. OS Ref TM 108839

SC SONNY DAY'S Baltic Farm, Cratfield, Halesworth, Suffolk, IP19 0BP

Ann Kingwell
Tel:-(098683) 297
Open all year
SC   £70-£95
        Sleeps 6

Originally a farm worker's cottage. Sleeps 6 in 3 bedrooms. Ground floor consists of bathroom/WC, kitchen, dining room and sitting room. Washing machine, night storage heaters, electric fires, 1 open fire, TV. Roomy garden. Good starting point for east coast, Norwich, Bressingham Gardens and steam museum, Otter Trust, R.S.P.B. reserve at Minsmere and Norfolk Broad. OS Ref TM 243874

SC LODGE FARM Algar Road, Bressingham, Diss, Norfolk, IP22 2BQ

David & Pat Bateson
Tel:-(037988) 629
Open all year
SC   £50-£135
        Sleeps 12
Tent   50p
Van   £1.75

Delightful 17th Century beamed maisonette in farmhouse and 18th Century coachhouse set in 10 acres of gardens, woodland and pasture. Can cater for groups of 4 to 12. Close to famous Bressingham Gardens and Steam Museum and the market town of Diss. Centrally situated in historic East Anglia. Fishing, riding, zoos, nature reserves, beaches in the area. Brochure available. OS Ref TM 077827

SC STABLE COTTAGES Chattisham Place, Nr Ipswich, Suffolk, IP8 3QD

Margaret Langton
Tel:-(047387) 210
Open all year
SC   £90-£150
        Sleeps 2/6

2 Well equipped flats converted from stables situated in SE facing courtyard, one designed for wheelchair users. Central heating, fitted kitchen, colour TV, linen, towels, electricity included. Games room and laundry facilities on site, swimming and tennis by arrangement. Chattisham is a quiet rural village near Constable country and the wool towns of Lavenham and Kersey. OS Ref TM 420093

SC WHISPERING WILLOWS BUNGALOW St Andrews Hall, Ilketshall St Andrews, Nr Beccles, Suffolk, NR34 8NS

Mrs Jessie Cannell
Tel:-(098681) 204
Open Easter-Oct
SC   £135-£160
        Sleeps 5

Modern red-brick bungalow, surrounded by farmland in unspoilt village in Waveney district of Suffolk. Large garden with lawn, garage, private grounds, convenient centre for historic town of Bungay and the attractive rural Georgian town of Beccles. Near River Waveney and within easy reach of the broads and coast. Sleeps 5 people. Linen available. Ideal for enjoyable, quiet, happy holiday. Children by arrangement. No dogs. OS Ref NG 395866

SC HOLLY COTTAGE Collin Green Farm, Lyng, Norwich, Norfolk, NR9 5LH

Kay Thomas
Tel:-(0603) 880158
Open Easter-Sep
SC   £100-£150
        Sleeps 6

Lyng is situated in central Norfolk 10 miles west of Norwich in the Wensum Valley. The property is within 1 mile of the village, near to a working farm. 1 double room and 2 twin rooms. Fitted kitchen/dining area, comfortable lounge, colour TV, bathroom. Covenient coast and Broads - peaceful rural setting. (Non group member) OS Ref TG 082164

Suffolk & Norfolk ENGLAND

COME AND VISIT
THE Clare Craft Pottery
WIZARD SHOP.

OPEN 10AM~4PM 7 DAYS A WEEK.

BROOMHILL LANE, WOOLPIT, BURY ST EDMUNDS. SUFFOLK. 0359 41217

CAMBRIDGESHIRE & HERTFORDSHIRE

CAMBRIDGESHIRE

Cambridgeshire is a county of contrasts with plenty to attract the visitor. Best known is Cambridge itself one of Britain's oldest university cities, but other areas of the county have their own attractions. Particularly striking is the flat landscape of the Fens, with its peat black soil criss-crossed by dykes and views dominated by the sky. The area around the river Great Ouse, once the county of Huntingdonshire consists of a string of attractive market towns and villages fronting the river.

The geology and geography of the county ensures wildlife abounds making it a haven for birdwatchers, fishermen, walkers, cyclists and boat enthusiasts. There is much for the lover of architecture and the admirer of historic buildings.

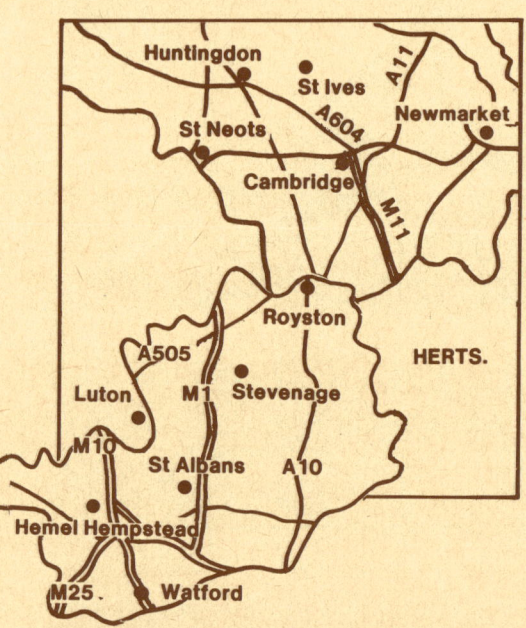

HERTFORDSHIRE

Hertfordshire — often referred to as the 'home county' — is rich in country houses, parks and fine churches famous for their spires, and is only a 30 minute train journey from central London. Houses such as Hatfield House, and Knebworth House are worthy of a visit. Others include Moor Park Mansion, home of the famous Moor Park Golf Club and Shaw's Corner, home of George Bernard Shaw.

(FH) MOLESWORTH LODGE FARM   Molesworth, Huntingdon, Cambs, PE18 0PJ

Rhona Page
Tel:-08014 309
Closed Xmas-New Year
B&B   £9-£10   Listed
Sleeps 5

A warm welcome awaits you at this fully central heated farmhouse, standing in 316 acres of peaceful Cambridgeshire countryside. There are places of interest in the area, and Grafham Water for the fishing & boating enthusiasts. The farm also has a caravan club C.L. 1 double room & a large double with cot &/or single. Reduced rate for children. EM by arrangement. OS Ref TL 069 739

(SC) SOUTHFIELDS FARM COTTAGE   Southfields Farm, Throcking, Nr Buntingford, Herts, SG9 9RD

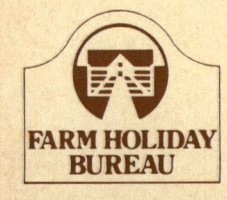

Irene Murchie
Tel:-(076381) 224
Open all year
SC   £65-£90
Sleeps 4

Self-catering farm cottage in the heart of prime agricultural land fully equipped, fitted carpets, double glazing, central heating. Heating, hot water & linen inclusive. Three bedrooms, bathroom, kitchen/diner and living room with open fire. Children welcome, cot available. OS Ref TL 3330

BEDFORDSHIRE

BEDFORDSHIRE

Easily accessible from both M1 and A1 Bedfordshire is ideally placed between Oxford and Cambridge and its heritage offers some first class attractions making it ideal for a short break. The County is perhaps best known as Bunyan country but is famous too for the Great Ouse, one of England's most attractive rivers. There is something to suit most tastes, with country houses like Woburn Abbey, Luton Hoo and Hinwick House, or Whipsnade Zoo for the children. Garden enthusiasts can visit The Swiss Garden, Wrest Park or Willington Garden Centre.

Nature lovers may go to the R.S.P.B. Nature Reserve, Stagsden Bird Gardens or the Country Parks. Walkers will find the newly-established Greensand Ridge Walk conveniently divided into three smaller circular routes based on the most attractive areas Those keen on aeroplanes will head for The Shuttleworth Collection or watch the airships passing over the countryside around Cardington. Even holidaymakers leaving from Luton Airport will find a few days here will help them unwind in preparation for their holiday.

At the end of their stay guests might find themselves going home laden with quantities of fresh fruit and vegetables picked at one of many of Bedfordshire's "pick-your-own" units.

Whatever your interests we're sure you'll enjoy your stay in Bedfordshire.

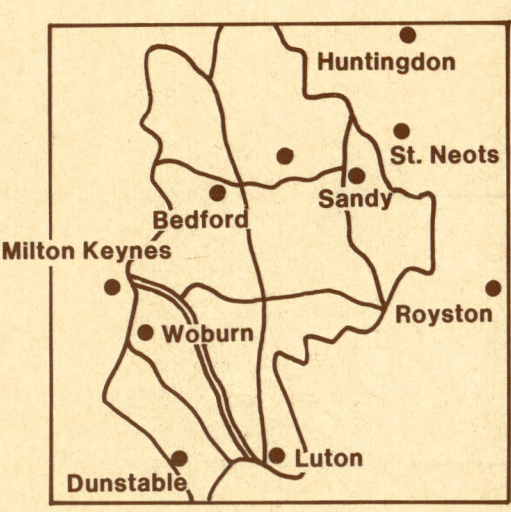

VACANCY SECRETARY:
Judy Tookey (0525) 712316

(FH) POND FARM   7 High Street, Pulloxhill, Bedford, MK45 5HA

Judy & Phil Tookey
Tel:-(0525) 712316
Open all year
B&B   £10   Listed
EM   £5
       Sleeps 6

Ideal base for touring Woburn Abbey/Safari Park, Whipsnade Zoo, Luton Airport, Shuttleworth collection of historic aircraft. An arable farm of 70 acres, although we have horses grazing on the meadowland & we keep Great Dane dogs. 3 miles from the A6 & 5 miles from the M1. 9 miles from Luton Airport. Most bedrooms with H/C and all with TV. OS Ref TL 063341

(FH) CHURCH FARM   41 High Street, Roxton, Bedford, MK44 3EB

Janet Must
Tel:-(0234) 870234
Open all year
B&B   £10-£12.50   Listed
       Redn given for
       3 consecutive
       nights or more
       Sleeps 6

A traditional farmhouse in a quiet village ½m from the A1. A Grade II listed building, part 16th Century part Georgian, it's bedrooms reflect it's past. Accommodation in guest wing overlooks garden and small orchard. The bedrooms are separate from the family's accommodation having their own staircase & bathroom. Tea/coffee making facilities in bedrooms. Full English breakfast served in the 16th Century dining room. OS Ref TL 153545

(FH) NEW ENGLAND FARM   Tadlow, Nr Royston, Herts, SG8 0EN

Mrs Angela Wilson
Tel:-(076723) 247
Closed Xmas and New Year
B&B   £10-£12.50   Applied
       Sleeps 6
SC   £80

We are located on the B1042 between Bedford and Cambridge, our farmhouse is situated in the centre of our 300 acre arable farm. an ideal base for visiting Cambridge, Duxford, Shuttleworth, Wimpole Hall, Woburn, RSPB Sandy and 10 golf courses within 30 minutes drive. OS Ref TL 276 486

(SC) PRIESTLEY FARM   Church Road, Flitwick, Bedford, MK45 5AN

Mrs Angela Little
Tel:-(0525) 712978
Open all year
SC   £75-£120
       Sleeps 6

Attached to the main farmhouse, set in peaceful countryside, the house offers 3 double bedrooms, bathroom, large lounge, and kitchen/diner. Electric cooking and heating. Large garden and ample car parking. Covenient for M1, Woburn Abbey, Whipsnade Zoo and many other places of interest. A working family dairy farm with 90 Jersey cows and youngstock. Pleasant walks around the farm. OS Ref TL 020333

(SC) SCALD END FARM   Thurleigh, Bedford, Beds

James Towler
Tel:-(0234) 771996
Open all year
SC   From £60
       Sleeps 6

Thatched cottages with pleasant views over open countryside - Scald Farm is working farm of 171 acres with cattle, sheep, pigs, horses and offers free-range eggs and fresh vegetables in season. Thurleigh is just north of Bedford and easy access to major roads. OS Ref 54911

100

THAMES VALLEY   26

Thames Valley ENGLAND

THAMES VALLEY

The Thames Valley is at the heart of historical England

Farms and homes are situated in the area stretching from the Chiltern Hills above Henley through the rich farmland of the Vale of Aylesbury and on to the west of Oxford to the Cotswolds.

Oxford is at the centre of the region and its dreaming spires and great buildings which include mediaeval colleges and Renaissance masterpieces such as the Sheldonian Theatre can provide great historical interest. You can take guided tours of Oxford, Windsor and Burford or enjoy browsing in antique shops and bookshops.

Woodstock has many historical associations and is the site of Blenheim Palace, Sir John Vanburgh's magnificent home for the Dukes of Marlborough. Sir Winston Churchill was born there and is buried in the nearby churchyard of Bladon.

The area includes the moated castle at Broughton near Banbury and many other Tudor and 18th century manors and country houses. Items of interest for children include the Cotswold Wildlife Park, Birdland, Cogges Farm Museum and a steam railway centre and activities such as boating, pony trekking and brass rubbing are available.

VACANCY SECRETARY:
Anne Amor (0367) 52620

(FH) MANOR FARM Shabbington, Aylesbury, Bucks, HP18 9HJ

Joan Bury
Tel:-(0844) 201103
Open all year
B&B £11-£15   Listed
Sleeps 6
🐎 (8) ♿

This 188 acre grazing farm is in a quiet pastoral setting with lovely views. Bounded by the River Thame. Twelve miles from Oxford, Manor Farm is conveniently situated for Chilterns, Cotswolds, Thames Valley and London. Accommodation in modern, well equipped bungalow with lounge, kitchen, bathroom, colour TV, CH. Breakfast served in adjacent farmhouse. Many good pubs and restaurants in area. OS Ref SU 664062

(FH) POLETREES FARM Brill, Nr Aylesbury, Bucks, HP18 9TZ

Anita Cooper
Tel:-(0844) 238276
Closed Xmas
B&B £12-£16   Listed
EM   £7
Sleeps 4

A 16th Century former coaching inn situated on the old Oxford to Buckingham Roman road. Retaining the original oak beams and open fireplaces. Overlooking peaceful green fields and English oak trees. Many delightful eating places by Brill Windmill. A round of golf for the man can be arrranged. Many other country interests for everyone. One double, 1 twin. OS Ref SP 663160

(FH) UPPER GREEN FARM Manor Road, Towersey, Thame, Oxon, OX9 3QR

Marjorie & Euan Aitken
Tel:-(084421) 2496
Closed Xmas-New Year
B&B £12-£14   Listed
Sleeps 5

A thatched 15th Century farmhouse. Winner of Farm Holiday Bureau Award. Beautifully restored, the house retains all its ancient character, beamed ceilings, wall timbers, a priest hole off one of the bedrooms, a Victorian Kitchen range, and an old bread oven. Close to Thame with a choice of eating places. Central heating. One twin, 1 double, 1 single room. Non-smokers. OS Ref SP 738051

(FH) MANOR FARM BRIMPTON Brimpton, Reading, Berks, RG7 4SQ

Mrs Jean Bowden
Tel:-0734 713166
Closed Xmas-New year
B&B £10-£15   Listed
Sleeps 4

Dairy/Arable family run farm, Georgian farmhouse with Norman chapel in the garden. Situated 45 miles West of London within easy reach of M4, M3, Heathrow,Gatwick airports & South Coast. Good pubs & restaurants locally. OS Ref SU 165 456

(FH) NEALS FARM Wyfold, Reading, RG4 9JB

Bridget Silsoe
Tel:-(0491) 680258
Closed Xmas
B&B £10-£12   Listed
EM   £6
     (Reductions
     for children)
Sleeps 6

A 100 acre livestock farm situated high in the Chilterns in an area of outstanding beauty. The spacious Georgian farmhouse is approached through beechwoods which open to reveal a wonderful view. Secluded, not isolated. Easy access Heathrow, Henley, Windsor and London. Informal, relaxed atmosphere. Guests treated as family. Swimming pool. Comfortable beds. Excellent home produced food. Non Smokers much preferred. OS Ref SU 685829

(FH) GLEBE FARM Spelsbury, Oxford, OX7 3JR

Jean & Helen Datson
Tel:-(0608) 810398
Open Easter-Oct
B&B £9-£12   Listed
Sleeps 4
🐎 (6)

We are a 320 acre mixed farm on the eastern edge of the Cotswolds. The farmhouse has full central heating and there are two bedrooms, both with tea making facilities. We offer a traditional breakfast with our own free range eggs and homemade marmalade! Spelsbury is a peaceful village within easy reach of Oxford, Burford, Woodstock and Bleinham Palace. OS Ref SP 349215

Thames Valley ENGLAND

FH SUGARSWELL FARM Shenington, Banbury, Oxon, OX15 6HW

Rosemary Nunneley
Tel:-(029588) 512
Open all year
B&B £12-£20
EM £12
Sleeps 6
(8)

Beautiful farmhouse overlooking fields and woodlands on the Oxfordshire/Warwickshire border with a luxurious interior where comfort is at the fore. Two bedrooms have king size beds, all have bathroom ensuite. Cordon-Bleu cooking, fillet steak in port & cream a speciality. recommended by Elizabeth Gundry in the Sunday Times. For the discerning guest who is looking for something rather special. Colour brochure. OS Ref SP 455420

FH HILL GROVE FARM Crawley Road, Minster Lovell, Oxford, OX8 5NA

Katharine Brown
Tel:-(0993) 3120/703120
Closed Xmas
B&B £10.50-£11.50
Sleeps 4

Hill Grove Farm is a mixed family run working farm of 250 acres, situated in an attractive rural setting overlooking the Windrush Valley and yet is within easy driving distance of Witney farm museum, Woodstock's Blenheim Palace, Burford, the gateway to the Cotswolds and Oxford. We offer bed and breakfast in a friendly atmosphere. Children welcomed. One double with shower, 1 twin with bath. OS Ref SP 335115

FH ASHEN COPSE FARM Coleshill, Highworth, Swindon, Wilts, SN6 7PU

Pat Hoddinott
Tel:-(0367) 20175
Closed Xmas
B&B £10-£12
Sleeps 6

Large, comfortable, National Trust farmhouse on a beef/arable farm amidst peaceful countryside on the borders of Oxfordshire, Wiltshire & Gloucestershire. Ideal centre for walking or touring the Cotswolds, Ridgeway, Oxford, Bath.- A wide variety of interesting places to visit locally. Riding, fishing, golfing, boating nearby. 2 light & airy double/family bedrooms with washbasins (1 has Shower & WC en suite). Small outdoor pool. Reduced rates for children. OS Ref SU 251933

FH MANOR FARM Kelmscott, Lechlade, Gloucestershire, GL7 3HJ

Anne Amor
Tel:-(0367) 52620
Open all Year
B&B £10-£15
Reductions for children
Sleeps 6

Working dairy farm in foothills of Cotswolds, ¼ mile from River Thames. Close to M4 exit 15. Ideally suited for touring, fishing, golfing, walking & cycling. 17th Century Cotswold stonehouse has large comfortable rooms all with washbasins and tea/coffee making facilities. Kelmscott is famous for the William Morris Manor. There are also many historic buildings and towns to explore nearby. OS Ref SU 251991

FH MORAR FARMHOUSE Weald Street, Bampton, (nr Witney), Oxon, OX8 2HL

Janet Rouse
Tel:-(0993) 850162
Closed Xmas
B&B £10-£15
EM £10
Sleeps 6
(6)

Morar is a NON-SMOKING, farmhouse in an area of honey coloured Cotswold homes and idyllic countryside. Our 450 acre farm has beef/dairy herds & arable crops. Ideally situated for Oxford, Cotswolds, Blenheim Palace, Didcot Steam Railway Museum, Cotswold weavers, swimming, sailing riding, fishing, golf. We like Morris Dancing, gardening, bellringing - and laughing! AA Relais Routiers & Elizabeth Gundrey recommended. OS Ref SP 320020

CH FOXHILL FARM Kingsey, Aylesbury, Buckinghamshire, HP17 8LZ

Mary-Joyce Hooper
Tel:-(0844) 291650
Open Feb-Nov
B&B £12-£13   Listed
(5)

This peaceful and substantial oak-beamed 17th Century, grade 2 listed farmhouse has a large garden with heated swimming pool. View to Chiltern Hills and some ducks and chickens. Foxhill is ideally located for Oxford, Windsor, Henley, Heathrow and only 1 hour from London. Nearby Thame has a choice of restaurants and pubs. Guests' lounge. 3 double/twin bedrooms with HC/shower. Central heating. OS Ref SU 748067

103

(CH) THE ELMS COUNTRY HOUSE Radnage, Nr. Stokenchurch, High Wycombe, Bucks, HP14 4DW

Pat & Bill Rowe
Tel:-(024 026) 2175
Open all year
B&B   £12.50-£15
EM   From £8.50
CH   Sleeps 6

The Elms, built in 17th Century, was formerly a farmhouse, now a comfortable home in the Chiltern Hills with magnificent panoramic views from the house, the grounds extend to 2 acres in an area of outstanding natural beauty. (2 Labradors and donkey). It is very well located being within easy reach of London, Oxford, Stratford, Windsor, Heathrow & Gatwick. the Cotswolds and many others. OS Ref SU 789 967

(FH) HAWTHORN FARM Calais Lane, Standlake, Witney, Oxon, OX8 7QU

Stella Pickering
Tel:-(086 731) 211
Open Apr-Oct
B&B   £9.50-£12
        Sleeps 4

Hawthorn Farm is situated on a quiet lane 1m from the nearest road. The house is old but has been recently modernised and offers ground floor accomodation suitable for the elderly. Spend a few days and try your hand at spinning, bottle feeding the lambs or milking the cow. Dogs and well behaved children welcome. AA listed. OS Ref SP 373048

(FH) NEW FARM Oxford Road, Oakley, Nr Aylesbury, Bucks, HP18 9UR

Binnie Pickford
Tel:-(0844) 237360
Closed Xmas-New Year
B&B   £10-£11   Listed
EM   From £6.50
        Sleeps 6
        (6)

A warm friendly atmosphere in fully modernised farmhouse with good food, comfortable accommodation. Working farm of 163 acres consisting of beef cattle, sheep, arable. Situated on Oxfordshire/Bucks border in peaceful surroundings on the edge of Bernwode Forest. 7m Oxford. Convenient for Waddesdon Manor, Blenheim Palace, Windsor and the M40 to London. Children over 6 welcome. OS Ref 138

(SC) HILL GROVE COTTAGE Hill Grove Farm, Minster Lovell, Oxford, OX8 5NA

Katherine Brown
Tel:-(0993) 3120/703120
Open all year
SC   £100-£180
        Sleeps 2/6

Hill Grove cottage is a large bungalow adjacent to our farmhouse. 2 double bedrooms, 1 twin, bathroom, WC, dining room, lounge with colour TV, fitted kitchen, fridge-freezer, washing machine, tumbledryer, CH, gardens. Situated above the Windrush Valley, excellent country walks yet within driving distance of Oxford, Woodstock, Burford, The Cotswolds. Cot & baby sitting by arrangement. Electricity free May-Sept. Linen free. Sorry no pets. OS Ref SP 335 115

Cotswold Wild Life Park
A World of Wild Animals

In 200 beautiful acres of gardens and woodland amidst the Cotswold Hills

PLUS: ● Picnic Areas ● Adventure Playground
● Narrow Gauge Railway ● Bar & Restaurant
● Brass Rubbing Centre

Open Daily from 10.00 am to 6.00 pm
Just off the A40 and A361 Junction

Burford, Oxfordshire. Tel: BURFORD 3006

Thames Valley ENGLAND

Cliveden - for a perfect day out

NEAR MAIDENHEAD, BUCKINGHAMSHIRE

Cliveden is a magnificent garden high above the Thames, with wonderful views. Explore miles of woodland walks, a Water Garden, Rose Garden and Parterre. Once the home of Nancy, Lady Astor. Shop and Orangery Restaurant.

OPEN: Grounds, March to end December, daily 11 a.m.-6 p.m. or sunset if earlier. **House,** April to end October, Thursday and Sunday, 3 p.m.-6 p.m.

LOCATION: Cliveden is 2 miles north of Taplow on the B476 from the A40. (M4 Junction 7 or M40 Junction 4). Telephone: **BURNHAM (06286) 5069.**

The National Trust

27 Cotswolds & Royal Forest of Dean, Gloucestershire

COTSWOLDS & ROYAL FOREST OF DEAN, GLOUCESTERSHIRE

The villages and scenic beauty of the Cotswolds are famed throughout the world. The many honey coloured villages include Bibury, Broadway, Painswick and Lower Slaughter while some of the finest churches in the country are at Northleach, Fairford and Winchcombe.
Along the River Severn the villages have black and white half-timbered cottages and cattle graze peacefully in the orchards and meadows. Gloucester with its cathedral, the elegant Regency town of Cheltenham and picturesque Tewkesbury with its 12th century Abbey are all in the Severn Vale. There are numerous visitor attractions in the main towns and villages while further afield are Berkeley Castle and Sir Peter Scott's Wildfowl Trust at Slimbridge.

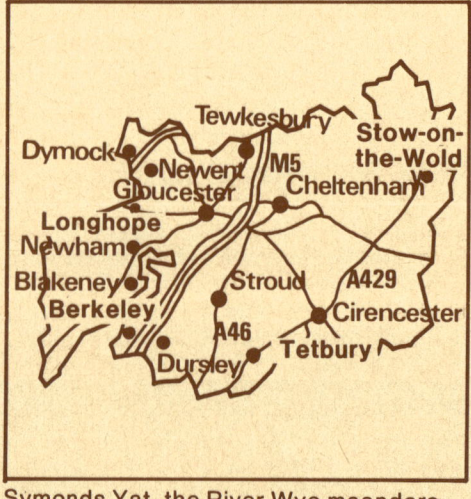

Bordered by two rivers, the Severn and the Wye, is the beautiful and romantic Forest of Dean, ancient hunting grounds of kings and still covered by oak woodlands. Scattered through the Forest are mining towns such as Cinderford, Coleford and Lydney. Below

Symonds Yat, the River Wye meanders dramatically in a most attractive wooded gorge.

GROUP CONTACT:
Barbara Evans (0453) 810348

Cotswolds & Forest of Dean ENGLAND

(FH) **TOWN STREET FARM** Tirley, Gloucester, GL19 4HS

Sue Warner
Tel:-(045278) 442
Open all year
B&B   £9.50-£13
Sleeps 4

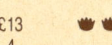

Town Street, a working farm close to the River Severn, within easy reach of Cheltenham & the M5. The red brick farmhouse is of a high standard with breakfast served in the sunlounge overlooking lawns & tennis court. Tirley village, within walking distance has several eating houses. Horses, ponies, chickens & dogs are to be found at Town Street. Horse riding & use of tennis court by arrangement. OS Ref SO 285 842

(FH) **MOAT FARM** Malleson Road, Gotherington, Cheltenham, Glos, GL52 4ET

Peter & Jo Tilley
Tel:-(024267) 2055
Open all year
B&B   £8.50-£9.50   Listed
Sleeps 6

(1)

Moat Farm is in the village of Gotherington in the heart of the Cotswolds. Between Cheltenham and Tewkesbury. Cheltenham racecourse, golf courses, village pubs. Prescott hillclimb for veteran cars and Sudeley Castle are nearby. Registered riding school. Swimming pool available for all guests in season. Blended cider made on the farm for sale. OS Ref SP 965296

(CH) **SEVERN BANK** Minsterworth, Gloucester, GL2 8JH

Ray & Shirley Carter
Tel:-(045275) 357
Closed Xmas
CH   Sleeps 20
B&B   £13-£16

(5)

A fine riverside country house in 6 acres of grounds, 4 miles west of Gloucester, with beautiful views over river and surrounding countryside. Full CH, residential licence, H/C, 6 bedrooms, 4 en-suite with TV and tea making facilities in all bedrooms. Central for Forest of Dean, Wye Valley and Cotswolds and at the recommended viewpoint for the Severn Bore. AA/RAC Highly Acclaimed. Free brochure on request. OS Ref SO 771171

(FH) **GILBERT'S** Gilbert's Lane, Brookthorpe, Gloucester, GL4 0UH

Jenny Beer
Tel:-(0452) 812364
Open all year
B&B   £12-£15
Sleeps 6

Beneath the Cotswold escarpment and only 10 minutes drive from Stroud or Gloucester, lies this organic smallholding. Gilbert's is a listed building 4 centuries old; guests also comment on the atmosphere, comfort and special wholefood breakfast. Accommodation for 6 guests in 4 bedrooms (including 2 rooms with their own bathrooms) combines modern amenities with antiques. Welcome to families, a group of friends, or individuals. OS Ref SO 837128

(FH) **BUTLERS HILL FARM** Cockleford, Cowley, Nr Cheltenham, Glos

Bridget Brickell
Tel:-(024287) 455
Open Mar-Oct
B&B   £9   Listed
EM   From £5
       Sleeps 6
SC   From £70
       Sleeps 4

(3)

Butlers Hill is a modern spacious farmhouse in a quiet unspoilt river valley. There are many attractive walks and is an ideal centre for exploring the Cotswolds. It is a working stock farm between Cheltenham and Cirencester. All rooms have H/C. Also available a self-contained flat with two twin bedrooms and living room. OS Ref SP 979136

(FH) **HARTPURY FARM** Chedworth, Nr Cheltenham, Gloucestershire, GL54 4AL

Peter & Peggy Booth
Tel:-(028572) 350
Open Apr-Oct
B&B   £9.50   Listed
EM   £5.50
       Sleeps 6
SC   Sleeps 6

17th Century farmhouse with splendid views, situated on 40 acre dairy farm with pedigree Jersey cows in the centre of the Cotswolds. Home grown food and special diets are prepared and guided tours on offer; Chedworth Roman Villa and Cotswold Water Park are local attractions. One double, 1 twin and 2 single bedrooms. TV lounge. Also self-catering 17th Century cottage, sleeps 6. OS Ref SP 056116

107

BIBURY TROUT FARM

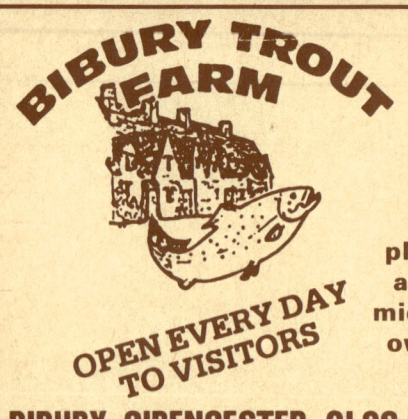

OPEN EVERY DAY TO VISITORS

This working farm is open all year and provides an ideal opportunity for people of all ages to learn about the Rainbow Trout and other wildlife which abounds in this glorious setting.

There is a farm shop where lovely gifts, plants, fresh and smoked trout, pâtés, etc. are on sale. A picnic area is situated in the middle of the farm. Now you can catch your own trout (between April and September). It's great fun for all — anyone can do it!

BIBURY, CIRENCESTER, GLOS GL7 5NL. Telephone: Bibury 215/212

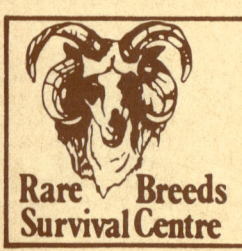

COTSWOLD FARM PARK

Guiting Power, Cheltenham — Telephone (045 15) 307

The most comprehensive collection of rare breeds of British farm animals in the country, displayed in a beautiful farm setting, high on top of the Cotswolds, with pets and baby animals to delight the children.

Open Easter to last week in September.
Please call for information on group rates. 10.30 a.m.-6.0 p.m.
Refreshments and Local Hand Crafts on sale
Free Car Park and Drive-in Picnic Area

Rare Breeds Survival Centre

COTSWOLD COUNTRYSIDE COLLECTION

Northleach

Award-winning museum for the Cotswolds. The Lloyd-Baker Collection of agricultural history includes wagons, horse-drawn implements and tools, acquired by the nation for display at Northleach. The museum's home was a House of Correction and its history is displayed in a reconstructed cell-block and courtroom. New displays include the history of man in the Cotswold countryside, plus a 'Below Stairs' gallery of domestic life

Open daily: 1st April-31st October

Tel: Cotswold 60715

Newent Butterfly & Natural World Centre

Free Flying Butterflies in Tropical Type Garden, Large Live Insect Collection

NATURAL HISTORY EXHIBITION
Displays of Snakes, Lizards, Amphibians and Hundreds of Exotic Water Creatures from All Over The World.

BIRCHES LANE, NEWENT GLOUCESTERSHIRE (0531) 821800

Easter to end October, 7 DAYS A WEEK
10 am to 5 pm (then enquire)

Cotswolds & Forest of Dean ENGLAND

(FH) LITTLE COLWAYS Hasfield, Nr Gloucester, GL19 4LE

Camilla Hope
Tel:-(045278) 250
Closed Xmas and New Year
B&B £9-£11   Listed
Sleeps 6

Colways Farm is a dairy farm of 186 acres with a herd of 150 Friesian cows, situated in the quiet village of Hasfield in the Severn Vale, within easy reach of Gloucester, Tewkesbury and Cheltenham. Views of the Cotswolds and an abundance of winter wildfowl on the bird sanctuary can be enjoyed from the comfortable farmhouse. Large garden with croquet available. OS Ref SO 827270

(FH) THE WHITE HOUSE FARM HOTEL Popes Hill, Nr Newnham, Gloucestershire, GL14 1LE

Ann & Brian Turner
Tel:-(0452-76) 463
Closed Xmas
B&B £15 ensuite
B&B £13 H/C
EM   £7.50
Sleeps 14
(8)

22 acre farm with superb panoramic views of River Severn, Royal Forest of Dean, Cotswold/Malvern Hills. Excellent walking, touring country, many interesting towns, villages, antique shops, markets, castles, museums. Most bedrooms ensuite, all with tea-making facilities. Tastefully furnished dining room. Relax in fully licensed lounge bar overlooking river, Gloucestershire countryside. Separate TV lounge. Choice menu, fire certificate, CH. Bar snacks available. OS Ref SO 685148

(FH) DOWN BARN FARMHOUSE The Camp, Stroud, Gloucestershire, GL6 7EY

Anita Morley
Tel:-(0452) 812853
Open Jan-Nov
B&B £9-£9.50   Listed
Sleeps 6

The farmhouse is on a smallholding with pygmy goats, calves and other small animals. Situated ¼ mile off the Cotswolds scenic leisure drive (B4070). All accommodation is on the ground floor and suitable for the immobile. Three bedrooms all with washbasins, visitors TV lounge with tea-making facilities, guest bathroom. Lovely views and peaceful setting. OS Ref SO 896094

(FH) LOWER HOUSE FARM Kempley, Dymock, Glos, GL18 2BS

Gill Bennett
Tel:-(053185) 301
Open Easter-Dec
B&B £9   Listed
Sleeps 6

Children's holiday 6-12 years on family run dairy farm. Small number taken as guests of family. Pony riding daily, fishing, swimming, trips to castles, Falconry Centre, Butterfly Farm. Good home cooked food, vegetables from garden. Feed calves, hens, collect eggs. Picnics & barbecues, fun & activities to suit individual children, making their first independent holiday enjoyable. From £120 per child per week all inclusive. OS Ref SO 662672

(FH) HARTS BARN FARM Monmouth Road, Longhope, Glos, GL17 0QD

Helen Few
Tel:-(0452) 830296
Open all year
B&B £10   Listed
Sleeps 6

Built in 11th Century by Johannes, Sargeant-at-arms to William the Conquerer, who kept 3 couples of hounds for the King to hunt the Hart in the Forest of Dean. The William and Mary facade and the Jacobean staircase were added in 1700. Harts Barn has been a dairy/fruit farm since 1600. Beautiful countryside and a warm welcome here! CH, drink facilities & TV lounge. OS Ref SO 676 184

(FH) GREEN ACRES FARM Breadstone, Berkeley, Glos, GL3 9HF

Barbara Evans
Tel:-(0453) 810348
Closed Dec, Xmas-New Year
B&B £10.50-£12.50
EM   £5.75
Sleeps 6

Beautiful Berkeley Vale. Twixt Cotswolds and River Severn. Privately run farm guesthouse, providing comfort and convenience in superb country setting; yet convenient for holidays of infinite variety. Golfing and horseriding close by. A warm welcome assured. Vegetables from the garden and all good home cooking. Bathrooms en suite. Tea/coffee making facilities in bedrooms. Inglenook fireplaces. OS Ref SO 308200

109

SPLASH OUT!
SANDFORD POOLS CHELTENHAM

- Two heated Outdoor pools
- Large lawns and sun decks
- Picnic and Childrens play area
- Cafeteria

Open every day from 11.00am – including Bank Holidays and FREE parking for pool patrons.

For further details phone (0242) 524430

Sandford Pools, Keynsham Rd., Cheltenham

Department of Recreation Centres
Making Recreation an Event in Cheltenham

SHEEPSKIN SWOP-SHOP
WE PART EXCHANGE

Sheepskin coats, so bring your old one for valuation and choose a super new Sheepskin or Leather coat whilst you are staying in the area.

THE Leather & Sheepskin SHOPS

9 Swan Street, Warwick Tel: (0926) 491571
33 Sheep Street, Stratford-Upon-Avon Tel: (0789) 293810
High Street, Chipping Campden Tel: (0386) 840437
High Street, Broadway Tel: (0386) 853493

Cotswolds & Forest of Dean ENGLAND

(FH) **PIXWOLD FARM** Cockleford, Cowley, Cheltenham, Glos, GL53 9NW

Pat Williams
Tel:-(024 287) 426
Closed Xmas-New Year
B&B   £10-£12
Sleeps 6

Part 17th Century cottage on 15 acre small holding in peaceful Churn Valley. Satisfying country breakfast, comfortable beds with duvets & electric blankets. Guests lounge with woodburner. You are welcome to relax in the lounge & garden during the day, or watch/help us with our animals, sheep, free range hens & driving pony. No smoking. OS Ref SO 142 969

(FH) **DAMSELS FARM** Painswick, Stroud, Glos, GL6 6UD

Mrs Burdett
Tel:-(0452) 812148
Closed Dec, Xmas & New Year
B&B   £10.50-£13.50
Sleeps 6

Damsel Farm may have been part of Painswick Manor, where Henry VIII hunted with Ann Boleyn. Set in a quiet part of the Cotswolds but within easy reach of Gloucester, Cheltenham, Cirencester and day trips to Bath, Slimbridge and the Malverns. Children are welcome to help feed ducks, geese, chickens, orphan lambs calves. OS Ref ST 113 876

(FH) **ABBOTS COURT** Church End, Twyning, Tewkesbury, Glos, GL20 6DA

Bernie Williams
Tel:-(0684) 292515
Closed Xmas
B&B   £10-£11
EM   £5.50
Sleeps 15

Lovely quiet farmhouse in 350 acres, between Cotswolds and Malverns. All bedrooms H/C, some en suite, colour TV, tea making facilities, large lounge, separate dining room. Excellent home cooked food. 3 games rooms with pool table, table tennis & childrens TV room. Grass tennis court, bowling green. Childrens play area on lawn. Superb centre for touring Cotswolds. OS Ref SO 894360

(FH) **HUNTING BUTTS FARM** Swindon Lane, Cheltenham, Glos, GL54 4NZ

Mrs Jane Hanks
Tel:-(0242) 524982
Closed Xmas and New Year
B&B   £9-£10
EM   By arrangement
Sleeps 6

Hunting Butts is a 200 acre beef and arable farm overlooking the racecourse within 1½m of Cheltenham town centre. Guests have a private wing of the farmhouse with breathtaking views of the surrounding countryside. Accommodation comprises 1 family room, 1 twin room and a double with ensuite. Swimming, tennis, squash and childrens playground are all within easy walking distance. OS Ref SO 952 248

(FH) **KILMORIE** Gloucester Road, Corse, Staunton, Nr Gloucester, GL19 3RQ

Sheila Barnfield
Tel:-(045284) 224
Open Mar-Nov
B&B   £6.50   Applied
EM   £3
Sleeps 10
TV   £2

Built in 1848 by the Chartists, Kilmorie is Grade 2 listed in a conservation area and is a smallholding keeping farm livestock, child's pony and fruit. Good home cooking, using own produce when available, 5 double bedrooms, large garden, situated in a lovely part of Gloucestershire countryside. There are many places of natural and historic beauty to visit. Children over 6 welcome. OS Ref SO 792286

(FH) **HOME FARM** Bredons Norton, Nr Tewkesbury, Glos, GL20 7HA

Anne & Mick Meadows
Tel:-(0684) 72322
Open Jan-Nov
B&B   £10   Listed
EM   £7
Sleeps 6

Mixed 150 acre family run farm on Bredon Hill with sheep, cattle, poultry and corn. The 18th Century farmhouse is comfortably furnished and has woodburning stoves and gas CH. Superb position for walking and an excellent base for touring or simply relaxing. Good home cooking. Evening meals by arrangement. Lounge, TV. Reductions for children. Also riding holidays for children, details on request. OS Ref SO 935389

(FH) CUTWELL FARM Tetbury, Glos, GL8 8EB

Jill Price
Tel:-(0666) 52026
Closed Xmas and New Year
B&B   £10-£12   Listed
Sleeps 5

A recently restored stone farmhouse, interior features created with local stone and timber (Elm). Within walking distance of Tetbury town centre. OS Ref OS 9091

(SC) SUNSHINE Staunton Court, Gloucester, GL19 3QE

Jerry Hawkins
Tel:-(0452) 84230
Open all year
SC   £110-£130
Sleeps 6

Attractive spacious 3 bedroomed bungalow situated in beautiful surroundings with fishing and country walks and pony hire available locally. The accommodation comprises 3 bedrooms, large lounge, dining room, kitchen, bathroom, separate toilet with garage and garden. There is mains water and electricity, central heating and immersion heater. Suitable for approximately 6 people. OS Ref SO 782292

(SC) WESTLEY FARM Chalford, Stroud, Glos, GL6 8HP

Julian Usborne
Tel:-(028576) 262
Open all year
SC   £60-£180
Sleeps 2/6

A traditional Cotswold stone farmhouse, with three converted cottages nearby. Set on the steep side of the Golden Valley with breathtaking views. Peace and seclusion guaranteed. Superb countryside for hill and woodland walks. Midway between Cirencester and Stroud. An excellent centre for touring the Cotswolds Cattle, sheep, chickens, geese. Orchard playground. Nearby golf, riding, gliding, watersports etc. Brochure.

(SC) THE COTTAGE AND THE WING Middle Farm, Stanley Pontlarge, Nr Cheltenham, Gloucestershire, GL54 5HE

Diana Prance
Tel:-(0242) 673119
Open Easter-Oct
SC   £95-£150
Sleeps 5

Middle Farm is a mixed 300 acre livestock farm near Winchcombe, Broadway, Tewkesbury, Bourton-on-the-Water, 45 minutes from Stratford-upon-Avon. A self-contained modernised wing of the farmhouse sleeps 2/5 and a uniquely built Cotswold stone cottage has 2 double bedrooms. Beautiful walks, riding nearby, near Prescott hillclimb and Sudeley Castle. Tennis Court for the energetic. Weekly Residential Hand and Machine Needlecraft Courses. OS Ref SO 390220

(SC) THE GRANARY Lower House Farm, Kempley, Dymock, Glos, GL18 2BS

Gill Bennett
Tel:-(053185) 301
Open Easter-Dec
SC   From £100
Sleeps 6

THE GRANARY, wing of farmhouse, sleeps 6, self contained, 2 bedrooms, lounge diner, kitchen, WC & shower room. Lovely walking and riding country. Farm adjoins 1300 acre wood with nature trails, bridle paths and course fishing lake. Golf course (18 hole) 2½m, market towns of Ledbury and Ross on Wye. Riding on farm can be arranged or horses accommodated. Local hunts, Ledbury farmers and Ross Harriers. OS Ref SO 295 668

(SC) FOLLY FARM COTTAGES Tetbury, Glos, GL8 8XA

Lindsay Harmer
Tel:-(0666) 52475
Open all year
SC   £100-£300
Sleeps 4/8

Seven purpose-built cottages border our picturesque Cotswold farmyard. Delightful in character with original timbers for homely living at your own pace, but not at hotel prices. Open all year. Full central heating, linen, logs, milk from our 160 cow herd at all-inclusive price close to the M4 and M5 motorways. Heathrow 1½ hours. OS Ref ST 896 929

Cotswolds & Forest of Dean ENGLAND

(SC) **WARRENS GORSE COTTAGES   Home Farm, Warrens Gorse, Cirencester, Glos, GL7 7JD**

Mrs Nanette Randall
Tel:-(028583) 261
Open Easter & Jul-Sept
          Xmas & New
          Year
SC   £60-£120
       Sleeps 3/6

Warrens Gorse is a hamlet 2½m from the Roman town of Cirencester (Corinium) between Daglingworth and Perrotts Brook, an ideal centre for touring the Cotswolds. The cottages are comfortable, well equipped and personally attended by the owners. They are quietly situated near the farmhouse, surrounded by fields belonging to the 100 acre family farm of beef cattle and sheep. OS Ref SP 006060

(SC) **CORNERWAYS   Home Farm, Bredons Norton, Nr Tewkesbury, Glos, GL20 7HA**

Anne & Mick Meadows
Tel:-(0684) 72322
Open all year
SC   £80-£160
       Sleeps 6

Cornerways is situated in a lovely small and peaceful village under Bredon Hill with superb views of the Avon and Severn valleys. Tythe barn opposite. Excellent base for touring, walking or relaxing. Comfortably furnished with fitted carpets throughout. Well equipped kitchen. Lounge with woodburner, TV, Dining room. Three double bedrooms, bathroom, storage heaters. Washing machine. Cot. Large garden. OS Ref SO 935389

(SC) **OATFIELD FARM COTTAGES   Gatcombe, Blakeney, Glos, GL15 4AY**

Liz & Gerald Hoinville
Tel:-(0594) 510372
Closed Jan-Feb
SC   £120-£280
       Sleeps 2-4

Luxury units converted from 17th Century listed buildings in 7 acres located on the edge of Forest of Dean. In a truly rural setting directly linked through woodland to new Severn River Walk. Ideal for exploring Wales & Cotswolds. All weather tennis court. Dining room with adjoining lounge. Gourmet meals on request. OS Ref SO 679058

FARM HOLIDAY BUREAU

(SC) **PLODDY LODGE   Ploddy House, Newent, Gloucestershire, GL18 1JX**

Mark & Hilary Davison
Tel:-(0531) 820240
Open Easter-Sep
SC   £60-£120
       Sleeps 5

Victorian lodge with 3 bedrooms, bathroom, living room, dining room, kitchen and garage. Situated on a 200 acre arable farm with a lake, facing a country lane, having pleasant views of the distant Cotswold hills and Severn valley. Many local attractions including falconry centre, Butterfly centre, Glassworks, May Hill and visiting Wye Valley, Forest of Dean, Cheltenham, Cotswolds. OS Ref SO 723230

SPECIAL OFFER

REDUCED ADMISSION TO NATIONAL TRUST PROPERTIES

When you book a farm holiday, in Gloucestershire, Warwickshire, Herefordshire and Worcestershire, you will automatically receive a free voucher for National Trust properties (open April – October).

This voucher entitles you to a third off the admission price at selected properties. Write for details of these and other properties to:–

The National Trust Severn Regional Office,
34 – 36 Church Street, Tewkesbury, Glos., GL20 6EB.

The National Trust

28 HEREFORDSHIRE

HEREFORDSHIRE

Herefordshire is a land of red earth, green meadows, quiet woods, streams and pretty black and white villages. In the South are the spectacular gorges of the River Wye and the silent woodland trails of the Forest of Dean; westward lies the quiet Golden Valley leading into Offa's Dyke. To the east, Elgar country rises to the Malvern Hills.

Herefordshire is rich in history and within reasonable travelling distance of the Black Mountains, Brecon Beacons and Elan Valley in Wales and the Clee Hills, Carding Mill Valley, Longmynd and Wenlock Edge in South Shropshire. The country itself has a range of sights that span every period in British history from Iron Age Hill forts, Roman remains, Norman castles and mediaeval manor houses to stately homes and their gardens and heritage museums.

At Kilpeck there are renowned twelfth century Herefordshire carvings or pagan Celtic figures. You may also like to wander through the street markets of the county which are **Tenbury Wells (Tuesday), Hay-on-Wye (Thursday), Leominster (Friday), Ross-on-Wye (Thursday and Saturday), Monmouth (Friday and Saturday), Ledbury (Friday)** and Hereford Cattle Market (Wednesday).

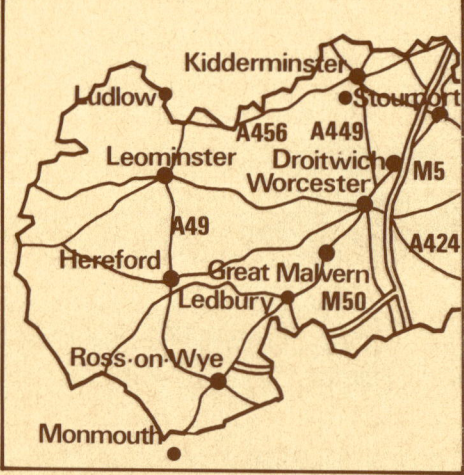

The Hereford group members offer special National Trust Mini Breaks, with reduced admission to Berrington Hall and Croft Castle.

VACANCY SECRETARY:
Liz Moore (0568 82) 239.

Herefordshire ENGLAND

(FH) DINEDOR COURT Dinedor, Nr Hereford, HR2 6LG

Rosemary Price
Tel:-(0432 73) 481
Open Mar-Nov
B&B £9.50-£10   Listed
EM   £5.50
Sleeps 6

Be sure of a warm welcome, peace and quiet with good farmhouse cooking at this 16th Century listed farmhouse. Large garden and beautiful views along the River Wye whilst only 3m from the Cathedral City of Hereford. Central for touring Wye Valley, Malvern Hills & Black Mountains. One double/family room, 2 twin-bedded. Table tennis & croquet. 'Herefordshire Hamper' OS Ref SO 545368

(FH) STRETFORDBURY Leominster, Herefs, HR6 0LP

Liz Moore
Tel:-(0568 82) 239
Open Feb-Nov
B&B £8.50-£9.50   Listed
EM   £6.50
Sleeps 6

A secluded, rambling farmhouse on a 200 acre dairy farm. Situated in a delightful valley alongside a tributary of the River Lugg. The extremely comfortable accomodation comprises twin, single, double & family rooms, visitors lounge/dining room complete with log fire. A varied selection of meals are available to suit individual requirements. Firm beds. OS Ref SO 353258

(FH) GRANGE FARM Newcastle, Monmouth, Gwent, NP5 4NX

Solveig Preece
Tel:-(0600) 2636
Open Mar-Nov
B&B £8-£8.50   Listed
EM   £4.50
Sleeps 4

Wye Valley district. Stock rearing farm. The farmhouse is 16th Century. Situated in quiet countryside within easy reach of Forest of Dean, the ancient border town of Monmouth and South Wales. Golf club and leisure centre nearby. Local produce used wherever possible. Good home cooking. OS Ref SO 453166

(FH) THE HILLS FARM Leysters, Leominster, Herefordshire, HR6 9HP

Jane Conolly
Tel:-(056887) 205
Closed Xmas
B&B £9   Listed
EM   £7
Sleeps 6

Amidst the beautiful North Herefordshire countryside "The Hills" offers friendly and exceptionally comfortable accomodation along with superb food, low ceilings and oak beams abound, guests enjoy the privacy of their own bathroom, lounge and dining room. Tea/coffee making facilities, colour TV and wood burner. Freshly prepared meals, we are happy to meet special requests, eg vegetarian or diabetic fare. OS Ref SO 563 638

(FH) WEBTON COURT Kingstone, Hereford, HR2 9NF

Gill & Robert Andrews
Tel:-(0981) 250220
Open all year
B&B £8-£10
EM   £5.50
10% redn for
OAPs & children
Sleeps 16

Webton Court is a Georgian black and white farmhouse with 280 acres mixed farm set in quiet and peaceful countryside in the heart of the Wye Valley. Local home farm produce is served to guests. Accommodation is spacious. 1 single, 2 family, 3 double rooms. AA listed, licensed, hacking, riding available. Washbasins, shavers, tea making facilities in all rooms. Reduced price for OAP's and children. 'Herefordshire Hamper' OS Ref SR 421366

(FH) WILTON OAKS Tarrington, Hereford, HR1 4ET

Jean Phillips
Tel:-(043279) 212
Open Feb-Nov
B&B £10
EM   £4.50
Sleeps 6

Wilton Oaks is set in beautiful gardens surrounded by 30 acres of ground which is grazed by sheep and cattle. It lies in an area of landscape beauty with views towards the Malvern Hills. The house is comfortably furnished with full central heating. Vanity units in all bedrooms. Separate dining room and lounge. Colour TV. OS Ref SO 621405

(FH) HAYNALL VILLA Little Hereford, Nr Ludlow, Shrops, SY8 4BD

Rachel Edwards
Tel:-(058472) 589
Closed Xmas
B&B   From £9
EM   From £5.50
Sleeps 6

Listed

Haynall Villa is situated near historic Ludlow in the Teme Valley. A warm welcome is made to guests who may enjoy private fishing, farm activities, relax in the spacious Victorian house with excellent facilities, or large well tended garden. Enjoy superb freshly prepared meals. Ideally situated for touring on foot, cycle or car. Children welcome. Reductions. 'Herefordshire Hamper' OS Ref 546 673

(FH) GRAFTON VILLA FARM Grafton, Hereford, HR2 8ED

Jennie Layton
Tel:-0432 268689
Open all Year
B&B   £8.50-£9.50
EM   £5
Sleeps 6

A farmhouse of great character & warmth, set in a large, peaceful garden, some 200 yards off A49 road. Panoramic views of our beautiful Herefordshire countryside, and yet only 2½ miles from city centre. All rooms have washbasins & TV. Enjoy farmhouse cooking using local, fresh produce with farmhouse proportions! Children very welcome. 'Herefordshire Hamper' OS Ref SO 500 361

(FH) GREAT HOUSE FARM Stoke Prior, Leominster, Herefs, HR6 0LG

Shirley Bemand
Tel:-(056882) 663
Closed Xmas
B&B   £8.50
EM   £5
Sleeps 6

Listed

Relax and enjoy our large homely 17th Century farmhouse in beautiful north Herefordshire set on 750 acres of family run farm. Friendly service, good farmhouse cooking and informal atmosphere. Fishing, horse riding, golf, swimming nearby and long walks in quiet pleasant countryside. Beamed lounge, dining room, TV, games room and tennis court. Babysitting arrangements. Two double, 1 twin. 'Herefordshire Hamper' OS Ref SO 524565

(FH) RATEFIELD FARM Kimbolton, Leominster, Herefs, HR6 0JB

Evelyn Mears
Tel:-(0568) 2507
Closed Mar & Xmas
B&B   £9.50
EM   £5.50
Sleeps 6

Listed

Traditional livestock farm in the north of the county near Berrington Hall, set amidst parkland landscaped by Capability Brown. Nature trail, National Trust breaks. Lots of animals. Guests welcome to watch and participate in farm chores. Home produce, home baking and local food a speciality. Family room and double room with washbasins. Twin and single rooms all with electric kettles. 'Herefordshire Hamper' OS Ref SO 515622

(FH) CHADWYNS FARM Forest Green, Walford, Ross on Wye, Hereford, HR9

Jane Sweet-Escott
Tel:-(0989) 63498
Open all year
B&B   From £8
Sleeps 6

Applied

A warm welcome awaits you, children and pets at this small working stock farm. Situated between Monmouth, Forest of Dean, Symonds Yat Gorge and having panoramic views over the Wye Valley and Welsh mountains. Ground floor room suitable for disabled. Breakfast served at times to suit residents. Local pub serves excellent evening meals. OS Ref 595198

(FH) ORCHARD FARM Mordiford, Nr Hereford, HR1 4EJ

Mrs Marjorie Barrell
Tel:-(0432) 73253
Closed Xmas
B&B   £9-£10
EM   from £5
Sleeps 6

Working farm with attractive 18th Century house peacefully situated with lovely views. Explore the picturesque local villages. Three double rooms with washbasins and tea making facilities, two sitting rooms, dining room, colour TV. Excellent food using local produce. Residential licence. AA listed. Fishing. Off-season bargain breaks. Wine & cider tasting week-ends arranged. OS Ref SO 576384

Herefordshire ENGLAND

(FH) THE ELMS   Eardisland, Leominster, Herefords, HR6 9BN

Mary Johnson
Tel:-(05447) 405
Open all year
B&B   From £10
EM   From £5
       Sleeps 6
TV   £2-£6
(10)

A friendly welcome awaits you in spacious, comfortable farmhouse. Separate lounge and dining rooms. All bedrooms H/C. 1 double, 1 twin, 2 singles. Bedtime drink, early morning tea. Traditional farmhouse fare, on edge of picturesque village within easy reach of many outdoor activities. Special terms for christmas, off season breaks Nov-March. A NO SMOKING HOUSE. AA Listed. 'Herefordshire Hamper' OS Ref SO 417585

(FH) PAUNCEFORD COURT   Much Cowarne, Nr Bromyard, Herefords, HR7 4JQ

Bob & Jenny Keenan
Tel:-(0432) 820208
Closed Xmas-New Year
B&B   £8-£10   Listed
EM   £4.50
       Sleeps 4

Pauneceford Court, a large country farmhouse dating back to the 11th Century makes an ideal touring centre for Ledbury, Bromyard, Hereford, Worcester, and Malvern Hills, while Gloucester, Ludlow, Hay etc are all within an easy hours drive. Children welcome, reduced rates, cot high chair, babysitting. No pets. 1 twin, 1 double with washbasin. Tea making facilities. CH, dining room, TV lounge, friendly atmosphere. OS Ref SO 624751

(FH) MOOR COURT   Stretton Grandison, Nr Ledbury, Hereford, HR8 2TR

Mrs Elizabeth Godsall
Tel:-(053183) 408
Open all year
B&B   £10   Listed
EM   £6
       Sleeps 6

A warm friendly welcome awaits you at this attractive 14th Century farmhouse, beautiful surroundings within easy access of main towns. We cater for all the family, spacious bedrooms, guests own bathroom, oak beamed lounge with open fire. Attractive garden ideal for barbeques. Guests may walk the 200 acre farm and surrounding woodland. Coarse fishing available. Home cooking a speciality, evening meal on request.

(SC) BROOKLYN, Leinthall Starkes   Marlbrook Hall, Elton, Ludlow, Shropshire, SY8 2HR

Valerie Morgan
Tel:-(056886) 230
Open Feb-Xmas
SC   £70-£120
       Sleeps 6

Three bedroomed detached house situated on the edge of a quiet rural village. Furnished to a good standard, including linen, fitted carpets, colour TV, washing facilities. Large secluded garden and garage with pleasant views of unspoilt countryside. Ideal for exploring the local market town of Ludlow with its historic buildings. Also local castles and Mortimer Forest. Local facilities personally supervised. 'Herefordshire Hamper' OS Ref SO 437710

(SC) LONGFIELD COTTAGE   Webton Court, Kingstone, Hereford, HR2 9NF

Gill & Robert Andrews
Tel:-(0981) 250220
Open Easter-Oct
SC   £60-£130
       Sleeps 7

This brick built semi-detached cottage midway between Hay-on-Wye and Ross-on-Wye has been modernised to provide a pleasant holiday home. The adequately furnished cottage has 3 bedrooms, 1 family and 2 doubles, bathroom, kitchen/diner and lounge. Washing machine, colour TV and payphone are included. In good touring area Forest of Dean and Wye Valley. OS Ref SR 421366

(SC) HIGH HOUSE FARMHOUSE   White House Farm, Preston Cross, Nr Ledbury, Herefs, HR8 2LH

Mrs G M Thomas
Tel:-(053184) 231
Open all year
SC   £120-£145
       Sleeps 6
       + cot

The High House is divided into 2 self-contained houses with own well kept gardens and furnished to a high standard. The original wing is 13th Century and beamed throughout, the other wing was added in Victorian times. Situated on A449, 3 miles from Ledbury. Ideal for touring Wye Valley, Malverns, Cotswolds and Forest of Dean. 'Herefordshire Hamper' OS Ref SO 671351

(SC) BANKY MEADOW BUNGALOW & MILL HOUSE FLAT, Woonton Court Farm, Leysters, Leominster, Herefs HR6 OHL

Elizabeth Thomas
Tel:-(056887) 232
Open all year
SC £55-£130
   Sleeps 4-6
TV Max 5

Beautifully situated bungalow on a mixed dairy farm in lovely North East Herefordshire, near Worcester/Shropshire border. Ideal for peaceful walks. Dairy produce from our farm. Bungalow sleeps 6 in twin bedded rooms. Open log fire. Enclosed garden suitable for the elderly. Dogs and children welcome. Mill House Flat sleeps 4, recently modernised, parking patio. 'Herefordshire Hamper' OS Ref SO 547624

(SC) THE VAULD HOUSE FARM   Marden, Hereford, HR1 3HA

Judith Wells
Tel:-(056884) 347
Open all year
SC £70-£100
   Sleeps 5

This peacefully situated converted Victorian oast-house is overlooking open farm land and apple orchards on working family stock farm. The large lawned and wooded gardens with moat and ponds extend to over an acre ideally positioned midway between Hereford and Leominster. The accommodation sleeps 5 + cot and high chair, 1 double, 1 twin, 1 single rooms. Brochure available on request. OS Ref 495 535

(SC) WARRYFIELD FARM COTTAGE   The Callow, Walford, Ross-on-Wye, Hereford, HR9 5QN

Diana Moore
Tel:-(0989) 64599
Open all year
SC £85-£135
   Sleeps 5

A quiet cottage in the Wye Valley, near Symonds Yat, Forest of Dean & the border castles. Many leisure activities available locally. 2 twin-bedded rooms, 1 single (cot available, some babysitting by prior arrangement). Kitchen, sitting room with colour TV, shower room. Own garden & parking. Equipped & decorated to a high standard. OS Ref SO 210 583

(SC) OLDCOURT FARM HOLIDAYS   Lower Maes-Coed, Longtown, Hereford, HR2 0HS

Tel:-(087387) 235
Closed Feb
SC £90-£230
B&B From £9   Listed
EM From £5.50

16th Century listed upper hall house sympathetically converted into 2 luxury cottages. Original features, central heating, modern conveniences. Superb views of Black Mountains. Working 90 acre livestock farm, rare Dexter cattle and sheep, own fishing. Ideal centre for country pursuits, historic towns and access to mid-Wales. Farmhouse accommodation and catering service available. 'Herefordshire Hamper' OS Ref SO 338304

(SC) WYE VIEW   Wyeside, Clifford, Hereford, HR3 5EJ

Barbara Mason
Tel:-(04973) 306
Open Easter-Oct
SC £80-£180
   Sleeps 8

Modern family house, perfectly situated for an unspoilt view overlooking a bend of the River Wye and surrounding valley. Standing in its own garden with garage and plenty of parking space, it is furnished and equipped to a high standard. Bed linen is included. It is an ideal for exploring the Wye Valley and Welsh Border country. 2 miles from Hay on Wye. 'Herefordshire Hamper' OS Ref SO 245458

(SC) WEST WING   Bircher Hall, Leominster, Herefordshire, HR6 0AX

The Lady Rosemary Cawley
Tel:-(056 885) 218
Open all year
SC £50-£150
   Sleeps 5

Wing of old Manor House. Thoroughly modernised, washing, dishwashing machines and tumble drier. All heating thermostatically controlled. Time clocks. Both oil and electric. Kitchen diner, sitting room, hall, 2 bathrooms, 2 double bedrooms, 1 single. Good riding, fishing, rambling. Common woods and National Trust properties. Duvets, sheets, cot, dogs and telephone extra. Garden, drive, courtyard. OS Ref SO 476657

118

Herefordshire ENGLAND

(SC) STABLE HOUSE Bircher Hall, Leominster, Herefordshire, HR6 0AX

The Lady Rosemary Cawley
Tel:-(056 885) 218
Open all year
SC   £50-£140
         Sleeps 3

Spacious 3 person house, 19th century. Modernised throughout. Kitchen - washing machine, fridge freezer, electric hob and oven. One twin, 1 single bedroom. Garden. Central heating. Wood burning stove and electric heating metered. Cot, linen and dogs extra. Riding, fishing, rambling. Lovely commons, forests. National Trust properties. Telephone on request. OS Ref SO 476657

Collection GALLERY

THE FINEST QUALITY POTTERY, WOODWARE, JEWELLERY AND GLASS BY BRITAIN'S LEADING CRAFTSMEN.

13 THE SOUTHEND, LEDBURY, HEREFORDSHIRE HR8 2EY
Tel: (0531) 4641   Telex: 35364 SHLED G

See England as it used to be

A quieter, slower more peaceful place
**THE BEAUTIFUL WYE VALLEY
GOLDEN VALLEY
THE ROYAL FOREST OF DEAN**
Designated an Area of Outstanding Natural Beauty, where every turn in the road brings a new vista of glorious countryside.
Leaflets and Accommodation List from:
(enclose 54p Cheque/PO/Stamps for P&P)
**The Wyedean Tourist Board, 20 Broad Street
Ross-on-Wye, Herefordshire. Tel: (0989) 62768**

29 WORCESTERSHIRE

WORCESTERSHIRE

To the north is Droitwich where salt has been mined since Roman times and a Pilgrim Father was born. Still further north are Kidderminster, the carpet town, and Bewdley, home of the Severn Valley steam railway, Bromsgrove which gave Guy Fawkes one of his Gunpowder Plotters and Redditch — now a new town which is traditionally the main centre of needle and fishing hook manufacturing.

In the south east is the beautiful market gardening town of Evesham, and in the south west rise the majestic Malvern Hills which gave the world such diverse benefits as Sir Edward Elgar, Malvern water and the throaty Morgan sports car.

Sprinkled throughout the county are other small towns such as Pershore, Upton-on-Severn, Tenbury Wells and Broadway where time has virtually stood still since the turn of the century.

They are all set in countryside where there are dozens of riding stables for the horse lover, small local brewers for real ale and cider enthusiasts, river boat trips, museums for the historian and 500 miles of public footpaths along which the walker can ramble for days.

National Trust Mini Breaks:

Most of the farmhouses operate a Mini Break scheme in conjunction with the National Trust. The farms offer free admission to certain specified National Trust properties to guests who book a National Trust Mini Break for a minimum of three nights. A discount scheme also operates for guests who stay for a shorter period. Full details from the farm of your choice on booking.

VACANCY SECRETARY:
Hilary Morgan (090 560) 252/839

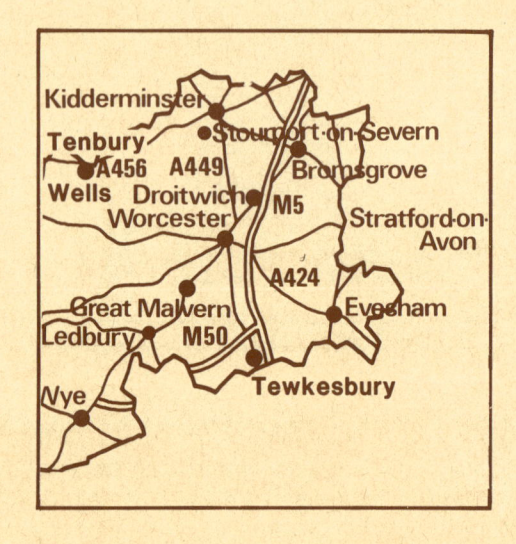

Worcestershire ENGLAND

FH LOWER DODDENHILL FARM Newnham Bridge, Tenbury Wells, Worcs, WR15 8NU

Joan Adams
Tel:-(058 479) 223
Open Mar-Nov
B&B £9.50-£11.50
EM   From £5.50
Sleeps 6
(6)

This 17th Century listed farmhouse set in 220 acres of mixed farmland, provides ideal opportunities for exploring the Heart of England, with extensive views across the Teme Valley, the heavily beamed farmhouse has central heating and ensuite or private bathroom facilities. Homely hospitality, imaginative cooking are assured. AA listed. OS Ref SO 669696

FH LITTLE LODGE FARM Broughton Green, Hanbury, Droitwich, Worcs, WR9 7EE

Jacqueline Chugg
Tel:-(052 784) 305
Open Easter-Oct
B&B £12-£16
Sleeps 6

This delightful 17th Century timbered farmhouse is beautifully furnished throughout & contains many special features. The bedrooms are spacious & comfortable & the co-ordinated fabrics & wallcoverings used convey the character of an English Country House. 3 guest bedrooms, 1 double with bath/ensuite & 2 Twin/Double rooms. The large garden has glorious views of the surrounding countryside making this an unusually quiet & scenic spot to stay. OS Ref SO 959 618

FH PHEPSON FARM Himbleton, Droitwich, Worcs, WR9 7J2

Tricia Havard
Tel:-(090569) 205
Closed Xmas-New Year
B&B £9-£10
EM   £6
Sleeps 6

Comfortable & relaxed atmosphere in our traditional 17th Century farmhouse with oak beamed lounge and dining room. Situated on peaceful family farm, where visitors may walk & see farm animals. Home cooking. Double, twin, family rooms, with washbasins, tea/coffee making facilities, electric blankets. AA listed. Featured on ITV's "Wish You Were Here". Convenient for M5 and touring Heart of England. OS Ref SO 941598

FH HUNTHOUSE FARM Frith Common, Tenbury Wells, Worcs, WR15 8JY

Jane Keel
Tel:-(029922) 277
Closed Xmas and New Year
B&B £9-£12
Sleeps 6
(6)

Relax and enjoy the comfort, peace and hospitality of our beautiful period farmhouse. Elevated amidst an 180 acre arable and stock farm, the house commands breathtaking views and provides an excellent base for walking, touring and exploring. 3 attractive bedrooms with en-suite or private bathroom facilities. Tea and home-made cakes. Full central heating and log fires. AA Listed. OS Ref SO 698701

FH VALLEY FARM Hanbury, Nr Bromsgrove, Worcs, B60 4HJ

Joyce & Harry Ulyet
Tel:-(052 784) 678
Closed Xmas-New Year
B&B £9-£12
EM   £3-£6
Sleeps 6

Originally a Malthouse and with a wealth of original beams and a magnificent inglenook in the lounge. Our farmhouse is set in lovely Worcestershire countryside only minutes from the M5 and M42. Our comfortable bedrooms all have colour TV and teamaker. Enjoy a warm welcome and traditional English cooking.

FH THE MOAT HOUSE STUD Longdon, Tewkesbury, Glos, GL20 6AT

Sue Virr
Tel:-(068481) 313
Closed Xmas-New Year
B&B £11.50-£13.50
EM   £7.50
Sleeps 6

Sue Virr invites you to stay at her Elizabethan Moat House set in its own secluded grounds. Evening meal available. Cordon Bleu & Farmhouse cookery. All bedrooms have tea/coffee facilities & H/C washbasins. Children welcome. Pony riding available & various wildfowl on grounds. Longdon is on B4211, 10 miles from Malvern & 5 miles from Tewkesbury.

121

The Domestic Fowl Trust

Honeybourne Pastures, Honeybourne, Nr. Evesham, Worcestershire WR11 5QJ
Telephone: (0386) 833083

*Over 130 breeds of ducks, geese, hens, turkeys on display.
Fowl for sale. Equipment, housing, books, feedstuffs.
Children's Farm, Adventure Playground.
Open daily all year round (except Fridays) – 10.30 a.m.-5.00 p.m.*

Dennis Hall
The home of Thomas Webb Crystal

Visit the factory and watch craftsmen at work. See glass masterpieces in the Thomas Webb Museum. Select a souvenir from the factory shop, and finally, relax over a coffee in the Thomas Webb Coffee Shop.

ADMISSION FREE

For details write to: Miss N. J. Elvin, Thomas Webb Crystal, Dennis Hall, King William Street, Amblecote, Stourbridge, West Midlands, DY8 4EZ.

More of an exploration than a visit
WINNERS OF A BRITISH TOURIST ASSOCIATION AWARD

The Jinney Ring Craft Centre

HANBURY
BROMSGROVE

TEL: HANBURY 272

Craft Workshops, Gallery, Gift Shop, Delicious home-made
Lunches, Evening Meals, Cream Teas and Coffee
Admission Free. Opening times: 10.30 am-5.00 pm Wed-Sat
OPEN ALL YEAR ROUND

Worcestershire ENGLAND

(FH) HILL FARM   Rocky Lane, Bournheath, Bromsgrove, Worcs, B61 9HU

Mrs Lily Rutter
Tel:-(0527) 72403
Open all year
B&B   £9-£10.50   Listed
EM   £5-£6.50
Sleeps 6

Our Georgian Listed farmhouse with medieval barn is just 1½m from M5 and M42 access. We offer very comfortable accommodation excellent food using much of our own produce and a warm welcome to all our visitors. All rooms are centrally heated with drink facilities available. Visitors Lounge has colour TV and looks out on to pleasantly landscaped gardens. OS Ref SO 977 395

(FH) WESSEX HOUSE FARM   Trench Lane, Oddingley, Droitwich, Worcs, WR9 7NB

Gwen Jackson
Tel:-(0905) 772826
Open Mar-Oct
B&B   £8-£9   Applied
EM   £4-£5
Sleeps 6

Our modern farmhouse in pleasant surroundings on stock and arable farm. 4m from M5 motorway, 3m from Droitwich. Easy reach of Cotswolds. Double and family rooms with washbasins. Children welcome, cot and high chair available. Guests are assured every comfort and good farmhouse food. Excellent food also available locally. Brochure on request. OS Ref SO 91 61

(FH) CHURCH HOUSE   Shelsley Beauchamp, Nr Worcester, WR6 6RA

Gill Moore
Tel:-(08865) 393
Open Apr-Oct
B&B   £10
EM   £5
Sleeps 4

Church House is a large 18th Century farmhouse situated on the banks of the River Teme, 10 miles from Worcester. We have a 200 acre family run farm with sheep, cattle and poultry. We are an hour's drive from the Cotswolds and the Welsh border. Farmhouse food with home grown meats and vegetables are served. Bedrooms have bathroom en suite or hand basins. OS Ref SO 220320

(FH) CHURCH FARM   Abberley, Nr Worcester, WR6 6BP

Sally & Roy Neath
Tel:-(029921) 316
Open Easter-Oct
B&B   £9-£11
EM   £6
Sleeps 5

You are invited to stay at our comfortable Victorian farmhouse on a traditional arable and beef farm whilst you discover our beautiful county, set in its own orchard the house overlooks a small nature pond and trout pool. All bedrooms decorated in Laura Ashley print have wash basins or ensuite bathroom. Hot drink facilities. Log fires. Evening meal by arrangement. AA Listed. Tel: Great Witley (0299) 896316. OS Ref SO 687510

(FH) MANOR FARM   Broughton Hackett, Worcester

Hilary Morgan
Tel:-(090560)252/839
Open Jun-Dec
B&B   £10-£15   Applied
EM   From £7.50
Sleeps 6
Van   £2
Max 5 vans

An exceptionally warm welcome awaits guests at our comfortable, well furnished, centrally heated farmhouse, on a beef, trout and arable farm in peaceful countryside. Charming twin and double bedrooms, some with private bathrooms. Excellent home cooking. Within easy reach of Worcester and M5, it is the perfect base from which to savour the delights of the Heart of England. OS Ref SO 924543

FARM HOLIDAY BUREAU

(FH) CHIRKENHILL   Leigh Sinton, Malvern, Worcs, WR13 5DL

Sarah Wenden
Tel:-(0886) 32205
Open all year
B&B   £10   Listed
EM   £5
Sleeps 6

David and Sarah Wenden welcome visitors to their attractive farmhouse sited on an arable/fruit farm amidst the beautiful Worcestershire countryside between the Malvern Hills and Worcester. Within easy driving distance are the Vale of Evesham, Stratford, Cheltenham, The Cotswolds and The Wye Valley. Dogs/horses housed by arrangement. Most country pursuits available locally. OS Ref SO 7750

Wyre Forest

Kidderminster Stourport-on-Severn Bewdley

History, heritage, natural beauty and a wealth of attractions blend together to delight the visitor to this intimate and beautiful corner of England.

★ **Bewdley:** A charming Georgian riverside town with a Craft Museum and working Brass Foundry.
★ **Stourport-on-Severn:** A unique canal and riverside town - a mecca for boating enthusiasts.
★ **Severn Valley Railway:** 16 miles of England's premier steam railway.
★ **West Midlands Safari and Leisure Park:** Exotic animals and thrilling rides.
★ **Kidderminster:** World-renowned carpet-making centre now boasting one of the country's finest Leisure Centres.
★ **Delightful countryside** - picturesque villages, the unspoilt banks of the River Severn and the ancient Forest of Wyre itself.

COME FOR A WEEKEND OR LONGER - YOU'LL FIND IT A REWARDING EXPERIENCE
EASY ACCESS FROM M5 AND M42 MOTORWAYS

Further information from the Tourism Officer, Wyre Forest District Council, Land Oak House, Chester Road North, Kidderminster, Worcs. DY10 1TA. Tel: (0562) 820505, Ext: 2552 or 2553.

Worcestershire ENGLAND

(FH) BULLOCKHURST FARM Rock, Nr Kidderminster, Worcs, DY14 9SE

Margaret Nott
Tel:-(029922) 305
Open Easter-Oct
B&B   £8.50
Sleeps 3

Listed

A warm welcome awaits you at Bullockhurst, a mixed family farm, its Georgian farmhouse having oak beams and open hearth and large pleasant gardens, enjoying superb views over the Worcestershire/Shropshire countryside. Situated on the edge of the Wyre Forest, close to the Worcestershire Way, and only 4 miles from Bewdley with its Severn Valley Railway and Safari Park. OS Ref SO 374 272

(FH) OLD HOUSE FARM Tibberton, Droitwich, Worcs, WR9 7NP

Pat Chilman
Tel:-(090 565) 247
Open Easter-Oct
B&B   £10-£11
EM   £5
Sleeps 6

Listed

Family run 100 acre dairy farm set in the peaceful village of Tibberton but only 1 mile from M5 junction 6. The farmhouse is tastefully furnished for comfort and relaxation with English breakfast our speciality. Evening meals to order. One double, 1 family, 1 single bedroom. Central for all the Heart of England including, Worcestershire, Herefordshire, Warwickshire, Gloucestershire and the Cotswolds. OS Ref SO 903567

(FH) LEIGH COURT Leigh, Nr Worcester, WR6 5LB

Sally Stewart
Tel:-(0886) 32275
Open Mar-Oct
B&B   £11-£12
EM   £8
Sleeps 6

A period manor house set beside the River Teme on a 270 acre sheep and arable farm with its famous tithe barn. Stratford Upon Avon, Welsh border country, Malvern Hills, lovely Severn and Wye valleys all within easy reach. Touring, walking and river fishing. Home cooking using local produce when available. Colour television. All bedrooms have washbasins and hot drink facilities. AA listed. OS Ref SO 784535

(SC) OLD YATES COTTAGES Old Yates, Abberley, Worcester, WR6 6AT

Sarah & Richard Goodman
Tel:-(029 921) 500
Open all year
SC   £60-£170
Sleeps 2/4

Our 4 cottages are comfortable and well equipped, standing in their own gardens on the edge of a wooded valley 300 yards from our dairy farm. Baby calves (July-Feb) and milking can be seen. Colour TV, electric central heating, log fires (3), table tennis room and laundry facilities. Price inclusive of electricity, linen and logs. Beautiful countryside. Fine fruit growing area. Excellent restaurants nearby. OS Ref SO 734 667

(SC) HALL FARM COUNTRY HOLIDAYS Lower Portway Farm, Sedgeberrow, Evesham, Worcs, WR11 6UB

Daphne Stow
Tel:-(0386) 881298
Open Apr-Oct
SC   £55-£245
sleeps 2/5

Three delightful cottages and a large Georgian farmhouse (skilfully converted into 4 self contained apartments). All properties have been carefully modernised. Furnished and equipped to a high standard and personally supervised by owner. Many lovely Cotswold beauty spots and interesting towns (Cheltenham, Stratord-upon-Avon, Worcester) to visit as well as stately homes, farm parks and pick-your-own produce from the Vale of Evesham. OS Ref SP 025385

(SC) OAKHURST COTTAGE Leigh Court, Leigh, Nr Worcester, WR6 5LB

Sally Stewart
Tel:-(0886) 32275
Open Mar-Oct
SC   £70-£90
Sleeps 4

In Bransford village, this comfortable modernised cottage is superbly placed for touring or an easy rural stay. Stratford-Upon-Avon, the Welsh border country, Malvern Hills and the lovely Severn, Teme and Wye valleys are all within easy reach. Cot available, television. Most sports and entertainment available in Malvern and Worcester. River fishing on farm. Winter lets by arrangement. OS Ref SO 791526

125

ANNARD WOOLLEN MILL

Handgate Farm, Church Lench, Evesham
Worcs. WR11 4UB
Telephone: Evesham (0386) 870270

A Working Woollen Mill To Visit in WORCESTERSHIRE...

Where a warm friendly welcome and free coffee awaits our customers.

Exclusive range of designer hand knit mohair sweaters, jackets & coats.

100's of colours & textures of designer mohair to knit a creation of your own!

Open 7 days a week 10.00 a.m. - 5.00 p.m.
Visitors always welcome
Party visits by appointment

FREE FACTORY TOURS AT STUART CRYSTAL

A fascinating insight into the glassmaking industry. Learn how beautiful Stuart Crystal is made. Free admission and weekday tours. Factory Shop. Museum. 200 year old glassmaking Cone. Free parking. Refreshments available.

For full details 'phone The Tourist Department on 0384 71161.

STUART CRYSTAL
Redhouse Glassworks, Wordsley, Stourbridge, West Midlands DY8 4AA.

WARWICKSHIRE

30

WARWICKSHIRE

The Heart of England . . . Shakespeare country . . . famous castle . . . country gardens . . . a Royal Spa . . . and a rural backcloth of unspoilt scenery — that's Warwickshire.

With so many attractions 'leafy' Warwickshire leaves you spoilt for choice. But starting with Shakespeare's Stratford-upon-Avon you've a town full of history and culture, with three theatres, half-timbered buildings, gardens and busy shopping centre.

A few miles up the river Avon there's Warwick with its magnificent mediaeval castle brought to 'life' by Madame Tussaud's vignettes. Kenilworth, just a stone's throw away has less castle — but these stark ruins are every bit as memorable — and another delightful town centre. Close to Kenilworth there's the Royal Showground, stage for the Royal Show each July and a year-round agricultural centre.

Royal Leamington Spa, an elegant town with wide Regency streets, crescents and fine gardens is, of course, famous for its healing waters — and the Royal Pump Rooms is as busy today as it was a century or so ago.

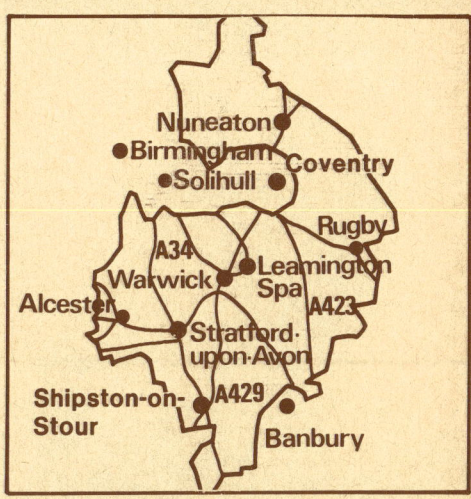

Between these towns — and dotted throughout the county — are some of the prettiest villages to be found. Stately homes abound — Packwood, Ragley, Charlecote, Baddesley Clinton, Coughton Court are just some of the names to look out for when you visit Warwickshire.

GROUP SECRETARY:
Deborah Lea (029577) 652

STRATFORD BRASS RUBBING CENTRE

ADMISSION FREE
Come and have a go! — OPEN 7 DAYS A WEEK
The Summer House, Avon Bank Gardens, Stratford-on-Avon. Tel: (0789) 297671

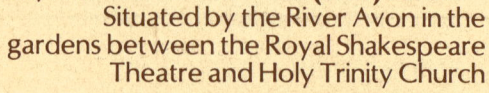

Situated by the River Avon in the gardens between the Royal Shakespeare Theatre and Holy Trinity Church

You too can make a beautiful brass rubbing from our collection of replica English Church brasses. No experience needed, we will show you how. Materials and instruction included in the price charged.

Historical gifts and souvenirs on sale

Easter to end of Sept 10 a.m. - 6 p.m. Oct 11 a.m. - 4 p.m. Nov, Dec and March Sat and Sun only 11 - 4 p.m. Closed January and February

---

Stoneleigh Abbey

Warwickshire's Finest Georgian Mansion

With Elizabethan Wing and Gatehouse
Home of the Leigh family for 400 years.

- ★ 15 acres of gardens originally laid out by Repton.
- ★ Nature Trail.
- ★ Woodland walks by the River Avon.
- ★ Children's playground.
- ★ Miniature steam railway (Sundays and bank holidays).
- ★ Licensed conservatory restaurant featuring home cooking.
- ★ Magnificent interiors.

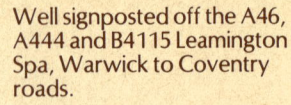

Well signposted off the A46, A444 and B4115 Leamington Spa, Warwick to Coventry roads.

Opening details and further information from The Estates Office, Stoneleigh Abbey, Kenilworth, Warwickshire CV8 2LF. Tel: 0926 52116.

Warwickshire ENGLAND

(FH) CRANDON HOUSE Avon Dassett, Leamington Spa, Warwickshire, CV33 0AA

Deborah Lea
Tel:-(029577) 652
Closed Xmas
B&B £9-£12
EM £5-£6
Sleeps 6

Guests receive a specially warm welcome at our farmhouse offering a very high standard of accommodation. Set in 20 acres of beautiful countryside. Small working farm with Jersey cows, calves, sheep, hens, ducks & geese. Own produce. Excellent food. Large Garden. Full CH, log fire. 1 double, 2 twin rooms, 1 en-suite. Ideal for exploring the Heart of England. Farm Holiday Bureau Member of the Year 1986. OS Ref SP 418506

(FH) NOLANDS FARM Oxhill, Warwick, CV35 0RJ

Sue Hutsby
Tel:-(0926) 640309
Closed Xmas-New Year
B&B £7-£12
EM From £6
Sleeps 14
(5)

Farmhouse situated off A422 from Stratford-on-Avon in tranquil valley surrounded by fields, woods & wildlife, with stocked trout lake. Double/family suite/single bedrooms. One romantic Tudor style four poster bedroom, all en-suite/colour TV, Tea/coffee facilities & central heating. On ground level overlooking peace & quiet of old stableyard. Use of garden, drawing room, separate dining room. OS Ref 312 469

(FH) HILL FARM Lewis Road, Radford Semele, Leamington Spa, Warwickshire, CV31 1UX

Mrs Rebecca Gibbs
Tel:-(0926) 37571
Closed Xmas & New Year
B&B £10-£12
EM £4-£8
Sleeps 6
TV Max 5
tent/vans

Hill Farm is a comfortable, friendly farmhouse situated in 350 acres of mixed farmland. Excellent food. Large garden. Attractive centrally heated bedrooms with tea/coffee making facilities. Comfortable TV lounge, guests bathroom. Children welcomed, babysitting available. 2 Doubles, 1 Twin/Family room. Past AA Award Winner. Camping/Caravanning club certificated site. Central for Warwick, Coventry, Stratford-Upon-Avon, Cotswolds, Birmingham, Kenilworth. OS Ref SP 344638

(FH) SUGARSWELL FARM Shenington, Banbury, Oxon, OX15 6HW

Rosemary Nunneley
Tel:-(029 588) 512
Open all year
B&B £12-£20
EM £12
Sleeps 6
(8)

Beautiful farmhouse overlooking field and woodlands on the Oxfordshire/Warwickshire border with a luxurious interior where comfort is at the fore. Two bedrooms have kingsize beds, all have bathroom ensuite. Cordon-Bleu cooking, fillet steak in port & cream a speciality. Recommended by Elizabeth Gundry in the Sunday Times. For the discerning guest who is looking for something rather special. Colour Brochure. OS Ref SP 450240

(FH) LITTLE HILL FARM Wellesbourne, Warwick, CV35 9EB

Charlotte Hutsby
Tel:-(0789) 840261
Open Mar-Nov
B&B £10
EM £7
Sleeps 6

Large rambling, William and Mary Farmhouse, set in 700 acres of arable/beef farmland. Spacious rooms, all with beams. Comfortable lounge with colour television and dining room. Friendly atmosphere, spacious garden with grass tennis court. Enjoyable walks around farm. Only 6 miles from Warwick, Stratford-upon-Avon and within easy reach of Cotswolds, Oxford, Coventry and other interesting places. OS Ref 00028575

(FH) SNOWFORD HALL Hunningham, Nr Leamington Spa, Warks, CV33 9ES

Rudi Hancock
Tel:-(0926) 632297
Closed Xmas-New Year
B&B £10-£13
EM £7.50
by arrangement
Sleeps 6

We offer a warm welcome and peaceful surroundings in our 18th Century farmhouse on a 300 acre mixed working farm set in rolling countryside. Near the Roman Fosse Way ideally suited for visiting Stratford, Warwick, Leamington, Cotswolds, NAC and NEC. 1 twin bedded room, 1 twin bedded/family room both with shower/washbasin. 1 double bedded room with washbasin. Centrally heated, good home cooking. OS Ref SP 386666

HAVE A MARVELLOUS DAY OUT AT THE HEART OF ENGLAND STEAM CENTRE

BIRMINGHAM RAILWAY MUSEUM
021-707 4696

★ Open daily 10 am–5 pm throughout the year.
★ Steam days every Sunday plus Bank Holidays from Easter to October.
★ Ample free parking.
★ Restaurant and Souvenir Shop.
★ Informative displays in the Visitor Centre.
★ Free train rides on steam days ★ Free Film Shows ★ Steam Gala events at Easter, Christmas and October.

See restoration work in progress in the workshop

WARWICK ROAD, TYSELEY, BIRMINGHAM B11 2HL   021-707 4696

RUGBY BOROUGH COUNCIL

THE JAMES GILBERT RUGBY FOOTBALL MUSEUM

Visit one of the tiniest museums in the Country!

Based in the original rugby football-maker's shop. A Museum brimming with rugby memorabilia.

OPEN
Monday to Saturday
10.00 a.m.–5.00 p.m.
(closed 1–2 p.m. Saturdays)

ADMISSION FREE
(A fine range of souvenirs on sale)
5 St. Matthews Street,
Rugby CV21 3BX
Tel: [0788] 536500

Warwickshire ENGLAND

(FH) CHURCH FARM Dorsington, Stratford-upon-Avon, Warks, CV37 8AX

Marian Walters
Tel:-(0789) 720471
Open all year
B&B £10-£12
EM £6
Redn for children
Sleeps 10

A friendly welcome awaits you with good farmhouse cooking at our Georgian farmhouse, open fires, CH. 1 family, 1 twin, 2 double bedroom, washbasins & electric blankets! Stratford-upon-Avon, Warwick, NEC, Royal Showground, Cotswolds Vale of Evesham all within easy reach. Guests are free to explore the beef, arable & horse farm. Gliding, fishing, boating, horse riding all nearby. AA/RAC Listed. Full Fire Certificate held. OS Ref SP 147498

(FH) SHARMER FARM Fosse Way, Radford Semele, Leamington Spa, Warwickshire, CV31 1XH

Nora Ellis
Tel:-(0926) 612448
Open Mar-Oct
B&B From £10
EM From £4
Sleeps 6

Guests are welcome to stay in our modern, comfortable farmhouse on 120 acreable and beef farm, in quiet countryside 4 miles from Leamington Spa. Trout fishing and horse riding available locally. Convenient for touring Shakespeare country and the Cotswolds. One twin bedded room, 1 family room both with washbasins, guests' bathroom, television lounge. Evening meals by arrangement. OS Ref SP 359625

(FH) LAWFORD HILL FARM Lawford Heath Lane, Nr Rugby, Warks, CV23 9HG

Susan Moses
Tel:-(0788) 2001
Closed Xmas
B&B £10
EM £5
Sleeps 6

Bed and breakfast all the year round in a spacious Georgian farmhouse which is situated on a 200 acre family farm. It has a small farm museum, children's farmyard where children can help look after the animals. Donkey riding and fishing. Two superior self catering units available from Easter 1988. Brochure on request. OS Ref SP 465747

(FH) MONWODE LEA FARM Over Whitacre, Coleshill, Warks, B46 2NR

Mollie Callwood
Tel:-(0675) 81232
Closed Xmas and New Year
B&B £11-£12.50 Listed
EM £5
Sleeps 5

Monwode Lea Farm is a spacious early Georgian farmhouse which is easily accessible from Coventry, Birmingham, M6/M42 and the National Exhibition & Agricultural Centres. It is situated on the B4114 very near to Bosworth Field and George Eliot country in North Warwickshire. The atmosphere is friendly and informal, guests are able to enjoy gardens where peacocks roam and private fishing. Children welcome. OS Ref SP 280401

(FH) GLEBE FARM Exhall, Alcester, Warks, B49 6EA

Margaret & John Canning
Tel:-(0789) 772202
Closed Xmas-New Year
B&B £9-£12 Listed
EM £6
Sleeps 5

Shakespeare named our village 'Dodging Exhall' and it has somehow 'dodged' the passing of time so, if you want a true taste of rural England, relaxed informal accommodation, come to our quaint old farmhouse & let us spoil you with log fires, wholesome food. Most is home produced including our own lovely fresh milk and free-range eggs, which children can collect. OS Ref SP 102551

(FH) MARTON FIELDS FARM Marton, Rugby, Warks, CV23 9RS

Pamela Dronfield
Tel:-(0926) 632410
Closed Xmas
B&B £10-£12
EM From £7
Sleeps 6/8

Guests receive a warm welcome at our period farmhouse. The working farm of 240 acres is surrounded by beautiful gardens and countryside. Bedrooms have CH, washbasins, electric blankets, tea/coffee facilities. Guests' bathroom, comfortable sitting room with colour TV, own dining room. We make our own bread. Lovely cottage for Self Catering. PAINTING HOLIDAYS AVAILABLE with full board. OS Ref SP

(FH) IRELAND'S FARM   Ireland's Lane, Henley in Arden, Solihull, Warks, B95 5AB

Pamela Shaw
Tel:-(05642) 2476
Closed Xmas and New Year
B&B   £10-£15
Sleeps 6
🐎 (10) 🐕

19th Century farmhouse set in 220 acres of peaceful countryside, 1m from main A34 Stratford to Birmingham Road. 1 double and 2 twin bedded rooms all with ensuite facilities, central heating and tea/coffee making facilities. Close to Stratford, Warwick, NEC and Royal Agricultural Show Ground.

(FH) PARK FARM   Spring Road, Barnacle, Shilton, Coventry, CV7 9LG

Richard & Linda Grindal
Tel:-(0203) 612628
Closed Xmas and New Year
B&B   £11   Listed
EM   £6
Sleeps 4
🐎 (10)

Park Farm is a listed building. Originally moated, offering comfortable fully centrally heated accommodation, within easy reach of the motorways linking Coventry, Birmingham and Leicester. 2 bedrooms, with TV, radio, tea/coffee making facilities and electric blankets. Guests' own bathroom. Good local pub food. OS Ref SP 847385

(SC) FURZEN HILL FARM COTTAGE   Furzenhill Farm, Cubbington Heath, Leamington Spa, Warks, CV32 6QZ

Christine Whitfield
Tel:-(0926) 24791
Open all year
SC   £60-£120
Sleeps 4-8
🐎 🐕

The cottage is part of Furzen Hill Farmhouse but is completely self contained. An arable farm, it is situated just off the A445 at Cubbington Heath, near to Stoneleigh. Fully equipped for 7-8 people. Large garden. Also two cottages at Radford Semele, near Leamington Spa, in quiet rural setting, each sleeping 4 guests. Open all year. Dogs by arrangement. OS Ref SP 346703

(SC) NOLANDS FARM   Oxhill, Warwick, CV35 0RJ

Sue Hutsby
Tel:-(0926) 640309
Closed Xmas and New Year
SC   £50-£110
Sleeps 2/5
🐎 (5)

15th Century Thatched cottage, full of character and charm fully furnished and all modern amenities, double bedded room and one with 3 single beds, bathroom, lounge, dining area and kitchen. Central heating, telephone, TV. Central to village. Farm Cottage has 1 double bedroom, bathroom, lounge cum dining area and kitchenette, central heating, TV. Quiet and peaceful, large garden and fishing.

(SC) SNOWFORD HALL FARM COTTAGE   Hunningham, Leamington Spa, Warks, CV33 9ES

Rudi Hancock
Tel:-(0926) 632297
Open all year
SC   £80-£180
Sleeps 5

Fully centrally heated spacious 2 bedroomed cottage on a quiet country road surrounded by well maintained lawns & farmland. Capable of sleeping 4/6 people. A comfortable lounge with TV and fitted kitchen makes this cottage an ideal base for touring the cotswolds, Shakespeare country and exploring Warwick, Kenilworth & Oxford. The NAC is 5m & NEC is 15m away. OS Ref Sp 386666

(SC) SHARMER FARM   Fosse Way, Radford Semele, Leamington Spa, Warks, CV31 1XH

Nora Ellis
Tel:-(0926) 612448
Open all year
SC   £80-£150
Sleeps 6
🐎

Well equipped self contained wing of modern farmhouse. 4 miles from Leamington Spa, set in peaceful countryside, yet convenient for Warwick, Stratford-Upon-Avon, NAC, NEC, and an excellent base for touring the Cotswolds. Sleeps 6. Ample car parking and play area for children. Brochure on request. OS Ref SP 359625

Warwickshire ENGLAND

(SC) **HILLESDEN HOLIDAY HOMES**   27 Meadow Sweet Road, Stratford-upon-Avon, Warks, CV37 OTH

Mrs Thelma Tunnicliffe
Tel:-(0789) 293518
Open all year
SC   £85-£170
Sleeps 6

Selection of 5 holiday homes, set in Warwickshire's rural heartland. Close to Stratford-upon-Avon and providing the ideal base for touring Shakespeare country and the Cotswolds. All houses are fully furnished, carpeted and equipped to Tourist Board standards. Each will accommodate up to 6 guests. Families very welcome. Also (0789) 66912. OS Ref SP 180586

(SC) **EDSTONE COTTAGES**   Yew Tree Farm, Wootton Wawen, Solihull, W Midlands, B95 6BY

Janet Haimes
Tel:-(05642) 2701
Open all year
SC   £90-£135
Sleeps 6
+ cot

Ideal for the country lover, located within the parklands of the Edstone Estate. These 2 delightful semi-detached houses are equipped to Tourist Board standard. Each with 3 bedrooms, large lawn, car park space, colour TV, telephone. 4m from Stratford-upon-Avon, near Cotswolds, National Exhibition Centre and the Royal Showground. OS Ref SP 162631

(SC) **SHEPHERDS COTTAGE**   Canada Farm, Kinwarton, Alcester, Warks, B39 6HA

Elizabeth Hartley
Tel:-(0789) 762456
Open all year
SC   £75-£135
Sleeps 4
+ cot

Attractive stonebuilt well equipped character cottage, situated in quiet country lane leading to River Alne, 1m from historic market town of Alcester. Heating by storage radiators and log fires. Linen included, cot, automatic washing machine, colour TV, telephone for incoming calls, coarse fishing. (1 rod and tackle provided), car space.

RYTON GARDENS

Unique in Britain!

Award Winning Organic Gardens as seen on TV's
'All Muck and Magic?' series.

Ten acres of gardens. Cafe with home cooking, shop,
play area, lake, wild flowers, guided tours.

Bring the family, open all year round
Sign posted off A45, 5 miles SE of Coventry.

Phone 0203 303517

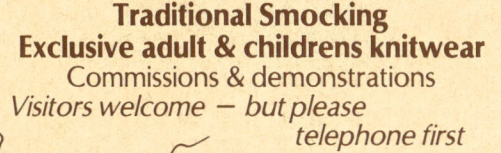

Traditional Smocking
Exclusive adult & childrens knitwear
Commissions & demonstrations
Visitors welcome — but please
telephone first

Thelma Watts,
Sinclair,
Avon Dassett,
Leamington Spa,
Warwickshire
CV33 0AL
Tel: 029589 362

31 SOUTH SHROPSHIRE

SOUTH SHROPSHIRE

If it's peace and quiet, unspoilt countryside, gently rolling hills, high desolate moorland and picturesque wooded valleys you're after — then South Shropshire is the place to come. Besides its exceptional countryside, there are bustling little market towns and a wealth of time-forgotten villages and historic buildings adding to South Shropshire's character.

Here on the Welsh borders, the area forms a buffer between the English Plains and the Welsh Mountains and contains some of the finest scenery you'll find in England. Part of the district is an 'Area of outstanding Natural Beauty', so don't forget your camera.

There are many places to see, from the Brown Clee — which is the highest point in Shropshire — to the rugged moorlands of the Stiperstones, the gentle slopes of Wenlock Edge and forested Clun Hills.

For the steam enthusiast, a ride on the Severn Valley Railway from Bridgnorth to Bewdley is a must. There are several National Trust properties in the area including a fine example of a fortified manor house at Stokesay and castles at Clun and Ludlow.

Ludlow has long been described as the most beautiful town in England and history is there for all to see in its old buildings and streets. Bridgnorth, set on the banks of the River Severn and with its cliff railway, is full of interest. So too are Bishops Castle, Church Stretton and Cleobury Mortimer.

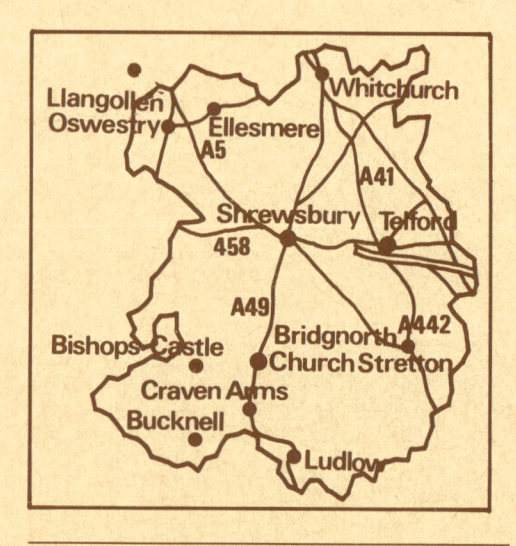

GROUP CONTACT:
Eileen Wilkes (058476) 221

South Shropshire ENGLAND

(FH) MALT HOUSE FARM   Lower Wood, Church Stretton, Shrops, SY6 6LF

Lyn Bloor
Tel:-(06945) 379
Open Easter-Oct
B&B £8-£9   Listed
EM   £6
Sleeps 6

Comfortable and homely accommodation in olde worlde farmhouse enjoying complete seclusion amongst the unspoilt Long Mynd Hills, yet only ten minutes drive from Church Stretton. Pretty bedrooms and generous home cooked meals, lots to do locally including golf, gliding, riding, museums and castles or just wander in the hills. 1 double, 1 twin and 1 family rooms. OS Ref SO 467978

(FH) NEW HOUSE FARM   Clun, Craven Arms, Shrops, SY7 8NJ

Luke & Miriam Ellison
Tel:-(0588) 638314
Closed Xmas and Mar
B&B £9.50   Listed
EM   £4.50-£5
Sleeps 6

Isolated 18th C farmhouse set high in the Shropshire Hills, near Offa's Dyke, ideally situated for walking and touring the Welsh Marches. On the hill farm, rising to 1200 ft you can find wild life in its natural habitat. Traditionally furnished farmhouse, guests are assured of a warm welcome, comfortable rooms and home cooking. Accommodation - 1 family, 1 twin and 1 single rooms. Pets by arrangement. OS Ref SO 275863

(FH) GLEBE FARM   Diddlebury, Craven Arms, Shrops, SY7 9DH

Michael Adrian & Eileen Wilkes
Tel:-(058 476) 221
Open Mar-Oct
B&B £17-£21
EM   £10.50
Sleeps 12
Tent £1-£1.50
Van   £2-£2.50

Glebe Farm is a 17th century stone and half timbered farmhouse. It is set in an Elizabethan garden by a stream in the shadow of the Saxo-Norman church. Glebe Farm lies in the centre of the Corvedale and is within easy reach of Ludlow, Much Wenlock and the beautiful unspoilt countryside of the Welsh Marches. Children over 10 only. OS Ref SO 508855

(FH) LOW FARM   Alveley, Bridgnorth, Shrops, WV15 6HX

Patricia Lawley
Tel:-(029 97) 206
Closed Xmas and New Year
B&B £8
EM   £5-£6
Sleeps 4/6

Peaceful and friendly atmosphere on this working farm in Shropshire located in Victorian farmhouse on 200 acres. Log fires. Ideal touring centre for Ironbridge Museum, Royal Worcester Porcelain, Severn Valley Steam Railway. Trout and coarse fishing within 2 miles. Situated on A442 Bridgnorth - Kidderminster road. Good home cooking in the evening by arrangement. 1 family room, 1 twin-bedded room. OS Ref SO 770826

(FH) MONEUGHTY POETH   Llanfair Waterdine, Knighton, Powys, LD7 1TT

Mrs Jocelyn Williams
Tel:-(0547) 528 348
Open Mar-Nov
B&B £9.50-£10   Listed
Sleeps 5

Victorian farmhouse, on site of old monastery. Working family farm on river Teme, Welsh border, overlooking wooded hillsides and meadows. Between picturesque villages of Llanfair-Waterdine and Knucklas, with Heart of Wales railway. Ideal base - Offa's Dyke, Glyndwr's Way, Mid-Wales, South Shropshire. Accommodation - 1 family, 1 double rooms, guests' bathroom, CH, TV, radios, tea/coffee facilities, wholesome breakfasts, fishing. Caravan site. OS Ref SO 748 955

(FH) STREFFORD HALL FARM   Strefford, Nr Craven Arms, Shrops, SY7 8DE

Caroline Morgan
Tel:-(05882) 2383
Open Easter-Oct
B&B £8.50-£9   Listed
EM   £5
Sleeps 6

Strefford Hall is a Victorian farmhouse with large comfortable rooms, nestling at the foot of the Wenlock Edge. A peaceful area of outstanding natural beauty. Ideal setting for walking or relaxing within easy reach of Ludlow, Ironbridge, the Long Mynd Hills, Shrewsbury. 1 double, 1 twin both with H/C, 1 family room, guests' bathroom, sitting room with log burner, TV, separate dining room. Non smoking household.

COURT FARM Gretton, Church Stretton, Shrops, SY6 7HU

Barbara Norris
Tel:-(06943) 219
Open Feb-Nov
B&B £9-£12   Listed
EM   £5-£6
Sleeps 6

Stone Tudor farmhouse on 325 acre arable and stock farm in idyllic peaceful, rural surroundings, north east of Church Stretton, 1m off the B4371. Within easy driving distance of Ludlow, Shrewsbury, Bridgnorth and Ironbridge. Seven miles from the Long Mynd Hills. Visitors are assured of a very warm welcome and every comfort (including CH). High quality cuisine. Non-smoking household. OS Ref SO 515953

MIDDLETON LODGE Middleton Priors, Bridgenorth, WV16 6UR

Mary Burton
Tel:-(074634) 228/675
Open Apr-Oct
B&B £12.50-£15.00
Sleeps 6
(10)

First class bed and breakfast accommodation in the quiet hamlet of Middleton Priors. Superb views. Trout stream. Ideal countryside for walking. Within easy driving distance of Bridgenorth, Ludlow, Ironbridge and Shrewsbury. Traditional open fires and central heating. Comfortable bedrooms (1 with four poster bed).

RECTORY FARM Woolstaston, Church Stretton, Shrops, SY6 6NN

Jeanette Davies
Tel:-(069 45) 306
Open Mar-Nov
B&B £10-£12
Sleeps 6
(12)

A friendly welcome awaits in this attractive half-timbered farmhouse built around 1620 situated on the lower slopes of the National Trust Long Mynd Hills with extensive views of Shropshire (good walking country). One double and 2 twins, all with bathroom en suite. Lounge and television room. Central heating. AA Recommended. OS Ref SO 453985

BUCKNELL HOUSE Bucknell, Shrops, SY7 0AD

Brenda Davies
Tel:-(05474) 248
Open Mar-Nov
B&B £9.50-£11
CH   Sleeps 6
Van Certificated
     Site
(12)

Mellow 'listed' Georgian Country House in secluded grounds on fringe of attractive village overlooking Teme Valley. Ideal base for exploring Welsh Marches, Medieval Ludlow, Housman Countryside, Herefordshire's 'olde-worlde' villages, Offa's Dyke. Comfortable spacious accommodation. Fresh country food. Friendly atmosphere, CH, TV, 2 double (washbasins), 1 twin-bedded. Guests' private bathroom. Tea/coffee facilities, shaving points, radios, fishing, tennis. AA Listed. OS Ref SO 355735

THE HALL Bucknell, Shrops, SY7 0AA

Christine Price
Tel:-(05474) 249
Open Mar-Nov
B&B £9-£10   Listed
EM   £5
Sleeps 6
(7)

The Hall is a 250 acre farm producing sheep and cereals, in the beautiful Teme Valley. Ideal centre for touring Welsh border country. The large Georgian farmhouse is located in a peaceful part of the picturesque village of Bucknell so giving the house and garden a relaxed atmosphere. The farmhouse offers 1 family, 1 double and twin-bedded rooms, lounge and colour television. OS Ref SO 356738

BECKJAY FARM Clungunford, Craven Arms, Shrops, SY7 0PY

Mary Bason
Tel:-(054 73) 281
Open Easter-Oct
B&B £9.50-£10.50   Listed
EM   £4
Sleeps 6

170 acre mixed working farm in beautiful peaceful part of county affording many delightful walks. Historic towns of Shrewsbury, Hereford, Ludlow within driving distance, also Welsh lakes, Offa's Dyke, Ironbridge, Severn Valley steam railway. Guests are offered wholesome farmhouse food, vegetarians catered for. One family, 1 twin-bedded, 1 single/bunk-bedded room. Reductions for children under 12 years. OS Ref SO 393776

South Shropshire ENGLAND

(FH) LOWER UPTON FARM — Little Hereford, Ludlow, Shrops, SY8 4BB

Mrs. Helen Williams
Tel:-(058472) 322
Closed Xmas and New Year
B&B £8.50
EM From £4.25
Sleeps 6

Impressive Victorian farmhouse set in pleasant garden, on peaceful, picturesque Shropshire/Herefordshire border, Ludlow 6½m. Friendly atmosphere with high degree of comfort. 160 acre mixed farm. Double, family and twin bedrooms, complete with washbasins and shaver points. Modern bathroom, separate WC, large comfortable television lounge. Extensive range of home cooked evening meals. AA Listed. Information desk - brochure. Ideal touring centre. OS Ref SO 546 662

(FH) CHARLCOTTE FARM — Cleobury North, Bridgnorth, Shrops, WV16 6RR

Wendy Green
Tel:-(074633) 238
Open all year
B&B £9-£10
EM £6.50
Sleeps 6

Charlcotte, a 300 acre family dairy, sheep and arable farm situated between Bridgnorth and Ludlow at the foot of the Brown Clee Hill, renowned for its woodland walks and panoramic views. 1 family room with ensuite bathroom, 1 double and 1 twin room with H/C. Tea/coffee making facilities in all rooms. Lounge with TV. Evening meals and picnic lunches by arrangement. OS Ref SO 633864

(FH) UPPER HOUSE FARM — Hopton Castle, Craven Arms, Shrops, SY7 0QE

Sue Williams
Tel:-(05474) 319
Open Mar-Oct
B&B £12.50
EM £7.50
Sleeps 6

Secluded Georgian farmhouse set in the beautiful Clun valley ESA near the Welsh border. Fishing available (River Clun), beautiful walks and many sites to see 12m Ludlow, 14m Church Stretton, 9m Knighton. Excellent food with home produced vegetables and meat used whenever possible, all bedrooms furnished to a high standard. Lounge, TV. Log fires. Ample parking. SAE for brochure. OS Ref 365777

(SC) STREFFORD COTTAGE — Strefford Hall Farm, Strefford, Nr Craven Arms, Shrops

Caroline Morgan
Tel:-(05882) 2383
Open all year
SC £70-£120
Sleeps 6/8
plus cot

Part Tudor semi-detached cottage, attached to 360 acre mixed farm in small hamlet of Strefford. Ideal setting for walking holidays. Close to many places of historical and scenic interest. Sleeps 6/8 in 1 double and 2 twin bedrooms. Sitting room with coal fire and bed settee. Colour television. Fully equipped kitchen/dining room. Large lawned garden with garage. OS Ref SO 444857

(SC) EUDON BURNELL COTTAGES — Eudon Burnell, Nr Bridgnorth, Shrops, WV16 6UD

Margaret Crawford Clarke
Tel:-(074 635) 235
Open all year
SC £65-£145
Sleeps 5/6

Victorian semi-detached 3 bedroomed cottages on a working dairy/arable farm. Sleeping up to 5/6 people, the cottages are comfortably furnished and very well-equipped with fitted carpets, washing machines, colour TV, duvets etc. Parkray solid fuel CH or economy 7 and log fires. Lovely peaceful countryside nearby. Severn Valley Railway, Ironbridge and many more places to visit. Large garden, ample parking. Dogs by arrangement. OS Ref SO 895800

(SC) LINNET COTTAGE — Camlad House, Lydham, Bishop's Castle, Shrops, SY9 5HB

Joan Sargent
Tel:-(0588) 638546
Open Jan-Nov
SC £60-£120
Sleeps 5/6

An ideal centre for exploring the Border country, this farm cottage, set in a large private garden, is 1½ miles from the market town of Bishop's Castle. Walks on the Long Mynd and Offa's Dyke are all nearby as is the picturesque town of Ludlow. A comfortable cottage with colour television and table tennis table. Horse-riding, swimming, hang-gliding nearby. OS Ref SO 326918

'A fascinating day out!'

Come and see over 60 colourful rare breeds of large fowl and other farm animals displayed in picturesque surroundings.

Chicks and other baby animals are waiting for you to make a fuss of them.

To complete your visit picnic in the natural tranquility of our 'Dingle'.

OPEN DAILY
Easter Saturday — October 30th.
Closed Mondays except Bank Holidays.
10.30 am-5.30 pm

Admission: Adults £1.35, Children 60p, Under 4 years free.

We are easy to find, only 1¼ miles off the A49 at Onibury.

THE WERNLAS COLLECTION
Green Lane, Onibury,
Nr Ludlow, Shropshire SY7 9BL

THE WERNLAS COLLECTION
A Living Museum Of Rare Poultry

Bromfield (058477) 318

MIDLAND MOTOR MUSEUM
On 458 Stourbridge Road, Bridgnorth, Shropshire

Over 100 superb sports and sports racing cars and motorcycles.

Beautiful grounds with Nature trail.

Refreshments, picnic and play area.

Open Daily 10 am-5 pm

STANMORE HALL CAMPING PARK

Idyllic setting in parkland around a lake for tourers
Tel: (0746) 761761

NORTH SHROPSHIRE & West Cheshire

32

NORTH SHROPSHIRE & WEST CHESHIRE

Shropshire is the largest county in the UK without a coast-line and as Shrewsbury and Telford are the only towns of any real size, there are many miles of unspoilt countryside to enjoy and explore.

Shropshire has its own lake district, comprising the meres centred around Ellesmere and for canal lovers, the Llangollen Canal winds through delightful rural scenery.

Hodnet Hall and Gardens is well worth a visit and the National Trust have several properties in the area including Attingham Park, Benthall Hall, Dudmaston and Wilderhope Manor. Also owned by the National Trust is Wenlock Edge and Long Mynd. The latter is a stretch of moorland rising to 1700 feet, providing magnificent views of the Shropshire and Cheshire Plains and the Black Mountains.

The Ironbridge Gorge and Museum Trust has established a museum in the birthplace of the Industrial Revolution close to the world famous Iron Bridge. Similarly, the Acton Scott Working Farm Museum recreates farm practices from the past.

Not to be missed is a day in Shrewsbury set in a loop of the River Severn, with its castle, its museums, the shuts or passageways and its wealth of old and historic buildings.

GROUP CONTACT:
Sue Clarkson (0939) 250289

(FH) CHURCH FARM Wrockwardine, Wellington, Telford, Shrops, TF6 5DG

Jo Savage
Tel:-(0952) 244917
Open all year
B&B   £11
EM   From £5
       Sleeps 8

Enjoy a warm welcome in our large 200 year old farmhouse with oak beams, log fires and spacious gardens in the centre of a pleasant peaceful village. The attractive and prettily furnished bedrooms have washbasins, tea trays and colour TV. 1m from A5 & M54. Giving easy access to Shrewsbury, Ironbridge, Birmingham, Ludlow, South Shropshire Hills and Wales. EM by arrangement. OS Ref SJ 625120

(FH) NEW FARM Muckleton, Nr Shawbury, Telford, Shrops, TF6 6RJ

Glynwen Evans
Tel:-(0939) 250358
Open all year
B&B   £9-£12
EM   £6
       Sleeps 6
(3)

A modernised brick farmhouse set amidst the beautiful, peaceful surroundings of the Shropshire/Welsh border country. The attractive & historic towns of Shrewsbury, Chester, Ludlow, Bridgnorth, Ironbridge & the Potteries are within driving distance. Guests are assured of every conmfort with good farmhouse food. All bedrooms have washbasins, 1 with shower en suite. TV, Tea/coffee facilities. OS Ref SJ 587215

(FH) THE DAY HOUSE Nobold, Shrewsbury, Shropshire, SY5 8NL

Tom & Tricia Roberts
Tel:-(0743) 860212
Closed Xmas & New Year
B&B   £12-£14
       Sleeps 6

This lovely house set in its own gardens is on a dairy/arable farm in a beautiful part of Shropshire. The Tudor town of Shrewsbury with its wealth of history is only 3 miles away, many other amenities close by. Bedrooms are large with all facilities provided including beautiful views of the Shropshire and Welsh Hills, ideal base for touring surrounding areas. OS Ref SJ 46491034

(CH) MILL HOUSE Higher Wych, Malpas, Cheshire, SY14 7JR

Chris & Angela Smith
Tel:-(0948 73) 362
Closed Xmas-New Year
B&B   From £9
EM   From £4
CH   Sleeps 6

Modernised mill house on the Cheshire/Clwyd border in a quiet valley convenient for visiting Chester, Shrewsbury and North Wales. The house is centrally heated and has a open log fire in the lounge. Bedrooms have washbasins, radios and tea-making facilities. One bedroom has an en-suite shower/WC. Reductions for children and senior citizens. OS Ref SJ 501435

(FH) CHURCH FARM Rowton, Wellington, Telford, Shrops, TF6 6QY

Virginia & Robert Evans
Tel:-(0952) 770381
Open all year
B&B   £9-£15
EM   £6
       Sleeps 6

Listed attractive 300 year old farmhouse with oak beamed ceilings and romantic 4 poster bed. Central heating, good home produced foods. A working dairy, pig, sheep farm. Central for visiting Ironbridge, Hawkstone, Golf, Hodnet Hall, Weston Park, The Potteries, Shrewsbury, Alton Towers, Chester and Ludlow. Guests welcome to join in farming way of life. Children welcome. Own playroom. Weekly terms available. OS Ref SJ 615199

(FH) LONGLEY FARM Stanton Heath, Shawbury, Shropshire, SY4 4HE

Chris & Sue Clarkson
Tel:-(0939) 250289
Closed Xmas
B&B   £8-£8.50   Listed
EM   £4
       Sleeps 6

A 15 acre smallholding set in beautiful countryside, rearing sheep and some arable. The brick farmhouse is close to the historic towns of Shrewsbury, Chester, Ludlow and the Long Mynd Hills. A special attraction is the Ironbridge Gorge and museums. Two family rooms and 1 double. Full central heating. OS Ref SJ 602228

North Shropshire & West Cheshire ENGLAND

FH CRUMPWELL   Maesbury Road, Oswestry, Shrops, SY10 8HB

Irene Lewis
Tel:-(0691) 653432
Open Easter-Oct
B&B   9.00
EM   £5 by prior
        arrangement
Sleeps 6

Listed

Close to market town of Oswestry (livestock market Wednesday, new leisure centre). Crumpwell a Georgian house with large garden on livestock/arable farm. Local attractions Wat's and Offa's Dykes. Seven Meres at Ellesmere. Golf courses, castles, fishing, riding. Narrow gauge railway and canal boat trips at Welshpool (15m). 1 double, 1 family, 1 single. Private bathroom, TV in drawing room. Evening meal by arrangement. OS Ref SJ 308268

FH BRADLEY HALL   Malpas, Cheshire, SY13 4RA

Theresa Mullock
Tel:-(0948) 860439
Closed Dec, Xmas and
          New Year
B&B   From £9
Sleeps 6

Listed

Spacious Victorian farmhouse attractively situated in unspoilt countryside. One mile from picturesque village of Malpas on B5395. Convenient for Chester, North Wales and Shropshire. Pleasant walks and many local sites of historical interest. OS Ref SJ 505460

FH THE WATERFOWL SANCTUARY   Bradeley Green Farm, Tarporley Road, Whitchurch, Shropshire, SY13 4HD

Ruth Mulliner
Tel:-(0948) 3442
Closed Xmas-New Year
B&B   £9.50-£12.50
        Under 12yrs ½
EM   £5-£6
Sleeps 6

Beautiful Georgian farmhouse on working dairy farm. Centrally heated, open fires, all rooms bathrooms en-suite. A favourite night-halt for travellers. Carp & trout fishing on farm, "prize winning" nature trail & extensive water gardens with large collection of waterfowl. Golf close by, an ideal spot for discovering Wales, Cheshire & Shropshire. We assure all guests of a warm friendly welcome. OS Ref SJ 537449

FH PERRY FARM   Whittington, Oswestry, Shrops, SY11 4PF

Hilary Ward
Tel:-(0691) 662330
Closed Jan-Feb
B&B   £10
EM   £5.50
Sleeps 4
(2)

We invite you to spend a night or longer on our working family farm on the Welsh border, 2m off A5 at Whittington. Convenient for touring Chester, Shrewsbury, Ellesmere, Mid North Wales. Enjoy riding (indoor school) walking, bird watching, fishing, cycling. Try a weekend break with dinner in a 13th Century castle. 1 family, 1 twin, 2 bathrooms with showers. OS Ref SJ 347304

FH ARGOED FARM   Gate Road, Froncysyllte, Nr Llangollen, Clwyd, LL20 7RH

Jane Roberts
Tel:-(0691) 772367
Open Mar-Oct
B&B   £9.50-£10.50
Sleeps 4
(10)

Situated in beautiful Vale of Llangollen on Welsh/English border, this modernised farmhouse retains its charm with oak beams, tasteful furnishings large garden, overlooking Telfords Aqueduct and River Dee. Guests have own lounge, private bathrooms. Ideal walking, (Offa's Dyke). Touring, N Wales, Chester, Shrewsbury. Fishing, riding, golf, leisure centre and pub meals available locally. 1 double-bedded, 1 twin-bedded. Pets by arrangement. OS Ref SJ 270817

FH THE SETT, VILLAGE FARM   Stanton-upon-Hine Heath, Shrewsbury, Shrops, SY4 4LR

Brenda Grundey
Tel:-(0939) 250391
Closed Xmas-New Year
B&B   £10-£18
EM   £8
Sleeps 14

A unique converted brick built barn on a 130 acre working farm. All double rooms have showers, WC ensuite and tea making facilities. Visitors' lounge with colour TV, separate dining room. Full central heating. Small animals & play areas. Farm trail through Britains first badger conservation area. Members of "6 Faces of Shropshire Farming". Central for Shrewsbury, Chester, Mid-Wales, Ironbridge, Potteries. 5 double, 1 family. OS Ref SJ 570240

FH LOWER HUNTINGTON FARM Little Wenlock, Telford, Shrops, TF6 5AP

Mrs Pauline Williamson
Tel:-(0952) 505804
Closed Xmas
B&B   £9-£12   Listed
Sleeps 6

Dairy farm with listed 17th Century black & white farmhouse. Exposed wattle & daub walls, beamed throughout, CH, quiet peaceful setting. Guests own bathroom and dining room. Bedrooms have TV, tea/coffee making facilities. Fishing in farm trout pools, 10 acres scenic wood with wildlife. 3½m from M54 Junction 7. Central for Ironbridge, Shrewsbury, Bridgnorth, 1 single, 1 twin bedded room, 2 double/family ensuite. 1 on ground floor. OS Ref SJ 653081

FH SUTTON HILL FARM Sutton Maddock, Nr Ironbridge, Shifnal, Shrops, TF11 9NL

Judy Palmer
Tel:-(095271) 217
Closed Christmas
B&B   £9.50-£10.50
EM   5.00
Sleeps 6

Our farmhouse has been beautifully refurbished to provide comfortable & welcoming accommodation for a relaxing holiday in Shropshire. All our rooms have wash-hand basins & tea/coffee making facilities. We are well situated for visiting Ironbridge, Severn Valley Railway, the historic towns of Much Wenlock, Bridgnorth, Shrewsbury. Guests are welcome to relax in the house & grounds during the day. Evening meals by arrangement. OS Ref 716029

FH WROCKWARDINE FARM Wrockwardine, Nr Wellington, Telford, Shrops, TF6 5DG

Mrs Margaret Carver
Tel:-(0952) 42278
Open all year
B&B   £9-£10
EM   £5
Sleeps 6

An early Georgian listed farmhouse on a 250 acre working farm, only 1½ miles from M54 motorway. Within easy reach of Shrewsbury, Chester, Ludlow, and the Ironbridge Gorge Museums. Private coarse fishing 1m, children's fishing pool on farm. 1 double, 1 twin and family room with shower en-suite. Home cooking, log fires OS Ref SJ 625121

FH ELSON HOUSE FARM Elson, Ellesmere, Shrops, SY12 9EZ

Patricia Sadler
Tel:-(069175) 276
Open Easter-Oct
B&B   £8-£9   Listed
Sleeps 6

A large farmhouse situated among the Shropshire Meres within easy reach of the Welsh border. The attractive farmhouse has open fires and is fully centrally heated. Guests have their own lounge with colour TV and separate dining room. Ellesmere is within easy reach of 3 golf courses, yachting lakes, stately homes and castles. A family atmosphere welcomes you. OS Ref SJ 385359

FH SAMBROOK MANOR Sambrook, Newport, Shrops, TF10 8AL

John & Eileen Mitchell
Tel:-(095279) 256
Open Mar-Oct
B&B   £9   Listed
Sleeps 6

Beautiful old farmhouse built in 1702 stands in 210 acres of mixed farm land, large comfortable rooms with tea/coffee making facilities, situated between Stoke potteries, Shrewsbury, Ironbridge & Wolverhampton along with canals running through local countryside and many places of beauty and historical interest.

SC THE GRANARY Mill House, Higher Wych, Malpas, Cheshire, SY14 7JR

Angela & Chris Smith
Tel:-(0948 73) 362
Open all year
SC   £65-£125
Sleeps 4

The Granary is a self contained bungalow adjacent to Mill House. Sleeps 4/5 in 2 double bedrooms. Kitchen/living area. Shower and W.C., colour TV central heating. Cot and babysitting available. Situated in a quiet valley with a small stream in the garden. Convenient for visiting Chester, Shrewsbury and North Wales. OS Ref SJ 501435

142

North Shropshire & West Cheshire ENGLAND

(sc) BOOLEY HOME FARM Stanton Upon Hine Heath, Shewsbury, SY4 4LY

Pauline & Tony Barrett
Tel:-(093924) 206
Open all year
SC £55-£75
    Sleeps 2
Van £1.50

The Studio Loft is a spacious open plan flat with a half glass roof admitting sun and warmth all day. Very private and peaceful with views of much unspoilt countryside. Double bed, fridge, cooker, colour TV, shower, open fire and other heating. Good pub food 1 mile, Shrewsbury 10 miles. Many activities and places of interest, or just plain peace and quiet. OS Ref SJ 569 257

(sc) BRADELEY GREEN FARM COTTAGE Bradley Green Farm, Tarporley Road, Whitchurch, Shrops, SY13 4HD

Ruth Mulliner
Tel:-(0948) 3442
Open all year
SC £80-£100
    Sleeps 4

Modernised and comfortably furnished cottage sleeps 4. Kitchen/diner, TV, electric heaters, meter 50p. All bed linen provided. Cot available. Situated in open countryside with glorious views. Ideal spot for touring N Wales, Cheshire, Shropshire. Trout and carp fishing on farm with access to waterfowl sanctuary and prize winning nature trail. Golf close by. Walking on Cheshire Sandstone Trail. OS Ref SJ 537449

(sc) LOWER HUNTINGTON FARM Little Wenlock, Telford, Shrops, TF6 5AP

Mrs Pauline Williamson
Tel:-(0952) 505804
Open Mar-Oct
SC £40-£90
    Sleeps 6-8

Spacious well equipped static 6/8 berth caravans on dairy farm. Situated near farmhouse in screened paddock. Views to Ironbridge Gorge. A brook runs through scenic 10 acre wood with wildlife etc. Fishing in farm trout pools. Central for Ironbridge museums, Shrewsbury. Caravans have double & bunk bedrooms, shower/bathroom, WC, fridge, TV, gas/electricity by meter. Linen hire. Indoor games area, sorry no pets. OS Ref SJ 653081

(sc) LLORAN ISAF Llansilin, Oswestry, Shrops, SY10 7QX

Pat Jackson
Tel:-(069170) 253
Open all year
SC £65-£120
    Sleeps 5

Beautiful detached bungalow on a farm in its own valley. Enclosed garden with barbecue, garden furniture. Well equipped kitchen, 3 bedrooms, WC, bathroom. Large lounge, woodburning stove, colour TV, fitted carpets. Wonderful scenery walk and trout fishing. Plenty of tourist attractions. Easy access for touring North & Mid Wales. Beautiful even in winter. Linen hire available. OS Ref WN 183278

Shropshire Trout Farm.

G. R. J. Sparrow
Tern Fisheries Ltd.
Broomhall Grange, Peatswood
Market Drayton, Shropshire
Tel: Market Drayton 3222

OPENING IN 1988

143

The Sett

Jim and Brenda Grundey have a well established reputation for welcoming visitors to their 130 acre farm and for sharing with them the peace and tranquility of this particularly beautiful part of Shropshire, England's last truly rural country. Their farmhouse accommodation and their enterprising farm trail are both extremely popular whilst their unique children's parties have been widely acclaimed. The Sett is their latest and most innovative venture.

The Sett is an attractive large brick built barn that has been sympathetically converted to provide accommodation of three star hotel standard. Each of the five double rooms and the two bedroomed family suite is equipped for tea and coffee making and have elegant en suite facilities.

Complete comfort has been ensured by selecting the best locally made furnishing and the decor throughout provides ample evidence of the Grundeys' concern for the conservation of the countryside and for the Shropshire way of life.

Both traditional country and healthy eater breakfasts are provided and evening meals are available on request as an alternative to the many and varied eating places in the immediate area. Vegetarians are entirely welcome.

For further information please contact:
Jim and Brenda Grundey, Village Farm, Stanton upon Hine Heath, Shrewsbury, Shropshire SY4 4LR. Tel: 0939 250591

ATTINGHAM PARK

SHREWSBURY SY4 4TP

Splendid mansion and park four miles SE of Shrewsbury on A5. House designed in 1785 for the First Lord Berwick by George Steuart; park landscape designed in 1797 by Humphry Repton; Nash picture gallery; magnificent state rooms; famous painted boudoir; splendid collection of Regency silver; good walks through deer park and grounds.
OS Ref: SJ542093.

The National Trust – Tel: (074377) 203
OPEN: April to September:
Saturday-Wednesday 2.00-5.30 (closed Good Friday).
Bank Holiday Monday 11.30-5.30.
October: Saturday & Sunday 2.00-5.30

Visit our Modern Dairy Farm. Watch the cows being milked. The milk is used to produce our delicious, additive free, Dairy Ice Cream, which you can buy at the shop.

The farm has several interesting Historical features which can be seen on the Farm Walk. These include an 18th Century Windmill and two unique Guillotine Locks situated on a branch of the Shropshire Union Canal.

**Hadley Park Farm,
Telford, Shropshire TF1 4GJ
Tel: Telford 3677**
9 a.m. - 7 p.m.

OPEN:
Shop, Picnic Area and Farm Walk open 10.00 am-6.00 pm all year.

Watch the cows being milked every Saturday, Sunday and all Bank Holidays. Easter — End of October 4.00 pm-5.30 pm.

ADMISSION: FREE

FACILITIES:
Car Parking,
Picnic Area,
Refreshments

HADLEY PARK FARM

STAFFORDSHIRE'S VALE of TRENT

33

STAFFORDSHIRE'S VALE OF TRENT

Drained by the River Trent and its tributaries, it is not difficult to understand why the Vale of Trent is becoming a popular place. Set in the Heart of England and easily accessible by road and rail, vast areas of the Vales still remain unspoilt by development and wealthy in local traditions. Twisting lanes, hawthorn hedges and forest separating undulating pastures are typical.

At its heart the Vale is dominated by the remains of the ancient hunting forests of Needwood, still heavily wooded, and Cannock Chase, a lovely area of forest where people can roam over thousands of acres. In addition to the forest there are many delights such as the picturesque villages of Abbots Bromley and Newborough still performing ancient ceremonies. Blithfield Reservoir, one of England's most important gathering points for migratory birds, the crumbling fortresses of Chartley and Tutbury Castles where Mary Queen of Scots was held, and the unique three spires of Lichfield Cathedral.

In the north the scenery changes dramatically as the land rises to form the southern extremity of the Pennines. Here the Dove forms a gorge-like valley well known to anglers through its association with Izaak Walton, whilst the heavily wooded Churnet Valley displaying its Rhineland quality plays host to Alton Towers, Europe's most popular theme park.

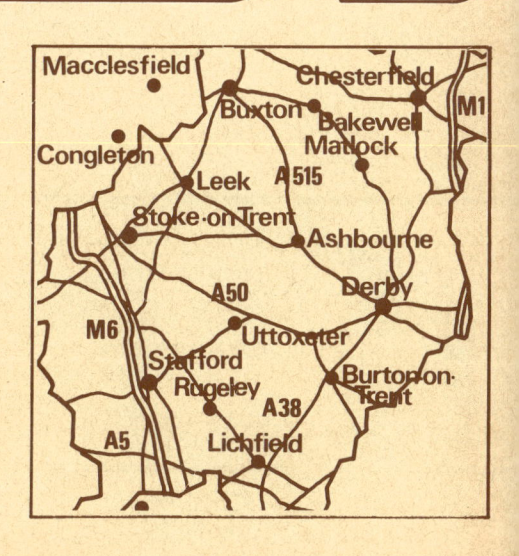

GROUP CONTACT:
Mrs. D. E. Moreton (09074) 2330

WESTON PARK

The 17th Century House is the Family Seat of the Earls of Bradford

SITUATED IN NEARLY 1,000 ACRES OF WOODED PARKLAND ON THE SHROPSHIRE/STAFFORDSHIRE BORDER

Woodland Adventure Playground, Aquarium, Studio Pottery, Museum of Country Bygones, Miniature Railway, Pets Corner, Architectural and Nature Trails,
Special Event Programme throughout the Season.
Licensed Bar and Restaurant.

Weston Park is at Weston-under-Lizard on the A5, 7 miles west of Junction 12 on M6 or 3 miles north of Junction 3 on M54.

For details of Opening Times:
Tel: (095276) 207 or write Weston Park, Shifnal, Shropshire TF11 8LE

AEROSPACE MUSEUM
ONE OF THE ROYAL AIR FORCE MUSEUMS

A major collection of over 60 historic aircraft on an active airfield site,.
Airliners, bombers, fighters, missles and aero engines.
Souvenir shop - cafe - picnic areas.
British Airways Hall and model displays.
GATES OPEN DAILY FROM 10 am to 4 pm
Closed at weekends from December to February.
ADMISSION: £2.50 Adults, £1 Children and Senior Citizens. Group rate available.
On A41 North West of Wolverhampton
JUNCTION 3 OFF M54

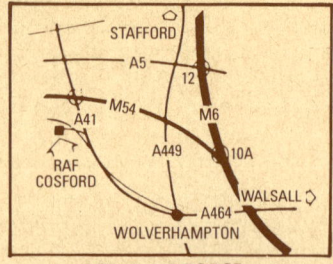

ROYAL AIR FORCE
COSFORD
WOLVERHAMPTON, WEST MIDLANDS WV7 3EX
Telephone: (090 722) 4872/4112

Vale of Trent, Staffordshire ENGLAND

(FH) FORESTSIDE FARM Marchington, nr Uttoxeter, Staffs, ST14 8NA

Janette & Chris Prince
Tel:-(0283) 820353
Closed Xmas and New Year
B&B   £8-£9   Listed
Under 3yrs £3
Under 13yrs
£5
Sleeps 6

A warm friendly welcome awaits you at Forestside Farm, which overlooks Marchington and offers 1 double/family room with handbasin and a twin-bedded room with bathroom and toilet adjacent. There is a comfortable lounge/dining room with colour TV and a large garden in which to relax, making it an ideal choice for a leisurely country holiday. Convenient for all of Staffordshire's many attractions. OS Ref SK 130 292

(FH) DAIRY HOUSE FARM Alkmonton, Longford, Derby, DE6 3DG

Andy & Dorothy Harris
Tel:-(033523) 359
Closed Xmas
B&B   £10
EM   £6
Sleeps 13

Dairy Farm, old farmhouse, oak-beamed rooms, comfortably furnished, spacious lounges, inglenook fireplace, colour TV, beautiful dining room. Washbasins in rooms. Tea making facilities, bathrooms, shower, toilets. Visitors can walk the farm and sit in pleasant garden. Enjoy good cooking. Home produced. Residential license. Gateway to Peak District, Dovedale, Chatsworth, Haddon, Hardwick, Keddleston, Sudbury Halls, Alton Towers. RAC/AA Listed. OS Ref SK 200400

(FH) MARSH FARM Abbots Bromley, Rugeley, Staffordshire, WS15 3EJ

Mary Hollins
Tel:-(0283) 840323
Closed Xmas and New Year
B&B   £8.50-£9.50
EM   £5
Sleeps 5

Now a stock rearing farm for the nearby dairy farm. Mary Hollins will make you welcome at this spacious farmhouse. 1m north of Abbots Bromley. While fully modernised, the farmhouse has retained its character, with large attractive dining room, comfortable lounge with TV, video and log fire. Traditional English food, Egon Ronay approved for the past Six years in the "Just a Bite Guide". OS Ref SK 261069

(FH) THE HOME FARM Woodseaves, Stafford, ST20 0LH

Mrs Joan Brown
Tel:-(078 574) 252
Open all year
B&B   £9.50-£12
EM   From £5
Sleeps 6
(4)

168 acre arable/dairy working farm (The Greenmarsh Herd Pedigree Friesians)on the edge of Woodseaves village in beautiful countryside, 6 miles junction 14, M6. Three storey house, very comfortable, tastefully decorated throughout, oak beams, inglenook fireplaces. Good home cooking, mostly local/home produce. Lovely gardens, grass tennis court. Convenient for Potteries, Severn valley, and Ironbridge museums. Two twin, 1 double/family rooms. OS Ref SJ 795258

(FH) FISHER'S PIT FARM Abbots Bromley, Rugeley, Staffs, WS15 3AL

Sylvia & Roy Aitkenhead
Tel:-(0283) 840204
Closed Xmas
B&B   £10-£11
EM   £5-£6
Sleeps 14
(5)

You are cordially invited to spend a pleasant, warm, friendly stay with Sylvia and Roy Aitkenhead. Picturesque Georgian farmhouse stands amid a 63 acre stock rearing farm in the heart of the Vale of Trent. Surrounded by scenic Staffordshire views. Ideally situated for Alton Towers, Stoke-on-Trent, Wedgewood, Bass Museum and Shugborough Hall. Good home cooking. 3 double or family rooms, 1 twin bed and 1 single. OS Ref SK 244097

(FH) POPINJAY FARM Stafford Road, Uttoxeter, Staffordshire, ST14 8QA

Kathleen Stockton
Tel:-(0889) 566082
Closed Xmas and New Year
B&B   £8.50-£10   Listed
EM   £4.50
Sleeps 4

Popinjay Farm is a small stock rearing farm overlooking a pleasant valley. The situation is one mile west of Uttoxeter on the Stafford Road making it within easy reach of Alton Towers, Pottery museums, Manifold Churnet and Dove Valleys. The 18th Century farmhouse has been pleasantly decorated and furnished but still retains its charm. All bedrooms have washbasins. Excellent traditional farmhouse cooking. OS Ref SK 075323

147

Stafford Art Gallery and Craft Shop

A major gallery for the visual arts with over 20 temporary exhibitions of painting, craft and photography throughout the year.

Craft Shop

The largest contemporary craft venue in the Midlands stocking work by over 150 British craftsmen displayed in an attractive gallery 'selected for quality' by the Crafts Council - jewellery, glass, ceramics, wood, toys and textiles and a distinctive range of cards and giftwrap.

Open all year: Tuesday-Friday 10 a.m.-5 p.m. and Saturday 10 a.m.-4 p.m.
Admission Free
Telephone or write for details of current exhibitions and events.

STAFFORD ART GALLERY
Lichfield Road, Stafford. Telephone: (0785) 57303

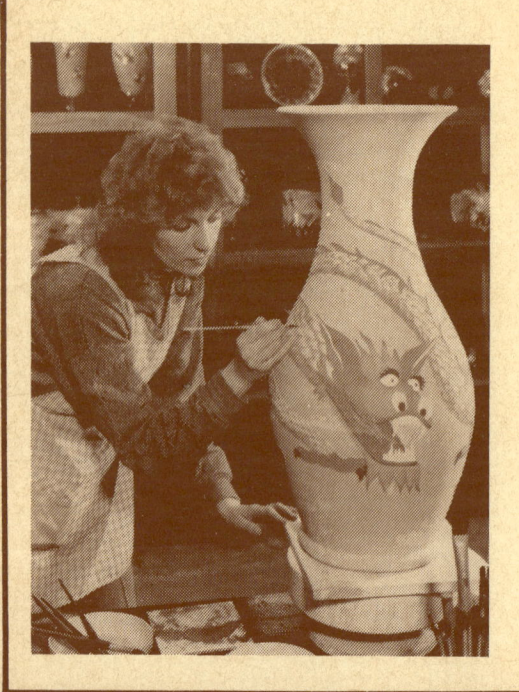

MOORCROFT POTTERY

Made by hand in England for collectors around the world

Visit the Bottle Oven where William Moorcroft created his world famous pottery ● See a pictorial display of the making of Moorcroft ● Buy an example from the large assortment of almost perfect pieces of pottery in the factory shop ● Free admission and car park ● Open Mon-Fri. 10 am-5 pm, Sat 9.30 am-12.30 pm ● Coach parties welcome ● Factory tours by arrangement ● Directions: from M6 junction 15 or 16 take A500 then A53 for 1½ miles, through traffic lights (A50) and, after Cobridge Park, keep straight on into Sandbach Road.

W. MOORCROFT LTD.
Sandbach Road, Cobridge, Stoke-on-Trent
Tel. Stoke-on-Trent 24323.

Vale of Trent, Staffordshire ENGLAND

(FH) FIELD FARM   Field, Uttoxeter, Staffs, ST14 8SG

Sally Williams
Tel:-(088 925) 202
Closed Xmas
B&B   £8.50-£12   Listed
Sleeps 6

The centrally heated 17th Century oak beamed farmhouse is situated on a dairy farm in open countryside 4 miles from Uttoxeter. The dining room features an inglenook fireplace and there is a cosy oak beamed sitting room with colour TV for guests use. All bedrooms overlook the large picturesque garden. Convenient for Alton Towers and all of Staffordshire's many attractions. OS Ref SK 027 335

(FH) CHANTRY VIEW FARM   Moat Lane, Newborough, Nr Burton on Trent, Staffs, DE13 8SS

Brenda Skipper
Tel:-(0283 75) 200
Closed Xmas
B&B   £8.50-£10   Listed
EM   £5
Sleeps 6

Small farm breeding pedigree Simmental cattle. Situated between Lichfield, Uttoxeter and Burton-on-Trent in a quiet country lane. The farmhouse is tastefully decorated with central heating and beautifully positioned, with exceptional views. Every modern convenience. Guest TV lounge. Guests bathroom. Convenient for Alton Towers, Shugborough, Bass Museum, Tutbury Glass and Staffordshire's many other attractions. Evening meal by arrangement. AA Inspected. OS Ref SK 1325

(FH) STANTON BARNS FARM   Stanton-by-Bridge, Derby, DE7 1HX

Julie Tavener
Tel:-(03316) 2346
Open all year
B&B   £8-£9   Listed
Sleeps 6

Picturesque stone farmhouse in secluded position on 42 acre dairy farm with land bordering the River Trent. Within 20 minutes of the East Midlands airport and M1. Riding and fishing are available. A convenient centre for visiting the Peak District and Charnwood Forest, Melbourne, Sudbury and Kedleston Halls, Calke Abbey and the Castle Donington race track. Evening meals available locally. Pets by arrangement. OS Ref SK 376275

(FH) CLAREMONT FARM   Alkmonton Lane, Boylestone, Derby, DE6 5AD

Christine Ferry
Tel:-(033 523) 616
Open all year
B&B   £9-£10   Listed
EM   £5.50
Sleeps 6
TV   £1.50

10 acre smallholding set in quiet countryside in the village of Boylestone 1 mile off A515 Ashbourne - Sudbury road. Comfortable, spacious accommodation within easy reach of the Peak District, Alton Towers, Donnington Park and the many stately homes of Derbyshire and Staffordshire. Optional evening meal available. Ponies and farm animals of particular interest to children. Dogs by arrangement. OS Ref SK 184359

(FH) MOORS FM & COUNTRY RESTAURANT   Chillington Lane, Codsall, Nr Wolverhampton, Staffordshire

Mrs D E Moreton
Tel:-(09074) 2330
Open all year
B&B   £11.50-£16
EM   From £6.50
Sleeps 16

We await the pleasure of your company at our livestock farm near Codsall on beautiful Shropshire border. First class home cooking using own produce. Restaurant welcomes non-residents. Oak beamed bar, dining room. TV lounge, 6 comfortable bedrooms with washbasins, tea/coffee facilities. Fire certificate. AA/RAC/British Relais Routiers approved. Ironbridge, Cosford Aerospace, stately homes nearby. Children over 4 welcome. Special 3-day Christmas Break. OS Ref SJ 864046

(FH) SOMERSAL FARM   Somersal Herbert, Doveridge, Derby

Bridget Noakes
Tel:-(028378) 265
Open all year
B&B   £9-£12   Applied
EM   From £6
Sleeps 6

Large Victorian farmhouse situated on the edge of the picturesque village of Somersal Herbert, near Staffordshire/Derbyshire border, 1½ mile from A50. Surrounding footpaths offer an abundance of country walks, a badger set is situated on farm, washbasins in rooms, guests' bathroom, guests shower room, lounge, colour TV, convenient for Alton Towers, Sudbury Hall, Dovedale, etc. OS Ref SK 354 135

FARM HOLIDAY BUREAU

149

(FH) MANOR FARM Kingstone, Uttoxeter, Staffordshire, ST14 8QH

Susan Stubbs
Tel:-(088 921) 391
Open all year
B&B   £8.50-£9.50   Listed
EM   £4
      Sleeps 6
Van   £1.60-£2

This 16th Century black and white farmhouse, situated in the village of Kingstone, 4 miles west of Uttoxeter, offers homely accommodation in half timbered rooms with log fires, on 40 acre farm. Within easy reach of Alton Towers, the Potteries and Uttoxeter racecourse. OS Ref SK 060296

(FH) DOMVILLES FARM Barthomley Road, Audley, Stoke-on-Trent, ST7 8HT

Eileen Oulton
Tel:-(0782) 720378
Closed Xmas
B&B   From £9   Listed
EM   £5
      Sleeps 6

Oak beamed staircase farmhouse set in large landscaped gardens, on a 120 acre dairy farm close to picturesque Barthomley. Ideal holiday for a family. Lots of animals to see, pigs, sheep, geese, tropical birds & rabbits. Games room, snooker table & large lawns for children to play on. Close to Alton Towers, Bridgmere Garden World & the Potteries. 3 mins from M6, J16. OS Ref SJ 1185177

(FH) OFFLEY GROVE FARM Adbaston, Nr Eccleshall, Stafford, ST20 0QB

Frazer & Margaret Hiscoe-James
Tel:-(0785 79) 205
Closed Xmas-New Year
B&B   £9-£10   Listed
EM   £3.75
      Sleeps 6
Tent £2
Van   £2.50-£4; Max 5

On the Staffordsire/Shropshire borders 5 miles from Newport & Eccleshall, within easy reach of M6, M54 & the potteries. 184 acres of beautiful farmland.Fishing, riding, canal boat trips within easy reach of farm which provides all home comforts, guest lounge, colour TV & excellent home cooking! We are now milking sheep & making cheese & yoghurt on the farm. OS Ref SJ 760271

(SC) ELMHURST DAIRY FARM Curborough Hall Farm, Lichfield, Staffs, WS13 8ES

Mrs Joan Hollinshead
Tel:-(0543) 262595
Open all year
SC   £65-£125
      Sleeps 4-6

Tastefully converted Drift House and Stable into 3 cottages each sleeping up to 6 persons. Approximately 2½ miles from the city of Lichfield in the unspoilt village of Elmhurst. An ideal base for visiting the Heart of the Midlands. Wide selection of pubs and restaurants within five miles. Something to suit all tastes. Brochure on request. OS Ref SK 120120

(SC) NOTHILL COTTAGES Nothill Farm, Crakemarsh, Nr. Uttoxeter, Staffs, ST14 5AT

Mary Brookes
Tel:-(088926) 210
Open all year
SC   £45-£135
      Sleeps 6

Adjoining farm cottages each sleeping 6 + cot. Fenced garden in pleasant country setting but convenient for Potteries, Peak District and Alton Towers. 3 bedrooms and bathroom. Downstairs toilet and cloakroom. Kitchen, lounge with colour TV. Open fire and storage heaters. Linen, towels, included in price. Logs and electricity extra. OS Ref SK 082475

(SC) GORTON LODGE FARM Farewell Manor, Farewell, Nr Lichfield, Staffordshire

Mrs L M Hammersley
Tel:-(05436) 2248
Open all year
SC   £70-£100
      Sleeps 5/7

A working farm with attractive ivy-covered farmhouse of great age. Sheep and beef are reared here in this beautiful peaceful part of Staffordshire. Large garden. An excellent touring base near to Lichfield and Cannock Chase. Lots of places to visit and personally recommended restaurants and pubs for people who like to eat out. OS Ref SK 083117

Vale of Trent, Staffordshire ENGLAND

(SC) PRIORY FARM FISHING HOUSE Priory Farm, Blithbury, Nr Rugeley, Staffordshire, WS15 3JA

John & Barbara Myatt
Tel:-(088922) 269
Open all year
SC   £45-£70
      Sleeps 4

Converted 18th Century fishing house overlooking River Blythe offering unique accommodation for 2/4 persons on secluded dairy farm. Ideal base for lovers of the countryside and wildlife. Close to Abbots Bromley, Blithfield Reservoir, Cannock Chase, Lichfield and Alton Towers. Comfortably and tastefully furnished accommodation includes large bed-sitting room with colour TV, modern kitchen and shower-room. OS Ref SK 091209

(SC) FISHER'S PIT FARM Abbots Bromley, Rugeley, Staffs, WS15 3AL

Sylvia & Roy Aitkenhead
Tel:-(0283) 840204
Open all year
B&B   £10-£12
EM   £5-£6
      Sleeps 10
SC   £80-£130
      Sleeps 4/5

63 acre working farm in the heart of the Vale of Trent surrounded by scenic Staffordshire views. Situated on the B5234, 1m from Abbots Bromley Village and Blithfield Reservoir. Also SC cottage in newly converted stable, in farm grounds. Sleeps 5/6 persons. Every facility provided. OS Ref SK 244097

(SC) ASHMORE BROOK COTTAGE Cross-in-Hand Lane, Lichfield, Staffs, WS13 8DY

Helen Broome
Tel:-(0543) 255753
Open all year
SC   £75-£110
      Sleeps 6

Close to Lichfield City, birthplace of Dr. Johnson, with good selection of shops and restaurants. In easy reach of Derbyshire Dales, many stately homes and museums, NEC and all Midlands attractions. Three bedrooms sleeping 6, with linen provided. Fully equipped kitchen, dining room, lounge with television, bathroom and cloakroom. Electricity by meter. Pets by arrangement. OS Ref SK 096110

(TV) SILVERTREES CARAVAN PARK Stafford Brook Road, Rugeley, Staffs, WS15 2TX

Mrs Susan Cooper
Tel:-(08894) 2185
Open Apr-Oct
SC   £95-£150
      Sleeps 2-4
Van   £3.50-£4.50
      Max 30
      vans

Eight luxury caravans with colour TV, shower, WC, etc. Set in the heart of Cannock Chase on a beautiful 30 acre quiet and peaceful park. Facilities include swimming pool, tennis court, games room with table tennis/football, video games, shop, laundry, play area, showers etc. The park also welcomes touring and motor caravans. OS Ref SK 015172

34 PEAK & MOORLANDS
Staffordshire / Derbyshire

PEAK & MOORLANDS OF STAFFORDSHIRE/DERBYSHIRE

The Peak District offers some of the most varied and lovely upland scenery in Britain and is remarkably unspoiled considering how accessible the area is. Limestone plateaux where a web of drystone wall divides meadows and pastures; high gritstone moorlands covered with peat and heather and marked by steep outcrops of rock; and a series of dales where swiftly flowing rivers have carved spectacular steep sided valleys.

The Dove threads a gorge-like valley well known to anglers; the Manifold is an elusive river, disappearing while the many-reservoired Derwent flows majestically down the eastern side of the Peak Park from its source on the high moorlands.

Places to visit include many attractive Peakland villages, some of which have well dressing festivals in spring or summer. There are fine houses and gardens and the many attractions of Matlock Bath are worth visiting, as are the interesting old market towns of Bakewell, Ashbourne and Leek.

Other specialised visits include the Gladstone Pottery Museum and the Wedgewood Visitor Centre in Stoke on Trent. For those interested in our industrial history the area abounds in fascinating sites such as Cromford, home of Arkwright's first cotton mills, James Brindley's mill in Leek, the Abbeydale Industrial Hamlet in Sheffield, the lead mining museum at Matlock Bath. Take a walk or hire a bicycle and ride along the converted railway lines of the Tissington and High Peak Trails, or ride behind a real steam train at Foxfield or Dinting.

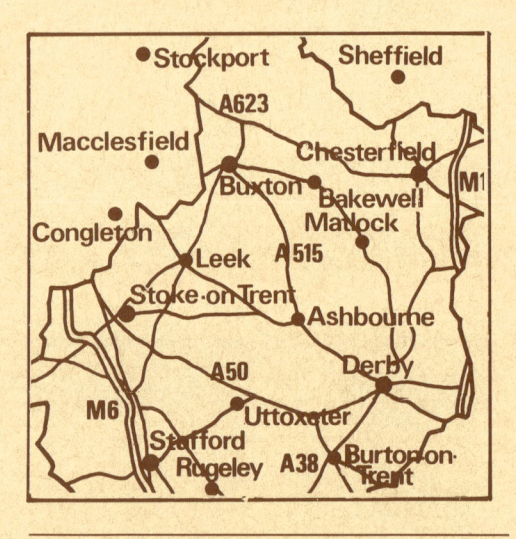

GROUP CONTACTS:
B&B — Angela Whatley (0298) 871175
Self Catering — Christine Pickford (0538) 383035

Peaks & Moorlands, Staffs/Derbyshire ENGLAND

(FH) OLD FURNACE FARM Greendale, Oakamoor, Stoke on Trent, Staffs, ST10 3AP

Maggie Wheeler
Tel:-(0538) 702442
Open all year
B&B   £11-£14
       Sleeps 6
SC   £50-£250
(10)

Farm is situated in unrivalled position at the head of Dimmingsdale Valley. Set in 40 acres of ground amongst hills and woods. Accommodation comprises 3 doubles each with bathroom ensuite. Also situated in the grounds, Spring Cottage and a chalet which are ideal for self-catering holidays. Local attractions include Alton Towers, Dovedale, Peak District, Wedgwood, Royal Dalton. Dogs in SC only. OS Ref SK 042 436

(FH) POOL HALL FARM Bradnop, Nr Leek, Staffs, ST13 7LZ

Barbara Clowes
Tel:-(0538) 382774
Closed Xmas and New Year
B&B   £8.50   Applied
EM   £5
       Sleeps 6

Pool Hall is an 18th Century 85 acre dairy farm 1½ m east of Leek within easy reach of Dovedale, and Manifold Valley, potteries, museums and Alton Towers. The bedrooms have washbasins, tea/coffee making facilities, guests bathroom with shower. Comfortable lounge, good home cooking and warm welcome.

(FH) HOLLINHURST FARM Park Lane, Endon, Stoke on Trent, Staffs, ST9 9JB

Sandra Clowes
Tel:-(0782) 502633
Open Easter-Oct
B&B   £8   Applied
EM   £6.50
       Sleeps 4/6
TV   £1

17th century farmhouse on working stock farm, easy reach to Potteries, Peak District, Alton Towers. Panoramic views, walking and touring. 2 bedrooms, shower room and w.c. T.V. lounge, dining area. Caravan site.

FARM HOLIDAY BUREAU

(CH) HENMORE GRANGE FARM Hopton, Carsington, Wirksworth, Derby, DE4 4JY

John & Elizabeth Brassington
Tel:-(062 985) 420
Open Apr-Dec, New Year
CH   Sleeps 20
B&B   £12-£20
EM   £8.50

28 acre arable farm between Ashbourne and Matlock, ideal for touring and walking in the National Park and Alton Towers. There are 7 bedrooms with private bathrooms and 3 with H/C. All have tea/coffee making facilities. Half price for children up to 16 when sharing parents room. Awarded Certificate Of Merit in "Come to Britain" BTA award. Good old fashioned country hospitality! OS Ref SK 262533

(FH) GLENWOOD HOUSE FARM Ipstones, Stoke-on-Trent, Staffs, ST10 2JP

Keith & Joyce Brindley
Tel:-(053871) 294
Open Mar-Nov and New Year
B&B   £9.50-£10.50
EM   £6.50
       Sleeps 6

This is a 58 acre working farm, where beef cattle are raised. The stone built farmhouse is very comfortable with central heating, washbasins and guests' own bathroom. One twin, 1 double, 1 family. We specialise in fresh farm produce and offer home comforts and country hospitality. Near to Alton Towers, the Peak Park and Wedgwood. Featured on TV "Wish You Were Here". OS Ref SK 005488

(FH) BEECHENHILL FARM Ilam, Ashbourne, Derbys, DE6 2BD

Sue & Terry Prince
Tel:-(033527) 274
Closed Xmas
B&B   £9-£10
       Sleeps 5

Situated in Dovedale between the pretty villages of Ilam and Alstonefield, our southfacing, traditional farmhouse (Grade II Listed) has central heating and offers family and double rooms with hot drink facilities. Friendly atmosphere, Lounge/dining room with TV. After fresh healthy breakfast, explore our 92 acre dairy farm with puzzling archaeological remains, many glorious walks lead from our door. OS Ref SK 149524

(CH) FOURWAYS DINER MOTEL Cleulow Cross, Wincle, Nr Macclesfield, Cheshire, SK11 0QL

Angela Webb
Tel:-(02607) 228
Open all year
CH Sleeps 30
B&B £15-£20
EM £5
SC £90-£180
TV £3/person

The Fourways Diner is a family owned motel, situated in the Peak National Park on the A54 Congleton-Buxton road, set high on the Southern Peaks with fine open views of the Dane Valley and Roaches. All rooms have television, tea making facilities and own bathroom. Single, twin, double and family rooms. Self catering units available - 2/6 persons. AA, RAC listed. Large garden for guests. OS Ref SK 869567

(FH) LITTLE PARK FARM Okeover, Ashbourne, Derbys, DE6 2BR

Joan Harrison
Tel:-(033 529) 341
Open Easter-Oct
B&B £8.50-£9
EM £4.50
Sleeps 6
(2)

Situated in the beautiful Dove Valley this 123 acre dairy farm offers delightful walks and an abundance of wildlife. Nearby Alton Towers, pony trekking and bike hire. The 300 year old listed farmhouse features oak beams and is tastefully furnished. All bedrooms have washbasins, comfortable visitors lounge, TV, central heating. Good wholesome farmhouse food served and a warm welcome. OS Ref SK 150480

(FH) LYDGATE FARM Aldwark, Grange Mill, Wirksworth, Derby, DE4 4HW

Joy Lomas
Tel:-(062 985) 250
Closed Xmas-New Year
B&B £8.50-£10 Listed
EM £6
Sleeps 6

A 250 acre dairy farm with a fine listed 17th Century house surrounded by the Derbyshire Dales. Situated in a small peaceful hamlet within the Peak National Park, a warm welcome awaits you with a high standard of accommodation and good food. Ideally situated for all that Derbyshire has to offer. One family room, 1 double, 1 twin. Two bathrooms. OS Ref SK 220570

(FH) HIGH HOUSE Foxlow Farm, Harpur Hill, Buxton, Derbys, SK17 9LE

Phil & Tina Heathcote
Tel:-(0298) 4219
Closed Xmas-New Year
B&B £10 Listed
EM £7
Sleeps 6

A 270 acre dairy farm, high on the outskirts of Buxton. The spacious farmhouse is traditionally furnished and has panoramic views over the town, and surrounding hills. 10 minutes from Buxton centre and with good walks in every direction. Chatsworth and National Trust properties nearby. Winner of the Golden Spoon Cookery Award (1987). Farmhouse holidays also gourmet weekends. (We love cooking!!) OS Ref SK 065715

(CH) THE HALL Great Hucklow, Tideswell, Buxton, Derbys, SK17 8RG

Angela Whatley
Tel:-(0298) 871175
Open Mar-Nov
CH Sleeps 6 Listed
B&B £10-£12
EM £7.50
(5)

A warm welcome is extended to share our unusual 17th Century country home for a tranquil holiday. Peaceful, south facing and surrounded by gardens and fields, the house is an excellent base from which to explore the area. Interesting menus combined with quality home cooking are provided for the six guests who can be accommodated in our spacious comfortable rooms. OS Ref SK 779179

(FH) HOLLY DALE FARM Bradnop, Nr Leek, Staffs, ST13 7NF

Michael & Dianne Needham
Tel:-(0538) 383022
Open Apr-Oct
B&B £7.50-£8 Listed
Sleeps 3

Holly Dale is a 72 acre dairy farm with a pedigree Ayrshire herd situated just off the A523 Leek to Ashbourne road 2 miles out of Leek. Holly Dale is ideally situated for Leek, the Potteries, Alton Towers and the surrounding countryside. The stone built farmhouse has 2 rooms to let, 1 double and 1 single, both with washbasins, plus a spacious lounge. OS Ref SK 019557

Peaks & Moorlands, Staffs/Derbyshire ENGLAND

(FH) HIGHFIELD FARM Ashford-in-the-Water, Bakewell, Derbys, DE4 1QN

Jean Brocklehurst
Tel:-(062981) 2482
Open Apr-Oct
B&B £10-£11   Listed
Sleeps 4

This traditional farmhouse with wonderful views is situated on the edge of the lovely village of Ashford. Beautiful Monsal Dale only 1 mile. Chatsworth House and Haddon Hall 4 miles. Spacious bedrooms with washbasins, tea making facilities, colour TV and shaver points. Beautifully appointed sitting room with TV. Sun lounge. A very high standard of accommodation is offered in a most peaceful setting. OS Ref SK 190690

(FH) LEY FIELDS FARM Leek Rd, Cheadle, Stoke-on-Trent, Staffs, ST10 2EF

Robert & Kathryn Clowes
Tel:-(0538) 752875
Open Easter-Oct
B&B £9-£10   Applied
EM £6
Sleeps 8

Listed Georgian farmhouse of character with large garden situated in beautiful countryside. 6m Alton Towers and close to Pottery Towns and the Peak District. Spacious, traditionally furnished accommodation includes visitors lounge with TV and separate dining room. Family and double rooms with washbasins and hot drink facilities, 2 visitors bathrooms, centrally heated throughout. Excellent home cooking and a warm welcome is assured. OS Ref SJ 994456

(FH) LANE HEAD FARM Holehouse Lane, Endon, Stoke-on-Trent, Staffs, ST9 9AF

Marjorie & Philip Brown
Tel:-(0782) 503096
Open Easter-Oct
B&B £7.50-£8.50   Applied
Sleeps 4

Beamed farmhouse on working dairy farm. Ideally situated for the Potteries, touring the Peaks, Moorlands, Alton Towers and the Stately Homes of the area. OS Ref 915551

(FH) BROOK HOUSE FARM Cheddleton, Leek, Staffs, ST13 7DF

Stan & Elizabeth Winterton
Tel:-(0538) 360296
Closed Xmas-New Year
B&B £9-£10
EM £5
Sleeps 9

A 180 acre dairy farm situated in a picturesque valley with scenic views and many pleasant walks. Convenient for Alton Towers, Peak District & pottery museums. 2 spacious family rooms with en suite facilities in a tastefully converted cowshed. 3 rooms in the farmhouse with guests bathroom. Tea/coffee facilities in all rooms. The attractive lounge has colour TV & patio doors. A warm welcome & good food a speciality OS Ref SJ 962512

(FH) PEAR TREE FARM Lea Bridge, Nr Matlock, Derbys

Dorothy Swindell
Tel:-(062984) 423
Open Mar-Nov
B&B £7.50-£8.50   Listed
EM £4-£5
TV
Sleeps

Early 18th Century stone farmhouse, once belonged to Florence Nightingale, standing in 70 acres of old pasture and woodland, the farming is mixed mainly sheep. Many and varied interests nearby from birdwatching to stately homes, trips on Cromford Canal, historic steam engine. Trout and coarse fishing in season. Pony rides free for children on farm. OS Ref SK 320560

(FH) FERNYDALE FARM Earl Sterndale, Buxton, Derbys, SK17 0BS

Mrs Joan Nadin
Tel:-(029883) 236
Open Easter-Oct
B&B £10-£12
EM £6
Sleeps 4

A 120 acre dairy farm in the village of Earl Sterndale, 5m from Buxton. Ideally situated for all the Dales & stately homes. We offer a high standard of accommodation, food & personal service, with warm & friendly hospitality made possible by our small size. Bedrooms have CH, washbasins, tea/coffee making facilities, shaver points. Lounge with colour TV. Separate dining room.

155

Do china in a day

*This special version of the Willow Pattern plate was designed and produced by the Gladstone Pottery Museum, where you can find out all about its hidden meanings.

*A*bove is a traditional Willow Pattern design.
 Or so it seems.
 In fact, it's actually a pictorial history of the world centre of "china," Stoke-on-Trent.* An area which, like the design, has more to it than meets the eye.
 Not only potteries galore (Wedgwood and Royal Doulton to name just two). But also gardens landscaped by Capability Brown and beautiful Victorian parks.
 Award-winning museums like the City Museum & Art Gallery and the unique Chatterley Whitfield Mining Museum.
 Or the delights of Europe's premier leisure park — Alton Towers.
 What's more, there are fast motorway and rail links with most English cities.
 So you really could do "china" in a day if you wanted.
 However, seeing all Stoke-on-Trent has to offer will take a little longer.

STOKE·ON·TRENT
THE CITY THAT FIRES THE IMAGINATION

For further information contact or visit the Tourist Information Centre, 1 Glebe Street, Stoke-on-Trent, ST4 1HP. Telephone: (0782) 411222

Peaks & Moorlands, Staffs/Derbyshire ENGLAND

(FH) **WINDMILL FARM** Biggin Lane, Hulland Ward, Derby, DE6 3FN

Mrs Muriel Bennett
Tel:-(0335) 70216
Open Easter-Sep
B&B   £9.50-£10   Applied
EM   £5.50
Sleeps 6
(2)

Situated in a landscape area with lovely views, a mixed working farm of 23 acres, including woodland with pond for fishing. A high standard of accommodation is offered with fresh home cooking. Twin and family room. Comfortable lounge with TV and CH. Excellent walking area, within easy reach of Peak District, Alton Towers, Chatsworth and Haddon Halls. OS Ref SK 267 473

(FH) **BANK END FARM MOTEL** Leek Old Road, Longsdon, Stoke-on-Trent, Staffs

Barbara Robinson
Tel:-(0538) 383638
Closed Xmas
B&B   £11-£17
EM   £5-£8
Sleeps 19
Van   £3

Bank End Farm Motel is a 62 acre livestock farm, situated 2m SW of Leek on the A53, enjoying extensive views, this 16th Century farm offers trout and coarse fishing, swimming in our indoor pool and a games room. All rooms en suite with colour TV. Residents lounge, restaurant & bar. OS Ref SJ 950540

(FH) **CLOUD HOUSE FARM** Cloudside, Congleton, Cheshire, CW12 3QF

Alec & Ruth Needham
Tel:-(02606) 272
Open Mar-Dec
B&B   £10
EM   £6
Sleeps 4

1612 Manor House, being stone built with half timbered interior walls. A quiet peaceful situation, nestling under the "Cloud", on the edge of the Peak District, Cheshire Plain and Potteries. The large family rooms are comfortable and tastefully furnished on this 120 acre dairy farm. Guests are ensured of a warm welcome in this family home. OS Ref SK 913639

(FH) **WEAVER FARM** Waterhouses, Stoke on Trent, Staffs, ST10 3HE

Kath Watson
Tel:-(0538) 702271
Open all year
B&B   £8-£10
EM   £4
Sleeps 14

A warm welcome awaits you at Weaver Farm, stone built, situated on the Weaver Hills, magnificent views over 5 counties. Easy access to Alton Towers, Manifold Valley, Dovedale, Peak District. All bedrooms have washbasins. Comfortable TV lounge. Good wholesome farmhouse cooking. Fire Certificate. Try your hand at spinning and weaving wool sheared from sheep reared on Weaver Farm. OS Ref SK 101467

(SC) **LIMESTONE VIEW FARM** Stoney Lane, Cauldon, Nr Waterhouses, Stoke on Trent, Staffs ST10 3JP

Wendy Webster
Tel:-(05386) 288
Open all year
SC   £50-£90
Sleeps 6

Staffordshire moorlands working dairy farm. Self contained cottage adjoining farmhouse. Overlooking open fields and away from main roads. Sleeps 6. Open fire giving full central heating. Close to Manifold valley, Dovedale and beautiful Peak District scenery. Local country pubs, market towns of Ashbourne, Leek and Uttoxeter. Potteries 15 miles, Alton Towers 2 miles. Ideal walking, touring, cycling, bird watching. OS Ref SK 064490

(SC) **PARK VIEW FARM** Stoney Lane, Cauldon, Nr Waterhouses, Stoke-on-Trent, Staffs ST10 3EP

Nancy Burndred
Tel:-(05386) 233
Open all year
SC   £70-£120
Sleeps 6
Van   £1.50/night

Self-contained cottage adjoining farmhouse on dairy/sheep farm centrally situated for Manifold and Churnet Valleys, Dovedale, Alton Towers and Pottery Museums. Shops and village inns nearby. Modern kitchen/diner including automatic washer. Lounge with TV, electric or open fire giving full central heating. Safe childrens play area. Parking 2 cars. Coal, electricity and bed linen inclusive. Caravan site. OS Ref SK 065487

157

KNAB HOUSE   Two Dales, Matlock, Derbys, DE4 2FJ

J S Williams
Tel:-(0629) 732367
Open Easter-Oct
SC   £80-£90
Sleeps 6

Impressive stone hall, built over 300 years ago stands in its own grounds surrounded by woodland. Mentioned in "Glover's history of Derbyshire" 1814 and connected with local history. Accommodation is simple but comfortable and includes lounge, kitchen/diner, bathroom and 3 bedrooms. Rough shooting available. OS Ref SK 409302

SHATTON HALL FARM   Bamford, Nr Sheffield, S30 2BG

Angela Kellie
Tel:-(0433) 20635
Open all year
SC   £60-£150
Sleeps 6

Paddock and Orchard cottages are recent farm building conversions with fine views of the Peak District. A centre for walking climbing and riding. Safe play area for children and private terrace and car park for each cottage. Comfortable accommodation for 4 and adequate for 6. Laundry facilities available. Fully equipped kitchen and linen provided. OS Ref SK 188823

GLENWOOD HOUSE FARM   Ipstones, Stoke-on-Trent, Staffs, ST10 2JP

Keith & Joyce Brindley
Tel:-(053871) 294
Closed Dec-Feb but open Xmas- New Year
SC   £80-£100
Sleeps 5/6

Although the address is Stoke-on-Trent, Glenwood is situated 5 miles from the Peak National Park, overlooking the beautiful Churnet Valley, within easy reach of Alton Towers and the pottery museums. This is a 58 acre working farm. A traditional stone farm building has been converted to provide two comfortable units. Games room, tennis court and children's play area. OS Ref SK 005488

CLOUGH HEAD FARM   Crowgutter Farm, Ipstones, Stoke-on-Trent, Staffs, ST10 2ND

Sheila Leeson
Tel:-(053 871) 428
Open all year
SC   £70-£120
Sleeps 5

Part of a working dairy farm, Clough Head is a large sandstone farmhouse, divided into spacious accommodation, completely self-contained. Comfortably furnished with central heating. It is in a quiet secluded spot but only ¼ mile from nearest village with inns and shops. Convenient to Peak District, Potteries and Alton Towers. Two bedrooms. Sleeps 5. OS Ref SK 300400

BEECHENHILL COTTAGE   Beechenhill Farm, Ilam, Ashbourne, Derbys, DE6 2BD

Sue & Terry Prince
Tel:-(033527) 274
Open all year
SC   £65-£115
Sleeps 2

Tiny peaceful stone cottage set in its pretty walled garden, west of Beechenhill Farm, overlooking Manifold Valley in the Peak National Park. Once a stallion pen, the cottage has been beautifully decorated and furnished and now offers a tranquil holiday for 2 people. Explore our 92 acre dairy farm, an ideal centre for walking and touring. Towels, fresh linen and heating are included. OS Ref SK 149824

COTE BANK COTTAGE   Cote Bank Farm, Buxworth, Stockport, Cheshire, SK12 7NP

Pamela Broadhurst
Tel:-(0663) 50566
Open all year
SC   £90-£170
Sleeps 6

18th Century stone cottage, with patio to rear, in secluded farmyard of 150 acre hill farm. Within easy reach of excellent walks and village amenities. Spacious accommodation comprises lounge (with open fire) separate dining room, downstairs toilet, modern kitchen, 1 double, 1 twin-bedded with washbasins, 1 single (bunk-beds available), large bathroom, separate shower, full CH, Bed linen, colour TV, and electricity inclusive. OS Ref SK 029827

Peaks & Moorlands, Staffs/Derbyshire ENGLAND

(SC) MERRYFIELDS FARM   Little Park Farm, Okeover, Ashbourne, Derbys, DE6 2BR

Joan Harrison
Tel:-(033 529) 341
Open Mar-Oct
SC   £60-£110
        Sleeps 6

Merryfields Farm is situated near the village of Kniveton in the beautiful Derbyshire Hills, ideal location for the Derbyshire Dales, Alton Towers and other places of interest nearby. Pleasant walks, bike hire and pony trekking. The farmhouse consists of 2 double, 1 twin bedded rooms. Bathroom, lounge, dining/kitchen. Electric cooker and fridge, calor gas fires. Pleasant garden and car space. OS Ref SK 200499

(SC) LYDGATE FARM COTTAGE   Aldwark, Grangemill, Wirksworth, Derby, DE4 4HW

Mary Lomas
Tel:-(062 985) 250
Open all year
SC   £80-£180
        Sleeps 8

Attractive listed 17th Century cottage, adjoining main farmhouse on working dairy farm, in peaceful hamlet. Ideal base for exploring Derbyshire. Very comfortable, spacious and well-equipped accommodation. 3 bedrooms (1 traditional gallery-type). Cot and high chair available. Log fire, Aga, electric cooker, fridge, washing machine, colour TV, central heating. Fuel, electricity, bed linen, use of facilities at local countryclub inclusive. OS Ref SK 220570

(SC) LOWER BERKHAMSYTCH FARM   Bottom House, Nr Leek, Staffs, ST13 7QP

Alwyn & Edith Mycock
Tel:-(05386) 213
Open all year
SC   £40-£80
        Sleeps 4

Converted farm building adjoining farmhouse on working dairy farm. Private shower room and toilet. Garden sitting area. Situated in the Staffordshire moorlands within 20 minutes drive of Alton Towers, Potteries, Peak District and all the moorlands beauty spots. Restaurant and pubs serving meals within walking distance. OS Ref SJ 308876

(SC) SITTINGLOW FARM   Dove Holes, Nr Buxton, Derbys, SK17 8DA

Ann Buckley
Tel:-(0298) 812271
Open Easter-Oct
SC   £55-£80
        Sleeps 3

Superior self-contained ground level farmhouse extension on 250 acre dairy farm in peaceful surroundings with magnificent views. Fitted carpets and double glazing throughout bedroom sleeps 2 (twin beds) Storage Radiator. Lounge, colour TV, fitted kitchen including fridge freezer. Bathroom including shower. Fixed Electric Fires (50p meter) folding bed available. Easy access from village of Dove Holes. Buxton 4 miles. OS Ref SK 071792

(SC) GATEHAM GRANGE FARM   Alstonefield, Ashbourne, Derbys, DE6 2FT

Robert & Theresa Flower
Tel:-(033527) 349
Open all year
SC   £60-£120
        Sleeps 6
        + cot

Situated 1½m north of Alstonefield, near Manifold Valley and Dovedale. Gateham Grange Working Farm is an ideal base for exploring the Peak National Park. Stay in a self contained cottage, adjoining the farmhouse, with kitchen, bathroom, living room (with sofa-divan and colour TV) and 2 bedrooms. Heated by night storage heaters (included in tariff). Other electricity on a 50p pre-payment meter. Bed linen inclusive. OS Ref SK 115569

(SC) STILE HOUSE FARM   Bradnop, Nr. Leek, Staffs, ST13 7LR

Shirley Plant
Tel:-(0538) 382463
Open Easter-Sep
SC   £95
        Sleeps 7

Imposing farmhouse on working farm with sheep, cattle and pigs which occupies a charming position on the edge of the Peak District National Park. (Leek 2m). Fully modernised, the farmhouse character and appeal has been retained to offer 3 bedrooms supplemented with a lounge/diner, kitchen and bathroom. Ideal location for touring and access to the unlimited beauty spots situated in the Staffordshire - Derbyshire countryside.

159

Discover the Moorlands

Beautiful Unspoilt Countryside.
Ideal for touring and walking. A wide variety of attractions including steam centres, canal boat trips, pony-trekking, craft shops, potteries and Alton Towers.
For more details, contact:
F. H. Rann, 1 Market Place,
Leek, Staffs.
Tel: (0538) 381000

STAFFORDSHIRE MOORLANDS

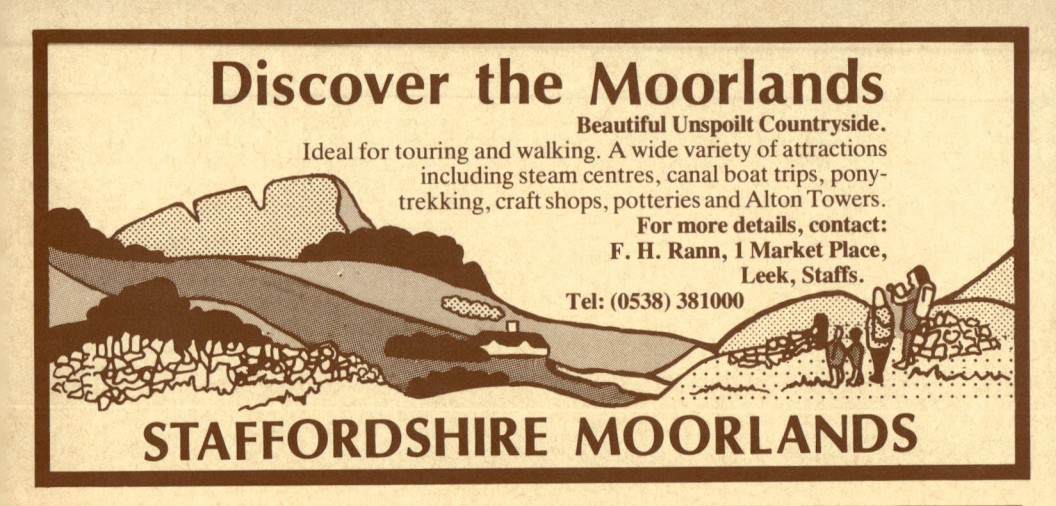

WEDGWOOD VISITOR CENTRE

The Home of Great British China

In our award-winning museum see the first wares Josiah Wedgwood made when he founded his famous firm in 1759, and in the craft centre see potters and decorators applying their skills making the Wedgwood ware of today. You can also see a colour film on Wedgwood History or Craftsmanship, and relax afterwards in the refreshment lounge before treating yourself in the souvenir shop.

You can visit us on your own, or as part of a family group or large party — all are welcome. We're open throughout the year (inc. Bank Holidays) Mon-Fri: 9am-5pm, Sat: 10am to 4pm (closed Christmas week and New Year's Day). There's plenty of free parking and a large coach park too.

Wedgwood
Barlaston, Stoke-on-Trent, ST12 9ES.
Telephone: (0782) 204218/204141

BOOKING TIPS

FARM HOLIDAY BUREAU

A WARM WELCOME

Some farm and country houses in this guide only take six guests — others take more; but wherever you stay, you'll be sure of a warm welcome.

Peaks & Moorlands, Staffs/Derbyshire ENGLAND

(sc) COLD SPRINGS FARM Buxton, Derbys, SK17 6ST

Sydney Booth Millward
Tel:-(0298) 2762
Open all year
SC £63.25-£105
    Sleeps 5-8
Tent £1
Van £1.50-£2.50

Cold Springs Farm is one mile from the elegant 18th Century town centre of Buxton, overlooking the surrounding hills. Choose one of the 5 well equipped and spacious flats, situated on a 100 acre dairy farm, adjacent the farmhouse. Sleeps 4/8 persons. Self contained accommodation includes fitted kitchen, bathroom, pleasant bedrooms and attractive sitting room all carpeted throughout. OS Ref SK 044747

(sc) OLD HOUSE FARM COTTAGE Friden, Hartington, Buxton, Derbyshire, SK17 0DY

Sue Flower
Tel:-062986 268
Open all year
SC £60-£120
    Sleeps 6

Tastefully renovated self-contained cottage adjoining farmhouse on a 400 acre Dairy/Stock farm with opportunity to watch farm activities. Accommodation - 2 large bedrooms with washbasins (1 double, 1 family room with full size bunk & twin beds). Lounge with colour TV, dining/kitchen with electric cooker & fridge. Downstairs bathroom including shower. Fitted carpets, storage heaters. Cot & high chair available. Ample parking. OS Ref SK 169 604

(sc) MEADOWFOLD Fold Farm, Onecote, Nr Leek, Staffs, ST13 7RG

Ann Poyser
Tel:-(05388) 396
Open all year
SC £65-£95

Meadowfold, situated in the village of Onecote, 6 miles from Leek, a stone built bungalow on a dairy farm in the Peak National Park. Accommodation comprises kitchen/diner, lounge, 1 double, 1 twin, bathroom, garden and ample parking. Ideally situated for walking and touring. Nearby beauty spots include Manifold Valley, Dovedale and the Roaches. OS Ref SK 051555

(sc) THE OLD STABLES Northfield Farm, Flash, Nr Buxton, Derbys, SK17 0SW

David & Elizabeth Andrews
Tel:-(0298) 2543
Open all year
SC £50-£160
    Sleeps 2/7

Situated in the highest village in England. We are an ideal centre for outdoor activities or the more leisurely holiday, with many attractions of the Peak Park and Potteries within easy reach. The farm is also BHS, POB approved riding centre. The three centrally heated well appointed flats accomodate 2/7. All facilities. Bed linen and electricity inclusive. Games room and laundry room. OS Ref SK 025672

(sc) PEAR TREE FARM Lea Bridge, Nr Matlock, Derbys

Dorothy Swindell
Tel:-(062984) 423
Open Mar-Nov
SC £65-£115
    Sleeps 4/6

This recently converted holiday accommodation attached to the main farmhouse stands in 70 acres of old pasture and woodland. Within a few miles of Chatsworth and Haddon and many other historical places. Kitchen, diner, lounge. Sleeps 4/6 in one double and 1 twin. Two other rooms available on request. OS Ref SK 320560

(sc) BANK TOP Mill Farm, Waterhouses, Stoke-on-Trent, Staffs, ST10 3HN

Bill & Jean Salt
Tel:-(053 86) 331
Open all year
SC £65-£110
    sleeps 5

Modernised stone cottage in village overlooking dairy and sheep farm and river Hamps. Fishing available. Within walking distance of Manifold Valley.Ideal for visits to Dovedale and Alton Towers. Sleeps 5 and cot. Fully equipped and carpeted. Electric and coal fires. CH. Coal, logs and bed linen provided. Lounge, kitchen/diner with electric cooker, fridge freezer, washing machine, colour TV.

161

LOWE HILL COTTAGES Lowe Hill Farm, Ashbourne Road, Leek, Staffs, ST13 7LY

Jim & Christina Pickford
Tel:-(0538) 383035
Open all year
SC £45-£150
Sleeps 2/8

Three 17th Century bargeman's cottages at Lowe Hill, a 160 acre dairy and stock farm 1 mile from Leek and 8 miles from Alton Towers. Tastefully modernised and retaining olde charm. Cottage No 1 sleeps 6 in 2 bedrooms. Tiny beamed Cottage No 2 sleeps 2 and Cottage No 3 sleeps 7 in 3 bedrooms. Ideal for large groups to use together. Open fires, fuel provided. Also Tel: (05388) 201. OS Ref SJ 996554

FOULD FARM Red Earth Farm, Rudyard, nr Leek, Staffs, ST13 8PT

Gill Heath
Tel:-(0538 33) 639
Open all year
SC £60-£150
Sleeps 9
+ cot

Fould farm is a beautiful old stone farmhouse on a working farm set in lovely countryside. It has been tastefully modernised to provide two spacious, fully equipped, centrally heated cottages. Ideally situated for walking, fishing (locally) and touring. Within easy reach of the Potteries, Alton Towers and the Peak Park. OS Ref 976521

BRAMHOUSE FARM Wetley Rocks, Stoke on Trent, Staffs

Mr Meakin
Tel:-(0782) 550527
Closed Xmas-New Year
SC From £65

Contained within this 110 acre dairy farm is the recently built Lodge House acquired when the farm was expanded. The house is delightfully located in 1 acre of landscaped gardens and lawns. The house, which is centrally heated throughout and tastefully furnished, provides the following accommodation: lounge, dining room, kitchen, laundry, 3 bedrooms, bathroom and double garage. Electricity by meter.

The Chatterley Whitfield Experience

- Underground Tours & Loco Rides
- Steam Winding Engine
- Steam Locomotives
- Pit Ponies
- Museum Shop
- 1930's Canteen

Unforgettable!

For further details contact **Chatterley Whitfield Mining Museum,** Tunstall, Stoke on Trent ST6 8UN. **Tel: (0782) 813337.**

DOVEDALE & Derbyshire Dales

35

DOVEDALE DERBYSHIRE

The countryside round the delightful old market town of Ashbourne, at the southern end of the Pennine Range in Derbyshire, is among the most beautiful in the whole of England. The spectacular scenery of Dovedale and the Manifold Valley, the rolling uplands with their scattered copses and stone walls and isolated traditional farmsteads are well known. Less dramatic but no less rewarding is the tranquil beauty of the unspoilt countryside and villages of the area.

These qualities have long been appreciated and there are strong literary connections. Izaak Walton and Samuel Johnson wrote in praise of the area and George Eliot based her novel Adam Bede on nearby Ellastone where her family lived. Handel wrote part of the Messiah while staying at Calwich Abbey near Ellastone.

Ashbourne itself is a small historic country town of distinction, with shops, hotels, restaurants, a swimming pool and other facilities of a very high quality.

The whole area is crisscrossed with footpaths providing ideal conditions for walking and there are ample facilities for pony trekking and cycle hire.

Within easy access are many well known places of interest, great country mansions, the Blue John mines near Buxton, the fascinating industrial archaeology of Derbyshire and Staffordshire and the varied delights of Alton Towers.

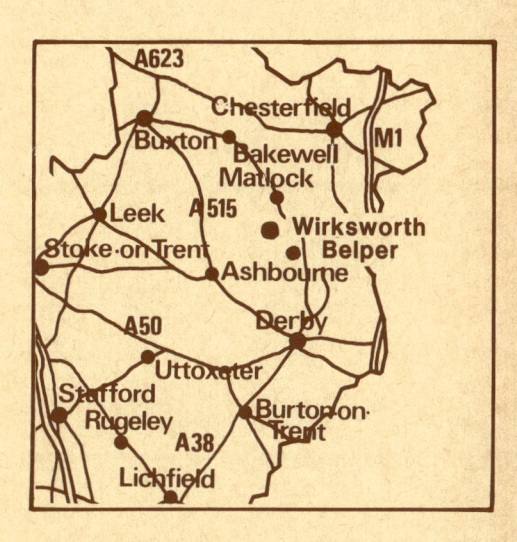

VACANCY SECRETARY:
Joan Slack (077389) 273

(FH) DANNAH FARM Bowmans Lane, Shottle, Nr Belper, Derbys, DE5 2DR

Joan Slack
Tel:-(077 389) 273
Closed Christmas
B&B   £9.50-£10.50   Listed
EM   £6.00
       Sleeps 6
Van   £2.50

Come and relax in our lovely old Georgian farmhouse, recently modernised. Traditional 128 acre mixed working farm set amidst beautiful countryside on Chatsworth Estate at Shottle. We offer a warm, friendly family welcome with good home cooking a speciality. Tea/coffee making facilities in all bedrooms. Ideally situated for visiting Chatsworth, Alton Towers etc. Ashbourne 6 miles. Reductions for children. Brochure available. OS Ref SK 313502

(FH) HOME FARM Norbury, Ashbourne, Derbys, DE6 2ED

Gillyan Prince
Tel:-(033524) 284/286
Closed Xmas-New Year
B&B   £8.50-£9.50   Listed
       Sleeps 6

This delightful farmhouse is situated in a quiet hamlet surrounded by woods, halfway between Alton Towers and Ashbourne. Easy access Dovedale and many stately homes. 1 twin bedded room on ground floor, cloakroom facilities adjacent. 1 family room on 1st floor. Visitors own dining/lounge. Separate TV lounge. Full central heating, coal fire in lounge. OS Ref SK 154443

(FH) SIDESMILL FARM Snelston, Nr Ashbourne, Derbys, DE6 2GQ

Catherine Brandrick
Tel:-(0335) 42710
Open Easter-Oct
B&B   £8.50-£9   Listed
EM   £5
       Sleeps 6

Peaceful dairy farm on banks of River Dove, a rippling millstream flowing past the 18th Century stonebuilt farmhouse. Good home cooking and warm welcome guaranteed. Own produce when available. Homemade bread. Within easy reach of Alton Towers, Dovedale and many other places of interest. Family, twin bedded rooms, own lounge, colour TV. Hot drink facilities. Visitors' bathroom. EM by arrangement. OS Ref SK 154443

(FH) WALDLEY MANOR Marston Montgomery, (nr Doveridge), Ashbourne, Derbys, DE6 5LR

Anita Whitfield
Tel:-(0889) 590 287
Open all year
B&B   £8.50-£10   Listed
       Sleeps 6

Come and spend a relaxing holiday in a 16th Century manor farmhouse. Oak beamed and oak timbered rooms, inglenook and open log fires. See the working dairy farm. In easy reach of the Peak District and 5 miles from Alton Towers. Full English breakfast. OS Ref SK 127371

(FH) PARKVIEW FARM Weston Underwood, Derby, DE6 4PA

Linda & Michael Adams
Tel:-(0335) 60352
Closed Xmas
B&B   £9-£10
       Sleeps 6

Lovely old Victorian farmhouse set in a large garden overlooking our 370 acre mainly arable farm and Kedleston Hall and Park. Well situated for Dovedale, Peak District and Alton Towers. The farmhouse is very comfortable with CH, washbasins, guests own bathroom, sitting room and delightful dining room. Country pubs and restaurants close by. 2 twin, 1 double room. OS Ref SK 323617

(FH) ROSTON HALL FARM Roston, Nr Ashbourne, Derbys, DE6 2EH

Mrs. Enid Prince
Tel:-(033524) 287
Open May-Sep
B&B   £9-£10   Listed
       Sleeps 6
(13)

Relax in our spacious traditional farmhouse in quiet village 6m SW of Ashbourne. Excellent centre for Alton Towers, Derbyshire Dales and many stately homes. Dining room with inglenook fireplace, comfortable lounge with wood burning stove and TV. 1 double/family room with washbasin, 1 twin bedded room. Tea/coffee facilities in bedrooms. Full English breakfast. Ploughmans suppers and snacks served 6-8pm. AA listed. OS Ref SK 134 409

Dovedale & Derbyshire Dales ENGLAND

(FH) SHIRLEY HALL FARM Shirley, Brailsford, Derby, DE6 3AS

Sylvia Foster
Tel:-(0335) 60346
Open Jan-Nov
B&B   £8.50-£11
EM   £6
Sleeps 6

Lovely listed farmhouse with half-timbered bedrooms, set in peaceful countryside on working farm, 4m from Ashbourne. Excellent for walking or visiting stately homes, Peak District and Alton Towers. 2 double bedrooms with washbasins & guests' bathroom, 1 double room ensuite, all with tea-making facilities. Guests' sitting room with TV. Annexe with 2 double rooms & bathroom or suitable as self-catering unit. Reductions for children. OS Ref SK 221418

(FH) CULLAND MOUNT FARM Brailsford, Derby, DE6 3BW

Carolyn Phillips
Tel:-(0335) 60313
Open Easter-Sep
B&B   £8.50-£9.50   Listed
Sleeps 4
(12)

Enjoy country life on our family dairy farm ideal for the Dales, Ashbourne and Alton Towers also business in Derby/Nottingham area. Beautiful front rooms, storage heaters, and log fire in lounge with colour TV. Dining room. Tea making facilities in bedrooms. Full English breakfast. Plenty of eating places locally. 1 family, 1 double. OS Ref SK 248395

(FH) PACKHORSE FARM Tansley, Matlock, Derbys, DE4 5LF

Margaret Haynes
Tel:-(0629) 2781
Closed Xmas-New Year
B&B   £9-£9.50
Sleeps 15
TV   £3-£4
(3)

Modernised farmhouse quietly situated in extensive grounds. Ideal for visitors to walk or just sit in; elevated south with extensive views. Mixed farm, 40 acres. 2 family rooms, 2 double, 1 twin bedded all with washbasins. Bathroom separate showers and 4 toilets. Lounge and dining room, colour TV open fires and CH. Fire Certificate. Dogs allowed in cars only. Cycle hire. Full English breakfast. SAE for replies. OS Ref SK 323617

(FH) NEW PARK FARM Bradley, Ashbourne, Derbys, DE6 1LQ

Carol Akers
Tel:-(0335) 43425
Closed Xmas and New Year
B&B   £8.50-£10.50
EM   5.00
Sleeps 6
SC   £60-£120
Sleeps 8

A comfortable modernised farmhouse in quiet surroundings and offering a warm welcome with good home cooking. Guests have their own dining room and lounge with TV and log fires. All bedrooms with washbasins, an ensuite available. A good base for Alton Towers, Matlock, Peak and Dale District. Children are most welcome and special diets are catered for. OS Ref SK 220530

(FH) SYCAMORE FARM Hopton, Wirksworth, Derbys, DE4 4DF

Bridget Corbett
Tel:-(062 982) 2466
Open May-Oct
B&B   £9-£10   Listed
EM   £5.50
Sleeps 4

A unique round fronted brick and stone Tudor Farmhouse situated on a 230 acre mixed farm. All the amenities of modern day living but still retaining its historical charm and peace associated with the countryside. Ideal situation for walking, touring close to the Peak District, Chatsworth, Bakewell and Ashbourne. A warm, friendly welcome assured. OS Ref 267535

(FH) CHEVIN GREEN FARM Chevin Road, Belper, Derby, DE5 2UN

Carl & Joan Postles
Tel:-(077 382) 2328
Open all year
B&B   £10-£14
Sleeps 8
SC   £60-£145
Van   £1.50-£2

Attractively converted farm buildings in beautiful yet peaceful situation on the Chevin overlooking the Derwent Valley. Very comfortable and luxurious accommodation offering family, ensuite & twin-bedded rooms. Lounge with colour TV & full English breakfast. Five superb self-catering cottages equipped to a high standard with colour TV. Excellent centre for walking, golf, touring, visiting local attractions & business in the area. OS Ref SK 339472

165

(FH) YELDERSLEY OLD HALL FARM   Yeldersley Lane, Bradley, Ashbourne, DE6 1PH

Mrs Janet Hinds
Tel:-(0335) 44504
Open all year
B&B   £8-£9
EM   £4.50
Sleeps 6

Listed

Yeldersley Old Hall farm is a family run dairy farm of 70 acres. The Grade II Listed farmhouse is situated in quiet surroundings just 3m from Ashbourne and is within easy reach of Alton Towers, Matlock and many stately homes. The accommodation consists of 1 double, 1 family & 1 twin bedded room. Reduced rates for children who are most welcome. OS Ref SK 449320

(CH) THE BEECHES FARMHOUSE   Waldley, Doveridge, Uttoxeter, Derby, DE6 5LR

Barbara Tunnicliffe
Tel:-(0889) 590288
Closed Xmas
B&B   £10-£16
EM   From £6.50
Sleeps 12 plus 4 children

160 acre working dairy farm with 200 year old beamed farmhouse, The Beeches is set in the beautiful Derbyshire countryside, close to Alton Towers and Dovedale. The farmhouse is fully centrally heated with 6 bedrooms. All have hand basins, televisions and two have ensuite facilities. Evening meals available in our licensed oak beamed dining room. Dogs by arrangement only.

(FH) MANOR HOUSE FARM   Prestwood, Denstone, Nr Uttoxeter, Staffs, ST14 5DD

Christine Ball
Tel:-(0889) 590415
Closed Xmas-New Year
B&B   £9-£12
Sleeps 6

Old world charm awaits you in this Jacobean farmhouse dating from the 17th century, overlooking the scenic Churnet Valley. Antique furnishings throughout, including a period 4 poster bed. Oak panelled breakfast room and beamed lounge. Relax in the terraced garden with Victorian summer house. Grass tennis court & croquet available. Ashbourne 6m, Alton Towers 3m. OS Ref SK 104424

(SC) HAYES FARM SELF CATERING   Hayes Farm, Biggin, Hulland Ward, Derby, DE6 3FJ

Audrey Gray
Tel:-(0335) 70204
Open all year
SC   £75-£122
Sleeps 6

Unwind in our peaceful valley, superb bungalow on small friendly dairy farm. Panoramic views of unspoilt countryside, join in farm activities. The Bungalow has its own garage and garden. It has utility room with automatic washing machine, toilet, modern fitted kitchen, pantry, Rayburn (free coal) and electric cooker, dining room, lounge, colour TV, bathroom with toilet. 2 double and 1 twin bedrooms. OS Ref SK 2548

(SC) ROSE COTTAGE   Snelston, Ashbourne, Derbyshire, DE6 2DL

Cynthia Moore
Tel:-(033 524) 230
Open all year
SC   £80-£160
Sleeps 5

Fully equipped, well appointed bungalow. 2 double bedrooms, bathroom (with shower) cloakroom with wc, pine kitchen and living area open plan. Carpeted throughout. Night storage heaters, TV, en-tout-cas hard tennis court. Beautifully situated with panoramic views. Quiet, secluded, but not isolated. Ashbourne 4 miles. OS Ref SK 148421

(SC) NEW BUNGALOW, SHIRLEY   Hall Farm Shirley, Brailsford, Derby, DE6 3AS

Sylvia Foster
Tel:-(0335) 60346
Open May-Sep
SC   £125
Sleeps 6
Van   £1

Our bungalow on edge of village close to our farm has large lawned gardens & excellent views. 3 bedrooms suitable for 6 adults. Bathroom. Open plan living area, open fire, fully carpeted, central heating, colour TV. Kitchen with fridge, cooker and washing machine. Ample parking. Convenient for Alton Towers, Stately homes, superb walking. Ashbourne 4m. OS Ref SK 218417

Dovedale & Derbyshire Dales ENGLAND

(SC) **CULLAND MOUNT FARM Brailsford, Derby, DE6 3BW**

Carolyn Phillips
Tel:-(0335) 60313
Open all year
SC   £75-£140
      Sleeps 6

Enjoy country life on our family dairy farm, ideal for the Dales, Ashbourne & Alton Towers also business in Derby/Nottingham. Whilst retaining many original features, the farmhouse is divided making a large luxury holiday home. Superb views from all windows. Colour TV, storage radiators in all rooms. Open log fire, washing machine, linen and electricity inclusive. Groceries ordered. OS Ref SK 248495

(SC) **THE HOLDING, DOVE ST. ELLASTONE,   Home Farm, Norbury, Ashbourne, Derbys, DE6 2ED**

Gillyan Prince
Tel:-(033524) 284/286
Open all year
SC   £70-£125
      Sleeps 2/4

The Holding is situated in Ellastone Village close to village stores and Post Office, River Dove and 4 miles to Alton Towers. Easy access to Dovedale and stately homes. Accommodation has 1 double and 1 twin bedrooms, dining/kitchen and separate lounge. Shower room on ground floor.

(SC) **WOODHEAD FARM Agnes Meadow Lane, Kniveton, Nr Ashbourne, Derbys, DE16 J18**

Norma Short
Tel:-(0335) 42274
Closed Xmas
SC   £60-£100
      Sleeps 6

Woodhead is a working beef/sheep farm situated at 750ft in the quiet Derbyshire hills. Only 3 miles from market town of Ashbourne & near to Alton Towers & Peak Park. The self-contained cottage within Tudor farmhouse provides sleeping arrangements for 5/6 - 1 large family bedroom, 1 twin bedroom, additional bed settee in sitting room. Open fire, electric heaters, colour television. Well equipped kitchen & bathroom. Use of walled garden.

ALL BED AND BREAKFAST PROPERTIES IN THIS GUIDE HAVE BEEN PERSONALLY INSPECTED.

ENGLISH TOURIST BOARD

WALES TOURIST BOARD

In England and Wales, the properties have been inspected and classified as 'Listed,' or '1, 2, 3 or 4 Crowns' by the English or Wales Tourist Boards. (See Introduction for details). The higher classification does not indicate that one property is better than another, but that it provides a greater range of facilities.

167

3G NORTHAMPTONSHIRE

NORTHAMPTONSHIRE

Northamptonshire, the county of 'squires and spires', has houses, monuments and fine churches too numerous to mention. There's Sulgrave Manor, home of George Washington's ancestors; Rockingham Castle which was 'Arnescote Castle' in the BBC TV series 'By the Sword Divided', Boughton House, modelled on Versailles; and Althorp, the home of the father of the Princess of Wales.

At the castle remains, by the river in picturesque Fotheringhay, you may ponder upon the execution of Mary Queen of Scots and the birth there of Richard III, and the Battle and Farm Museum will give you a taste of that decisive Civil War battle in 1645.

A firm hold has been kept on our heritage and at Brixworth and Earls Barton you will be able to see possibly the country's finest examples of a Saxon church and tower. Many of the county's villages and towns have splendid churches, well-preserved from Norman times through to the 15th century.

Traditional methods of transport and entertainment are well preserved. The Waterways Museum at Stoke Bruerne gives you a fascinating insight into life on the canals, and there are boat trips along the Grand Union canal. With the Nene Valley Steam Railway you can take a nostalgic trip down the line and study steam trains and rolling stock from all over the world.

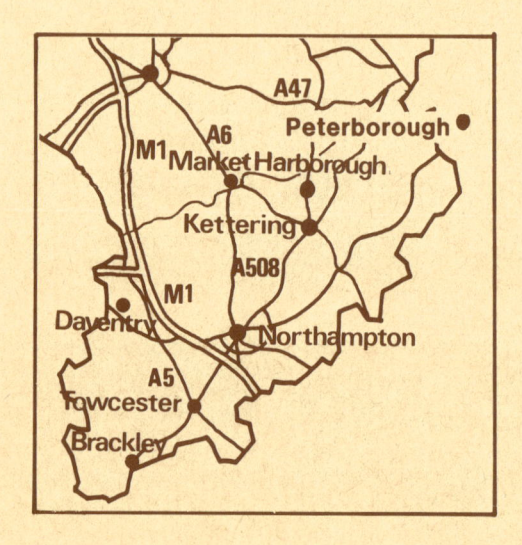

GROUP CONTACT:
Anne Engler (0604) 781258

Northamptonshire ENGLAND

(FH) WOLD FARM Old, Northampton, Northants, NN6 9RJ

Anne Engler
Tel:-(0604) 781 258
Open all year
B&B   £11-£12
EM   £7 Redn for children
Sleeps 6

18th Century farmhouse, oak beams, inglenook fireplace, open fires, snooker table, large garden, on a 250 acre beef/arable farm in a quiet rural village. Close to 7th Century Brixworth church, trout fishing, birdwatching & sailing at Pitsford Reservoir, Lamport Hall, Wicksteed Park. Excellent theatres in Northampton. 1 twin & 1 double with showers, 1 double room with bathroom. Reduced rates for children. 1 single with washbasin. Pets by arrangement. OS Ref SP 786732

(FH) BARWELL FIELDS Moreton Pinkney, Daventry, Nhants, NN11 6SQ

Margaret Lainchbury
Tel:-(029 576) 382
Open Feb-Nov
B&B   £10-£12   Applied
EM   £3.50-£6.50
Sleeps 4

Barewell Fields, situated in peaceful Moreton Pinkney, which lies in beautiful unspoilt countryside. National Trust properties & M1 make it an ideal touring centre. Guests welcome to relax in their drawing room & have the use of their own dining room & bathroom. Just 5 mins walk through the village is Home Farm, run by Margaret Lainchbury's son, where you are welcome to visit. OS Ref SP 493573

FARM HOLIDAY BUREAU

(FH) OLD WHARF FARM Grafton Road, Yardley Gobion, Towcester, Northants, NN12 7UE

Susie Bowen
Tel:-(0908) 542454
Open all year
B&B   £10.50-£12.50   Listed
Sleeps 6
SC   £86
Sleeps 4-6

A working wharf on the Grand Union Canal and 18th century farmhouse form opposite sides of a farmyard square of historic restored buildings now used for smallholding, self-catering accommodation and marine activities. Surrounding water meadow, canal and a mini Noah's Ark of different animals give a tranquil Arcadian atmosphere quite unique. A rowing skiff is available for exploration and fishing. Mentally handicapped welcome. OS Ref SP 767453

(FH) DAIRY FARM Cranford St Andrew, Kettering, Northamptonshire, NN14 4AQ

Audrey Clarke
Tel:-(053678) 273
Closed Xmas
B&B   £12.50-£16
EM   £7.50
Sleeps 6

Thatched Jacobean farmhouse with oak beams and inglenook fireplaces, log fires. Large garden with ancient circular dovecote and mature trees. Cranford is a beautiful Northamptonshire village ideal for visiting the many places of interest nearby or just for having a restful holiday. Good farmhouse food and individual attention at all times.

(FH) WOOLLEYS FARM Welford Road, Naseby, Northampton, NN6 7DP

Mrs Heather Jeffries
Tel:-(085881) 310
Closed Dec, Xmas-New Year
B&B   £10
EM   £5
Sleeps 3

A modernised Georgian brick farmhouse set in attractive Northamptonshire countryside. Close to the site of the Battle of Naseby 1645, midway between Northampton and Leicester and surrounded by beautiful rolling country. Twin bedded room with tea making facilities and shower. OS Ref SP 669787

169

FH WALLTREE HOUSE FARM Steane, Brackley, Northants, NN13 5NS

Richard & Pauline Harrison
Tel:-(0295) 811235
Closed New Year
B&B From £12
EM   £9
Sleeps 16

Lovely Victorian countryhouse recently modernised with warmth and comfort in mind. The farm is arable, we have gardens to relax in and 20 acres of woodland. Some bedrooms are in a recently completed courtyard development and most bedrooms have private bathrooms. We are in an ideal situation for touring The Cotswolds, Oxford, Blenheim, Althorp, Stratford-Upon-Avon and Warwick. Pets by arrangement. Licensed. OS Ref SP 542372

FH GRANGE FARM Brampton Ash, Market Harborough, Leics, LE16 8PE

Barbara Carpenter
Tel:-(085885) 215
Open all year
B&B From £9.50   Listed
Sleeps 4

Spacious 17th Century stone farmhouse with extensive views over Welland Valley on 240 acre dairy farm. Attractions include Elizabethan triangular lodge built by Thomas Tresham and the vast expanse of Rutland Water. Two twin bedded rooms with tea making facilities and guests' own bathroom and lounge. Substantial breakfasts with free range eggs and good nearby inns for evening meal. No dogs. OS Ref SP 791875

FH PRIESTHAY WOOD FARM Syresham, Nr Brackley, Northants, NN13 5PU

Jim & Joyce Ponting
Tel:-(02805) 663
Open Mar-Oct
B&B From £11
EM   From £5
Sleeps 4

A warm welcome awaits you at Jim & Joyce's Victorian Farmhouse, pleasantly situated 1½m from the A43, in quiet peaceful surroundings, where guests return year after year. Within easy reach of Cotswolds, Stratford upon Avon & many places of interest in Northamptonshire. Traditional farmhouse breakfasts are the order of the day, together with a hearty evening meal if required. OS Ref SP 635434

FH PEARTREE FARM Aldwincle, Nr Kettering, Northants, NN14 3EL

Mavis Hankins
Tel:-(08015) 614
Open Feb-Oct
B&B £10   Listed
EM   £5
Sleeps 4/5
(10)

Peartree Farm is a mixed 400 acre farm consisting of cattle, sheep, poultry, and arable. A relaxed family atmosphere, comfortably furnished, good home cooking. Excellent for walking, bird watching, fishing. Two bedrooms. Large garden for relaxing. OS Ref TL 000 810

SC PAPLEY FARM COTTAGES Papley Farm, Warmington, Peterborough, PE8 6UU

Joyce Lane
Tel:-(0832) 72583
Open all year
SC   £75-£200
Sleeps 2/5

On a large mixed farm 4 traditional stone cottages stand tucked away from 20th Century by a "lost" village site. Recently restored, each has an old world charm coupled with a high standard of modern comfort. There is also a modern bungalow near the main farm. All are fully equipped including linen. Cottages sleep 2/5. Five miles from A1. A "get-away" retreat or ideal touring base. OS Ref TL 107893

SC THE OLD VICARAGE Church Street, Blakesley, Towcester, Northants, NN12 8RA

Rosemary & Philip Burt
Tel:-(0327) 860200
Open all year
SC   £80-£200
Sleeps 6

Spacious split level 3 bed flat, complete with games room, part of lovely old Victorian vicarage. The property is set in formal gardens complemented by swimming pool and hard tennis court, private fishing. Conveniently situated for Milton Keynes, Northampton, Banbury, Silverstone racetrack, Towcester Racecourse, several fine stately houses, Althorp, Castle Ashby and the Cotswolds. Adjacent to motorway. OS Ref SP 406208

LEICESTERSHIRE

37

LEICESTERSHIRE

A short holiday in Leicestershire could be just the break you need. Easily accessible by road and rail, the County has much to offer.

The varied scenery provides many delights. To the west is Charnwood Forest, with its rugged, rocky landscape. There are several country parks here affording splendid views over this part of the County. The countryside of eastern Leicestershire is the typical image of rural England, with small stone built villages nestling in rolling hills. The market towns each have their own individual identities contrasting with the large bustling City of Leicester.

A good way to explore the County is by bicycle. If you haven't got your own they can be hired from Rutland Water, near Oakham. Why not make it a day out and take a picnic made from traditional Leicestershire food — Stilton and Red Leicester cheeses, Melton Mowbray Pork Pie, with locally brewed beer to wash it all down. Alternatively you could take a welcome break at a local inn. Cycles can also be hire for the week by prior arrangements enabling you to tour the County staying at different farms.

Leicestershire is an ideal base for visiting other attractions in the region. To the north and east there's Nottingham, Belton House (near Grantham) and Burghley House (Stamford), while the farms to the south are handy for Coventry Cathedral, the National Exhibition Centre at Birmingham and the Royal Agricultural Showground at Stoneleigh.

GROUP CONTACT:
Molly Knight (053758) 388

FH WHEATHILL FARM Church Lane, Shearsby, Lutterworth, Leics, LE17 6PG

Susan Timms
Tel:-(053 758) 663
Closed Xmas-New Year
B&B £10-£10.50   Listed
EM   £5.50
Sleeps 5

Centrally heated farmhouse rich in old beams & inglenook fireplaces on 133 acre working dairy farm. Good home-produce cooking our speciality (EM by arrangement). Easy distance from M1, M6 on outskirts of tiny Saxon village in Heart of England. Gliding, fishing, walking & many stately homes nearby. Guests' own bathroom, lounge & dining room. Bedrooms have shower or vanity unit & tea/coffee facilities. OS Ref SP 622911

FH THE GREENWAY, KNAPTOFT HSE FARM Bruntingthorpe Road, Nr Shearsby, Lutterworth, Leics, LE17 6PR

Mrs A M Knight
Tel:-(053758)718/388
Open all year
B&B From £9-£11
EM   From £5.50
Sleeps 6

A luxurious bungalow, very quietly set in the old farm orchard, overlooking our farmland. Spacious rooms, each with H/C basins, tea/coffee facilities, heating. All ground floor rooms, level access, sitting room, TV, separate dining room. EM by arrangement. Warmth, comfort, good home cooking. Coarse fishing on farm in restored medieval carp pools. Fridge and barbeque for guests use. OS Ref SP 619893

FH KNAPTOFT HOUSE FARM Bruntingthorpe Rd, Nr Shearsby, Lutterworth, Leics, LE17 6PR

Mrs A T Hutchinson
Tel:-(053 758) 388
Open all year
B&B £9-£11
EM   £5.50
Sleeps 6

Warm, friendly home with every comfort, peacefully set with lovely views. Tea/coffee facilities in each room. Ideal touring centre or overnight stop. Fishing in our own carp pools, drying facilities, barbecue and fridge for guests' use. Whole foods and diets prepared. Sunny rooms, colour TV, wood burner in sitting room. 9m south of Leicester. A50, M1 exit 20, M6 exit 1. OS Ref SP 619893

FH MANOR HOUSE Saxelbye, Melton Mowbray, Leics, LE14 3PA

Margaret A Morris
Tel:-(0664) 812269
Open Easter-Sep
B&B From £9.50
EM   £6
Sleeps 6

Manor House is situated in the quiet hamlet of Saxelbye. It is a stone built house of great character the unique oak stairway being 400 years old. Surrounded by lawns & with ample parking it is ideal for the visitor seeking peace & tranquility. The food served is traditional English fare of excellent quality - AA award 1978. AA listed.

FH THREE WAYS FARM 1578 Melton Road, Queniborough, Leicester, LE7 8FN

Janet Clarke
Tel:-(0533) 600472
Closed Xmas-New Year
B&B £10-£14   Listed
Sleeps 6

In the picturesque village of Queniborough. Spacious modern bungalow, surrounded by fields with views to Charnwood Forest. Covenient for M1 or A1, Leicester, Loughborough, Nottingham Castle & Water Sports Centre, Melton Mowbray & Belvoir Castle, Oakham & Rutland Water. 2 Twin-bedded rooms/family rooms, 1 double, cot, visitors' bathroom, colour TV. Excellent evening meal facilities near by. Some very comfortable accommodation via a Slingsby loft staircase. OS Ref SK 600 150

FH THE OLD RECTORY Belton-in-Rutland, Nr Uppingham, Oakham, Leics, LE15 9LE

Mr & Mrs D E Renner
Tel:-(057286) 279
Closed Xmas
B&B £10-£17
EM   £5
Sleeps 12
SC   £50-£55 Sleeps 2
TV   £2-£3 Max 5 Van

Superb accommodation, ideal holiday setting especially for families. Homely Victorian Rectory in beautiful gardens overlooking picturesque pastoral parkland. Luxurious lounge & dining room, and delightful bedrooms including a 4 poster bedroom with ensuite. Retail Country Craft Centre where craftspeople instruct at times. Country bygones on display, pedigree miniature farm animals. Children's play area and picnic facilities. Rutland Water nearby. Evening meal by arrangement. OS Ref SK 815 012

Leicestershire ENGLAND

(SC) VALLEY VIEW FARM Leire, Lutterworth, Leicestershire, LE17 5EY

Mrs P Cooke
Tel:-(0455) 209369
Open all year
SC   From £70
      Sleeps 2 +

Well appointed cottage by farm entrance with views all around the valley. Hall, fitted kitchen/breakfast room, spacious lounge, double bedroom and bathroom. Craftsman made wrought ironwork and carved woodwork. Located at the end of quiet village lane, with peaceful walks along bridlepaths from the farm gate. Perfect for 2. OS Ref SP 532911

(SC) RUTLAND HOLIDAY COTTAGES 5 Cedar Street, Braunston, Oakham, Leics, LE15 8QS

John & Connie Beadman
Tel:-(0572) 2049
Open all year
SC   £90-£100
      Sleeps 5
B&B   £11-£12
      Sleeps 5

Rutland Holiday Cottages are situated in the delightful conservation village of Braunston near Oakham. Only 3 miles from Rutland Water with its trout fishing, sailing, picnic spots and cycle hire. The cottages are fully equipped & spotlessly clean. If available, bed and breakfast guests can stay in one of the nearby cottages, allowing them to use the amenities of a self-catering situation.

BOSWORTH BATTLEFIELD

Visit the historical site of the Battle of Bosworth Field, 1485

★ **Award winning Battlefield Visitor Centre** with exciting exhibitions and models giving an insight into the Battle and mediaeval life; film theatre, book and gift shops, cafeteria.

★ **Centre open every afternoon** Easter to last Sunday in October: Adults £1.20, Children/OAPs 80p, Cars 30p. (Special Event Days excepted).

★ **Illustrated Battle Trails** through picturesque countryside (open all year).

★ **Series of Mediaeval Attractions** July-September.

★ **Follow road signs** off A447, A444, A5 and B585 in vicinity of Market Bosworth, Leicestershire.

Project Manager: Director of Property, Land Agency Division, LEICESTERSHIRE COUNTY COUNCIL

Enquiries: Market Bosworth (0455) 290429
Bosworth Battlefield, Sutton Cheney
Market Bosworth, Leicestershire.

An Enterprise of Leicestershire County Council

38 SHERWOOD FOREST, Nottinghamshire

SHERWOOD FOREST, NOTTINGHAMSHIRE

Sherwood Forest itself is nowadays much smaller than it used to be, but near Edwinstowe you can still find Robin Hood, at the Sherwood Forest Visitor Centre where his story is told in a walkthrough exhibition. There are also films, guided walks in the Forest and lots of other activities here together with a fair to enjoy at Edwinstowe or perhaps a village cricket match, close to the church where Robin Hood is said to have married Maid Marion.

Worksop is a pleasant market town with a fine priory and 14th century gatehouse — both well worth a visit. Retford has a small museum and some interesting Georgian buildings around its market square. The open air markets at Newark and Mansfield are both popular with visitors as well as local residents and each town has its local museums. Newark's parish church has a fine spire and interesting treasury but the nearby Minster at Southwell is on a larger scale even though Southwell itself is hardy more than a village.

In Nottingham itself Robin Hood's statue stands outside the Castle, which houses the city's fine arts museum, and there's a small Robin Hood exhibition at the gatehouse. At the foot of Castle Rock, beside the ancient Trip to Jerusalem Inn, is the Breweryhouse Yard Museum illustrating the city's social history, while nearby the Canal Museum of Costume shows other aspects of the city's heritage. The Lace Centre, in an attractive timbered building, shows off a range of Nottingham's finest work, which you can buy as a souvenir.

GROUP CONTACT:
Joy Shaw-Browne (0623) 823132

Sherwood Forest, Nottinghamshire ENGLAND

(FH) NORTON GRANGE FARM   Norton Cuckney, Nr Mansfield, Notts, NG20 9LP

Jacqueline Palmer
Tel:-(0623) 842666
Open Easter-Nov
B&B   £9
Sleeps 6

Listed

A Georgian, stone farmhouse situated on the edge of Sherwood Forest with sitting room for guests' use. One family room, 1 double and 1 twin-bedded room. Soap and towels provided. Bathroom and toilet separate. Ample parking. Reduction for children under 12. OS Ref SK 573722

(FH) MOORGATE FARM   Laxton, Newark, Notts, NG22 ONU

Lizzie Rose
Tel:-(0777) 870274
Closed Xmas
B&B   £8-£9
EM   £4
Sleeps 6

Listed

A warm welcome awaits you at Moorgate Farm, a family run farm of 145 acres producing beef and cereals. Situated in the mediaeval village of Laxton where the last remaining open field system of farming still exists. Laxton is on the edge of Sherwood Forest and within easy reach of many historic towns. One double, 1 twin and 1 single. OS Ref SK 717266

(FH) BLUE BARN FARM   Langwith, Mansfield, Notts, NG20 9JD

June Ibbotson
Tel:-(0623) 742248
Closed Xmas
B&B   From £9
Sleeps 6

Listed

Welcome to Blue Barn, a family run 250 acre, mixed arable farm on Welbeck Estate, in quiet countryside off A616 near Cuckney. Sherwood Forest, Clumber Park, Creswell Crags, Hardwick Hall and the Peak District are a short car journey away. Guests welcome to walk round farm and lawned garden CH, 1 double, 1 twin, a family room all with tea/coffee facilities. OS Ref SK 539714

(SC) THE WILLOWS   Top House Farm, Mansfield Road, Arnold, Nottingham, NG5 8PH

Ann Lamin
Tel:-(0602) 268330
Open all year
SC   £80-£110
Sleeps 6

"The Willows" is a self contained unit, being half of a 19th Century farmhouse. Tastefully furnished, it has 3 bedrooms, a well equipped kitchen and night storage heaters throughout. Large, attractive gardens surround this country residence, which is within easy reach of Nottingham, Newstead Abbey, The Dukeries, Sherwood Forest, Southwell Minster, Derbyshire and the National Water Sports Centre. Pets by arrangement. OS Ref SK 579481

(SC) THE COTTAGE AND THE MEWS   Eastwood Farm, Hagg Lane, Epperstone, Nottingham, NG14 6AX

Susan Santos
Tel:-(0602) 663018
Open all year
SC   £60-£80
Sleeps 4/5

Eastwood Farm, 170 acres producing cereals and beef, is situated on a private road, ½m from the village, 10 miles from Nottingham. The accommodation forms part of the 150 year old range of brick and pan-tiled buildings. Each well-equipped unit comprises 2 bedrooms, living room, kitchen and bathroom. Goat's milk, free-range eggs and home baked bread available. Central heating included. OS Ref SK 661492

(SC) SHERWOOD FOREST CARAVAN PARK   Clipstone Park Estate, Old Clipstone, Mansfield, Notts, NG21 9BS

Joy Shaw-Browne
Tel:-(0623) 823132
Open Apr-Sep
SC   £70
Tent   £5.50
Van   £6.00

FARM HOLIDAY BUREAU

Clipstone Park, a family farm of 1,000 acres with 400 acres of Woodland has been a farming manor since 1068. Beautiful, quiet retreat in heart of Robin Hood country. Situated along wooded valley of River Maun, boating lake, coarse fishing, woodland walks. Two holiday caravans for hire, double bedroom, on award winning Caravan Park. Warm welcome. OS Ref SK 590650

(SC) 1 - 2 NORWOOD COTTAGES Hardwick Park Farm, Teversal, Sutton-in-Ashfield, Notts, NG17 3JR

Sheena White
Tel:-(0246) 850271
Open all year
SC £55-£85
Sleeps 5

Comfortable, semi-detached stone cottages set in open parkland surrounding historic Hardwick Hall, on 320 acre beef, sheep and corn unit. Each has double, twin and single bedrooms. Cot. Sittingroom, open fire, colour TV Kitchen, fully equipped. Bath, shower. Supplementary radiators. Electricity metered. Garden. Pets by arrangement. Easy parking. Convenient M1, Sherwood Forest, Dukeries, Peak District, Derby, Nottingham and Sheffield. OS Ref SK475633

(SC) NO. 3 FRANDERGROUND BUNGALOW Franderground Lane, Kirkby Lane, Pinxton, Nottingham, NG16 6JB

Ruth Bunting
Tel:-(0623) 752158
Open all year
SC £60-£95
Sleeps 5

150 acre farm on Nottinghamshire/Derby border offering easy access to both areas. Located 3 miles off Junction 28, M1. The modern detached fully furnished self-catering accommodation offers a relaxing holiday comprising 2 double bedrooms, 1 single bedroom, kitchen, lounge, bathroom. Electric heaters, solid fuel central heating, TV.

(SC) WOLDS FARM Fosse Way, Cotgrave, Nottingham, NG12 3HG

Joan Hinchley
Tel:-0602 892227
Open all year
SC £75-£110
Sleeps 2/5
Van £2

A family farm situated south of Cotgrave with open fields to the south it is set against a 500 acre forest, very peaceful with wooded walks. Each unit is centrally heated & all linen is provided. The 3 bedroom cottage sleeps 5 with own garden. A ground floor flat attached to farmhouse sleeps 2 with garage for car.

(SC) BLUE BARN COTTAGE Blue Barn Farm, Langwith, Mansfield, Notts, NG20 9JD

June Ibbotson
Tel:-(0623) 742248
Open all year
SC From £150
Sleeps 8

Original 18th Century farmhouse recently completely and tastefully restored. Situated on family run 250 acre mixed arable farm in quiet countryside off A616 near Cuckney on edge of Sherwood Forest. Many places of interest, Chatsworth House, Peak District, Clumber Park, Newstead Abbey all easily accessible by car. 1 double, 1 twin, 1 family, 1 single, cot available. CH, linen & servicing provided. Electricity by 50p meter. OS Ref SK 539714

BOOKING TIPS

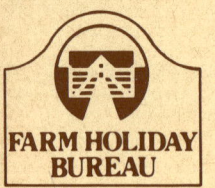

FARM HOLIDAY BUREAU

PLEASE MENTION...

Please mention the Farm Holiday Bureau's Guide when making a booking.

176

Lincolnshire ENGLAND

LINCOLNSHIRE

39

LINCOLNSHIRE

Visit one of the market towns, especially on market day when you join the bustle and activity and bid at the auctions for country produce which is brought in from the surrounding villages. Buy some Lincolnshire sausages, pies and cooked meats from a local butcher to eat either on holiday or to take home.

Tennyson Country forms the southern part of the Lincolnshire wolds that have been designated as an area of outstanding natural beauty.

Halt a while to visit a Saxon Church or a perfectly preserved 18th century chapel, or go for a walk along part of the Viking Way which stretches the length of the county. Alternatively you can enjoy short walks in picnic places such as Tattershall, Stickney and Willingham Ponds near Market Rasen, along the Spa Trail — A disused railway line that runs between Horncastle and Woodhall Spa, and in a nature reserve as at Snipe Dales near Spilsby. All have signed walks and trails with interpretation boards that help you to understand and appreciate the surroundings.

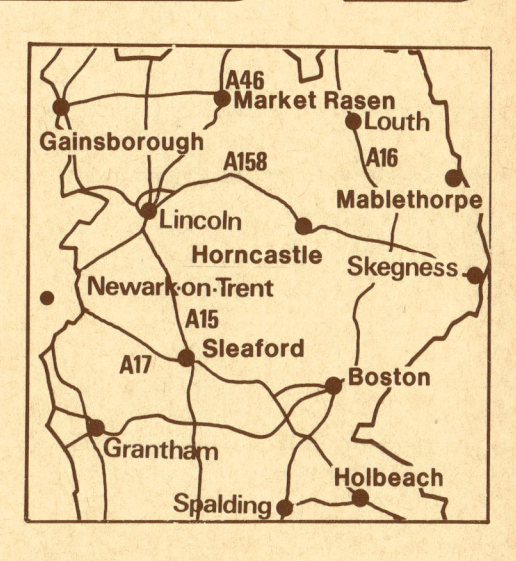

You can get a taste of the countryside by visiting one of the five windmills that are still in working order in the country at Alford, Burgh le Marsh, Heckington, Lincoln and Sibsey. Then go on to either the Museum of Lincolnshire Life in Lincoln or the Church Farm Museum, Skegness, which vividly illustrate the agricultural and social life of old Lincolnshire.

GROUP CONTACT:
Anne Thompson (0406) 22239

(FH) THE VILLAGE FARM Sturton-by-Stow, Lincoln, LN1 2AE

Sheila Bradshaw
Tel:-(0427) 788309
Open Easter-Oct
B&B   £10-£13
EM   £6.50
      Sleeps 6

(10)

Come & stay in a lovely 19th Century farmhouse in the centre of the village. We give caring personal service in our fully modernised CH home. Enjoy good food including home produced beef & lamb. 9m from Lincoln. 400 acre mixed farm with beef cattle, sheep & large garden. Guests are assured of every comfort. All bedrooms have washbasins, tea/coffee facilities. 2 doubles, 2 singles. AA listed. OS Ref SK 890804

(FH) MIDDLE FARM Valley Lane, Long Bennington, Newark, Notts, NG23 5EE

Phil Baggaley
Tel:-(0400) 81324
Open Apr-Oct
B&B   £8.50   Listed
      Sleeps 4

(5)

Phil and Jeff Baggaley welcome you to their 15 acre smallholding just off the A1 between Newark and Grantham. The farmhouse was built between the wars and is surrounded by a colourful garden and greenhouse. Tea and homemade cakes always available. The breakfasts are truly farmhouse style. Private trout and coarse fishing available. OS Ref SK 300400

(FH) ABBEY FARM North Ormsby, Nr Louth, Lincs, LN11 0TJ

Marjory Findlay
Tel:-(0472) 840272
Closed Xmas-New Year
B&B   £10-£12.50
EM   From £5
      Sleeps 6

This spacious Georgian farmhouse nestles idyllically in a secluded little valley on a large mixed farm in the Lincolnshire Wolds. Ideal for touring & walking. Within easy reach of Louth, Lincoln, Humberbridge & coast. Many public footpaths locally and Viking Way approx 6m. Also coarse fishing. Bedrooms have CH, H/C, tea facilities & radios. Guests bathroom with shower, lounge with TV. Morning papers. OS Ref TF 931280

(CH) HOE HILL Swinhope, Nr. Binbrook, Lincoln, LN3 6HX

Erica Curd
Tel:-(047283) 206
Closed Xmas-New Year
B&B   £8.50-£11
EM   £5-£6
CH   Sleeps 6

Come to the Lincolnshire Wolds & disprove the image of a completely 'flat county'. Hoe Hill, an old farmhouse offers attractive & comfortable rooms, a large garden, substantial English breakfasts & evening meals by arrangement. Cookery demonstrations are also offered at weekends. Louth, Grimsby & the Humber Bridge, gateway to the North, are within a few miles. OS Ref TF 2295

(FH) GELSTON GRANGE FARM Gelston, Grantham, Lincs, NG32 2AQ

Janet Sharman
Tel:-(0400) 50281
Open all year
B&B   £8.50-£9.50   Listed
EM   £5.50
      Sleeps 6

(2)

Janet and Bob welcome you to their comfortable Georgian farmhouse. Enjoy the friendly relaxing atmosphere, good home cooking and pleasant large garden. Guests rooms all with tea/coffee facilities, TV. Situated approximately 5 mins from the A1 between Grantham and Newark. Within easy reach of Lincoln Cathedral, Belton House, Belvoir Castle and many places of interest. OS Ref SK 855467

(FH) THE GRANGE Grange Lane, Covenham St Bartholomew, Louth, Lincs, LN11 0PD

Phyllis Shaw
Tel:-(0507) 86678
Closed Xmas-New Year
B&B   £10-£12   Listed
      Sleeps 6

Phyl and Jim welcome you to share the interests of their 700 acre mixed farm and the comfort of their old farmhouse. Phyl serves a traditional farmhouse breakfast and can recommend local pubs for evening meals. Ideally situated for touring the Lincolnshire Wolds and coast, visiting Lincoln, Louth and old market towns. Bird watching, fishing, horse riding not far away. OS Ref TF 350952

Lincolnshire ENGLAND

(SC) PENFOLD FARM   Old Beer House, Normanby-by-Spital, Lincoln, Lincs, LN2 3HE

Richard & Pip Hassell
Tel:-(067 37) 345
Open all Year
SC   £100-£175
         Sleeps 6

Warm comfortable country cottage in friendly village. Central heating, open fires, traditional furniture, colour TV, large garden, plus enclosed rear area. Pets and children welcome; babysitter available. Meals including breakfast can be supplied by an excellent cook at the cottage. Historic Lincoln is nearby, within easy reach of Wolds and coast. York via Humber Bridge makes a really interesting day out. OS Ref TF 002882

(SC) NEWPORT FARM HOUSE   The Old Hall, North Carlton, Lincoln, LN1 2RR

Mrs Jean Heneage
Tel:-(0522) 730262
Open all year
SC   £100-£140
         Sleeps 5

Four miles from historic Lincoln at the gates of the 16th Century Old Hall (Henry VIII really did sleep here) sits an attractive double fronted farmhouse sleeping 5 with 2 bathrooms open fire and night storage heaters, on a 300 acre working farm. Tennis and swimming. OS Ref SK 943775

(SC) PINGLES COTTAGE   Grange Farm, Broxholme, Nr Saxilby, Lincoln, LN1 2NG

Pat Sutcliffe
Tel:-(0522) 702441
Open all year
SC   £100-£130
         Sleeps 5

Pingles is comfortable, well equipped for 5 people - a 19th Century farm cottage with its own lawn and garden, surrounded by fields, in hamlet of Broxholme, 6 miles from historic Lincoln. Over ½ mile of coarse fishing in the River Till which is part of the family run cereals/stock farm. The Lincolnshire Edge, Wolds and coast, Nottinghamshire, Humberside are all within easy reach. OS Ref SK 910782

(SC) PANTILES COTTAGE   The Old Hall, Potterhanworth, Lincoln, LN4 2DS

Mrs. Susan Battle
Tel:-(0522) 791338
Open all year
SC   £90-£130
         Sleeps 5

Pantiles is a charming oak-beamed cottage. It has been tastefully furnished to accommodate 5 people and its quiet secluded garden overlooks fields and a duckpond. Situated 7 miles south of Lincoln, it is within easy reach of many places of interest. Linen is provided and there is central heating. A log fire and TV.

(SC) CARRIER'S FARM COTTAGE   Carrier's Farm, Broxholme, Lincoln, LN1 2NG

Irene Gilkison
Tel:-(0522) 702976
Open all year
SC   £75-£100
         Sleeps 6

Set in a quiet hamlet and only 10 minutes from Lincoln, the sympathetically restored and furnished Victorian 3 bedroomed cottage has all modern amenities. The farm has a horticultural bias with it's own nursery and private fishing on the River Till is close by. Fully centrally heated accommodation and log fires makes it an ideal holiday home any time of the year. OS Ref SK 909781

40 CHESHIRE

CHESHIRE

Cheshire is dominated by the Roman and mediaeval city of Chester. It displays its heritage in fine style atop the sandstone city walls, in the Grosvenor Museum and at other exhibitions in the city. Down by the Dee, there are boat trips and regattas and its banks make ideal picnic spots. Cheshire is a magic, fairy-tale county with traditional black and white houses. It has stately homes — Tatton Park — with a country estate in a thousand acres of deer park. At Danesbury the windows of the church pay tribute to its famous son, Lewis Carroll by portraying characters from Alice in Wonderland in stained glass.

There are many things to do and see in Cheshire. There are day trips on canals, riding, walking some well-known trails — like the Gritstone Trail or the Sandstone Trail. At Ellesmere Port there is the Boat Museum with traditional narrow boats and exhibition hall. At Styal Quarry Bank Mill the story of cotton spinning is told with the added attraction of a country park. And for industrial archaeology you can move straight into space-age technology with Jodrell Bank and its planetarium and garden.

VACANCY SECRETARY:
Anne Read (0625) 25759

Cheshire ENGLAND

(FH) LITTLE HEATH FARM Audlem, Crewe, Cheshire, CW3 0HE

Hilary Bennion
Tel:-(0270) 811324
Closed Xmas-New Year
B&B   £8-£10   Listed
EM   £5
Sleeps 6

A working dairy farm, 5 mins walk from centre of canal-side village offering numerous shops. On the Cheshire, Staffordshire, Shropshire border. Ideal for touring, Stapeley Water and Bridgemere Gardens close by. Good home cooking and a warm welcome awaits you in the beamed farmhouse. Guests own TV lounge, dining room. 1 family, 1 double, bathroom with shower. Evening meal by arrangement. OS Ref SJ 661443

(FH) BURLAND FARM Wrexham Road, Burland, Nr Nantwich, Cheshire, CW5 8ND

Sandra Allwood
Tel:-(0270 74) 210
Open all year
B&B   £10-£18
EM   £6
Sleeps 6

Beautiful Victorian farmhouse in lovely gardens on 200 acre dairy farm. Comfortable sitting, dining rooms. 1 double, 1 twin ensuite, 1 double with H/C. Period furnishing and central heating throughout. Superb food using fresh local produce – homemade bread a speciality. Evening meals provided with pleasure. Near several areas of outstanding natural beauty and historical interest. AA Listed. Special winter breaks. OS Ref SJ 604534

(FH) ELM HOUSE FARM Saighton Lane, Saighton, Nr Chester, Cheshire, CH3 6EN

Sheila Thomas
Tel:-(0244) 335093
Closed Xmas-New Year
B&B   £9.50-£10   Listed
      Reductions for children.
Sleeps 4-6

Cosy 17th Century listed farmhouse on 75 acre working dairy farm, overlooking open pastureland & Peckforton Hills. 4m south of historic City of Chester; 15 minutes from Welsh border and within easy reach of Liverpool & motorways. Heating throughout. Guests dining room, bathroom and open fired TV lounge. Full farmhouse breakfast. Tea/coffee facilities in bedrooms. Single, double, twin or family. OS Ref SJ 444619

(FH) HENHULL HALL Welshmans Lane, Nantwich, Cheshire, CW5 6AD

Philip & Joyce Percival
Tel:-(0270) 624158
Closed Xmas-New Year
B&B   £10-£15   Listed
EM   £5
      Reductions for children.
Sleeps 6

On the site of the Battle of Nantwich, this 200 acre dairy farm borders the historic town. The rosy double room has luxury shower room en suite. The Green Room is a spacious family or twin room. The Pink Room is a pretty single. Families are very welcome to enjoy our comfortable warm home with TV lounge, dining room and bathrooms. OS Ref SJ 642534

(FH) STOKE GRANGE FARM Chester Road, Nantwich, Cheshire, CW5 6BT

Georgina West
Tel:-(0270) 625525
Open all year
B&B   £10
Sleeps 6

Modern comfortable canalside farmhouse set in 120 acres of Cheshire dairyland. 1 twin/family and double room with washbasin, tea making facilities and central heating. Guests own television lounge with log fire, games room, bathroom and dining room. Central for Nantwich, Chester and N Wales. Convenient for Bridgemere Nurseries, Stapeley Water Gardens, Jodrell Bank, Beeston and Cholmondeley Castle. OS Ref SJ 623559

(FH) BANK FARM Wrenbury Frith, Wrenbury, Nantwich, Cheshire, CW5 8HJ

Caroline Hockenhull
Tel:-(0270) 780253
Closed Xmas-New Year
B&B   £8.50-£10   Listed
EM   £4
Sleeps 2

Modern comfortable farm house in quiet countryside. A working dairy farm within easy reach of Chester, Nantwich and North Wales. Two miles off the A49. Good home cooking and a warm welcome. Open fire places. Charming canalside pub and restaurant 1 mile. Places to visit: Bridgemere Nurseries, Stapeley Water Gardens, Wedgewood Pottery. Golf course 7 miles away. Guests have own lounge/dining room with TV. OS Ref SJ 576487

181

HIGHER ELMS FARM   Minshull Vernon, Crewe, Cheshire, CW1 4RG

Mary Charlesworth
Tel:-(027 071) 252
Open all year
B&B   £9-£10
Sleeps 6

A farmhouse of character set in attractive gardens alongside the Shropshire Union Canal in the heart of rolling Cheshire countryside. Oak beamed dining room and sitting room. Spacious bedrooms with H/C and colour TV. Kiddies play area. This 200 acre dairy farm has 10 acres of woodland and lovely opportunities for fishing (River Weaver), birdwatching and walking. OS Ref SJ 671613

ROUGH HEY FARM   Leek Road, Gawsworth, Macclesfield, Cheshire, SK11 0JQ

Phyllis Worth
Tel:-(02605) 2296
Closed Xmas and New Year
B&B   £9-£10   Listed
Sleeps 5

(3)

Rough Hey Farm dates back as early as the mid-sixteenth Century and is 800ft above sea level. 3 miles from Macclesfield and 12 miles from Buxton. Ideal for walking and a small coarse fishing pond. Pony trekking near by. Family room, twin bedded room and single room. Bathroom with toilet and shower room with toilet. Guests are assured of a warm welcome. OS Ref SJ 919688

GREEN FARM   Deans Lane, Balterley, Nr Crewe, Cheshire, CW2 5QJ

Geoff & Chris Hollins
Tel:-(0270) 820214
Open all year
B&B   £8.50-£9.50   Listed
Sleeps 6

145 acre working dairy farm. An attractive, comfortable farmhouse in peaceful surroundings. Guests own lounge with colour TV, shower room and toilet. Twin bedded room on ground floor suitable for disabled. Tea making facilities. Situated on the Cheshire/Staffordshire border, 2 miles from junction 16 (M6) and ½ mile from A52. Enjoy the beauty and many attractions in the surrounding area. OS Ref SJ 761510

BEECHWOOD HOUSE   206 Wallerscote Rd, Weaverham, Northwich, Cheshire, CW8 3LZ

Janet Kuypers
Tel:-(0606) 852123
Closed Xmas-New Year
B&B   £9-£10.50   Listed
EM   £4
Sleeps 4

Comfortable 1830's farmhouse on 19 acre stockfarm in peaceful surroundings. CH, home cooking, adaptable mealtimes. Good sports facilities nearby: golf, tennis, squash, swimming, windsurfing, fishing etc, tackle and drying room. Within easy reach of M6, M56. 1 twin, 2 single rooms. OS Ref SJ 632 735

LEA FARM   Wrinehill Road, Wybunbury, Nantwich, Cheshire, CW5 7NS

Mrs Jean Callwood
Tel:-0270 841429
Closed Xmas-New Year
B&B   £8.50-£9   Applied
EM   £4
Sleeps 6

A pleasant farmhouse, set in a landscaped garden, on 150 acre dairy & arable farm, in the Heart of the Cheshire countryside, offering many attractions. Near to Bridgemere Wild Life Park & Stapeley Water Gardens. Convenient for Crewe, Nantwich, Chester M6 Motorway (Junction 16). 1 double/family room, 1 twin bedded room, tea/coffee facilities. Guest TV lounge & dining room. OS Ref 72 49

PITTS FARM   Malpas, Cheshire, SY14 7AJ

Doris Bevin
Tel:-(094881) 224
Closed Xmas and New Year
B&B   £10   Listed
Sleeps 4
SC   £80-£160
Sleeps 6

Self catering cottage comprising 3 bedrooms, 1 bathroom, 1 shower room, fitted kitchen and lounge. Sleeps 4 to 6. Inclusive of linen. Electricity 50p metered. TV, fridge-freezer, electric cooker, toaster, washing machine, iron and ironing board. Storage heaters included in rent (towels not included). 2 miles from shops. Pets by arrangement. Also available Bed & Breakfast in farmhouse. OS Ref SJ 459466

Cheshire ENGLAND

FH HARDINGLAND FARM Macclesfield Forest, Macclesfield, Cheshire, SK11 0ND

Anne Read
Tel:-(0625) 25759
Open Easter-Nov
B&B   From £10   Listed
EM   From £7
      Sleeps 6

Good food and a warm welcome await you in this secluded stone built, tastefully modernised, 18th Century farmhouse, on hillside in the Peak National Park. (8m from Buxton) with panoramic views over the Cheshire plain. Ideal centre for touring in the Peak District and Cheshire. 1 double en suite, 1 twin, 1 family en suite. Gourmet weekends out of season. OS Ref SJ 958726

FH COOLE HALL FARM Hankelow, Crewe, Cheshire, CW3 0JO

Carolyn & Franklin Goodwin
Tel:-(0270) 811232
Closed Xmas-New Year
B&B   £9-£10
      Sleeps 5

Come and relax on our 160 acre beef/arable farm, with ample opportunities for birdwatching, fishing and walking. The spacious oak-beamed 18th Century farmhouse, overlooking the River Weaver will provide all the comforts of home. Sample the warm hospitality and good home cooking which we offer in our peaceful surroundings. 1 family/double room, 1 twin, both with vanity units. OS Ref SJ 658458

FH CURTIS HULME FARM Bradwall Road, Middlewich, Cheshire, CW10 0LD

Philip & Miriam Williams
Tel:-(060 684) 3230
Closed Xmas
B&B   £8.50   Listed
      Sleeps 6

A warm welcome is assured at this 160 acre dairy farm between historic market town of Sandbach and Middlewich. Three miles from motorway. Very quiet with large gardens. Comfortable and relaxing surroundings. One family room, 1 double, 1 twin. Lots of space for children, swings, etc. Dining room, 2 sitting rooms. Television. Old oak beams and open fireplaces. OS Ref SJ 732643

FH OLDHAMS HOLLOW FARM Manchester Road, Tytherington, Macclesfield, Cheshire, SK10 2JW

Brenda Buxton
Tel:-(0625) 24128
Closed Xmas
B&B   £11.50   Listed
      Sleeps 6
      (6mths)

A warm welcome is assured in this large 16th Century restored 3 storey farmhouse on a 60 acre dairy and sheep farm. Two twin and 1 single bedded room each with own washbasin. Large comfortable lounge with colour TV and open log fire. Separate dining room. All rooms with oak beams. One mile from the market town of Macclesfield. Dogs by arrangement. OS Ref SJ 915757

FH GOOSE GREEN FARM Oak Road, Mottram St Andrew, Macclesfield, Cheshire, SK10 4RA

Dyllis Hatch
Tel:-(0625) 828814
Closed Xmas-New Year
B&B   £12-£14
      Sleeps 6

50 acre beef/arable family run farm in beautiful countryside with panoramic views. Just off A538 in easy reach of M6 and Manchester Airport. Convenient for fishing, horse riding and walking, bird watching. Comfortable and homely with log fire in guest lounge. Separate dining room. 1 family, 1 twin, 2 single rooms with washbasins, TV, CH, and tea/coffee facilities. OS Ref SJ 875782

FH THE GOLDEN CROSS FARM Siddington, Nr Macclesfield, Cheshire, SK11 9JP

Hazel Rush
Tel:-(026 04) 358
Closed Xmas and New Year
B&B   £9-£10   Listed
      Sleeps 4

Small, organic dairy farm, 100 yards from the A34 on the B5392. In picturesque surroundings. Central for Macclesfield, Congleton, Holmes Chapel and Alderley Edge. Places of local interest include Capesthorne Hall, Gawsworth Hall, Tatton Hall and Park, Dunham Massey Hall, Styal Mill and Nether Alderley Mill. Double bedded room. Two single rooms. OS Ref SJ 846708

183

SPROSTON HILL FARM Wrenbury, Nr Nantwich, Cheshire, CW5 8HH

Janet Wilkinson
Tel:-(0270) 780241
Open all year
B&B   £9.50-£10   Listed
       Sleeps 8

Comfortable oak beamed farmhouse, situated only 300 yards from Llangollen Canal and canalside pub/restaurant. Nantwich 5 miles, ½ hours drive from Chester. Convenient for North Wales. Bridgemere Garden World and Stapeley Water Garden, biggest of their kind in Europe. One twin-bedded and two double with vanity units. Own lounge with colour TV, tea/coffee making facilities. OS Ref SJ 588484

HATTON HALL Hatton Heath, Chester, Cheshire, CH3 9AP

Shirley Woolley
Tel:-(0829) 70601
Open all year
B&B   £12-£15
       Redn for child
       Sleeps 6
Van   £1.50-£2;
       Max 3
(10)

Elegant Georgian listed farmhouse within a Norman moat on peaceful 250 acre dairy farm. 1 mile off A41, 5 miles from Roman walled city of Chester. First class B&B. Spacious comfortable rooms, one en-suite, others with vanity units. Cotton bed linen, quality towelling, tea/coffee with fine china. Colour TV, radio alarms, electric blankets in each room. Central heating throughout. OS Ref SJ 472 611

STAPLEFORD HALL Tarvin, Chester, CH3 8HH

Margaret Winward
Tel:-(0829) 40202
Open all year
B&B   £12-£15   Listed
       Sleeps 6

Beautiful Georgian farmhouse on 250 acre dairy farm 6 miles from Chester, listed for historical and architectural interest. Large gardens in peaceful and attractive countryside, tennis and croquet on the lawn. Attractively furnished dining room and drawing room with colour TV. Spacious comfortable bedrooms with tea/coffee facilities. One bedroom has private bathroom and colour TV. Also 2 bedroom self-catering cottage. OS Ref SJ 4867

DEAN BANK COTTAGES Manor Farm, Peckforton, Tarporley, Cheshire, CW6 9TJ

Frances Dakin
Tel:-(0829) 260353
Closed Feb-Mar
SC   £90-£140
       Sleeps 6

The cottage is ¾ mile from Beeston Castle and the Sandstone Trail and less than ¼m off the A49, between the towns of Nantwich and Chester. It has 3 bedrooms, lounge with TV, well equipped kitchen and a bathroom. Heating is by storage heaters and an open fire. Fuel, electricity provided but no bed linen. Cot available if required. OS Ref SJ 541565

STAPLEFORD HALL COTTAGE Stapleford Hall, Tarvin, Chester, CH3 8HH

Margaret Winward
Tel:-(0829) 40202
Open all year
SC   £90-£175
       Sleeps 6

Self-catering cottage 6 miles from Chester, in the grounds of historic Stapleford Hall. In peaceful and attractive countryside on 250 acre dairy farm with views of Peckforton and Beeston Castles. Recently completely renovated, this character cottage has two bedrooms (sleeps 6), bathroom, beamed sitting room with open fire and colour TV and large fully equipped kitchen. 50p slot meter, electric heating. OS Ref SJ 4867

Cheshire ENGLAND

SEE CANDLES IN THE MAKING

ENJOY A DAY OUT IN THE HEART OF THE BEAUTIFUL COUNTRYSIDE

In an area steeped in History, lies Cheshire Workshops, one of the largest manufacturers of hand sculptured candles in Europe. Come along and see for yourself just how this ancient craft has been revived and developed by Cheshire Workshops

You will be completely absorbed and fascinated watching our craftsmen achieve such intricate detail with their hand carving. Each item is an individual work of art. We make every effort to ensure that your visit is enjoyable and memorable.

★ Hayloft Restaurant ★ Children's Play Area ★ Free Admission
★ Craftshop ★ Demonstrations ★ Free Parking.
Coaches Welcome – Please Book.

OPENING HOURS: Workshops & Craftshop –
Every day including Sunday: 10am-5pm.
Evening Coach Parties by prior booking.
Hayloft Restaurant Daily – (including Sat. & Sun.): 10am-4.30pm.
For further details on how to find us,
please contact: Burwardsley, Nr. Chester CH3 9PF.
Tel: Tattenhall (0829) 70401.

Cheshire Workshops
RURAL ENGLISH EXPERIENCE

THE GREATEST GARDENING DAY OUT IN BRITAIN

25 acres of fascinating plants and gardens

NEW NEW **... THE GARDEN KINGDOM**

Bridgemere — more than a mere garden centre
— now with more than ever to see

BRIDGEMERE GARDEN WORLD

Between Woore and Nantwich on the A51

★ COFFEE HOUSE
  Egon Ronay Recommended
★ EASY ACCESS
  & LEVEL GROUND
★ FACILITIES FOR THE
  ELDERLY & DISABLED
★ IDEAL FOR PARTY VISITS
  & COACH TOURS
★ INFORMATON PACK
  FOR PARTY VISITS
★ EVENTS THROUGHOUT
  THE YEAR

● MORE THAN AN ACRE UNDERCOVER
(So forget about the weather)

● FREE ADMISSION Car & Coach Parking Open Mondays to Saturdays 9 am to dusk and Sundays 10 am to dusk(dusk: Summer 8.30 pm latest and Winter 5 pm)

Bridgemere Garden World
Bridgemere, Nr Nantwich
Cheshire CW5 7QB
Tel: (09365) 239/381

● We are only ½ hour drive away from Stoke on Trent
● Only 45 minutes from the historic city of Chester
● 20 minutes from Junction 15 & 16 on M6

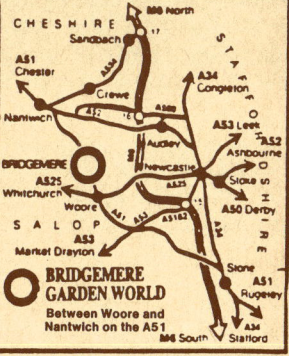

41 RIBBLE VALLEY, Lancashire

RIBBLE VALLEY, LANCASHIRE

The forest of Bowland, the largest area of upsoilt countryside in Lancashire 1827 feet high Pendle Hill, and the fringes of the Pennines, afford the visitor to the area a chance to appreciate Lancashire at its most beautiful.

Complementing such countryside are a number of towns and villages, all with their own individual character: Clitheroe, with its castle and museum; Whalley its Cistercian Abbey (founded in 1296) and Georgian and Tudor Houses; the old market town of Skipton and Ribchester, with its Roman Museum. Barley, at th foot of Pendle Hill, with its connections with the Witch Trials of 1612, Slaidburn, the gateway to the Forest of Bowland, once a Royal hunting ground.

There is something here to suit all tastes. For example places of historic interest, such as Browsholme Hall, the home of the Parker family, which houses a display of thirteenth century domestic articles, can be contrasted with the new Preston Guild Hall with facilities for many social cultural and educational activities.

If you prefer a quiet, more sedate pace, you can enjoy one of the several country parks and picnics in the area, such as Beacon Fell, Spring Wood, Barley or Wycoller.

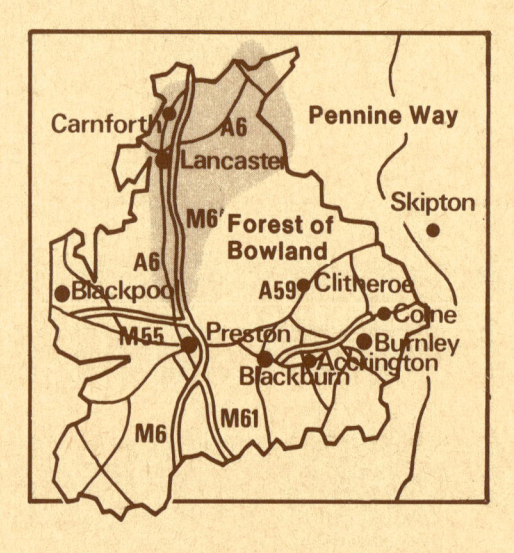

A holiday in the farms of the Ribble Valley will also leave you within easy reach of the Yorkshire Dales, the Lake District, Haworth and the Bronte country.

GROUP CONTACT:
Frances Oliver (02005) 295

Ribble Valley, Lancashire ENGLAND

(FH) CAPPER FARM Wellhead Rd, Sabden Fold, Burnley, Lancs, BB12 9LR

Nigel & Glad Taylor
Tel:-0282 602092
Open Easter-Oct
B&B £14.50-£18.50
EM By arrangment
Sleeps 6

Cappers Farm, (which runs a flock of Polled Dorset Sheep) is situated in the heart of Pendle Witch Country - good walking & cycling & easy access to the Yorkshire Dales & Lancashire Towns. Comfortable log-fired lounge with oak beams. Heated indoor swimming pool with sun lounge. Bedrooms with en-suite bathrooms - choice of Jacobean Four Poster or Brass Bed.

(CH) MYTTON FOLD FARM HOTEL Whalley Road, Langho, Blackburn, Lancs, BB6 8AB

Frank & Lilian Hargreaves
Tel:-(0254) 48255
Closed Xmas
B&B £16-£30
EM From £6
CH Sleeps 26

Situated at the gateway to the Ribble Valley, Mytton Fold Farm Hotel was originally stables, built in 1880 of random stone. Converted in 1982 to a luxurious hotel, run by the Hargreaves family with daughter Carole being the 4th generation to farm the 100 acre beef/sheep farm. Only 200 yds from the A59. A peaceful oasis in todays busy world. OS Ref SD 712348

(FH) PAGES FARM Woodhouse Lane, Slaidburn, Nr Clitheroe, Lancs, BB7 3AH

Mrs Brenda Cowking
Tel:-(02006) 205
Open all year
B&B £11
Sleeps 6

This 17th Century farmhouse is situated on Woodhouse Lane ⅓ of a mile west of the lovely village of Slaidburn. The farmhouse has old oak beams, is fully centrally heated and has a very comfortable lounge with open fire. Accomodation comprises 2 double rooms with bathrooms en suite and 1 twin-bedded room. Shaver points and tea-making facilities are provided. OS Ref SD 700529

(FH) HIGHER WANLESS FARM Red Lane, Colne, Lancs, BB8 7JP

Carole Mitson
Tel:-(0282) 865301
Closed Xmas-New Year
B&B £12.50-£15
EM Approx £6
    (Red'n for
    children)

A warm welcome awaits you at this beautiful farmhouse with oak beams, log fires & luxurious bedrooms. Nestling in a peaceful rural area within 10 minutes drive from "Pendle Witch" & Bronte country & within easy reach of Yorkshire Dales. Pendle Heritage Centre 1m. The farm is used mainly for breeding Shire horses & sheep. Several country inns nearby offering wide range of meal facilities. AA Listed. OS Ref SD 872413

(FH) HORNS FARM Church Street, Slaidburn, Nr Clitheroe, Lancashire, BB7 3ER

Sheila Parker
Tel:-(02006) 288
Closed Xmas
B&B £9-£10   Listed
Sleeps 4

96 acre dairy/sheep farm on bank of River Hodder has 17th Century farmhouse in cobbled main street of small, quiet, unspoilt village. Within easy reach of Dales, Lakes and seaside. Fishing at Stocks reservoir 2m. Large family room with tea making facilities, private bathroom, lounge/dining room, TV. Second room only available to members of same family or party of friends. OS Ref SD 713522

(FH) NEW HOUSE FARM Bracewell, Skipton, Yorks, BD23 3JG

Sheila Mattinson
Tel:-(0282) 813026
Closed Xmas & New Year
B&B £9
Sleeps 6

A warm welcome to our 17th Century farmhouse on a family run farm situated on the edge of a small village, just off the A59 midway between Skipton and Clitheroe. Easy reach of the Yorkshire Dales, Bronte country and Pendle. Easy reach of the Lake District. 2 double rooms and 1 twin with washbasins. 1 single. Lounge with TV. OS Ref SD 860486

(FH) **WYTHA FARM   Rimington, Clitheroe, Lancs, BB7 4EQ**

Frances Oliver
Tel:-(02005) 295
Closed Xmas-New Year
B&B   £9-£12.50   Listed
EM   £6
Sleeps 6

This 176 acre dairy farm near Pendle Hill gives panoramic views of the Ribble Valley. It is an ideal touring and walking centre. A warm welcome awaits every guest with plentiful good farmhouse food, open fire, central heating and television. We offer double and family rooms with washbasins. Public health and hygiene certificate. Pets by arrangement only. OS Ref SD 827449

(FH) **FALICON FARM   Fleet Street Lane, Hothersall, Longridge, Preston, Lancs PR3 3XE**

Katie Johnson
Tel:-(025484) 583
Open Feb-Nov
B&B   £16-£22
EM   £11.50
Sleeps 6

Peacefully situated, luxurious oak-beamed farmhouse. AA listed. Country Homes Host. Highly personal, friendly service. 4 course English country breakfast provided. Excellent freshly prepared, imaginative cuisine, 5 course dinner, wine inclusive. No smoking. No TV. 2 double rooms, 1 twin, all with private bathrooms. Reduced price breaks available. 15 mins exit 31, 32 & M6 to peace and tranquility. OS Ref SD 628360

(FH) **PARKGATE FARM   Cow Ark, Forest-of-Bowland, Nr Clitheroe, Lancs, BB7 3P7**

Mrs Elsie Calvert
Tel:-(020 08) 229
Open Mar-Nov
B&B   £9-£11   Listed
Sleeps 6

300 year old listed house on 200 acre beef/sheep farm nestling amongst Pennine Hills at gateway to Trough-of-Bowland, Lancaster, Lakes. Clitheroe market town nearby. Within easy reach of north Lancashire coast. Many beautiful villages close by, Slaidburn, Chipping and Waddington. Car essential. Home cooking and friendly atmosphere. Tea/coffee facilities. 1 family, 1 double, 1 single all with washbasins, open fires. Visitors lounge & bathroom. OS Ref SD 670458

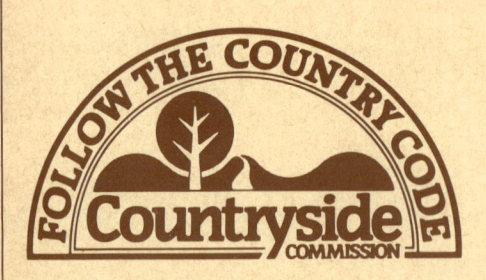

FOLLOW THE COUNTRY CODE
Countryside COMMISSION

TAKE CARE OF THE COUNTRY

Enjoy the countryside and
respect its life and work.
Guard against all risk of fire.
Fasten all gates.
Keep your dogs under close control.
Keep to public paths across farmland.
Use gates and stiles to cross fences,
hedges and walls.
Leave livestock, crops and machinery alone.
Take your litter home.
Help to keep all water clean.
Protect wildlife, plants and trees.
Take special care on country roads.
Make no unnecessary noise.

VALE OF LUNE, Lancashire

VALE OF LUNE, LANCASHIRE

Rising in the hills of Cumbria the Lune flows through richly pastoral countryside; one of it's first ports of call is Kirkby Lonsdale an attractive and unspoilt market town with its 13th century church and Devils Bridge. To the south east lies the busy moorland market town of High Bentham with its Wednesday cattle market and Ingleton famous for its show caves and spectacular waterfall glens. To the North West lies the unique Limestone Crags of Arnside and Silverdale with its many splendid coastal walks. The area is a haven for birdwatchers with the RSPB bird Sanctuary at Leighton Moss and for railway enthusiasts "Steam Town" at Carnforth will take you back in time. The Lune then flows down to the Roman City of Lancaster with its castle and museums including the newly opened Maritime Museum, Museum of Childhood and the Judges Lodgings. At the end of the Lune Valley lies Morcambe Bay.

The River Wyre starts its journey to the sea high in the fells of the ancient hunting Forest of Bowland and flows down through unspoilt villages such as Marshaw, Abbeystead and Dolphinholme to the market town of Garstang. Beacon Fell Country Park is on the doorstep and well worth a visit. Both the River Lune and the Wyre offer plenty of opportunities for coarse fishing.

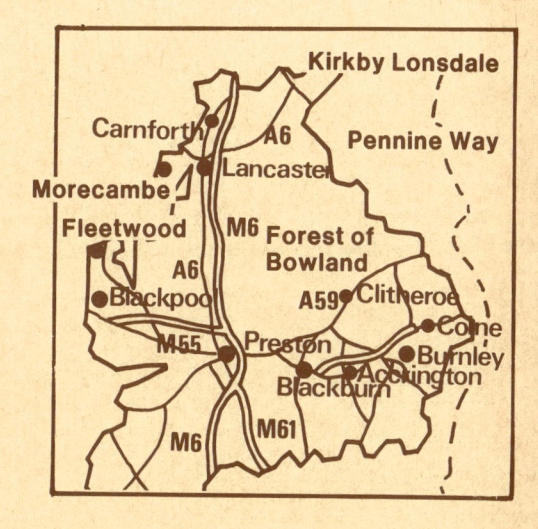

GROUP CONTACT
Jean Fowler (09952) 2140

STIRZAKERS FARM Barnacre, Garstang, Preston, Lancs, PR3 1GE

Ruth Wrathall
Tel:-(09952) 3335
Closed Xmas-New Year
B&B £8-£9 Listed
Sleeps 6

A warm welcome awaits you at this 130 acre dairy farm, with its old beamed farmhouse and log fire. Help with the milking and feed the calves, or explore the beautiful wooded Pennines, Forest of Bowland, Lake District, Blackpool and the coast or nearby shopping centres. Double, family and single rooms with CH, visitors' lounge, colour TV and bedtime drink. OS Ref SD 519442

COTESTONES FARM Sand Lane, Warton, Carnforth, Lancs, LA5 9NH

Gill Close
Tel:-(0524) 732418
Closed Xmas
B&B £8 Listed
EM £5
Sleeps 6
Van £1.75

Situated on the north Lancashire coast near to the M6 junction 35 on the Carnforth to Silverdale road. This is a family run dairy and beef farm which adjoins Leighton Moss RSPB Reserve, also very near to Steamtown Railway Museum. Situated between Lancaster/Morecambe and the Lake District, it is an ideal place for touring the area. OS Ref SD 487715

LANE HOUSE FARM Bentham, Nr Lancaster, LA2 7DJ

Betty Clapham
Tel:-(0468) 61479
Open Mar-Oct
B&B £8
EM £6
Sleeps 6

Lane House is a 100 acre dairy farm. 17th Century beamed farmhouse has beautiful views of Yorkshire Dales. Guests assured of every comfort, with good farmhouse food. Bedrooms have washbasins. Also separate visitors' lounge. Situated 1 mile from the market town of High Bentham, and ½ hour from M6. Ideal for local caves, waterfalls, walking, touring or relaxing in the countryside. Pets by arrangement. OS Ref SD 672676

LUND HOLME Ingleton, Carnforth, Lancs, LA6 3HN

Nancy Lund
Tel:-(0468) 41307
Closed Xmas-New Year
B&B £8-£9
EM £6
Sleeps 6

A warm welcome awaits you at Lund Holme, a working dairy and sheep farm at Ingleton in the Dales National Park. Tour the Dales, ramble in the Lake District or laze on the coast. Family, double or twin room with hot and cold water. Separate visitors' lounge with TV. Golf, fishing, swimming and horse riding in surrounding area. Good farmhouse cooking. Weekly reductions. OS Ref SD 685729

GREENHALGH CASTLE FARM Castle Lane, Garstang, Preston, Lancs, PR3 1RB

Mrs Jean Fowler
Tel:-(09952) 2140
Open all year
B&B £8.50
Redn for children
Sleeps 6

150 acre dairy/sheep farm, with 300 year old, low beamed farmhouse. Secluded but close to small market town. Ideal touring centre or perfect for relaxing, walking or getting the feel of life on a busy farm. Very comfortable guest accomodation. Lounge with colour TV, dining room, separate bathroom, shower room. All bedrooms with washbasins. Canal fishing on farm. Variety of sports facilities nearby. OS Ref SD 501450

FOWGILL PARK FARM High Bentham, Nr Lancaster, LA2 7AH

Shirley Metcalfe
Tel:-0468 61630
Open Easter-Sep
B&B £7.50-£9 Listed
EM £5
Sleeps 4

Fowgill is situated in an elevated position with beautiful views of the Dales. Ingleton 2½ miles away is known for its caves & waterfalls. A good centre for touring the Dales, Coast & Lakes. Good farmhouse cooking, 4 course evening meal by arrangment. Evening drink included. Bedrooms have washbasins & shaver points. Beamed ceiling in lounge & dining room. Reductions for children. OS Ref SD 678 691

Vale of Lune, Lancashire ENGLAND

(FH) GARGHYLL DYKE Cowan Bridge, Kirkby Lonsdale, Carnforth, Lancs, LA6 2HT

Gillian Burrow
Tel:-(0468) 71446
Open Easter-Nov
B&B £9-£10.50   Listed
Sleeps 4

A warm, homely welcome to Garghyll Dyke. A family run 260 acre dairy, beef and sheep farm for over 4 generations. Set in the Lune Valley, close to the old market town of Kirkby Lonsdale with its picturesque Devils Bridge, an ideal base for Lakes, Dales and coast. One double and 1 twin room each with washbasin and tastefully furnished. OS Ref SD 762632

(FH) COLLINGHOLME FARM Cowan Bridge, Via Carnforth, Lancashire, LA6 2JL

Anne & Peter Burrow
Tel:-(0468) 71775
Open Mar-Oct
B&B £8.50-£9   Listed
Sleeps 4

For a break from the hustle and bustle, Collingholme is the place for you. It is a 250 year old farmhouse nestling by a pretty stream, mountains and fells are its backdrop. Between Dales, Lakes only 3 miles from the market town of Kirkby Lonsdale. We offer guests a warm, friendly home, giving guests a feeling of wellbeing where they can relax and feel at home. OS Ref SD 637748

(SC) KEEPERS COTTAGE Brackenthwaite Farm, Yealand Redmayne, Carnforth, Lancs, LA5 9TE

Susan Clarke
Tel:-(04482) 3276
Open all year
SC £60-£135
Sleeps 4-6

Our original cottage sleeps 4, a newly converted barn provides 2 cottages sleeping 4 & 6. Part of an attractive limestone building complex. Fully equipped with colour TV & storage heaters. Situated midway between Lancaster & Kendal with easy access to the lakes & Dales. Lovely walking area near nature and bird reserves. Watersports & riding nearby. Facilities for own horse. Short lets out of season. OS Ref SD 492772

(SC) THE COTTAGE Oxenforth Green, Tatham, Lancaster, LA2 8PL

Barbara Mason
Tel:-(0468) 61784
Open all year
SC £75-£170
Sleeps 4/5

Enjoy farm life in this recently converted double glazed cottage adjoining farmhouse of 56 acre dairy farm. Cosy accommodation for 4 plus cot, with well equipped fitted kitchen, lounge with gas fire and colour television, 2 shower rooms and storage heaters. Within easy reach of Lancaster, Morecambe, Blackpool, the Lake District and the Yorkshire Dales. Also orchard caravan. OS Ref SD 685644

(SC) TARNACRE HALL FARM St Michaels-on-Wyre, Preston, Lancs, PR3 0TB

James & Frances Whewell
Tel:-(09958) 217
Open Easter-Oct
SC £60-£100
Sleeps 6

A warm welcome awaits you on our 150 acre dairy farm (nr Garstang) with sheep, goats and hens. The first floor self contained flat in the farmhouse has unrestricted views of the countryside. Double bedroom, twin bedroom, shower room, kitchenette/lounge with double bed settee. All electric with storage heating. Bed linen provided. Central for visiting the many contrasting places in the area. OS Ref SD 470422

43 SOUTH PENNINES
W. Yorks/Lancs/Cheshire

**SOUTH PENNINES
(W. YORKS/LANCS/CHESHIRE)**

'Last of the Summer Wine', Emmerdale Farm', 'In Loving Memory', 'Juliet Bravo' and the novels of the Bronte Sisters may have already introduced you to this area.

Here, walkers along the Pennine Way will experience some of the most dramatic Pennine scenery. For those who wish to rest a while, towns such as Marsden and Hebden Bridge have lots to offer. Hebden Bridge is a typical bustling Pennine town. Nearby Hardcastle Crags is a popular beauty spot and Heptonstall, an ancient hilltop village, is completely unspoiled.

Other routes include Blackstone Edge, the best preserved section of Roman road in Britain, circular walks such as the Calderdale Way, the Rossendale Way and the Colne Valley Circular. There is even a Bog Dodgers Way above Marsden for a real challenge!

Bronte enthusiasts can soak up the atmosphere in the Parsonage Museum, Haworth and the village's much photgraphed main street bustles with activity. Take the family for a ride on the Worth Valley Railway, recalling locations in the film "The Railway Children". The Bury-Rawtenstall line is being restored and re-opened as a steam railway. The South Pennines textile heritage is also magnificently illustrated. At the Colne Valley Museum, Golcar you can see life as it was in a domestic weavers cottage of the 1840's or watch clog making and hand loom weaving at the fascinating craft weekends. At Helmshore Textile Museum near Haslingden, the 18th century fulling mill and waterwheel depict the history of the Lancashire textile industry.

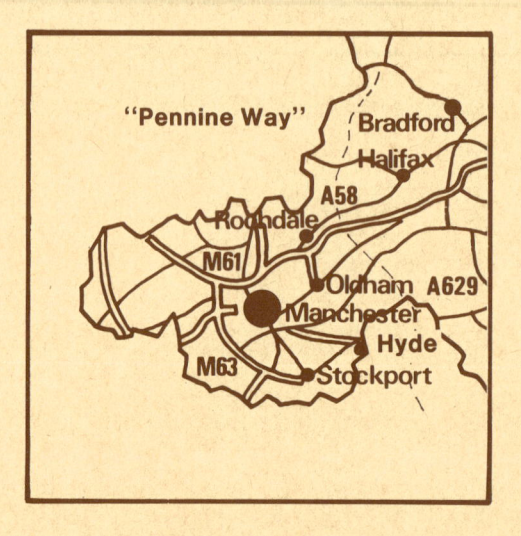

GROUP CONTACT
Jean Mayall (04577) 3040

South Pennines ENGLAND

(FH) UPLANDS FARM Werneth Low, Gee Cross, Hyde, Cheshire, Sk14 3AG

Freda Beaumont
Tel:-(061) 368 6559
Open all year
B&B   £10-£12   Listed
EM   £4-£5
Sleeps 6/8
Tent   £1
Van   £2; Max 5

Step back in time in an 18th Century stone built farmhouse with wooden beams stripped pine. Roaring log fires, brass beds, & feather mattresses ooze comfort. Wedged between Werneth Low & Etherow Country Parks, adjoining Golf course with super views of Cheshire, Derbyshire and Staffordshire. Good basic home cooking or 5 minutes to Pub Grub/Restaurant. Convenient for Manchester Centre, Airport, Stockport.

(FH) LEACHES FARM Ashworth, Rochdale, Lancs, OL11 5UN

Jane M Neave
Tel:-(0706) 41116
Closed Xmas-New Year
B&B   £10   Listed
Sleeps 6

Beautiful 18th Century beef and sheep hill farm with unrestricted views over Lancashire, Cheshire and Derbyshire. Comfortable lounge with open fire, twin bedded and family rooms and central heating throughout. Ideally situated for exploring the local countryside and Northern beauty spots. Only 4 miles from M62, Junction 19. OS Ref SD 8314

(FH) SHIRE COTTAGE Ernocroft Farm, Benches Lane, Marple Bridge, Stockport, Cheshire SK6 5NT

Monica Sidebottom
Tel:-(061427) 2377
Open all year
B&B   £10-£13
EM   £4.50
Sleeps 8

New farm cottage in rural surroundings adjoining Hill Farm. H/C, shaver point in each room. Family room, shower, toilet. Magnificent views overlooking Etherow Country Park. Licensed farm restaurant 5 minutes and other good inn food locally. 30 minutes drive from Derwent Dams, Castleton Caverns and the Blue John Mines. Sports facilities nearby. AA Listed. 20 mins Manchester City centre. Also (04574) 66536. OS Ref SJ 981 912

(FH) CRIB FARM Luddendenfoot, Nr Halifax, West Yorkshire, HX2 6JJ

Pauline Hitchen
Tel:-(0422) 883285
Open Mar-Oct
B&B   £8.50-£10
EM   £6
Sleeps 6

17th Century farmhouse in Heart of Pennines. Tastefully modernised yet retaining olde worlde atmosphere. Fifteen minutes drive from Junctions 22 or 24 on M62. Family run 200 acre dairy farm commanding breathtaking view of Calder Valley. Only few minutes walk to unspoiled heather clad moorland. AA Listed. OS Ref SE 026344

(FH) HIGHER QUICK FARM Lydgate, Oldham, OL4 4JJ

Mrs Annis Heathcote
Tel:-(045 77) 2424
Closed Xmas
B&B   £10   Listed
EM   £4
Sleeps 6

Farmhouse accommodation on 40 acre beef farm. One double, 1 twin, visitors' bathroom. Central heating, television, drying room and bedtime drink. Magnificent views, close to Uppermill (craft centre, museum, golf club, swimming baths), lovely walking area. Evening meals if requested. Within easy reach of Manchester airport and M62. (Members of the Saddleworth Tourist Association) OS Ref SD 968033

(FH) GLOBE FARM Huddersfield Road, Delph, Nr Oldham, OL3 5LU

Jean Mayall
Tel:-(04577) 3040
Closed Xmas-New Year
B&B   £9.50   Listed
EM   £3.50
Sleeps 5
SC   £3.75/night
Tent   £1

Globe Farm offers wide opportunities for walking either on one of the many local footpaths or on the nearby Pennine Way. We have 2 twin, 2 single and 1 family room with CH, hot and cold and a large open fired lounge. With real northern hospitality and good home cooking. We also have a 27 person Bunkhouse with meals or self catering. OS Ref SD 012 097

(sc) **LOWER HILL TOP COTTAGE** Lower Hill Top Farm, Grains Road, Delph, Nr Oldham, OL3 5RL

Alice Dyrom
Tel:-(045 77) 2357
Open all year
SC   £40-£75
          Sleeps 2

Situated on a small farm near to the Pennine Way and the Saddleworth Moors, three miles from Uppermill which is the centre of a group of 7 villages with its own craft centre and museum. Fully modernised cottage with all mod cons. Sleeps 2 people. Close to shops and restaurants. Bedding provided. OS Ref SD 979078

(sc) **BOWERS HALL FARM** Saddleworth Road, Barkisland, Halifax, HX4 0BG

Christine Haigh
Tel:-(0422) 72529
Open all year
SC   £90-£100
          Sleeps 6 + cot

Attached to 1614 manor house, 2 bedroomed accommodation with bath and shower. Sitting room with cooking facilities. Situated beside the farmyard and stables. Not isolated and within easy distance of Halifax, Huddersfield, Bradford and Leeds. Local pubs and shops nearby. Could sleep 6 with cot available. Linen and electricity inclusive. Good facilities for town, country and cultural life. Idyllic setting. OS Ref SE 0520

YORKSHIRE DALES
ß Bronte Country

44

YORKSHIRE DALES & BRONTE COUNTRY

This beautiful region extends from Haworth, home of the Bronte sisters in the south, to beyond Kettlewell in the Yorkshire dales to the north — and in between there's something to please everyone.

Those keen to do their exploring on foot will head for the network of pathways in and around the National Park, the Pennine Way — the 'backbone' of England — and the dales with their lovely valleys, deep woods, clear streams and waterfalls — plus many a welcoming inn.

If history and heritage are more in your line you'll make for Haworth and the Bronte Parsonage; the slate-roofed stone-built cottages and steep cobbled streets lead you straight into the pages of the sisters' family classics.

Also on the visiting list must be Skipton with its mediaeval castle and enchanting Tudor courtyard; the semi-ruined splendour of Bolton Abbey; and Fountain Abbey — biggest, and some claim, the most beautiful of all the ruined abbeys in Britain.

For a real touch of nostalgia take a ride on the North Valley Steam Railway or the Yorkshire Dales Railway; or stop at the famous Five Rise Locks on the Leeds/Liverpool Canal near Bingley.

Or simply enjoy the beautiful dales, villages such as Kettlewell, Burnsall, Malham or Lothersdale — all have a charm of their own, and will make you want to return for more.

GROUP CONTACT
Self Catering —
Wendy Carr (0535) 44568

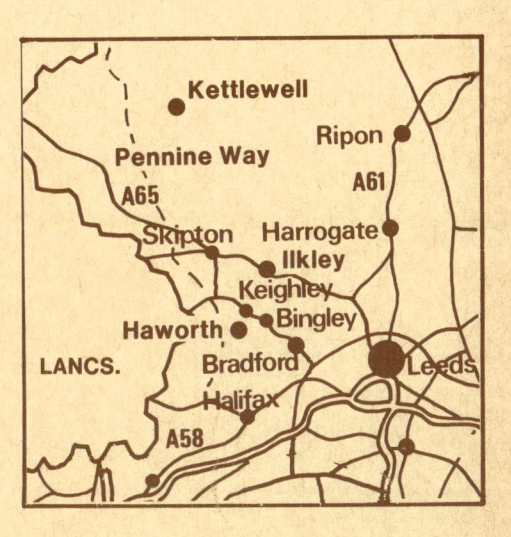

BONDCROFT FARM Embsay, Skipton, North Yorks, BD23 6SF

Christine Clarkson
Tel:-(0756) 3371
Open all year
B&B £9-£10
EM £5
Sleeps 6

Listed

Bondcroft Farm is a working dairy/sheep farm. It is in a beautiful area of the Yorkshire Dales National Park with excellent walks & car drives in all directions. It has a visitors' lounge and visitors' bathroom. Mrs Clarkson is an excellent cook and the family makes everyone welcome. Breakfast at 8.30 and EM at 6pm Late night drinks 9.45pm OS Ref SE 012547

MARCH COTE FARM Cottingley, Bingley, West Yorks, BD16 1UB

George & Jean Warin
Tel:-(0274) 487433
Closed Xmas & New Year
B&B £9-£11
EM £6
Sleeps 6

A friendly atmosphere awaits you on our 200 acre dairy/sheep farm. The 17th Century farmhouse is fully modernised, but enjoys oak beams & mullioned windows - private bathroom available. Farmhouse cooking mostly home grown produce. Peaceful surroundings with plenty of woodland and countryside walks. Ideal for visiting dales & Bronte country. One double, 1 twin, 1 family. Comfort is our aim. AA listed. OS Ref SE 103372

CRAVEN HEIFER FARM Grassington Road, Skipton, North Yorkshire, BD23 3LA

Dorothy Hundsdoerfer
Tel:-(0756) 3732
Open Easter-Oct
B&B £8-£10
EM £6
Sleeps 6

Visitors most welcome to our family dairy farm, 1½ miles from the market town of Skipton on the B6265, main route to the heart of the Dales. Cosy bedrooms (some on ground floor) with H/C, tea/coffee facilities & lovely views. CH, visitors lounge, bathroom and shower room. Enjoy hearty breakfasts in the dining room & by arrangement, excellent home cooked evening dinner. OS Ref SD 983534

KNOTT FARM Lothersdale, Skipton, North Yorkshire, BD20 8HX

Pauline Lambert
Tel:-(0535) 32517
Open Mar-Nov
B&B £9-£10
Sleeps 4

(10)

Listed

Visit our charming 17th century farmhouse as seen on TV, set in delightful garden with superb views across the valley. The farm is situated on hillside overlooking Lothersdale village, 1 mile from shop and pub. Accommodation-1 twin bedded with washbasin, 1 double bedroom, heaters in all rooms. Visitors' sitting room with TV. Convenient for Skipton. Gateway to the Dales and Bronte country. OS Ref SD 953465

MIRESFIELD FARM Malham, Skipton, N Yorks, BD23 4DA

Vera & Peter Sharp
Tel:-(07293) 414
Open all year
B&B £7.50-£9
EM £6
Sleeps 18
SC £60-£210
Sleeps 6-8

Listed

Miresfield Farmhouse stands in a beautiful garden bordering the village green and a tumbling stream. We welcome visitors and their children to our accommodation which provides a superb base for a holiday in the national park. Malham is said to be the prettiest village in the Yorkshire Dales, amid green meadows and white limestone hills. OS Ref SD 901628

FOLD FARM Kettlewell, Nr. Skipton, N Yorks, BD23 5RJ

Barbara Lambert
Tel:-(075676) 886
Open Easter-Oct
B&B £10
EM £6
Sleeps 6

Listed

Fold Farm is a hill sheep farm, situated within the village, behind the Church and, nearby, are two excellent shops and three hotels/pubs. The farmhouse is comfortable and warm and has lovely oak beams and coal fires. There is a separate guests' sitting room with colour TV. Good home cooking. OS Ref SD 972722

Yorkshire Dales & Bronte Country ENGLAND

(SC) SEAT HOUSE FARM Eshton, Skipton, North Yorks, BD23 3QL

Kath Wellock
Tel:-(07293) 217
Open Easter-Nov
SC £70-£120
Sleeps 4-6

This pine lined, single storey, self contained accommodation for 4/6 persons is situated on a quiet section of our dairy and sheep farm. The cottage offers warmth and comfort providing an ideal base for touring and walking in Malhamdale and Wharfedale. OS Ref SD 929571

(SC) WESTFIELD FARM COTTAGES Tim Lane, Haworth, West Yorkshire, BD22 7SA

(Mrs) Wendy Carr
Tel:-(0535) 44568
Open all year
SC £70-£160
Sleeps 2-6

Enjoy the comforts of home in one of our delightful cottages. 100 acre farm with Galloway cows and sheep, ½ mile from Haworth. 4 cottages to sleep 2 to 6 people; disabled unit for 2; all with beautiful south-facing aspect. Colour TV, automatic washer, microwave in each. Dogs by arrangement. Farm trail and safe river for fishing or play. OS Ref SE 026380

(SC) CAWDER HALL Cawder Lane, Skipton, N Yorks, BD23 2QQ

Anne Pearson
Tel:-(0756) 61579
Open Mar-Nov
SC £70-£150
Sleeps 4

Disabled people are especially welcome at our three newly converted single storey cottages. Each has vehicular access, is comfortable, heated and well equipped. Each caters for 2 to 4 persons and has extensive views. Utility room and telephone are available. Linen provided. 1m from the castle and market town of Skipton. An ideal centre for touring & walking in the Dales & Bronte country. OS Ref SD 997503

(SC) KNOTT FARM Lothersdale, Skipton, North Yorkshire, BD20 8HX

Pauline Lambert
Tel:-(0535) 32517
Open Easter-Oct
SC £95-£120
Sleeps 4
(5)

Delightful, single storey cottage adjoining 17th Century farmhouse with panoramic views, set in charming gardens, patio and garden furniture. Conveniently situated for Dales, Bronte country and many places of interest. Accommodation, living room with open fire, exposed stonework and colour TV Separate kitchen area, 1 twin, 1 double bedroom. Heaters throughout. Electricity on 50p meter. Pub/shop 1 mile. Sorry no pets. OS Ref SD 953465

(SC) FOLD COTTAGE & GHYLL Fold Farm, Kettlewell, Nr Skipton, North Yorkshire, BD23 5RJ

Barbara Lambert
Tel:-(075676) 886
Open all year
SC £130-£180
Sleeps 2/7

Fold Farm is a typical Dales hill sheep farm. Two delightful old stone-built holiday cottages are available in Kettlewell, beside the stream and within easy walking distance of excellent shops, hotels/pubs and the lovely old church. Each cottage is well equipped, fully heated and has a garage and garden and sleeps 6/7 people. OS Ref SD 972722

(SC) LOW GROUND FARMHOUSE ELSLACK Ivy House Farm, Gargrave, Nr Skipton, North Yorkshire, BD23 3RT

Nancy Harrison
Tel:-(075678) 214
Open all year
SC £65-£160
Sleeps 2/6

Guests are welcome on our family dairy/sheep farm ideally situated for exploring Dales and Bronte country. Ancient market town of Skipton 5 miles away. Pennine Way close by and Roman Road on door step. While retaining many original features, the farmhouse is divided into 2 large self contained apartments, tastefully furnished for comfort sleeping 5/6+ cot in each. Also cosy cottage sleeps 2. OS Ref SD 940501

45 HERRIOT COUNTRY, North Yorkshire

HERRIOT COUNTRY, NORTH YORKSHIRE

Take a trip around North Yorkshire and sample for yourself the delights of this area as portrayed in James Herriot's "All Creatures Great and Small'.

Start with the ancient city of York and wander through narrow streets to the Minster, ride up river to the Bishop's Palace or visit the Railway Museum and Jorvik Centre. Or drive from Helmsley, over Sutton Bank — a favourite for hang-gliders — to the market town of Thirsk where James Herriot still practices.

A day all the family will enjoy is a visit to the Lightwater Valley Theme Park where modern farming exhibits combine with an adventure play area. Or maybe you prefer the peace and tranquility of the romantic abbeys, stately homes, gardens and deer parks found here.

In Wensleydale, home of the famous cheese, you can fish or picnic by the waterfalls and enjoy real ale in friendly village pubs. Locally, many craftsmen display their skills, the most famous being the Mouseman of Kilburn.

Walkers can follow the Pennine Way past the Buttertubs, through panoramic Swaledale where shepherd and sheepdog work the hills, to the cobbled streets and Norman castle of Richmond, towering over the river below.

Whatever the weather, whatever your interest, you are spolit for choice. There is something for everyone in North Yorkshire!

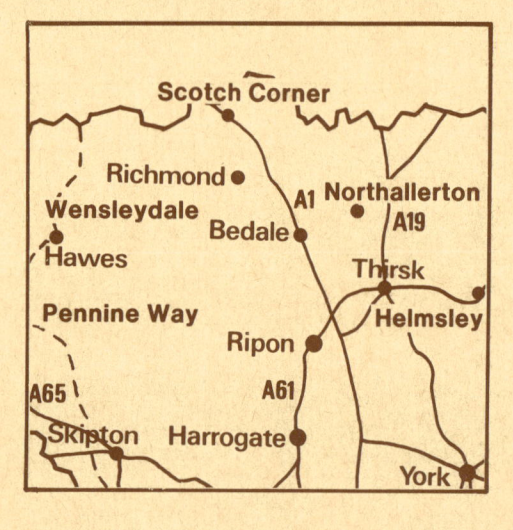

VACANCY SECRETARY:
Rosemary Metcalfe (060981) 291

Herriot Country, North Yorkshire ENGLAND

(CH) ELMFIELD HOUSE   Arrathorne, Bedale, N. Yorks, DL8 1NE

Edith Lillie
Tel:-(0677) 50558
Open all year
B&B   £10
EM   £6
CH   Sleeps 6

Elmfield House is located approximately 5 miles from the market towns of Bedale & Richmond, with magnificent views of surrounding countryside. Adjacent to Wensleydale and Swaledale - "Herriot country". Ideal for walking or touring. Horse riding available. Warm friendly atmosphere and excellent farmhouse cooking. 2 double or family bedrooms - with private shower & WC, 1 twin bedroom. Centrally heated throughout. TV lounge and residential licence.

(FH) MILL CLOSE FARM   Mill Close, Patrick Brompton, Bedale, N Yorks, DL8 1JY

Doris Knox
Tel:-(0677) 50257
Open Easter-Oct
B&B   £9   Listed
EM   £6
       Sleeps 4

(8)

This lovely old house is surrounded by an attractive garden and set in the middle of a family run dairy farm of 230 acres. One double room, 1 twin bedded room, dining room, TV lounge. Situated at the gateway to the Yorkshire Dales and Herriot country. A true Yorkshire welcome with home cooking a speciality. Evening meals at nearby inns and restaurants. OS Ref SE 230922

(FH) CARR HOUSE   Ampleforth, York, N Yorks, YO6 4ED

Anna Taylor
Tel:-(03476) 526
Closed Xmas-New Year
B&B   £8-£9   Listed
EM   £6
       Sleeps 6

(7)

Sunday Observer recommend "fresh air fiend's dream, good food, walking, warm welcome" Come and enjoy your stay in our 16th Century farmhouse. Part of 400 acre mixed family farm in unspoilt Herriot countryside, ½ hour York. 2 bedrooms ensuite. Romantics will love the 4 poster bedroom. Winter log fires. CH Good home cooking. Relaxing & informal atmosphere. Ideal touring centre. Children over 7. OS Ref SE 567788

(FH) AINDERBY MYERS FARM   Nr Hackforth, Bedale, N Yorks, DL8 1PF

Valerie Anderson
Tel:-(0609) 748668
Closed Xmas-New Year
B&B   £9-£9.50 Listed
EM   from £7
       Sleeps 5

This historical farmhouse, set amidst rolling countryside offers comfortable accommodation with a warm welcome for visitors. An ideal base for touring Herriot country, moors, dales, castles, abbeys and historical towns. There is a small kitchen for guests use suitable for preparing picnics or snacks. Milk, tea, coffee and biscuits provided. Good cooking our speciality. Local facilities for pony trekking. OS Ref SE 2593

(FH) HAREGILL LODGE   Ellingstring, Masham, Ripon, N. Yorks, HG4 4PW

Rachel Greensit
Tel:-(0677) 60272
Open Mar-Nov
B&B   £9.50-£11
EM   £5.50
       Sleeps 6

This attractive 18th Century stone farmhouse set on a large working mixed farm, with large Victorian staircase and fire places. Large secluded garden in peaceful surroundings overlooking the Hambleton Hills. Good base to explore the Dales and Herriot country. Good home cooking with supper tray for all guests. Fishing & pony trekking nearby. OS Ref SE 184833

(FH) OXNOP HALL   Low Oxnop, Gunnerside, Richmond, N Yorks, DL11 6JJ

Annie Porter
Tel:-(0748) 86253
Open Mar-Nov
B&B   £9-£9.50 Listed
EM   £6.50
       Sleeps 6

Oxnop Hall is a working hill farm situated in the heart of beautiful Swaledale within the Dales National Park & James Herriot country. The house dated 1685 is a listed building with many features including mullion windows and oak beams. It has panoramic views from every way you look. Ideal for walking & touring. Home cooking and a warm welcome awaits you. OS Ref SD 931974

EAST FARM East Farm, Little Smeaton, Northallerton, N. Yorks, DL6 2HD

Rosemary Metcalfe
Tel:-(060981) 291
Open Easter-Nov
B&B   £9-£10   Listed
Sleeps 5
(12)

Discover our favourite drives and walks after a real Yorkshire breakfast in our warm friendly home. Visitors lounge, family & single bedroom, guests own bathroom with shower. Overlooking garden to Hambleton Hills. Country inns offering excellent meals. Home baking for picnics, supper trays. York & coast 1 hours drive. Close to golf and race courses, stately homes, Moors and Dales. OS Ref NZ 352033

WELLFIELD HOUSE FARM North Otterington, Northallerton, N Yorks, DL7 9JF

Dorothy Hill
Tel:-(0609) 2766
Open all year
B&B   £8.50-£10.50
EM   £6
Sleeps 6

Relax in comfortable farmhouse part of which dates back to 17thC on sheep, cattle, arable working farm. Large garden where croquet can be played; coarse fishing available. Unspoilt views from all angles. Ideally situated for touring Dales/Moors. Accommodation, double room with hand basin, double or family room with hand basin, 1 twin bedded room with handbasin. Home cooking & warm welcome awaits you. OS Ref SE 369895

WHASHTON SPRINGS FARM Richmond, N Yorks, DL11 7JS

Gordon & Fairlie Turnbull
Tel:-(0748) 2884
Closed Xmas and New Year
B&B   £11-£14
EM   From £8
Max guests 18
(5)

300 acres beef and sheep, family working farm in the heart of Herriot country. This delightful Georgian farmhouse, featured on "Wish You Were Here", has unusual bay windows overlooking lawns sloping down to a sparkling stream. A real Yorkshire breakfast starts the day-home cooking using local produce-most of our 8 comfortable bedrooms have en suite bath/showers. Historic Richmond only 3 miles away. OS Ref NZ 148049

NURSERY COTTAGE Leeming Bar, Northallerton, N Yorks, DL7 9BG

Edna & David Braithwaite
Tel:-(0677) 22861
Open Easter-Oct
CH   Sleeps 5
B&B   £9-£12
(12)

A warm welcome, every comfort awaits you in old converted cottage adjacent to our Nursery Garden Centre - bliss for plant lovers. 1 family, 1 double room with washbasins, separate bathroom, shower. Overlooking attractive gardens, lounge, dining room have CH, log fire, colour TV. Ideal centre, follow our routes provided for your pleasure, explore Yorkshire replete after full Yorks ham breakfast with homemade bread. OS Ref SE 284897

THORNTON MANOR Helperby, York, N Yorks, YO6 2RH

Ann Hebblethwaite
Tel:-(0423) 360648
Open Easter-Oct
B&B   £9   Applied
EM   £6
CH   Sleeps 6

An attractive and interesting Georgian country house on an historic site mentioned in the Domesday Book. Peacefully situated near to the River Swale. An ideal base for touring the Dales and Moors, close to York, Harrogate, Ripon and Thirsk. Guests are assured of a warm welcome in a most comfortable family home. Non Smokers welcome. OS Ref SE 431716

BAXBY MANOR Husthwaite, York, YO6 3SW

Elaine & David Smith
Tel:-(03476) 572
Closed Xmas and New Year
B&B   £9.50-£10
Sleeps 6

Interesting 13th Century farmhouse - peaceful but not isolated. 1½m from A19 between York & Thirsk. Beamed guest lounge with inglenook. CH throughout. Bedrooms have washbasins and lovely views. Tea/coffee making facilities. Large walled garden. Explore our family run traditional mixed farm with its trout stream. Arrangements made for evening meals at nearby inns & restaurants. AA Listed. Dogs by arrangement, not in house. Stairlift. OS Ref SE 513752

Herriot Country, North Yorkshire ENGLAND

(FH) LASKILL FARM   Laskill, Hawnby, Helmsley, York, YO6 5NB

Susan Smith
Tel:-(04396) 268
Open Mar-Oct
B&B   £10   Listed
EM   £8
Sleeps 6

Amidst beautiful North Yorkshire moors, in heart of "James Herriot country", in one of England's finest national parks. Attractive farmhouse, large, pretty secluded garden for visitors. Oak furniture handcarved by local craftsmen. High standard, generous meals, mostly homegrown produce. Pony-trekking, fishing, rambling, birdwatching nearby. York 45 mins away. Many places historic interest - Rievaulx Abbey, folk museum at Hutton-le-Hole. OS Ref SE 610830

(SC) WREN COTTAGE, KIRKBY FLEETHAM   Street House Farm, Little Holtby, Northallerton, Nrth Yorks, DL7 9LN

Jennifer Pybus
Tel:-(0609) 748622
Open all year
SC   £90-£130
Sleeps 4

This cosy cottage for four set in the heart of Herriot country, overlooks the village green where cricket is played in the summer. Nearby is a well-stocked village shop and a local pub providing both bar snacks and full restaurant meals. The cottage with its traditional oak beams and open fire in the lounge has a fully equipped kitchen. OS Ref SE 285947

(SC) GREEN GABLES   Lime Kilns Farm, Bedale, N Yorks, DL8 2SH

Cynthia Johnson
Tel:-(0677) 22842
Open Easter-Sep
SC   £110-£130
Sleeps 6

Stone built bungalow opposite farmhouse. Large garden. Between Bedale and Masham. Near the Dales, Pateley Bridge, Fountains Abbey, Harrogate, York and the coast. Fitted carpets, electricity, coal included. Owner maintained. Well equipped kitchen suitable for disabled. Sleeps 6. Open fire, coal and logs included. OS Ref SE 246851

(SC) STANHOW FARM BUNGALOW   Great Langton, Northallerton, North Yorkshire, DL7 OTJ

Lady Mary Furness
Tel:-(0609) 748614
Open all year
SC   £80-£160
Sleeps 6

Herriot's Yorkshire. Enjoy the peace of our comfortable detached farm bungalow. Well equipped, heating, CTV, modern facilities, lounge with open fire. 1 double, 2 twin bedrooms; level garden, garage, electricity included. Linen hire. Lovely views. Walk on our farm. See sheep, cattle & horses. Ideal for touring the Dales & Moors, villages, market towns, country houses, historic cities: good local hospitality & recreations. OS Ref SE 295981

(SC) BRIDGE COTTAGE & THE LODGE   Boville Park, Osmotherley, Northallerton, N Yorks, DL6 3PZ

Jean Lamb
Tel:-(060983) 208
Closed Xmas-New Year
SC   £75-£175
Sleeps 4-6

2 cottages in 142 acres of farmland with trout stream within national parks. Offering tranquility, ideal for totally relaxing holiday, 1m from Osmotherley village. Open fires, well equipped kitchens, sleep 2/6. Linen provided. Beautiful countryside for rambling, bird watching. Pony trekking nearby. Each cottage has own garden and holidaymakers may wander over farmland, fish in stream. En-tout-cas tennis court. OS Ref SE 449965

(SC) DALES FARMHOUSE AND COTTAGES   Shaw Ghyll Farm, High Shaw, Simonstone, Hawes, N Yorks

Brenda Stott
Tel:-(09697) 359
Open all year
SC   £55-£199
Sleeps 2/10

Our farmhouse and cottages are located on our 50 acre smallholding 2 miles north of Hawes in Wensleydale. All are fully equipped to the highest standard with open fires and central heating, offering an opportunity for a relaxed and peaceful holiday summer and winter. Activities include fishing, birdwatching, walking, near Pennine Way. Very central position for exploring the Yorkshire Dales. OS Ref SE 870919

201

KEEPERS COTTAGE Lansdowne Farm, Sowerby Road, Islebeck, Thirsk, N Yorks, YO7 3AL

Doreen Hebdon
Tel:-(0845) 401335
Open Easter-Nov
SC   £80-£110
Max guests 5

Explore Moors, Dales, browse round historic cities of York, Ripon or visit quaint fishing villages on the east coast. Then relax in the comfort of this pleasant, well equipped detached farm cottage and garden, on perimeter of a 72 acre arable farm, overlooked by the famous "White Horse" on the Hambleton hills. Sleeps 4 plus Z-bed or cot. Open Nov-Apr by arrangement. OS Ref SE 458787

THE LODGE East Farm, Little Smeaton, Northallerton, N Yorks, DL6 2HD

Rosemary Metcalfe
Tel:-(060981) 291
Open all year
SC   £80-£150
Sleeps 4

The Lodge-bungalow style, no steps, warm, fully carpeted (telephone, linen, electricity inclusive). 1 double, 1 twin bedded room. Lounge, open fire, colour TV bathroom, shower, WC. Electric kitchen/dining room, stable door opening onto garden, overlooking 215 acre family farm. 1m Great Smeaton with shops, church, inns. Discover historic York, Durham. Romantic abbeys, stately homes, golf, racing, Dales, coast. Brochure on request. OS Ref NZ 352033

INGLENOOK Wellfield House Farm, North Otterington, Northallerton, N Yorks, DL7 9JF

Dorothy Hill
Tel:-(0609) 2766
Open Easter-Oct
SC   £80-£130
Sleeps 2-4

Beautifully decorated ground floor flat attached to dwelling house on 350 acre mixed farm with ewes, lambs and beef cattle. Ideally situated for touring moors, dales and historical towns, the flat sleeps 2/4, fitted carpets, bed linen provided. Dining/kitchen with stable door, oak beamed ceiling, sitting room with inglenook fireplace, french window opening onto patio. OS Ref SE 369895

WHASHTON SPRINGS Richmond, North Yorkshire, DL11 7JS

Gordon & Fairlie Turnbull
Tel:-(0748) 2884
Open Mar-Nov
SC   £90-£140
Sleeps 7

A delightful farmhouse, approached through gated fields, set high in the hillside, with wonderful views. Freedom and peace can be enjoyed from this comfortably furnished house sleeping 7 + cot. Children who love the countryside will be in their element. The farm was filmed for the James Herriot series. OS Ref NZ 148049

CISSYS COTTAGE HARDRAW HAWES Southolme Farm, Little Smeaton, Northallerton, N Yorks, DL6 2HJ

Belinda Metcalfe
Tel:-(060981) 302
Open all year
SC   £85-£160
Sleeps 4

Nestling under the fells in Hardraw village is this delightfull 18th Century Cottage. Traditionally built, retaining beamed ceilings & pine panelling it has been furnished with antique pine and Laura Ashley prints. Heated with an open fire & storage heaters, coal/electricity included. Sleeps 4 in comfort plus cot, equipped to highest standards. South facing garden and patio with rear paddock. Trout fishing available. OS Ref SE 865 912

HARDSTYLES COTTAGE Park Top Farm, Marske, Richmond, N Yorks, DL11 7LS

Jean Wallis
Tel:-(0748) 3712
Open all year
SC   £80-£120
Sleeps 6/7

Bungalow type cottage with spacious rooms. Situated at the gateway to Swaledale. Peaceful surrounding yet within easy reach of historical venues. Ideal base for walking and touring. OS Ref NZ 107006

202

(SC) **26 HIGH STREET, HELMSLEY** Laskill Farm, Hawnby, Helmsley, N Yorks, YO6 5NB

Susan Smith
Tel:-(04396) 268
Open Easter-Sep
SC £60-£150
Sleeps 5

Delightful cottage in attractive market town of Helmsley. Nearby, York, Norman Castles and Churches, N. York moors, coastal resorts. No. 26 is cosy, clean comfortable, having been modernised yet maintaining many interesting features and character. 1 double, 1 twin bedded rooms, with cot if necessary. Also St. Ceadda, charming, stone built, 3 bedroom cottage Nr Kirkbymoorside. Linen can be hired. OS Ref SE 616835

ALL BED AND BREAKFAST PROPERTIES IN THIS GUIDE HAVE BEEN PERSONALLY INSPECTED.

ENGLISH TOURIST BOARD

WALES TOURIST BOARD

In England and Wales, the properties have been inspected and classified as 'Listed,' or '1, 2, 3 or 4 Crowns' by the English or Wales Tourist Boards. (See Introduction for details). The higher classification does not indicate that one property is better than another, but that it provides a greater range of facilities.

4G

RYEDALE
North Yorkshire

RYEDALE, NORTH YORKSHIRE

Upper Rydale is the western part of the North Yorkshire Moors National Park, where the efforts of man to wring a living from the hillsides has enhanced the natural beauty of the classical glacial valleys. It is a place which appeals particularly to the walker.

There are two nationally famous Walks passing through the area, The Lyke Wake and the Cleveland Way, but, for those who want to see the abundant wildlife, the network of unnamed footpaths, through woods and over wild moorland, will be more inviting. There is also trout fishing in the Rye.

The area also has three well known monastery ruins and several stately homes, headed by Castle Howard. York, with its magnificent selection of museums, historic Minister and its encircling walls, is an hour away by car. Literary pilgrimages can be made to Coxwold, where Lawrence Sterne preached, or the Thirsk, where James Herriot has his practice. Music lovers can take advantage of Ryedale Festival, in Helmsley for the first week in August.

The seaside towns of Scarborough, Whitby and Filey are within easy reach. Close by are Lightwater Valley and Flamingoland, plus the slightly more sedate pleasures of a ride on the North Yorkshire Moors Steam Railway.

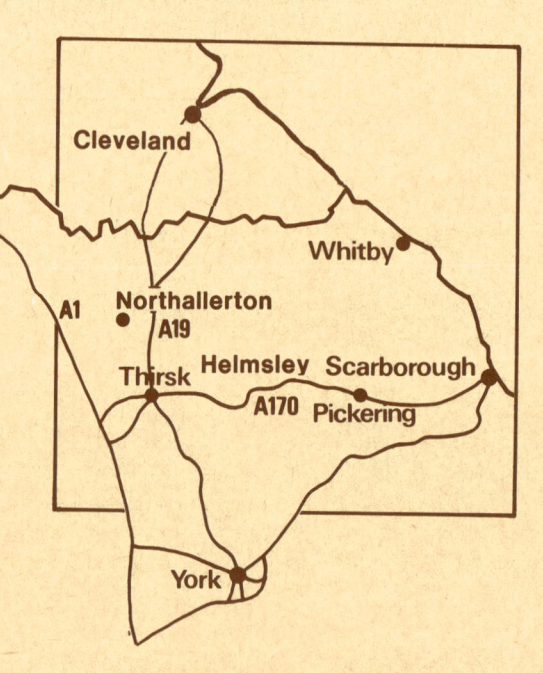

VACANCY SECRETARY:
Sally Robinson (04396) 221

Ryedale, North Yorkshire ENGLAND

(FH) HILL END FARM   Chop Gate, Bilsdale, Cleveland, TS9 7JR

Brenda Johnson
Tel:-04396 278
Closed Xmas-New Year
B&B   £8-£9   Listed
EM   £6
Sleeps 5

The farm stands on high ground with beautiful views of Bilsdale & is situated halfway between the market towns of Helmsley & Stokesley. Good home cooking, lounge/dining room with colour TV & log fire. 1 family & 1 double bedrooms with supplementary heating. Evening meals by arrangement. OS Ref SE 576 967

(FH) MIDDLE FARM   Cold Kirby, Thirsk, YO7 2HL

Mrs Ruth Clough
Tel:-0845 597349
Open all year
B&B   £8.50-£9.50   Listed
EM   £6
Sleeps 6
Tent 50p-£1
Van   £4

Relax & enjoy the comfort & peace of our 17th Century farmhouse situated in a small peaceful hamlet. 1 mile from Sutton Bank. Friendly atmosphere & Yorkshire hospitality. Middle Farm is a family run stock farm, where Shire horses are bred & worked. 3 attractive bedrooms. Private guest bathroom. Beamed lounge with log fire. Full central heating. OS Ref SE 533 845

(FH) CRINGLE CARR FARM   Hawnby, Helmsley, York, YO6 5LT

Susan Garbutt
Tel:-04396 264
Open Easter-Oct
B&B   £8.50-£9.50   Applied
EM   £5.50
Sleeps 5

Working dairy farm situated in glorious scenery, with the River Rye running along the edge of the farmland. Ideal for peaceful walks & nature observation. The comfortable central heated accommodation comprises twin & family room with wash basins & shower room for visitors' exclusive use, dining/sitting room with colour TV. Home produce. Home baking. OS Ref SE 563 880

(FH) BARN CLOSE FARM   Rievaulx, Helmsley, Yorks, YO6 5LH

Joan Milburn
Tel:-043 96 321
Closed Dec-New Year
B&B   £9-£10   Listed
EM   £5
Sleeps 5

Barn Close is set in a wooded valley with the River Rye running through it. A 1 mile private tarmac road, mixed hill rearing farm. Lounge/dining room. 1 double, 1 family with wash basins. Storage heaters in rooms. Good food home produce, meat, eggs & home made bread. OS Ref SE 566 872

(FH) VALLY VIEW FARM   Old Byland, Helmsley, York, YO6 5LG

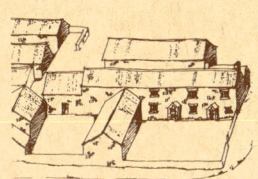

Sally Robinson
Tel:-04396 221
Closed Xmas-New Year
B&B   £10-£11   Listed
EM   £6
Sleeps 4

Comfortable, relaxed atmosphere in our 17th Century farmhouse. Situated in peaceful family farm on the edge of a small unspoilt village. Where visitors may see farm animals & walk on the Cleveland Way. Area particularly good for wild flowers. Good home cooking. Double or twin/family room each with its own en-suite shower etc. Tea/coffee making facilities. Central heating. OS Ref SE 551 858

(FH) MANOR FARM   Old Byland, Helmsley, York, YO6 5LG

Mrs Joyce Garbutt
Tel:-04396 247
Open Easter-Oct
B&B   £8.50-£9.50   Listed
EM   £6
Sleeps 4

You are assured of a warm welcome at Manor Farm. Situated in the picturesque village of Old Byland. Ideally placed for walking & touring the N York Moors. Guests are welcome to browse around the family run dairy & sheep farm. 2 comfortable bedrooms with washbasins. Private guest bathroom. Lounge with log fires. Full central heating. Good home cooking. OS Ref SE 551 858

47 YORKSHIRE COAST, Moor ß Wolds

YORKSHIRE COAST, MOORS & WOLDS

When you come to stay with us on our farms you have the opportunity to visit the seaside and yet enjoy the countryside inland as well.

The coast offers sandy beaches, secret caves, pretty fishing villages and thirty miles of Heritage Coast with bird sanctuaries and wildlife. The resorts of Scarborough, Whitby and Bridlington offer lively entertainment in the evenings for all tastes.

There are over 1,000 miles of public footpaths and bridleways in the area and recognised walks like the White Rose Walk, the Cleveland Way, and the Lyke Wake Walk. Or perhaps pony trekking through the National Park appeals to you.

Those interested in historic heritage will find much to enjoy. There is Castle Howard designed by Vanbrugh and Hawksmoor in the grand baroque style, where 'Brideshead Revisited' was filmed. At Pickering, the parish church is famous for its unique 15th century wall painting of St George and the Dragon. Whitby and Rievaulx Abbeys and the Minsters of Yark and Beverley are other examples of the magnificent religious architecture of the area. Ancient castles can also be explored at Helmsley, Pickering and Scarborough.

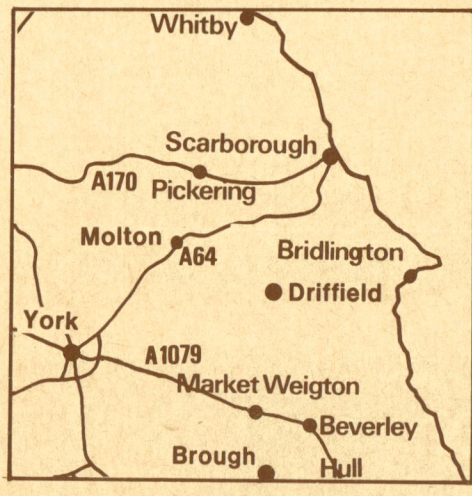

The Yorkshire Museum of Farming at Murton, near York, and the Folk Museum at Hutton-le-Hole are both fascinating places.

GROUP CONTACT
Anne Barrett (0751) 73131

Yorkshire Coast, Moor & Wolds ENGLAND

(FH) COTE BANK FARM   Aislaby, Whitby, N Yorks, YO21 1UQ

Mrs. B.A. Howard
Tel:-(0947) 85314
Closed Xmas
B&B   £9.50-£10
EM   £6.50
Sleeps 6

Large, comfortable 18th Century house peacefully located in the National Park 5m from the coast. Guests are welcome to watch farming activities on our 300 acre family run dairy/mixed hill farm. Excellent home cooking. Special diets available. Bedtime drink inclusive. Bedrooms with washbasins, shaver points & heating. Family atmosphere. Splendid area with superb scenery. Lots to see & do. AA Listed. OS Ref NZ 825069

(CH) INTAKE FARM   Egton Road, Aislaby, Whitby, North Yorkshire, YO21 1SX

Jacqueline Roberts
Tel:-(0947) 810817
Open all year
B&B   £10-£11
EM   £6
CH   Sleeps 6
(5)

A country house of distinction on a small stock farm, an amazing view, a southerly aspect and gardens of peacefulness await our guests. Tastefully furnished accommodation of ample proportions. A magnificent sitting room and a spiral stairway to gallery landing. A host of interesting recreational pursuits include Captain Cook Museum. Forest Drives, Sandy Beaches and fossiled coves, and walks for both novice and experienced. OS Ref NZ 850080

(FH) KELLEYTHORPE   Driffield, N Humbs, YO25 9DW

Tiffy Hopper
Tel:-(0377) 42297
Closed Xmas-New Year
B&B   £8.50-£11   Listed
Red'ns for children.
Sleeps 4

Imagine peacocks strutting, ducks swimming and trout rising. Our lovely Georgian farmhouse is set on the banks of a crystal clear shallow river amidst large attractive gardens. Although secluded it is easily accessible off the A163 with a large choice of evening meals locally. A mixed farm, Aberdeen Angus Cattle, horses, pony, aviary, fly fishing, croquet & swings. Central for York & Coast. OS Ref TA 012565

(FH) CROSS BUTTS FARM   Whitby, N Yorks, YO21 1TL

Eileen Morley
Tel:-(0947) 602519
Open May-Oct
B&B   £10-£12
Sleeps 4
(5)

240 acre family working farm, dairy/mixed. This 16th Century farmhouse consists guests TV lounge, dining room with original flagstoned floor, beamed & panelled bedroom with original 4 poster bed, wash basin, 1 twin, 1 single 2' 6" bed suitable for child. Furnished traditionally throughout. Situated on A171, 2m from historic town of Whitby. Famous Captain Cook connections. Close to Moors, beaches, golf course. AA recommended. OS Ref NZ 487510

(FH) THE GRANGE   Glaisdale, Whitby, N Yorks, YO21 2QW

Heather Kelly
Tel:-(0947) 87241
Closed Xmas
B&B   £9-£11   Listed
EM   £5
Sleeps 6

Beautiful stone manor house with a magnificent hilltop view. It lies in the midst of our sheep/arable farm, bordering the Esk River which boasts the best salmon fishing in the country. Home grown produce used in our generous meals. Excellent position for walks, steam railway & Whitby. Bathrooms en suite or shared between 2 rooms. Packed lunches and fishing by arrangement.

(FH) CROFT FARM   Fylingthorpe, Whitby, North Yorkshire, YO22 4PW

Pauline Featherstone
Tel:-(0947) 880231
Open May-Oct
B&B   £8.50-£9.50
Sleeps 6
(5)

A comfortable modernised farmhouse of character on a working dairy farm overlooking the old smuggling village of Robin Hood's Bay with wonderful views of the sea, moors and countryside. Within easy reach of coastal resorts, Moors Railway and many historic attractions. Ideal for walking and touring the beauty spots of North Yorkshire. One family and 1 double room. All home comforts. OS Ref NZ 941051

207

FH SEAVY SLACK   Stape, Pickering, N Yorks, YO18 8HZ

Anne Barrett
Tel:-(0751) 73131
Open Easter-Oct
B&B   £8-£9   Listed
EM   From £6
Sleeps 6

A family dairy farm with comfortable farmhouse situated on the edge of the North Yorkshire moors offering good home cooking with mainly home produced food. Close to the market town of Pickering and North York Moors Railway and only ½ hour's drive from the east coast or historic city of York. OS Ref SE 923798

FH HALL FARM   Low Hawsker, Whitby, N Yorks, YO22 4LE

Mary Sedman
Tel:-(0947) 880239
Open Easter-Oct
B&B   £8.50-£9.50
EM   From £5
Sleeps 4
(3)

A small dairy farm with comfortable modernised farmhouse with exposed beams, situated in North York Moors National Park, midway between Whitby and Robin Hood's Bay, the Moors and the sea. Excellent walking country. Within easy reach of many pretty moorland and coastal villages and the market towns of Pickering and Helmsley. Excellent farmhouse cooking. OS Ref NZ 923 076

FH ACRES   Clay Lane, Shiptonthorpe, (nr Market Weighton), York, YO4 3PH

Mrs Gill Sergison
Tel:-(0696) 73474
Open Mar-Oct
B&B   £8.50   Applied
EM   £6
Sleeps 6

Join us in our comfortable home. Set in large pleasant gardens nestling at the foot of the Wolds. Centrally placed for visits to York, Beverley, Malton, Hull and Humber Bridge, with many local walks. Good home cooking, with a little bit extra. Afternoon tea, bedtime drinks, tea/coffee facilities in all rooms. Regret no smoking. Disabled guests welcome. OS Ref SE 8741

FH SUNLEY COURT   Nunnington, York, YO6 5XQ

Mrs Joan Brown
Tel:-(04395) 233
Open Easter-Oct
B&B   £7.30-£8.30   Listed
EM   £6
Sleeps 6

A comfortable modern farmhouse with open views. All bedrooms have tea making facilities. One has shower/toilet en suite. Good home cooking with mainly home produced food. Central for York, Moors and Coast.

FH HARDWICK FARM   Harwood Dale, Scarborough, N Yorks, YO13 0DS

Christine Macer
Tel:-(0723) 870348
Open Feb-Nov
B&B   £8.50-£9.50
EM   £6.50
Sleeps 6

This impressive farmhouse has been tastefully restored to provide a very high standard of comfort. Our speciality menus give variety and satisfaction - diets can be catered for. The 190 acre arable/stock farm is situated within the North Yorkshire Moors National Park close to forests, moors, coast, and historic towns, providing guests with a wide variety or interests. OS Ref SE 958754

FH THE GRANGE   Bempton Lane, Flamborough, Bridlington, YO15 1AS

Joan Thompson
Tel:-(0262) 850207
Closed Xmas-New Year
B&B   £7.25-£7.75   Listed
Sleeps 6
Tent £1.50
Van   £2.50-£3

A spacious Georgian farmhouse near the sea, with large garden and grass tennis court. This working farm with 125 dairy cows, is an excellent centre, for exploring the cliffs, birdwatching, golf, fishing or pony trekking. OS Ref TA 223710

Yorkshire Coast, Moor & Wolds ENGLAND

(SC) COTEBANK FARM   Aislaby, Whitby, N Yorks, YO21 1UQ

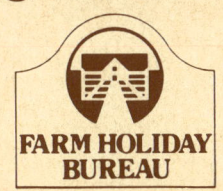

Mrs Barbara Howard
Tel:-(0947) 85314
Open Mar-Oct
SC   £65
          Sleeps 6
Tent   £2

Peacefully located in National Park 5 miles from coast, in a well kept garden on a 100 acre dairy/mixed hill farm, 1 six berth caravan. Fully carpeted and equipped. (Linen for hire). Gas cooking and heating, electric light, toilet, double bedroom. Washroom and freezer facilities at house. Nearest shops and North York Moors Steam Railway 2 miles. Guests welcome to watch farming activities. OS Ref NZ 825069

(SC) CROFT FARM COTTAGE   Croft Farm, Fylingthorpe, Whitby, N Yorks, YO22 4PW

Pauline Featherstone
Tel:-(0947) 880231
Closed Christmas
SC   £65-£130
          Sleeps 4

Attractive self contained accommodation on a working dairy farm, overlooking Robin Hood's Bay. A cottage full of character with modern facilities. Enjoy the wonderful views of sea, moors and countryside. Within easy reach of coastal resorts, Moors Railway and places of historic interest. Two bedrooms, 1 double and 1 with built-in bunk beds. Fully equipped except linen. (Hire Service available). OS Ref NZ 941051

(SC) THE GRANGE   Sinnington, (Nr Pickering), York, YO6 6RB

Mary Turnbull
Tel:-(0751) 32612
Open all year
SC   £60-£85
          Sleeps 4 +

Country views, private site. Easy access on dairy/mixed farm. Trout farm. Near market towns of Pickering and Kirbymoorside. North Yorks Moors, coast, York, Castle Howard, Flamingo Fun Park, zoo, steam railway, fishing, pony trekking. 4 berth fully equipped static caravan (no linen). Mains electricity, WC, shower, double room, bunk beds. Extra guests accepted.

(SC) FIELD HOUSE   Field House, Sewerby, Nr Bridlington, North Humberside, YO16 5YG

Angela Foster
Tel:-(0262) 674932
Closed Xmas
SC   £80-£170
          W/ends £40
          in winter
          Sleeps 6 + cot

Lovely self-contained Georgian property. Very comfortable, tastefully furnished and equipped to the highest standard. 3 bedrooms, living/dining room with open fire, TV, heating throughout. Delightful walled garden with croquet and clock golf. Our large dairy/arable farm is nearby the "Heritage Coastline", offering cliffs, caves, sandy beaches, bird reserve, Sewerby Park, golf. Easy access historic York, Moors. OS Ref TA 190710

(SC) POND FARM CARAVAN   Pond Farm, Fylingdales, Whitby, North Yorkshire, YO22 4QJ

Grace Cromack
Tel:-(0947) 880441
Open Easter-Oct
SC   £50-£90
          Sleeps 6

Pleasantly situated on a mixed hill farm, on the edge of the North Yorkshire Moors and near to Robin Hood's Bay. The 6 berth caravan is sited in a walled garden with pleasing views, it has mains services. Well equipped, with double room and bunk bedded room. Ideal for visiting coastal and country villages and sites of historic interest. OS Ref NZ 922013

(SC) WOLDS WAY COTTAGES   Rudstone Walk Farm, South Cave, Brough, N Humbs, HU15 2AH

Pauline Greenwood
Tel:-(04302) 2230
Open all year
SC   £90-£240
          Sleeps 5

Two attractive cottages at the foot of the Wolds on medieval Domesday site. Each has panoramic views, spacious lounge with inglenook fireplace, kitchen/diner, 3 bedrooms and bathroom. CH and linen is included. Surrounded by pretty villages, close to historic Beverley and York. Within easy reach of the Moors and coast. (2½m from M62.) OS Ref SE 918343

(SC) WHIN CLOSE   Hasholme Grange, Holme on Spalding Moor, (Nr Market Weighton), York, YO4 4DD

Sally Williamson
Tel:-(0696) 60329
Open all year
SC   £80-£120
Sleeps 6

A comfortable, well equipped, detached house with garden, set in peaceful countryside near to our farmhouse. The 200 acre farm has breeding sheep in addition to mixed arable cropping. There are pleasant walks & fishing available on the farm. Historic York, the market town of Beverley, east coast and M62 motorway are within easy driving distance. Sleeps 6. Linen and cot provided. OS Ref SE 824330

(SC) MANOR FARM COTTAGE   Butterwick on Wolds, Weaverthorpe, Malton, N Yorks, YO17 8HF

Betty Taylor
Tel:-(0377) 87245/87212
Open May-Sep
SC   £75
Sleeps 4
+ cot

Our comfortable cottage with beamed ceiling is attractively situated on 460 acre farm carrying sheep, cattle and growing cereals. Ideally placed for E coast resorts, Moors and many interesting places - Stately homes, Pickering Steam Railway, York, Beverley Minster and Transport Museum, PoW camp and museum, Malton. Accommodation: 1 double room, sitting room with double bed settee, cot available. OS Ref SE 986713

(SC) BLACKMIRES FARM   Danby Head, Whitby, N Yorks, YO21 2NN

Gillian & Lewis Rhys
Tel:-(0287) 60352
Closed Xmas-New Year
SC   £60-£110
Sleeps 6
Tent   £1-£6

Cottage attached to farmhouse, adjacent to moors in an area of outstanding beauty. Ideal centre for walking and touring N Yorks Moors by road and rail. Sea fishing and seaside at Whitby. A day at Flamingo Zoo, Castle Howard, Rievaulx Abbey, folk museums. Picturesque villages. Fishing in River Esk. Moorland and valley birds. 6 berth caravan. OS Ref NZ 688048

LAKE DISTRICT GUIDE

The handy pocket guide which makes more of your holiday

£3.95

from bookshops and newsagents, or in case of difficulty from the address below

NICHOLSON   16 Golden Square, London W1R 4BN

SOUTH LAKELAND 48

SOUTH LAKELAND

From a base in South Lakeland one can find interesting occupations for every member of the family within easy reach whatever the season or weather. Spring and Autumn are particularly lovely in the fell country, the Spring blossom and wild daffodils, immortalised by Wordsworth, are a delight not to be missed, as are the green pastures where new born lambs gambol in the Spring sunshine. In Autumn the rich carpet of bracken and the varied golden tints of the leaves contrast with the blue sky to provide a sightseer's delight and a photographer's paradise.

One of the major attractions of the area is fell walking and the southern fells such as Coniston Old Man, the Langdales, Fairfield, Kentmere and Longsleddale provide many interesting routes for walkers of varying stamina. Or if you would prefer to see the views in comfort why not take to the 'Mountain Goat', a scheduled mini-bus service connecting many of the small, remote villages via spectacular mountain passes.

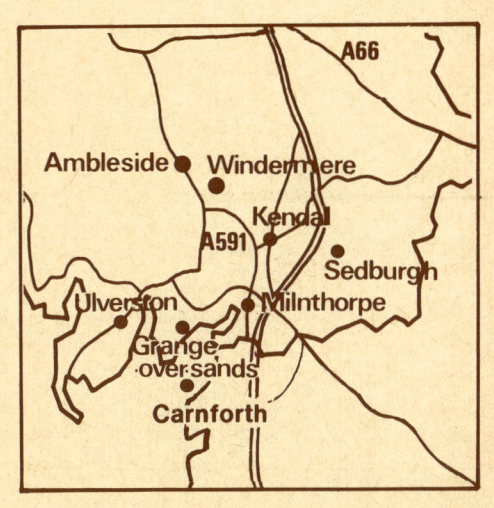

For rock climbers there are crags giving a variety of climbs in the Langdale Pikes, Coniston Fells and many other locations.

Those knowledgeable enough to tackle potholing will know that one of the country's major networks is in easy reach in Ingleton in neighbouring Yorkshire.

GROUP CONTACT:
Mrs C. M. Simpson (04488) 318

(FH) GARNETT HOUSE FARM Burneside, Kendal, Cumbria, LA9 5SF

Sylvia Beaty
Tel:-(0539) 24542
Closed Xmas-New Year
B&B   £8.50-£9.50
EM   £4
Sleeps 14

An AA/RAC 15th Century farmhouse on large dairy/sheep farm. Situated ½m from A591 (Kendal to Windermere road). Bedrooms have washbasins, shaver points, tea making facilities. Bathroom & shower room. Oak panelled colour television lounge, dining room with separate tables, English breakfast & 5 course dinner. Home produced lamb and beef, meringues, trifles etc. Child reductions. Featured in "The Times". SAE please. OS Ref SD 500959

(FH) GATESIDE FARM Kendal, Cumbria, LA9 5SE

Mrs June Ellis
Tel:-(0539) 22036
Closed Xmas-New Year
B&B   £9-£9.50
EM   £4.75-£5
Sleeps 10

Traditional Lakeland Dairy & Sheep Farm with 16th Century farmhouse fully modernised in traditional style washbasins, teamaking facilities & colour TV in all rooms. Bath & shower room. Fire certificate. Good parking. 2 miles from Kendal on the main Windermere Road, the main Tourist Route through Lakes, easily accessible from M6 Junction 36. AA recomended. Short or weekly stays welcome. OS Ref SD 495955

(FH) PATTON HALL FARM Kendal, Cumbria, LA8 9DT

Mrs Margaret Hodgson
Tel:-(0539) 21590
Open Feb-Nov
B&B   £8-£8.50
EM   £4.50-£5
Sleeps 6

Friendly farmhouse accommodation in comfortable clean rooms with good home cooking available on this 200 acre dairy/sheep farm. Rural position overlooking Kendal 3 miles away. Two bedrooms, with hot and cold water, guests bathroom and separate toilet, lounge with colour television. Dining room. River fishing. Dogs by arrangement. Weekly slide show, life on the farm. Easy reach of Lakes & Dales. OS Ref SD 548960

(CH) FIELD END Brigsteer, Nr. Kendal, Cumbria, LA8 8AN

Pat & Bill Evans
Tel:-(04488) 570
Open Mar-Oct
B&B   £8.50-£9
EM   £4.50
CH   Sleeps 4

Brigsteer is a small attractive village in the Lyth Valley, close to M6, Yorkshire Dales and South Lakes. Twin and double ground floor bedrooms with washbasins, tea/coffee facilities. EM optional. Central heating, plus open fire in TV lounge. Packed lunches on request. Ideal for country and fell walking - or enjoy our terraced garden, should you wish a quiet leisurely day. Dogs by arrangement. OS Ref SD 483 896

(FH) PLUMTREE FARM Brigsteer, Kendal, Cumbria, LA8 8AR

Chris Sykes
Tel:-(04488) 271
Open Easter-Oct
B&B   £8-£8.50
Listed
Sleeps 5
(2)

A working dairy farm, built 125 years ago of local limestone, on edge of attractive village with views of the lovely Lyth Valley. Close to M6, the Southern Lakes and coastal areas, ideal for country and fell walking and touring. Comfortable accommodation in one double room with washbasin and one family room, tea/coffee making facilities. OS Ref SD 482894

(FH) HIGH GREGG HALL FARM Underbarrow, Kendal, Cumbria, LA8 8BL

Mrs Cicely Simpson
Tel:-(04488) 318
Open Apr-Oct
B&B   £7.50-£8.50
EM   £4
Sleeps 4

High Gregg Hall is a 100 acre dairy and sheep farm on the main road looking towards Scout Scar. Lovely country walks. Good local Inns. Home produced food. Open log fires. Ideal for touring lakes. Windermere 6 miles. Kendal 4 miles. Children welcome. Reduced rates for children. Come and try us. OS Ref SD 465914

South Lakeland, Cumbria ENGLAND

(FH) OLD BARN FARM Fiddler Hall, Newby Bridge, Ulverston, Cumbria, LA12 8NQ

Peter & Edna Waterworth
Tel:-05395 31842
Closed Xmas-New Year
B&B £10
       Sleeps 6

A non-working farm situated 1½ miles from Lake Windermere, just off the A590. Within easy reach of Southern Lakes, Cartmel & Furness Peninsulas. All bedrooms have en-suite shower room & tea making facilities. Separate dining room & lounge with colour TV for guests. Central heating & log fires for cooler months. Garden & parking available. OS Ref SD 340490

(CH) BRIDGE HOUSE Garnett Bridge, Kendal, Cumbria, LA8 9AZ

Brenda White
Tel:-(0539 83) 288
Open all year
B&B £9-£10
EM   £5.50
CH   Sleeps 6

Bridge House stands in the peaceful hamlet of Garnett Bridge near Kendal at the foot of the unspoiled Longsleddale Valley. Now a smallholding. Ideal for lakes touring/walking. Good accommodation provides hot and cold water in all rooms, free tea/coffee making facilities, guest lounge TV. Separate dining room. We offer imaginative cooking at sensible prices. Our pleasure is to make your stay enjoyable. OS Ref NY 525994

(FH) LOW HUNDHOWE FARM Burneside, Kendal, Cumbria, LA8 9AB

Marjorie Hoggarth
Tel:-(0539) 22060
Closed Xmas
B&B £8.50-£9
EM   £3.75
       Sleeps 6

Family working farm with farmhouse over 350 years old in peaceful location. Four miles from Kendal and 5 miles from Windermere, pleasant walks. Fishing available. Rooms all with washbasins, radiators and tea making facilities. Lounge with colour television. Bedtime drink included in price. Packed lunches available. Good food and a warm welcome awaits you. OS Ref SD 493978

(FH) MURTHWAITE FARM Longsleddale, Kendal, Cumbria, LA8 9BA

Mrs Nancy Waine
Tel:-(0539) 83 634
Closed Xmas-New Year
B&B £8-£8.50   Listed
EM   £4.50
       Sleeps 6

A friendly welcome awaits you at Murthwaite, our hill farm nestling in Longsleddale, one of Lakelands loveliest valleys. Secluded and peaceful yet only 1½m from the A6. This 17th Cenury stonebuilt farmhouse has been tastefully modernised. Full central heating, guests own bath/shower room. Colour TV lounge, separate dining room. High standard, home cooked generous meals. Packed lunches available. OS Ref NY 515007

(CH) RIVERBANK HOUSE Garnett Bridge, Nr Kendal, Cumbria, LA8 9AZ

Julia H Thom
Tel:-(0539) 83 254
Closed Xmas-New Year
B&B £8-£9   Listed
EM   £4
CH   Sleeps 6

Riverbank House is situated just off the A6 at the foot of the beautiful Valley of Longsleddale. Standing at the head of 20 acres of pasture land bordered by a ¾m of the River Sprint, providing private fishing. Comfortable bedrooms with washbasins. Tea/coffee facilities. Guests sitting room with TV & open log fire. Background CH. Good food and a warm welcome awaits visitors. OS Ref NY 525994

(FH) LOW SIZERGH FARM Sizergh, Nr Kendal, Cumbria, LA8 8AE

Marjorie Park
Tel:-(05395) 60426
Open Easter-Nov
B&B £9-£10
       Sleeps 6

Situated adjacent to Sizergh Castle and 4 miles south of Kendal (gateway to the Lakes), this working dairy farm with its spacious, oakbeamed 18th Century farmhouse lies only 10 minutes from junction 36 (M6). Facilities are available on the farm for horses and/or riders and close at hand are tennis courts, fishing and delightful walks through deer inhabited parks. OS Ref SD 503875

(FH) TRANTHWAITE HALL   Underbarrow, Nr Kendal, Cumbria, LA8 8HG

Doreen Swindlehurst
Tel:-(04488) 285
Closed Dec
B&B £9-£10
Sleeps 6

Applied

A warm welcome awaits you at this beautiful old world farmhouse with its magnificent oak beams, doors and original fireplace. This dairy/sheep farm is situated ½m up an unspoilt country lane where deer and other wildlife can be seen. Several country Inns nearby offer a wide range of meals. Kendal 3m, Winderemere 6m. 1 double, 1 twin and 1 family rooms. OS Ref SD 469 930

(FH) HEVERSHAM HALL   Heversham, Nr Milnthorpe, Cumbria, LA7 7EE

Jean Handley
Tel:-(04482) 3571
Open Easter-Sept
B&B £8
Sleeps 6

Applied

Heversham Hall is a working Dairy and Sheep farm situated on the tip of the beautiful Kent Estuary ideal location for birdwatching, walking, or touring Lakes and Yorkshire Dales. We offer you a warm welcome, comfortable accommodation. Lounge with TV, 1 double, 1 twin, 1 family room. Reductions for children under 12 sharing with 2 adults. OS Ref SD 4983

(SC) PRESTON PATRICK HALL COTTAGE   Preston Patrick Hall, Crooklands, Milnthorpe, Cumbria

Jennifer Armitage
Tel:-(04487) 200
Open all year
SC £80-£125
Sleeps 4

This self contained wing of a medieval manor house, now a working farm near Crooklands, is an ideal touring centre. Accomodation comprises kitchen, sitting room with TV log fire and double sofa bed, bedroom with twin beds, bathroom and WC. (Further bedroom sleeping 3 optional extra.) Children welcome. Swimming, fishing and riding available locally. Ring for brochure. OS Ref SD 543837

(SC) STOCKS COTTAGE   Stocks Farm, Scalthwaiterigg, Kendal, Cumbria, LA9 6PL

Jean Chapman
Tel:-(0539) 24901
Open Easter-Oct
SC £55-£90
Sleeps 4

Comfortable 2 bedroomed cottage adjoining the farmhouse, set in peaceful surroundings with extensive views of the Lakeland Fells, yet only 2m from the busy market town of Kendal. Sitting room with electric fire, TV. Shower room with toilet. Kitchenette, cooker, fridge. Both bedrooms have washbasins, fully equipped except linen. Electricity extra. OS Ref SD 539949

(SC) THE LODGE FLAT   High Gregg Hall Farm, Underbarrow, Kendal, Cumbria, LA8 8BL

Cicely Simpson
Tel:-(04488) 318
Open Apr-Oct
SC £60-£90
Sleeps 2/4
1 Unit

The Lodge Flat is the ground floor of a converted barn. It contains kitchen with electric cooker & fridge; bathroom with shower; 1 family bedroom (with double bed & bunks); lounge with bed settee, colour TV, electric fire. Linen hire. Hot water is supplied, electric radiators if required. Electricity by 50p meter. Ideal for touring Lakes, Windermere 6m, Kendal 4m. OS Ref SD 465914

(SC) WOODSIDE   Hollin Cragg, Underbarrow, Nr Kendal, Cumbria, LA8 8AY

Mrs Valerie O'Loughlin
Tel:-(04488) 655
Open all year
SC £55-£100
Sleeps 2

Woodside is situated in a quiet and secluded spot 3 miles from Kendal and 6 miles from Bowness-on-Windermere. This single-storey country cottage comprises lounge/kitchenette with electric fire, colour TV, fridge and electric cooker. One bedroom sleeps two adults. Shower, washbasin and toilet. Bed linen not provided. OS Ref SD 610940

South Lakeland, Cumbria ENGLAND

(SC) LOWER ROWELL COTTAGE Lower Rowell Farm, Milnthorpe, Cumbria, LA7 7LU

Mavis Robinson
Tel:-(04482) 2270
Open all year
SC   £60-£110
Sleeps 6

18th century 2 bedroomed cottage adjoining farmhouse, sleeps 6 plus cot. Large lounge, colour TV, open or electric fire. Fitted kitchen, fridge and washer. Bathroom with shower. Storage heaters, fitted carpets, oak panelling and beams. Beautiful views across open countryside. Peaceful surroundings. Excellent for touring Lake District, Morecambe Bay, Yorkshire Dales or relaxing in our garden. Electricity and heating extra. OS Ref SD 470370

(SC) CRAGG FARM COTTAGE Cragg Farm, Burneside, Kendal, Cumbria, LA8 4HH

Rosalie Dodgson
Tel:-(0539) 821249
Closed Jan-Feb
SC   £40-£100
Sleeps 4

Cragg Farm Cottage adjoins the 17th Century farmhouse and is set in quiet rural surroundings, overlooking the Kent Valley, ¾ mile from main Kendal to Windermere road. Kendal 4 miles. Windermere 6 miles. The cottage is comfortable, clean and well-equipped. Sleeps 4, 1 double, 1 twin-bedded room. Bed linen provided. OS Ref SD 485975

(SC) POUND FARM Crook, Kendal, Cumbria, LA8 8JZ

Mrs Margaret Lister
Tel:-(0539) 821220
Open Mar-Oct
SC   £45-£110
Sleeps 4/8

This small spacious farm site is ideally situated 10m from M6, yet is set in the peace and tranquility of a picturesque Cumbrian village. Easy access from the B5284 to the rest of Lakeland. Less than 30 mins to the Yorkshire Dales. Modern shower and toilet block. (Some caravans, own facilities.) Laundry room. Childrens playground, fishing, sailing, riding, golf nearby. OS Ref SD 953473

(SC) GREENGATE FARMHOUSE & COTTAGE Byranbarn, 85 Greengate, Levens, Kendal, Cumbria LA8 8NE

Eileen Edmondson
Tel:-(05395) 60930
Open May-Oct
SC   £85-£120
Sleeps 4/8

An old Westmorland limestone farmhouse on the fringe of Levens village, surrounded by outstandingly beautiful countryside. House and cottage tastefully modernised to retain Old World charm. Excellent base for exploring Lakes, Dales and Morecombe Bay areas. Playing field, tennis, bowls adjacent. Good village shops. Choice of good local "pub food". Not a working farm, owner supervised. Dog by arrangement. OS Ref SD 205480

(SC) BRUNT KNOTT FARM Over Stavely, Kendal, Cumbria

RD & SFJ Wolstenholme
Tel:-(0539) 821030
Closed Jan-Feb, Dec
SC   £90-£180
Sleeps 2/4
(5)

2 detached cottages on elevated beautiful Lakeland hill farm. Fantastic views over 60m, 1m from village, 4m from Windermere. Privacy and comfort. Lovely walking country, yet convenient for all local tourist attractions. Both cottages comfortably furnished, all usual facilities, colour TV etc. Easy access from M6 Lakeland Link. OS Ref NY 476003

(SC) GRAYGABLES COTTAGE Grayrigg, Nr Kendal, Cumbria, LA8 9BU

Susan Bindloss
Tel:-(053984) 649
Open Mar-Oct
SC   £80-£130
Sleeps 6

Graygables Cottage, luxury conversion adjoining main house, old world charm, retaining oak beams. One double bedroom and lovely bathroom on ground floor. Open plan lounge with Dales stone fireplace, colour TV. Fully equipped kitchen. Minstrel's gallery accommodating 2 single and 1 double bed. CH available. Personal attention and high standard of maintenance assured. OS Ref SD 579976

HORNSBARROW NEW END Hornsbarrow Farm, Lupton, Carnforth, Lancs, LA6 2PS

Elsie M Braithwaite
Tel:-04487 618
Open all year
SC £65-£150
Sleeps 4

Hornsbarrow New End Bungalow luxuriously appointed adjoins farmhouse with uninterrupted views from all the double glazed windows. Dining kitchen, larder & fridge. Spacious lounge, electric fire, colour TV, patio. Two bedrooms - double & twin. Extra fold-up bed, cot & chair. Bed linen available for small charge. Electricity charges by meter, oil heating. Ideal for lakes & Dales. Further details from Hornsbarrow Farmhouse. OS Ref SD 681 106

LOW SIZERGH FARM CARAVAN Low Sizergh Farm, Sizergh, Nr Kendal, Cumbria, LA8 8AE

Marjorie Park
Tel:-(05395) 60426
Open Easter-Nov
SC £55-£70
Sleeps 6

FARM HOLIDAY BUREAU

This 6 berth caravan with end double bedroom, mains electricity, flush toilet, shower, fridge etc is situated on the farm in a beautiful historic area (adjacent to Sizergh Castle). Facilities available for horses and close by are tennis courts, fishing and delightful walks through deer inhabited parks. Ideal base for touring Lakes & Yorkshire Dales. Linen not included. OS Ref SD 503875

MAKE THE MOST OF THE COUNTRY

40 beautiful walks in the Lake District for all the family, with clear maps and route descriptions.

from all good bookshops, or in case of difficulty from the address below.
£3.50

BARTHOLOMEW Duncan Street, Edinburgh EH9 1TA

A full list of the complete Walk the... series can be obtained from the same address.

WALK THE LAKES — 40 EASY WALKS SELECTED & DESCRIBED BY JOHN PARKER

CUMBRIA – NON-GROUP MEMBER.

HILL FOLD FARM Burneside, Kendal, Cumbria, LA8 9AU

Mrs Eleanor Bell
Tel:-(0539) 22574
Closed Xmas
B&B £8-£8.50   Applied
EM   £4.50
Sleeps 6

FARM HOLIDAY BUREAU

Hill Fold is a 400 acre dairy/sheep farm, 3 miles north of Kendal, near the rolling hills of Potter Fell. There are many quiet walks on the hills or by the river, within easy reach of lakes and sea. Colour TV, log fire in lounge. One double, 2 family bedrooms. H/C water, bathroom, separate toilet. Fishing available. Genuine hospitality. OS Ref SD 517977

Eden Valley & Alston Moor, Cumbria

49

EDEN VALLEY & ALSTON MOOR, CUMBRIA

The area lies between the Yorkshire Dales National Park and Hadrian's Wall and is bounded by the Pennine Fells on one side and the mountains of the Lake District on the other.

It is a walkers' and climbers' paradise. There are over 100 guided walks in the Cumbrian Pennines, Eden Valley and Yorkshires Dales National Park.

You don't need a guide to climb Cross Fell or up to High-Cup-Nick and enjoy the panoramic views. The more intrepid (properly equipped and shod, of course) can pit themselves against the mountains of the Lake District. Likewise, others less energetic will enjoy the Nunnery Walks through narrow footpaths cut from vertical sandstone cliffs to take you past beautiful waterfalls, mature shady trees and the Croglin Beck tumbling through its deep gorge into the Eden.

High in the Cumbrian Pennines we find Alston, the highest market town in England, with its distinctive market cross. The cobbled road that climbs steeply through the town leads off into lanes and yards enclosed by old houses that have outside staircases clinging to the walls.

Alston Moor was the centre of northern lead mining in the 19th century and industrial archeologists will find much to interest them.

VACANCY SECRETARIES:
B & B Pat Dent (0498) 81383
Self Catering:
Anne Ivinson (06996) 230

(FH) MIDDLE BAYLES FARM   Penrith Rd, Alston, Cumbria, CA9 3BS

Pat Dent
Tel:-(0498) 81383
Open all year
B&B   Up to £8.50   Listed
EM   Up to £4.50
      Sleeps 6

300 acre hill farm with cattle & sheep where visitors can wander & a garden for relaxing and admiring breathtaking views. Ideal base for walking and touring. Warm comfortable 17th C farmhouse, CH, 1 double & 1 family room with handbasins, cotton sheets, electric blankets. Tourist Board, AA listed. Good home cooking. Tea making facilities. Friendly welcome, reductions weekly & for children under 14. SAE for brochure. OS Ref NY 707451

(CH) ASHLEY BANK   Newbiggin-on-Lune, Kirkby Stephen, Cumbria, CA17 4LZ

Iain & Nazig Hickman
Tel:-(05873) 214
Closed Xmas-New Year
B&B   £10-£11
EM   £6
CH   Sleeps 6

A large, comfortable house peacefully located near the head of the Ravenstonedale Valley, in 2 acres of wooded gardens with a magnificent view of the Howgill Fells. The house is tastefully furnished. The residents' lounge has a colour TV and marble fireplace. Delicious home cooking and relaxed friendly atmosphere await all visitors. Residential courses in photography. OS Ref NY 701055

(FH) LOATBURN FARM   Alston, Cumbria, CA9 3LQ

Edith Jopling
Tel:-(0498) 81544
Open Apr-Oct
B&B   £7.50-£8   Listed
EM   £4
      Sleeps 6

A lovely area, we would like to share its beauty. Our 17th Century farmhouse is full of character with original pine beams, situated near the Northumberland/Durham border within easy access of the Lake District. Small, stockbearing farm which visitors can explore. We offer warm welcome, good beds, home cooking. Ideal for motorists, ramblers, geologists or botanists. Pets by arrangement. OS Ref NY 753454

(CH) HOWSCALES   Kirkoswald, Penrith, Cumbria, CA10 1JG

Elaine & Colin Eade
Tel:-(0768 83) 666
Closed Xmas-New Year
B&B   £9.50-£10.50   Listed
EM   £5
CH   Sleeps 5
  (12)

A warm welcome awaits you at Howscales, which is a retired farmstead set in the beautiful, tranquil countryside between the Eden Valley and the Pennines. Our 17th Century house, with exposed beams, offers 1 double, 1 twin, with washbasins and 1 single. All have tea/coffee facilities, colour TV and easy chairs. Ours is a non-smoking establishment. OS Ref NY 580413

(FH) GAISGILL FARM   Gaisgill, Tebay, Via Penrith, Cumbria, CA10 3UA

Mrs Joyce Leak
Tel:-(05874) 634
Open all year
B&B   £9
EM   £5
      Sleeps 6
  (7)

This attractive 18th Century farmhouse with beamed ceilings is situated in the peaceful hamlet of Gaisgill yet only 1¼ miles from the M6. Alan is a sheep dog trialist and grazes sheep on this 9 acre smallholding. Two double, 1 twin, washbasins, central heating, tea making facilities. Children over 7 years welcome. Excellent home cooking. Very central for Lakes, Dales, Borders. OS Ref NY 638053

(FH) GROVE FOOT FARM   Watermillock, Penrith, Cumbria, CA11 0NA

Mrs Shiela Hunter
Tel:-(08536) 416
Open Easter-Oct
B&B   £8-£8.50   Applied
EM   £4
      Sleeps 6
Van   £1.50

Grove Foot Farm a 90 acre dairy farm, situated 2½m from Ullswater, 4m from M6. It is within easy reach of all other Lakes and places of interest including historic houses, gardens and a wildlife park.

Eden Valley & Alston Moor, Cumbria ENGLAND

(FH) AUGILL HOUSE FARM Brough, Kirkby Stephen, Cumbria, CA17 4DX

Jeanette Atkinson
Tel:-(09304) 305
Closed Xmas-New Year
B&B   £9.50
EM   £6
Sleeps 6

(12)

A warm welcome awaits you at our Georgian farmhouse, situated in the lovely Eden Valley. Handy for visiting The Lakes, Yorkshire Dales, Teesdale & Hadrians Wall. Comfortable bedrooms with washbasins, shaver points TV, coffee/tea facilities. Bathroom, separate shower and toilet, comfortable lounge & dining room. Good farmhouse fayre, homebaked bread, local butter and cheese. Excellent fishing. AA listed. Children over 12 welcome.

(FH) MEABURN HILL FARM Maulds Meaburn, Penrith, Cumbria, CA10 3HN

Mike & Ruth Tuer
Tel:-(09315) 205
Open Easter-Oct
B&B   £8.50   Applied
Sleeps 5
Tent £1
Van   £2

Relax at our traditional 16th Century Cumbrian Longhouse, overlooking the tranquil Lyvennet Valley. Guests are welcome to explore the 200 acre suckler beef & sheep farm which offers outstanding views across to the Pennines. The farmhouse retains many of its original features of beams, panelling and fireplaces, making a warm and comfortable base for touring and exploring. OS Ref NY 165 625

(CH) HOWHILL GUEST HOUSE Garrigill, Alston, Cumbria, CA9 3DF

Jeannette Wood
Tel:-(0498) 81519
Open all year
B&B   £8-£10
EM   £5.50
Sleeps 6

Friendly, family run guest house, tastefully modernised from a 17th Century stone barn, retaining a feature stone arch window in the comfortable guests' lounge. Set on a hilltop in open countryside, Howhill enjoys spectacular views of the Pennines. Bedrooms have wash hand basins, electric blankets, one ensuite. High standard and wide choice of meals, including cordon bleu, vegetarian. OS Ref NY 729433

(SC) CROSSFIELD FARM & FISHERY Kirkoswald, Penrith, Cumbria, CA10 1EU

Richard & Patricia Massingham
Tel:-(076 883) 711
Open all year
SC   £65-£202
Sleeps 3-5
(+ cot)

Accessible seclusion amidst beautiful Eden Valley countryside. Comfortable new warm quality cottages, centrally located for visiting Lakes, Pennines, Scotland's borderland, Hadrians Wall etc. Fish in well stocked pools. Cleanliness guaranteed. Immaculately maintained. Safe, well fenced interesting farm. Short breaks welcome. Babysitting, cots, linen available. OS Ref NY 5641

(SC) SKIRWITH HALL COTTAGE Skirwith Hall, Skirwith, Penrith, Cumbria, CA10 1RH

Laura Wilson
Tel:-(076 888) 241
Open all year
SC   £69-£161
Sleeps 8

Situated on a 400 acre dairy farm, this cottage, half the Georgian farmhouse, stands in a large garden landscaped down to the Briggle Beck, a tributary of the River Eden. Exposed beams in the lounge and open fire, colour TV, storage heaters. Lakes and Yorkshire Dales easily accessible. Ideal for anyone touring, walking, fishing or simply enjoying idyllic rural surroundings. Accommodates 2/8 people. OS Ref NY 610327

(SC) THE SMITHY Skirwith Hall, Skirwith, Penrith, Cumbria, CA10 1RH

Laura Wilson
Tel:-(076 88) 241
Open Easter-Oct
SC   £75-£115
Sleeps 4

Situated on the outskirts of a fellside village, this cottage was originally the house for the village smithy. Comfortable & well equipped, there is one double bedroom & one twin-bedded room, storage heaters & open fires (coal provided) colour TV. Shops two miles, thirty minutes Lakes and easy access Yorkshire Dales. Golf, riding and fishing nearby. Superb fell walking and birdwatching country. OS Ref NY 610327

219

(sc) PARK HOUSE Gale House, Roman Road, Appleby-in Westmorland, Cumbria

Mary Wood
Tel:-(0930) 51380
Open Easter-Nov
SC   £100-£140
Sleeps 6

Park House, former farmhouse is beautifully situated off the Roman Road with the Fells in the background. Sleeps 6 in 3 large double bedrooms, bathroom, lounge/dining room, kitchen, downstairs cloakroom. Heating-night storage heaters and electric fires. All electricity on slot meters. Colour TV, bed linen, electric blankets. Open air heated swimming pool, bowls, squash, golf, pony trekking available locally. OS Ref NY 695207

(sc) STAFFIELD HALL Kirkoswald, Penrith, Cumbria, CA10 1EU

Beverley & Alan Dawson
Tel:-(076883) 656
Open all year
SC   £67-£150
Sleeps 2/5

Magnificent 19th Century Mansion built in 1848 of local red sandstone. Two acres of wooded grounds with superb views of the lovely Eden Valley. perfect for lovers of beauty and tranquillity. Four self contained well appointed suites. Ideal for couples and small families. Central for Lake District and Scottish borders. Fully inclusive prices. Central heating. Resident proprietors. Colour brochure. OS Ref NY 544 426

(sc) WELL COTTAGE Green View, Welton, Nr Dalston, Carlisle, Cumbria CA5 7ES

Anne Ivinson
Tel:-(06996) 230
Open all year
SC   £80-£195
Sleeps 6

17th Century, remodernised, double glazed, oil CH, electric fires, fitted carpets, lounge, kitchen/dinette. 3 bedrooms. 2nd WC downstairs. Sun lounge at rear. Equipped to high standard. Cottage has unspoilt views over farmland to Caldbeek Fells, 20 mins Ullswater, easy reach Hadrian's Wall, Scottish borders. Winter breaks, warm for your arrival. Welton is tiny hamlet, craft shop, pub, shop. Car essential. OS Ref NY 353444

(sc) GREEN VIEW LODGES Welton, Nr Dalston, Carlisle, Cumbria, CA5 7ES

Anne Ivinson
Tel:-(069 96) 230
Open all year
SC   £80-£195
Sleeps 4/6

3 peacefully situated Scandinavian pine lodges, new 1984, set in our large garden on edge of picturesque hamlet. Triple glazed, fully insulated, 2-3 bedrooms, fitted carpets & heaters in all rooms. 1 or 2 WC's. Spacious lounge/diners completely pine panelled with matching furnishings. Equipped to a very high standard. Large verandah not overlooked. Three Danes came over from Denmark to build these for us. OS Ref NY 353444

(sc) HOWSCALES Kirkoswald, Penrith, Cumbria, CA10 1JG

Elaine and Colin Eade
Tel:-(076883) 666
Closed Jan-Feb-March
SC   £85-£205
Sleeps 2, 3 & 4
(12)

Come and enjoy your holiday in the peaceful surroundings of our newly converted cottages situated between the Eden Valley and the Pennines. The 3 cottages, for 2, 3 & 4 people, are equipped to a very high standard and in an ideal location from which to explore Cumbria, Borders, Dales and Northumberland. All inclusive price (linen, towels, electricity, gas, insurance). Ours is a non-smoking establishment. OS Ref NY 580413

(sc) HILL VIEW Augill House Farm, Brough, Kirkby Stephen, Cumbria, CA17 4DX

Jeanette Atkinson
Tel:-(09304) 305
Open all year
SC   £110-£140
Sleeps 4
EM   £6

This luxury chalet is nicely situated on our working farm in the lovely Eden Valley. Equipped to a high standard with 2 bedrooms, bathroom, coloured suite, shaver point. Fitted kitchen with microwave. Lovely lounge with colour TV & dining area. CH and fitted carpets. Ideally situated for visiting the Lakes, Yorkshire Dales & Teesdale. Fishing. Dinner available in farmhouse £6.

Eden Valley & Alston Moor, Cumbria ENGLAND

(SC) HOWHILL COTTAGE Howhill Farm, Garrigill, Alston, Cumbria, CA9 3DF

Jeannette Wood
Tel:-(0498) 81519
Open all year
SC   £60-£115
Sleeps 4

FARM HOLIDAY BUREAU

Set in beautiful open countryside, this single storey compact stone cottage, converted from 17th Century buildings, has been tastefully modernised to give a high standard of comfort. Spectacular views of the South Tyne Valley. CH, fitted carpets, 2 double bedrooms with electric blankets, lounge with colour TV, lunch and evening meals available. Private fishing. Golf course nearby. Linen provided. Not suitable for wheelchairs. OS Ref NY 729433

BOOKING TIPS

FARM HOLIDAY BUREAU

PLEASE REMEMBER... Telephone or write to check prices and other details
— and confirm your booking in writing.

50 HADRIAN'S WALL
Cumbria ß N'humberland

HADRIAN'S WALL, CUMBRIA & NORTHUMBERLAND

Go North . . . and enjoy the lakes, lochs, mountains, moorlands, Hadrian's Wall — and generous helpings of history.

These romantic borderlands have a rich heritage — there's Lanercost Abbey and its Priory, Carlisle and Naworth castles, Heritage Castle where Mary, Queen of Scots rode to meet the Earl of Bothwell, and Gretna Green famous for eloping lovers . . .

Edinburgh — the Athens of the North — is only a couple of hours drive away, and not to be missed. The amazing castle on its rocky heights looks down on some of the most fashionable stores outside Paris.

Across and down into West Northumberland you can call at Housesteads, the biggest and best of the Roman forts created by Hadrian to accompany his incredible wall — a 15ft high and 7½ft thick deterrent to all known invaders!

If you come to walk, tour or bird-watch you will find the border country a wild wonderland of moorland landscapes.

There is also excellent fishing for sea trout and salmon — and while we're on water you'll marvel at Keilder, the largest man made lake in England with its magnificent forest forming a natural backdrop.

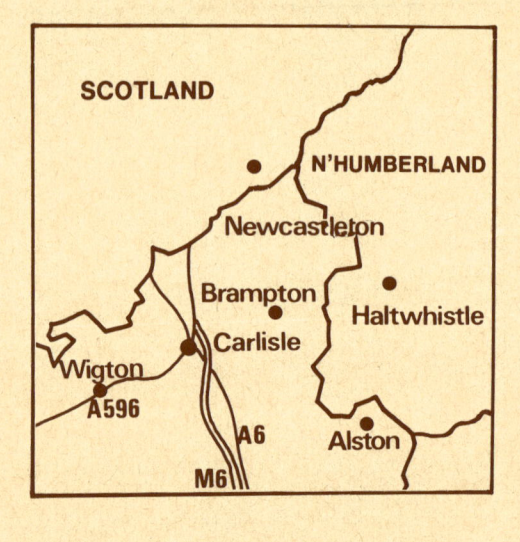

It's an area of country inns, market towns, woollen and tweed mills, sheep dog trials, crafts and other traditional skills — an inviting experience if you've never travelled these parts before, and one you'll be keen to repeat if you have.

VACANCY SECRETARIES:
B & B: Georgina Elwen (022877) 308
Self Catering:
Pamela Copeland (06978) 617

222

Hadrian's Wall, Cumbria & Northumberland ENGLAND

(FH) BANK END FARM Roadhead, Carlisle, Cumbria, CA6 6NU

Dorothy Downer
Tel:-06978 644
Open all year
B&B £12.50-£14
EM £7
Sleeps 2

Relax as a house guest in a luxurious self contained suite (twin bedroom, private sitting room, and bathroom) on small peaceful hill sheep farm close by the Scots Border. Meal times and packed lunches by arrangement. Marvellous centre for touring, walking and fishing. Phone for brochure with colour photo and leaflet on what to do and see while staying. OS Ref NY 513775

(FH) HULLERBANK FARMHOUSE Talkin, Brampton, Cumbria, CA8 1LB

Sheila Stobbart
Tel:-(06977) 668
Open Feb-Nov
B&B £8-£8.50   Applied
EM £5
Sleeps 6

Hullerbank is a Georgian farmhouse standing in its own grounds. A working sheep smallholding near Talkin Tarn with panoramic views of the borders & Solway. 9m from Carlisle. Junction 43, M6. 2 twin, 1 double, extra beds, cot and high chair available. Electric blankets, tea trays in rooms. We also have facilities for BB for up to 4 horses. OS Ref NY 555 579

(FH) NEW PALLYARDS Hethersgill, Carlisle, Cumbria, CA6 6HZ

Georgina Elwen
Tel:-(022877) 308
Open all year
B&B £8.50-£10.50
EM £5.50
Sleeps 10

We would like to welcome you to our beef/sheep farm, a wonderful area to visit and ideal base for Lakes and Scottish borders. Local salmon and sea trout fishing. Every home comfort with CH, tea/coffee making facilities. 1 family room and 2 double rooms with ensuite, 1 single and 1 twin H/C. Disabled welcome, plenty of room for wheelchairs. OS Ref NY 469713

(FH) WHITE CRAIG FARM Shield Hill, Haltwhistle, Northumberland, NE49 9NW

Isobel Laidlow
Tel:-(0498) 20565
Open Easter-Oct
B&B From £10
EM £6
Sleeps 6

17th Century croft-style farmhouse, clean and comfortable on edge of Northumberland National Park. 1 mile Hadrian's Wall, ½m A69. Kielder Water, forests, abbeys, castles and walks nearby. We keep prizewinning pedigree and commercial sheep, rare Longhorn cows and a Clydesdale mare, also interested in spinning. 1 twin en-suite, 2 doubles (1 en-suite), all have tea making facilities, CH TV etc. AA listed. OS Ref NY 713649

(FH) HIGH NOOK Low Row, Brampton, Cumbria, CA8 2LU

Annabel Forster
Tel:-(06976) 273
Open Apr-Oct
B&B £6-£7   Listed
EM From £3
Sleeps 6

This is a working hill farm, rearing sheep and beef cattle. Situated 4m east of Brampton in peaceful Irthing Valley, near Hadrian's Wall and Lanercost Priory. Convenient for Scottish Borders, Northumberland and English Lakes. Interesting walks, Talkin Tarn Country Park nearby. River fishing. Comfortable farmhouse, home cooking. One double and 1 family room. Lounge, TV. Reduction for children. OS Ref NY 589644

(FH) WILLOW HILL FARM Kirklinton, Carlisle, Cumbria, CA6 6DD

Ida Tailford
Tel:-(022875) 201
Closed Xmas-New Year
B&B £7-£9
EM £4.50
Sleeps 6

Willow Hill is a 100 acre working dairy and sheep farm with farmhouse built in the 18th Century. Just 10 minutes from exit 44 of the M6 and situated on A6071 (set well back from the road). A convenient break when heading north or south. Central for the Borders, Lakes and Hadrian's Wall. One family room, 1 double, 1 single, (H/C all rooms). OS Ref NY 417657

FH CRACROP FARM Kirkcambeck, Brampton, Cumbria, CA8 2BW

Marjorie Stobart
Tel:-(06978) 245
Closed Xmas-New Year
B&B £9-£10
EM £6
Sleeps 6

Comfortable accommodation in clean rooms with CH throughout. H/C & tea/coffee making facilities. Picturesque scenery from all rooms. Best home cooking. Cracrop is a busy mixed farm of 425 acres. Pedigree Ayrshire & Charolais herds and sheep. Excellent base for touring (Scotland, Lake District, Roman Wall, Kielder), walking (farm trail) or relaxing (large garden, games room). Situated 1m from B6318 at Kircambeck. AA listed. OS Ref NY 521698

FH CRAIGBURN FARM Catlowdy, Penton, Carlisle, Cumbria, CA6 5QP

Jane Lawson
Tel:-(0228 77) 214
Open Easter-Oct
B&B £10-£11
EM £6
Sleeps 12

A friendly atmosphere with personal attention awaits you at this spacious 18th Century farmhouse, in a quiet rural setting. A family run farm of 250 acres. Delicious home cooking with fresh produce. All bedrooms with bathrooms en suite. Central heating. Residential licence. Pool table/darts board. Swings, ponies for hire. Excellent for touring walking, fishing and shooting. OS Ref NY 476471

FH BESSIESTOWN FARM Catlowdy, Penton, Carlisle, Cumbria, CA6 5QP

Margaret Sisson
Tel:-(022877) 219
Open all year
B&B £12.50-£13
EM £7
Sleeps 18

AA Award Winner, RAC listed. Registered Cumbria and English Tourist Board. Residential licence. Small sheep/beef rearing farm offering friendly relaxing atmosphere combined with delicious home cooking in delightful 7 bedroom - all en-suite - farmhouse overlooking Scottish border 15 miles north Carlisle. Convenient Lake District, Scottish Borders, Kielder Reservoir, Roman Wall. Indoor heated pool (mid May/mid September). Pony riding. Games room. OS Ref NY 458769

FH THE BREAKS FARM Newtown of Irthington, Carlisle, Cumbria, CA6 4PE

Ann Bell
Tel:-(022875) 229
Open all year
B&B £6.50   Listed
EM £5.50
Sleeps 2/4

Lovely ivy-clad farmhouse on old border mixed farm. Panoramic views of the Pennines. Ideally situated for Hadrian's Wall, Lakes, Scotland, Carlisle city and small market town of Brampton. Excellent area for bird-watching and walking. Farm trail. Personal service and friendly atmosphere with tea on arrival. One double (2 extra beds available). Pets by special arrangement only. Self-catering caravan available. OS Ref NY 493647

FH HOWARD HOUSE FARM Gilsland, Carlisle, Cumbria, CA6 7AN

Elizabeth Woodmass
Tel:-(06972) 285
Closed Xmas-New Year
B&B £9
EM £6
Sleeps 6

Howard House, 150 years old is situated on elevated site overlooking Roman Wall country. 240 acre stock rearing family farm lies near Gilsland village. We keep a flock of Jacob sheep and spin the wool, also private fishing. Visitors are assured of a friendly service and comfortable accommodation. An ideal base for walking or touring. One twin; 1 family room; both H & C. OS Ref NY 632668

FH HIGH RIGG Walton, Brampton, Cumbria, CA8 2AZ

Margaret Mounsey
Tel:-(06977) 2117
Closed Xmas and New Year
B&B £7-£8   Listed
EM £4.50
Redn for children
Sleeps 6

Visitors welcome on this 144 acre dairy/sheep farm 1m from Hadrian's Wall, 18th Century farmhouse (listed building), on roadside. Central for Lakes, Pennines, Scotland. Near Lanercost Priory, Brampton, Talkin Tarn Country Park (water sports). Local fishing & riding. Home cooking, excellent views, large garden, patio, play area, pool/snooker table, TV, CH, 1 double, 1 family, separate dining room. Drink in evening & on arrival. OS Ref NY 527657

Hadrian's Wall, Cumbria & Northumberland ENGLAND

(sc) **OLD FARM AND BARN COTTAGES** Bank End Farm, Roadhead, Carlisle, Cumbria, CA6 6NU

Dorothy Downer
Tel:-(06978) 644
Open all year
SC £68-£200
Sleeps 4-8
plus
cots

Two warm, well-equipped cottages welcome you to a quiet, peaceful and relaxing holiday on a small farm close by Scots Border. Sleep 4/8. Home baking and meals available from farm kitchen. Utility room and freezer. Rental includes fuel. Ideal for fishing, walking, touring. AA listed. ETB category 3. Please phone for free brochure with colour photo. OS Ref NY 513775

(sc) **SMITHY COTTAGE** White Craig Farm, Shield Hill, Haltwhistle, Northumberland, NE49 9NW

Isobel Laidlow
Tel:-(0498) 20565
Open all year
SC £65-£180
Sleeps 4/7

Stone built cottages on edge of Northumberland National Park on working sheep farm. 1 mile Hadrian's Wall, ½ mile A69. Nearby attractions best parts Hadrian's Wall, Kielder Water, forests, abbeys, castles, heated pool 1 mile, golf 3½ miles. Superb base for touring. Personally maintained high quality accommodation. Log stove, CH, modern facilities, children's play area. AA listed, brochure on request. OS Ref NY 713649

(sc) **BESSIESTOWN FARM** Catlowdy, Penton, Carlisle, Cumbria, CA6 5QP

Margaret Sisson
Tel:-(022877) 219
Open all year
SC High Season:
£195
Winter breaks:
£50-£60
Sleeps 4/6

AA Award winner. Registered Cumbria & English Tourist Board. Three cottages tastefully converted from farm stable & barn retaining many original oak beams & stonework, offering comfortable accommodation for 4/6 people. Situated on small sheep/beef rearing farm overlooking Scottish Borders. Ideal walking touring country. Indoor heated swimming pool (mid May/mid Sept). Pony riding. Games room. Dogs by arrangement. Out of season breaks OS Ref NY 458769

(sc) **THE STORE LOFT MILL & GRANARY** Bailey Mill, Bailey, Newcastleton, Roxburghshire, TD9 0TR

Pamela Copeland
Tel:-(06978) 617
Open all year
B&B £7.50-£8.50
SC £68-£238
Max guests 30

Bailey Mill, 5 acre small holding nestled on border of Cumbria/Roxburghshire. Centrally situated for touring Hadrian's Wall, Gretna Green, Lake District, surrounding Scottish mill towns. Originally working grain mill, recently extended, converted into 5 well equipped s/c apartments. CH,linen,electricity included. We have 2 ponies, 3 horses for trekking, sauna, solarium, games room for wet weather, play area, OS Ref NY 517785

FOLLOW THE COUNTRY CODE

Countryside COMMISSION

TAKE CARE OF THE COUNTRY

Enjoy the countryside and
respect its life and work.
Guard against all risk of fire.
Fasten all gates.
Keep your dogs under close control.
Keep to public paths across farmland.
Use gates and stiles to cross fences,
hedges and walls.
Leave livestock, crops and machinery alone.
Take your litter home.
Help to keep all water clean.
Protect wildlife, plants and trees.
Take special care on country roads.
Make no unnecessary noise.

51 TEESDALE, Co. Durham

TEESDALE, CO. DURHAM

Teesdale with its wealth of history and outstanding scenery lies south-west of Durham city. Its gentle dales and rolling moorland abound with features of geological, geographical and historical interest.

The river Tees itself rises at Cross Fell and courses down the valley and includes the impressive 'High Force,' England's highest waterfall with a dramatic 70ft. drop over Great Whin Sill. Ancient stone quarries and disused lead mines in the upper dale mark industries dating back to Roman times and many public footpaths in the dale include a magnificent scenic stretch of the well known Pennine Way.

Teesdale makes an excellent base for exploring the nearby Yorkshire Dales, the Roman wall, Northumberland and the Lake District, all of which are within an hour's drive. For the holidaymaker interested in castles and museum's there are plenty to choose from; Barnard Castle dating back to the 12th century, the famous French style Bowes Museum, and the historic Raby Castle, seat of Lord Barnard. A little further across the county is the now famous Beamish Open Air Museum and many other interesting places too numerous to list.

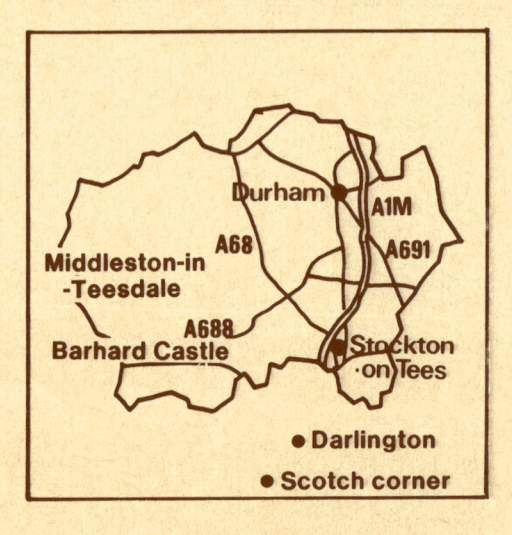

Visit Teesdale to discover its scenic beauty and historic sights for yourself.

GROUP CONTACT:
Gwen Wall (0833) 50794

Teesdale, Durham ENGLAND

(FH) WYTHES HILL FARM Lunedale, Middleton in Teesdale, Co Durham, DL12 0NX

June Dent
Tel:-(0833) 40349
Open Easter-Oct
B&B   £7.50-£8.50   Listed
EM   £3.50
Sleeps 6

Wythes Hill is a working hill farm. All rooms have panoramic views. Situated on Pennine Way route. Many picturesque walks in Teesdale. The Bowes Museum, Raby Castle and High Force are all famous places to visit. Trout fishing and Horse riding nearby. Good plain cooking with free range eggs. One double, 1 twin and family room. Lounge with coal fire. OS Ref NY 922228

(FH) GRASSHOLME FARM Lunedale, Middleton in Teesdale, Barnard Castle, Co Durham, DL12 0PR

Alison Sayer
Tel:-(0833) 40494
Open Easter-Oct
B&B   £7   Listed
EM   £3.50
Sleeps 4

Grassholme Farm is a small family run farm with home bred beef cattle and Swaledale sheep in Lunedale, 3 miles out of Middleton one mile off the B6276 Brough Road overlooking Grassholme Reservoir which is stocked with Brown and Rainbow Trout we offer a full English breakfast and evening meal with free range eggs and home produced meat. OS Ref NY 925216

(FH) SNAISGILL FARM Middleton in Teedale, Barnard Castle, DL12 9UP

Mrs Susan Parmley
Tel:-(0833) 40343
Open Easter-Oct
B&B   £8-£9   Listed
Sleeps 4

This warm recently modernised old farmhouse occupies a magnificent position overlooking the valley of Upper Teesdale. One mile from the village of Middleton-in-Teesdale. Large private lounge and supper tray for all guests. Ideal for walking and touring. Evening meals available at a number of village pubs. OS Ref NY 954 271

(FH) TOBY HILL FARM Egglesburn, Eggleston, Barnard Castle, Co Durham, OL12 0BD

Mrs Sheila Tarn
Tel:-(0833) 40016
Open Easter-Oct
B&B   £8-£8.50   Listed
Sleeps 4

A family run farm of 700 acres with dairy cows, sheep and cattle. The farmhouse dated 1802 is located in a peaceful setting with beautiful views. Good homecooked breakfasts, with excellent opportunities for eating out at local inns and restaurants. Ideal for walking and touring Dales. OS Ref NY 982 244

(FH) GREENGATES Lunedale, Middleton in Teesdale, Co Durham, DL12 0NV

Mary Body
Tel:-(0833) 40447
Open Easter-Oct
B&B   £7.50-£8   Listed
EM   £3.50
Sleeps 4

Stone built farmhouse on the main B6276 road to Brough and the lake district. Greengates overlooks the lower dales and in the distance Grassholme Reservoir. One double and one twin room available, bathroom/toilet, lounge/dining room with colour TV, fishing, pony trekking, sailing and windsurfing are all available nearby. Ample car parking. OS Ref NY 935 234

(FH) WEST PARK FARM HOTEL West Park, Lunedale, Middleton in Teedale, Barnard Castle, DL12 0PS

MM or BJ Killen
Tel:-(0833) 40380
Closed Xmas, New Year & Jan
B&B   £9.50
EM   £7
Sleeps 12

West Park, a stock rearing farm with riding facilities and once part of the Earl of Strathmore's Estate lies in a secluded valley ½m from the B6276 overlooking Grassholme Reservoir and has extensive views of Teesdale. The centrally heated modernised farmhouse offers the very best in comfort & service. Licensed, the Cellar Bar offers a selection of moderately priced bottled ales and wines. OS Ref NY 929 229

(SC) PINEDALE, DENT BANK Wythes Hill, Lunedale, Middleton in Teesdale, Co Durham, DL12 0NY

June Dent
Tel:-(0833) 40349
Open all year
SC £75-£120
Sleeps 4/5 + cot

Situated next to River Tees. Lounge with colour TV, dining/kitchen, coal fires or electric heating. Modern bathroom. 2 bedrooms (1 double, 1 twin, plus cot). All fuel, electricity, linen and towels included in rent. Shops and pub 1 mile. Car parking space for 2 cars. One well behaved pet welcome. OS Ref NY 934259

(SC) SNAISGILL FARM COTTAGE Middleton in Teedale, Barnard Castle, Co Durham, DL12 0RP

Mrs Susan Parmley
Tel:-(0833) 40343
Open Easter-Oct
SC £65-£125
Sleeps 4

A small cottage situated next to the owners farmhouse on a 19 acre working farm approximately 1m from Middleton-in-Teesdale. The cottage occupies a magnificent position overlooking the valley of Upper Teesdale and is ideal for a peaceful holiday yet many places of interest are within easy driving distance. 1 double bedroom, 1 full size bunk bed. Fridge, colour TV. All linen, & coal provided. Electricity by 50p meter. OS Ref NY 954271

(SC) GREEN ACRES Moorhouse Farm, Newbiggin in Teesdale, Barnard Castle, Co Durham, DL12 0UF

Glennis Scott
Tel:-(0833) 22217
Open all year
SC £80-£150
Sleeps 6

Detached bungalow with outdoor swimming pool set in ½ acre of gardens, lounge with open fire and colour TV, dining room, fully equipped kitchen, bathroom with shower, double bedroom, twin bedroom. Bed settee in lounge. All bedding and linen provided. Electricity charged for. Situated beside the Holwick to Middleton-in-Teesdale Road. An area of outstanding beauty ideal for nature lovers. OS Ref NY 910267

(SC) WILDEN HOUSE, Doe Park, Cotherstone, Barnard Castle, Co Durham, DL12 9UQ

Muriel M Lamb
Tel:-(0833) 50302
Open all year
SC £75-£150
Sleeps 6

Comfortable spacious detached farmhouse in own garden, good access and parking. Situated in wooded dales countryside near village and all services. Beamed living room with open fire, colour TV, fully equipped for 6 plus cot. Part nightstorage heating, 2 double and 1 twin bedrooms, separate bathroom and toilet. Ideal walking and touring. Private trout fishing. Guests very welcome on farm. OS Ref NZ 005203

(SC) THE BUNGALOW Wether Hill Farm, Winston, Darlington, Co Durham, DL2 3PZ

Liz Atkinson
Tel:-(0833) 27263
Open Mar-Nov
SC £60-£120
Sleeps 4/6

Holiday cottage in peaceful surroundings on working dairy farm. Fully equipped modern kitchen. Bathroom, 3 bedrooms plus cot & highchair available. Lounge with coal fire & colour TV, electric heating in bedrooms, ample space for children to play in garden 4½m from historical market town of Barnard Castle 2½ miles from Winston Village. Ideally situated for touring Yorkshire Dales. Lake district 1 hour. OS Ref NZ 105175

(SC) LOW GREEN FARM HOUSE Kleine Cottage, Romaldkirk, Barnard Castle, Co Durham, DL12 9ED

Gwen Wall
Tel:-(0833) 50794
Open all year
SC £90-£170
Sleeps 8 + Cot

Children are made especially welcome on our family farm. The detached stonebuilt farmhouse is both spacious & homely, with an open fire & partial central heating all included in the rent. It has 3 comfortable bedrooms, lounge, dining room, kitchen & bathroom. The front faces south & has ample parking, the back has a large enclosed garden. It is situated in the beautiful village of Romaldkirk. OS Ref NY 997221

Teesdale, Durham ENGLAND

(SC) FROG HALL & HONEY POT Raby Estate Office, Middleton-in-Teesdale, Barnard Castle, DL12 OQH

The Upper Teesdale Estate
Tel:-(0833) 40209
Open all year
SC £40-£155
Sleeps 4/6

2 well-equipped cottages in Harwood-in-Teesdale. Frog Hall has dining room, sitting room, kitchen, bathroom, WC, 2 double bedrooms. Honey Pot has living room, kitchen, bathroom, WC, 2 bedrooms. Both cottages have electric cooker, fridge, TV, electric storage heaters, open fires or immersion heater 50p meter. Linen not provided. Dogs by arrangement. Brochures available on request. NY 828317. OS Ref NY 807341

52 NORTHUMBERLAND

NORTHUMBERLAND

Nortumberland is England's best kept holiday secret. It is an area of beauty and yet of dramatic contrast, which has altered little during history. On the east it is bordered by the sea and where countryside meets it there are vast empty beaches; to the west there are the massive sprawling forests and three national parks.

The comparative geographical isolation has preserved in this northern corner of England some of the most lovely open countryside.

As England's most northerly county and the site of the once mighty Roman Empire, Northumberland is the proud possessor of Emperor Hadrian's 'left-overs' — and what a legacy he left. Now just a shadow it its former self the Wall is still something to wonder at . . . And wander over. There are plenty of visitor centres and museums for those keen to find out more.

There are castles galore — Alnwick, Dunstanburgh, Bamburgh and Raby — and many stately homes. There is an abundance of wildlife; you can take a boat out to the Farne Islands (known as the 'cradle of English Christianity') to look at the birdlife, visit wildfowl parks, follow forest trails and admire the Chillingham wild cattle, native Northumbrians for centuries.

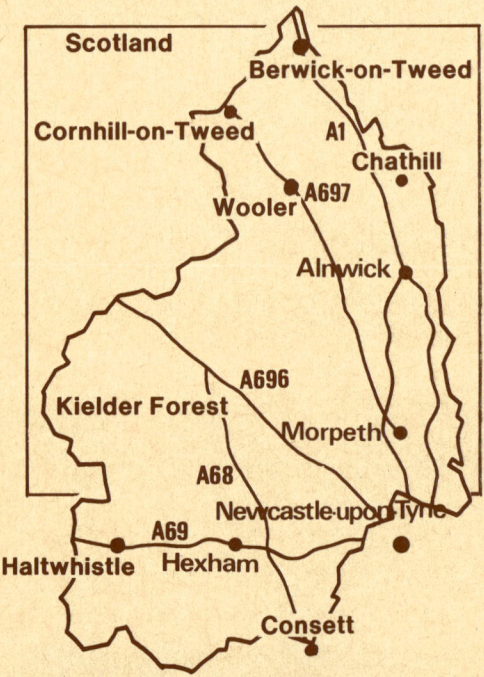

Tyne and Wear offers lively towns, bustling centres of commerce and superb shopping facilities where traditional markets mingle with modern shopping precincts.

Properties marked by * are members of the North Northumberland Group.

GROUP CONTACT:
Mrs J. Smalley (0289) 81279

Northumberland ENGLAND

(FH) EARLE HILL HEAD FARM   Wooler, Northum, NE71 6RH ✱

Sylvia & Charles Armstrong
Tel:-(0668) 81243
Open Jan-Mar, Jun-Nov
B&B   £10-£12   Listed
        Sleeps 6
Tent   £2-£5

Earle Hill Farm, a stock farm of 4000 acres, is in the National Park at the foot of the Cheviots. We give everyone a warm welcome both in our comfortable farm house and outside. Lovely walks in the nearby picturesque valleys. Household and farming museum for our guests to browse around.

(FH) THRUNTON FARMHOUSE   Whittingham, Alnwick, Northum, NE66 4RZ ✱

Mrs Phyllis Campbell
Tel:-(066574) 220
Open May-mid Oct
B&B   From £9   Listed
EM   £6
        Sleeps 4/5

A warm welcome awaits you on this 600 acre mixed farm. Thrunton is ideal for a country holiday having magnificent views' across Whittingham Vale to the Cheviots and being central for the county's numerous beauty spots and places of interest. Thrunton Woods are popular with walkers and nature lovers. Hearty meals are served in the guests' dining room. TV lounge. OS Ref NT 091109

(FH) DOXFORD FARMHOUSE   Chathill, Northum, NE67 5DY ✱

Douglas Turnbull
Tel:-(066579) 235
Closed Xmas and New Year
B&B   £10-£12
EM   £5
        Sleeps 6

Doxford Farm is situated centrally in 420 acres of unspoilt wooded countryside, four miles from the sea midway between the market town of Alnwick and Belford. It is ideally placed for visiting other parts of Northumberland, being between the foothills of the Cheviots and the lovely heritage coastline. The farm is about a mile from the main road. Reductions for children under 15yrs. OS Ref NU 181 233

(FH) THE FARM HOUSE   West Ditchburn, Eglingham, Alnwick, Northum, NE66 2UE ✱

Avril Irene Easton
Tel:-(066578) 337
Open Mar-Oct
B&B   £11.50-£12.50
EM   £7-£8
        Sleeps 8

17th Century stone-built farmhouse situated between the beautiful Cheviot Hills & unspoilt sandy beaches of Northumberland. Ideal for touring, castles, museums or participating in outdoor activities. 2 double, 2 family bedrooms, all with washbasins, teasmades, hair dryers, TV, 2 with showers. Bathroom with separate toilet, CH, fire certificate. Traditional meals, dining room, separate lounge. AA/RAC listed and Elizabeth Gundrey "Staying Off The Beaten Track". OS Ref NU 131208

(FH) ALNDYKE FARM   Alnwick, Northum, NE66 3PB ✱

Anne Davison
Tel:-(0665) 602193
Open May-Oct
B&B   £11-£12
EM   £6.50
        Sleeps 8

Georgian Farmhouse with panoramic views, offering friendly, relaxing atmosphere with delicious home cooking, family, double or twin rooms, all with H/C, drink making facilities. Bathroom/shower, 2 toilets. Lounge with TV, woodburning stove. Dining room. Excellent centre for touring Northumberland from the coast to the Cheviot hills. Situated near A1068 1m from Alnwick, 3m to the sea. AA listed, fire certificate, Brochure on request. OS Ref NU 208125

(FH) BILTON BARNS   Alnmouth, Alnwick, Northum, NE66 2TB ✱

Dorothy Jackson
Tel:-(0665) 830427
Open Easter-Oct
B&B   £10-£11   Listed
EM   £6.50
        Sleeps 6

Our spacious farmhouse has beautiful panoramic views, over Alnmouth and Warkworth Bay, set in lovely countryside we are excellently situated for the many magnificent beaches, castles, walks and recreational activities Northumberland can offer. Rooms are centrally heated, guests have their own lounge and dining room, bedrooms have washbasins, TV and tea/coffee making facilities. Good food and a warm welcome. OS Ref NU 224100

(FH) BEUKLEY FARM   Great Whittington, Newcastle-upon-Tyne, NE19 2LD

Tom & Alice Southern
Tel:-(043472) 225
Open May-Oct
B&B   £11-£12.50
EM   £6.50
Sleeps 6

Beukley - a 400 acre mixed farm in the heart of Roman Wall country. The modernised farmhouse offers spacious accommodation of a very high standard: private lounge, 1 twin bedded room with private facilities and a family room with luxurious bathroom adjoining. Good food, excellent accommodation and a warm welcome are always assured by hosts Tom and Alice Southern. OS Ref NZ 984709

(CH) THE COACH HOUSE   Crookham, Cornhill-on-Tweed, Northum, TD12 4TD

Lynne Anderson
Tel:-(089082) 293
Open Mar-Oct
B&B   £15-£20
EM   £8
CH   Sleeps 19

Set in rolling country near the Scottish border, a most comfortable base from which to explore north Northumberland. Most bedrooms have private bathrooms and are suitable for disabled guests. The house is centrally heated, with log fires in the public rooms. Fresh local produce, border beef, salmon from River Till and Northumbrian lamb are served with garden grown vegetables. OS Ref NT 914381

(CH) BISHOP FIELD FARM   Allendale, Hexham, Northum, NE47 9EJ

Keith or Kathy Fairless
Tel:-(043483) 248
Open Jan, Mar-Dec
B&B   £15-£20
EM   £10
Sleeps 18

17th Century farmhouse full of character, all rooms have ensuite facilities, telephones & full CH. Guests dine over log fires, with selection of fine wines. All food is fresh and prepared on the farm. Bishop Field is the ideal place for peace amidst comfort and high standards. Facilities include private fishing, full size snooker table and many outdoor pursuits, 7 twins, 2 doubles.

(FH) BRANDON WHITE HOUSE   Powburn, Alnwick, Northum *

Margaret Chisholm
Tel:-(066578) 252
Closed Dec-New Year
B&B   £9-£11   Listed
EM   £6
Sleeps 6

550 acre sheep & arable farm, attractive farmhouse set in large garden 1 mile north of Powburn village on A697. Within easy reach of beautiful sandy beaches & Cheviot Hills. Ideal for walking & touring. Friendly & comfortable with full English breakfast. Visitors' own dining room & lounge with colour TV. OS Ref 0506 18

(SC) DOXFORD FARM COTTAGES   Chathill, Northumb, NE67 5DY *

Douglas Turnbull
Tel:-(066579) 235
Open all year
SC   £60-£180
Sleeps 3/10

There is a terrace of stone built cottages on the farm, and five of them are available to let. They have all been modernised, and are simply furnished clean and comfortable. We also have a charming farmhouse annexe to let and it has accommodation for up to four people. Fuel for fires and electricity included. OS Ref NU 184233

(SC) WEST KYLOE   Berwick on Tweed, Northumberland, TD15 2PF *

Mrs Teresa Smalley
Tel:-0289 81279
Open all year
SC   £55-£150
Sleeps 2-4

A family farm of 600 acres situated in a peaceful, secluded position, 1 mile off the A1. Overlooking Holy Island. The recently converted flat within the farmhouse (sleeps 2-3) & terraced cottage (sleeps 4) have magnificent views of the coast & are warm & comfortable. Scenic farm walks & ideally situated for touring the historic border country. OS Ref NU 049 404

Northumberland ENGLAND

(sc) WEST KYLOE Berwick-upon-Tweed, Northum, TD15 2PF ✱

Mrs Sandra Leyland
Tel:-0289 81295
Open Easter-Oct
SC £50-£100
Sleeps 4-6

Secluded, peaceful farm caravan site in picturesque setting adjacent to old Mill Pond. 2 comfortable well-equipped, 6 berth, static caravans with separate double bedroom, mains electricity, water & flush WC's. Close to Holy Island, beautiful unspoilt beaches & Cheviot Hills. Linen not provided. Prices inclusive of electricity & gas. OS Ref NU 049 404

(sc) BRACKENSIDE BUNGALOW Brackenside Farm, Bowsden, Berwick-on-Tweed, Northum, TD15 2TQ ✱

Mary & John Barber
Tel:-(0289) 88293
Open all year
SC £70-£140
Sleeps 6

Attractive and comfortable bungalow with its own garden and young woodland. Enjoy the view to the Cheviot Hills and magnificent coast. Feel welcome to walk around the fields, woods and conservation areas. See the sheep & lambs, cows, calves and growing crops. 3 bedrooms, open fire, central heating, well equipped. Cot and high chair available. OS Ref NT 978402

BOOKING TIPS

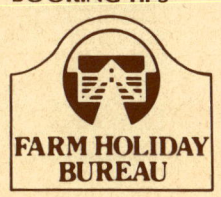

A WARM WELCOME

Some farm and country houses in this guide only take six guests — others take more; but wherever you stay, you'll be sure of a warm welcome.

53 PEMBROKESHIRE Dyfed

PEMBROKESHIRE, DYFED

Pembrokeshire is the south western corner of Wales, now part of the larger modern county of Dyfed. A large portion of Pembrokeshire is covered by the National Park, including most of the coastal strip and Preseli Mountains.

The countryside is unspoilt with an abundance and variety of wild flowers everywhere from the coast to the banks that skirt the miles of narrow country lanes.

The beaches vary from long sandy stretches to small rocky coves — but you could see them all if you walked the coastal footpath from St. Dogmeals in the north to Tenby in the south — 167 miles! You would also see the islands off the coast including Skomer and Skokhom which are nature reserves; and Caldy inhabited by the monks. Some of these islands can be visited and you may see seals here or indeed off any part of the coastline.

The variable terrain from coast to mountain, moorland to marsh provides an agreeable habitat for a wide variety of birds, insects and animals.

The area is full of history from ancient to modern, with Iron Age settlement remains, cromlechs and standing stones right up to more recent times the many castles, and of course the fine cathedral at St. Davids.

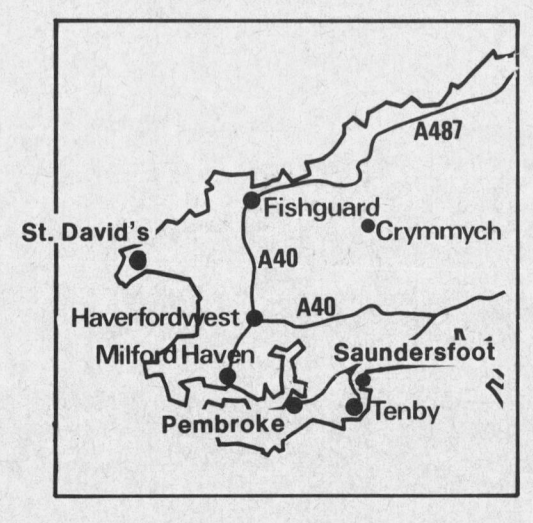

GROUP CONTACT:
Olive Evans (0437) 721382

Pembrokeshire WALES

(FH) TREARCHED FARM GUEST HOUSE Croes Goch, Haverfordwest, Pembs, Dyfed, SA62 5JP

Mrs M B Jenkins
Tel:-(03483) 310
Open Mar-Oct
B&B   £10-£12
EM   £5.50
Sleeps 12

Trearched is an arable 100 acre farm. The comfortable, centrally heated old farmhouse is down farm lane off A487 in Croes Goch village. Seven bedrooms, TV lounge, reading lounge, patio, dining room. Nearest beach 2¼ miles by road. Good home cooking. Ideally situated for touring N/S Pembrokeshire and coastal footpath. AA and RAC listed. Fire Certificate. WTB Farmhouse Award. OS Ref SM 828304

(FH) UPPER VANLEY FARM Solva, Haverfordwest, Pembs, SA62 6LJ

Morfydd Jones
Tel:-(03483)418/7728
Open all year
B&B   £8-£10
EM   £4-£6
Sleeps 15

150 acre dairy farm, central for St David's peninsula, situated 2m from coastal path. 4m from Solva Harbour. Comfortable, centrally heated, award winning farmhouse with log fires. Play area. Various farm pets. Choice of menus traditional evening dinner & vegetarian meals. Spacious bedrooms with colour TV, tea making facilities, H/C, heating and electric blankets. 4 bedrooms with private bathrooms. OS Ref SN 860268

(FH) LLANDDINOG OLD FARMHOUSE Solva, Haverfordwest, Dyfed, SA62 6NA

Sarah Griffiths
Tel:-(03483) 224
Open all year
B&B   From £9
EM   £4.50
Sleeps 12

Peacefully situated in spacious grounds, this 16th Century farmstead is an ideal base for sandy beaches, fishing, riding, walking or visiting historic St Davids, the Preseli Mountains or nearby fishing villages. Homely atmosphere (log fires). Substantial fayre from mainly home-grown produce. Picnics, Welsh cawl lunches and teas. Three family, 1 single. Central heating. Colour TV, play area for children. 50% redn for children sharing. OS Ref SM 831271

(FH) OLMARCH FARM Llandeloy, Nr Haverfordwest, Dyfed, SA62 6NB

Gloria Davies
Tel:-(03483) 247
Open Apr-Oct
B&B   £8-£9
EM   £4
Sleeps 6

Listed

Recently modernised stone-built farmhouse situated within 6 miles of St David's city and 10 minutes drive from many beautiful sandy beaches. Bedrooms are comfortable and spacious, 1 with en suite shower and washbasin, 1 family room, and 1 twin-bedded room. The farm is 175 acres family worked mixed dairy. Good home cooking is provided, using much of our own produce. Lawns for children's use. OS Ref SM 834278

(FH) LITTLE NEWTON FARM Kilgetty, (nr Saundersfoot), Dyfed, SA68 0YD

Sadie James
Tel:-(0834) 812306
Open Apr-Sep
B&B   £8.50-£9.50
EM   £3.50-£4
Sleeps 18

7 acre small holding with a lovely modern house, situated 5m from Tenby, 2½m Saundersfoot. All bedrooms have H/C heating, shaver points. 2 bathrooms, 2 shower rooms, 4 WC's. Dining room with separate tables. Lounge with colour TV & video. Excellent meals, licenced club, cricket played within 50 yards. Excellent communications, buses and trains only minutes away. AA listed. OS Ref SN 121073

(FH) TORBANT FARM GUEST HOUSE Croesgoch, Haverfordwest, Pembs, Dyfed, SA62 5JN

Barbara Charles
Tel:-(03483) 276
Open Easter-Oct
B&B   £10-£11.50
EM   £5
Sleeps 18

Torbant is a 110 acre dairy farm, 1½ miles from dramatic scenery and wildlife of Pembrokeshire coast. Guests welcome to watch milking in the modern parlour and walk through the farm. Although modernised the farmhouse retains its traditional character. 7 bedrooms, all with central heating & H/C. Fully licensed bar. Good home cooking. Wide range of activities and local crafts nearby. AA listed. OS Ref SM 844993

(FH) PENYCRAIG FARMHOUSE Puncheston, Haverfordwest, Dyfed, SA62 5RJ

Betty Devonald
Tel:-(034882) 277
Open Easter-Oct
B&B £8.50-£10   Listed
EM   £5
Sleeps 6

Penygraig is a modern 300 acre mixed farm situated in the picturesque Preseli Hills. The modernised farmhouse is on the edge of the village of Puncheston, Centrally situated for the North Pembrokeshire coastline. In the spacious dining room good wholesome cooking is served. There is 1 double room with shower, WC en suite. 1 family room with H/C. Reductions for children sharing. OS Ref SN 030130

(FH) FELIN TYGWYN Crymych, Pembs, SA41 3RX

Tom & Beryl Hazelden
Tel:-(023979) 603
Open all year
B&B +EM £87-£97 /wk
Other prices on request
Sleeps 9

Have a relaxing summer holiday or out of season break in a farmhouse at the foot of the Preseli mountains, 8m from a safe beach. Enjoy the unspoilt countryside with its wide variety of flora and fauna. We offer freshly cooked food from our own (organically grown) and local produce. Vegetarians especially welcome. Diets also provided for. Children and dogs welcome. Residential licence. OS Ref SN 162356

(FH) TREVACCOON FARM St Davids, Haverfordwest, Pembrokeshire, SA62 6DP

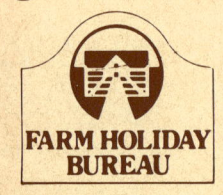

Mayrid Rees
Tel:-(03483) 438
Open all year
B&B £10
EM   £5
Sleeps 10

FARM HOLIDAY BUREAU

Trevaccoon is a 60 acre working farm. Modernised farmhouse situated on the beautiful coast of Aberiddy Bay and Porthgain. Spacious rooms all have private bathrooms and sea views. TV lounge, annex for guests. Tea/coffee making facilities, parking and safe playing area. Horse riding, fishing etc nearby. Free golf to guests. Farmhouse Award. Fire certificate. BB/EM at £95 to £105 per week. OS Ref SM 814308

(FH) TREPANT FARM Morvil, Rosebush, Clynderwen, Pembs, Dyfed, SA66 7RE

Marilyn Salmon
Tel:-(09913) 491
Open Apr-Nov
B&B £8.50-£9.50   Listed
EM   £5
Sleeps 6

Guests receive a warm welcome at Trepant, delightfully situated in the Preseli mountains with attractive views of the surrounding countryside. 1 family room, 1 twin, 1 double (all H/C) and television lounge. Imaginatively prepared meals will tempt your palate. Within easy reach of sandy beaches, Trepant is a focal point for all your holiday interests including pony trekking, walking and fishing. Ideal for touring and relaxing. OS Ref SN 044 319

(FH) GILFACH GOCH FARMHOUSE Fishguard, Pembrokeshire, Dyfed, SA65 9SR

June Devonald
Tel:-(0348) 873871
Closed Xmas-New Year
B&B £8.50-£10
EM   £6
Sleeps 10

A warm Welsh welcome and good home produced food await you at our smallholding. Superbly positioned in the National Park overlooking a magnificent landscape of sea, villages and countryside. Relax in attractive beamed rooms of this 18th Century stone built farmhouse. From here choose to explore the hills, walk flower strewn stretches of the coastal path or laze on sandy beaches. WTB Award. OS Ref SM 831271

(FH) LOWER HAYTHOG Spittal, Haverfordwest, Pembs, SA62 5QL

Nesta Thomas
Tel:-(043782) 279
Closed Xmas
B&B £8.50
EM   From £4.50
Sleeps 7 plus children

Escape to our centuries old farmhouse, peacefully located in the centre of county 5m north of Haverfordwest, set in 246 acres, the visitor can enjoy wooded walks, private fishing in trout ponds, pony rides for children. The house is within walking distance of Scolton Country Park. Delicious home cooking and relaxed friendly atmosphere. Log fires in winter. WTB Farmhouse Award. OS Ref SM 996 214

(FH) SPITTAL CROSS FARM Spittal, Haverfordwest, Pembs, SA62 5DB

Mary Evans
Tel:-(0437 87) 253
Open May-Sep
B&B £9-£10   Listed
EM £4.50
Sleeps 8

If you like to visit all parts of Pembrokeshire without driving for miles, enjoy peace and quiet in beautiful countryside, a warm welcome to a working farm, hearty breakfasts, imaginative evening dinners and comfortable accommodation, then this is the place to stay. If you like quality and value for money then this is the holiday for you. WTB Farmhouse Award. OS Ref SM 966 232

(FH) PENRALLT MEREDITH Eglwyswrw, Crymych, Dyfed, SA41 3SA

Nal Rees
Tel:-(023979) 228
Open all year
B&B £7.50
EM £4

A warm Welsh welcome awaits you on our working farm situated in the Pembrokeshire National Park Land. Guests are welcome to participate in farm activities. Fishing available on the farm. Wales Tourist Board Farmhouse Award. OS Ref SN 143 367

(FH) HIGHLAND GRANGE FARM GUEST HOUSE Robeston Wathen, Narbeth, Pembs, SA67 8EP

Naomi and Ken Jones
Tel:-(0834) 860952
Open Jan-Xmas
B&B £10-£11.50
EM £4
Sleeps 10

220 acre beef and sheep farm, excellent situation on the A40 in a central position for touring the Pembrokeshire Peninsula. Superior modern farmhouse, delicious home cooking with accent on healthy eating - home-made bread, muesli etc. Organic vegetable garden. All ages welcome, babysitting, also suitable for elderly or disabled. Beach 8 miles, inn 200 yds, golf, fishing, leisure complex nearby. Brochure on request. OS Ref SN 081156

(SC) "Y LODGE" Trearched Farm, Croes Goch, Haverfordwest, Dyfed, SA62 5JP

Mrs M B Jenkins
Tel:-(03483) 310
Open all year
SC £85-£110   Approved
Sleeps 2

"Y Lodge" is a unique single storey cottage situated at Trearched Farm Lane entrance on A487 in Croes Goch village. Sleeps 2. Comprising bed-sitting room with studio couch, kitchenette, bathroom, coal/log fire, storage heater, convector heater, TV, all linen, etc. Fuel provided. Ideally situated for touring lovely coastal footpath walks. Abereiddy Beach 2¼ miles. OS Ref SM 828304

(SC) TORBANT FARM GUEST HOUSE Croesgoch, Haverfordwest, Pembs, SA62 5JN

Barbara Charles
Tel:-(03483) 276
Open all year
SC £50-£250   Approved
Sleeps 2-6
EM £5

Torbant now has 3 self contained well appointed apartments, sleeping 4/6 persons. Attached to the main guest house. All the facilities of the guest house are available including childrens suppers & dinners in the main dining room with a fully licensed bar. Linen provided and electricity by meter.

54 DYFED, COAST & COUNTRY

DYFED COAST & COUNTRY

Dyfed — covering as it does more than 2,200 square miles, a good quarter of Wales, has more than its share of holiday attractions. Sandy beaches, rugged coastline, vast expanses of rolling open countryside and mountains. Dyfed really does mean do-as-you-please.

But lovely as the beaches and landscapes are, you will want to visit some of the old towns that dot this part of Wales; all have fascinating stories to tell in a part of Wales that has become an important cornerstone of its national heritage.

Carmarthen, for example, the oldest of the Welsh towns abounds with legends of Merlin, King Arthur's wizard. And if you doubt what you hear, remember that Carmarthen's Welsh name 'Caerfryddin' means 'City of Merlin.' Here the local fishermen go after their catches of salmon in the ancient and traditional coracle.

Not far from Carmarthen, lies the 'timeless, mild, beguilling, island of a town' — Laugharne — where Dylan Thomas wrote, lived and died.

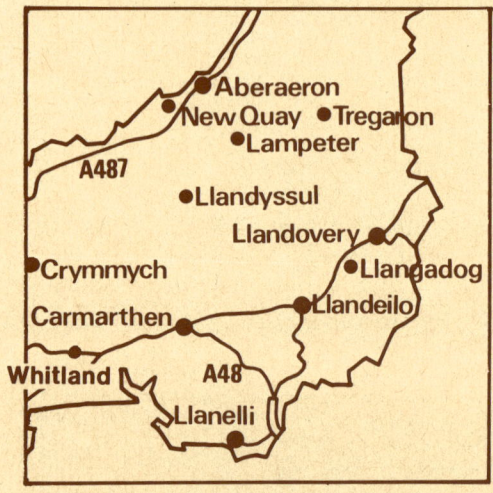

Around the coast a bit further you come to Tenby, where the medieval walls still hold a cluster of old buildings that almost touch across narrow, crooked strets.

Further west again you come to Milford Haven, an inlet 20 miles long, which Nelson described as one of the world's finest natural harbours.

GROUP CONTACT:
Ronnie Kelly (0545) 560346

Coast & Country, Dyfed WALES

FH NANTERNIS FARM Nanternis, New Quay, Dyfed, SA45 9RP

Joan White
Tel:-(0545) 560181
Open Easter-Oct
B&B £8-£10
EM £4
Sleeps 6
SC £95-£195

5 Dragons

Stock farm in peaceful village with lovely views 1½m from sea at Cwmtudu, 2½m from picturesque harbour of New Quay. Many activities, beauty spots within short distance of our Edwardian farmhouse. Drink making facilities, good home cooking. Goats milk available. Guests using our self-catering cottage (open all year) invited to help themselves to eggs, garden produce without extra charge. WTB Award. OS Ref SN 374 567

FH GLOG FARM Glog, Llangain, Llanstephan, Carmarthen, Dyfed SA33 5AY

Maureen Gribble
Tel:-(026783) 271
Closed Xmas-New Year
B&B £10
EM £4.50
Sleeps 8

Friendly working 40 acre livestock farm in Dylan Thomas country situated 4m from quiet sandy beach at Llanstephan, 4m from market town of Carmarthen. Norman Castle at Llanstephan, beautiful walks. Home produced eggs, veg, locally produced meat used whenever possible. Morning tea brought to your room. Choice of breakfast, 4 course evening meal and bedtime milk drink. Beautiful situation and views. WTB Farmhouse Award. OS Ref SW 366157

FH TREHOWELL FACH FARM GUEST HOUSE Glandwr, Hebron, Whitland, Dyfed, SA34 0YJ

Sian & Brian Gunstone Lowans
Tel:-(09947) 346
Open Mar-Nov
B&B £8-£10   Listed
EM £4
BB&EM
£80/week
Sleeps 8

Our 19th Century renovated farmhouse is situated at foot of the Preseli Mountains & ideally positioned for you and your family to explore the many coves, castles and craft centres of Pembrokeshire. Children and adults are welcome to help in feeding the animals & poultry and to walk through the pinewoods. Enjoy generous portions of excellent, mainly home produced food. OS Ref 184287

FH BROOK HOUSE FARM Pendine Road, Laugharne, Carmarthen, Dyfed, SA33 4NX

Miss Rhian James
Tel:-(099421) 239
Open all year
B&B £8.50-£9.50   Listed
EM From £4.50
Sleeps 6
SC £90-£180
TV £2-£4.50

Dairy farm in quaint wooded hamlet of Brook, between Laugharne (home of Dylan Thomas) and Pendine (7m of golden sand). Splendid open views, terraced lawns, children's play area. Comfortably furnished 3 bedroom cottage for self-catering/B&B (sleeps 8) & small 5-caravan site also available. 200 acres, rough shooting, birdwatching, walking. A warm welcome awaits all visitors, good food, licensed restaurant. OS Ref SN 268095

FH CWM IAGO Whitehill, Carmarthen, Dyfed, SA32 7HH

Doris Tarling
Tel:-(0267 84) 637
Open Easter-Sep
B&B £8-£10   Listed
EM From £2
Sleeps 4

Converted cottage set in 3 acres with lovely views and only 6m from Carmarthen. Comfortable rooms with separate shower room for guests, friendly and informal. Family run, helped by dogs, cats and horses. OS Ref SN 268473

FH CWMDWYFRAN FARM Cwmdwyfran, Bronwydd, Carmarthen, Dyfed, SA33 6JF

Mrs Joan Brandrick
Tel:-(026787) 419
Closed Xmas-New Year
B&B £8.50-£9   Listed
EM £4-£5
Sleeps 6
SC £72-£173   Approved

25 acre farm, 3m from Carmarthen, overlooking the beautiful Gwili Valley with breathtaking views. An assortment of farm animals, abundance of birdlife - the Buzzard being a common sighting in this area. Nearby fishing, golf, pony-trekking, forest walks. Scenic routes to the mountains and coast. Full farmhouse breakfast. Also self-catering cottages (open all year) fully equipped, southerly aspect, beautiful views. OS Ref SN 409249

239

(FH) TY HEN FARM   Llwyndafydd, Nr. New Quay, Llandysul, Dyfed SA44 6BZ

Mrs Roni Kelly
Tel:-(0545) 560346
Open Mid-Feb - Mid-Nov
B&B £13-£20
EM   £7.50
Sleeps 10
SC   £90-£350   Approved

Small working farm, variety of livestock, set in beautiful part of West Wales between New Quay, Llangranog, 1½m to Cwmtudu Cove. In farmhouse non-smokers, all bedrooms ensuite, CTV, drink making facilities. Charming s/c cottages (open all year) grouped round farmyard. Stone-built, beamed, well equipped. 2 1-roomed cottages suitable for wheelchair access (s/c or B & B). EM optional. Dogs by arrangement. OS Ref SN 365 553

(FH) GLANGRAIG FARM   Llangrannog, Llandyssul, Dyfed, SA44 6AQ

Jill Griffiths
Tel:-(023978) 554
Closed Xmas and New Year
B&B £9.50-£13.50   Listed
EM   £4.50
Sleeps 6

Glangraig farm is a beautifully situated Welsh farm with magnificent sea views. There is access to a private headland where seals and seabirds can be seen. The nearest sandy beach is only 1½m away. All rooms are comfortable and pleasantly furnished. There are panoramic views from the lounge and dining room. Full English breakfast, warm welcome, children and pets welcome. OS Ref SN 333 552

(SC) CWMCYNON   Llwyndafydd, Llandysul, (nr New Quay), Dyfed, SA44 6LE

Catherine Ann Davies
Tel:-(0545) 560426
Open Mar-Oct
SC   £80-£150   Approved
Sleeps 5

Cwmcynon a 100 acre farm set between New Quay & Llangranog. A friendly Welsh speaking family farm, animals such as milking herd & sheep. Guests are welcome, at owners discretion, to watch milking etc. Accommodation is part of farmhouse, with a front & back door, large sitting room, kitchen/diner. 3 bedrooms, 2 family rooms with double bed & 2 single beds, 1 single room, large bathroom. Play area for children. Babysitting by arrangement.

(SC) CEFN CANOL DEER FARM   Crymych, Nr Cardigan, Dyfed, Wales

Caroline Clark
Tel:-(023973) 526
SC   £80-£150   Applied
Sleeps 6
Tent £2-£2.50
Van   £3-£4

The cottage is traditional Welsh structure adjoining the main house. It is situated on a working Deer farm, horses are kept for trekking on the Preseli mountains. The farm has two small trout pools. The coast is about 8 miles away and completely unspoiled. OS Ref 32 18

CEREDIGION, Dyfed

55

CEREDIGION, DYFED

Through the ages travellers have come to Ceredigion: the Romans built roads here, and the Celtic saints constructed many churches along the coast. Some 500 years ago Henry Tudor travelled through on his way to Bosworth, staying for one night near Cwm Tudu — and somewhat later, the Victorians arrived by pony and trap for their holidays beside the fine beaches.

The 'Cardis' as the district's native inhabitants are known, have guarded their heritage well — many still speak Welsh, Europe's oldest living language. And the birthplace of St. David, patron saint of Wales is here.

Ceredigion's 52 mile coastline looks out on the expanse of Cardigan Bay; yachts and dinghies take to the waters from small harbours like Aberaeron and New Quay, and the many sandy beaches — among them Mwnt, Tresaith and Llangrannog — are a haven for sunbathers and swimmers, inland, around Tregaron, you might be lucky enough to spot rare birds like the red kite, whilst the River Teifi at Cenarth produces some fine catches of salmon.

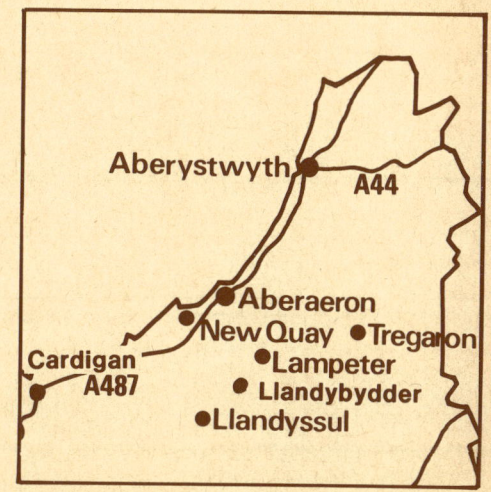

Between the mountains and sea is an unspoilt patchwork of farmland; there are villages and small market towns where market days are still occasions well worth experiencing.

Other places of interest include the narrow gauge railway from Aberystwyth to Devil's Bridge, the National Library of Wales and Arts Centre also at Abersytwyth.

VACANCY SECRETARY:
Carol Jacob (023975) 261

FH HENDRE Llangranog, Llandysul, Dyfed, SA44 6AP

Bethan Williams
Tel:-(023 978) 342
Open Mar-Oct
B&B £9-£10
EM £5
Sleeps 6

100 acre mixed farm, overlooking Cardigan Bay, 2 miles from Llangranog's sandy beaches with coastal footpaths, bird watching, country walks. Warm Welsh welcome given in our comfortable 19th Century stonebuilt farmhouse. Tastefully furnished throughout with carpets and central heating. Three pretty bedrooms with washbasins, 1 en-suite. Excellent home cooked meals using fresh local produce. WTB Farmhouse Award. AA Listed. OS Ref SN 344538

FH PENLAN FAWR Plwmp, Llandysul, Dyfed, SA44 6HR

Mrs Fernleigh Smith
Tel:-(023 975) 205
Open Easter-Oct
B&B £8.50-£9.50
EM From £5
Sleeps 6

Penlan Fawr - a comfortable and well maintained farmhouse on 200 acre dairy and Shire horse farm. Overlooking unspoilt countryside. Farm trail, through scenic valley and lots of animals. Situated just off A487 coast road midway between Cardigan and Aberaeron. Ideally placed for countryside and coast. Llangrannog beach 4 miles. A warm welcome, individual attention and freshly produced farmhouse cooking. OS Ref SN 3552

FH PENTRE FARM Llanfair, Lampeter, Dyfed, SA48 8LE

Mrs Eleri Davies
Tel:-(057045) 313
Open Easter-Oct
B&B £10-£12
EM £6
Sleeps 6

Sample true Welsh hospitality with generous home cooked meals using fresh farm produce. Comfort assured in large stonebuilt farmhouse, fully carpeted and centrally heated. Double, twin & family-size bedrooms each with own fully fitted bathroom. See cattle, sheep, pigs & pets on 300 acre working farm overlooking Teifi Valley. Near mountains and coast. Pony trekking, free fishing & shooting available to guests. WTB Farmhouse Award. OS Ref SN 624506

FH BRONIWAN Rhydlewis, Llandysul, Dyfed, SA44 5PF

Carole Jacobs
Tel:-(023975) 261
Open all year
B&B £10-£11
EM £5.50
Sleeps 6

Enjoy a warm welcome on our small farm 5m from the sea. Ideal centre for walking, bird watching & exploring the little market towns of the Teifi Valley. Our Victorian farmhouse has 3 comfortable bedrooms, one with private facilities, sitting room with lovely views & dining room with delicious home cooked food. Playroom in barn. Children's participation welcome. WTB farmhouse award. OS Ref SN 348475

FH ABERMEURIG MANSION Lampeter, Dyfed, SA48 8PP

Mallo Rogers-Lewis
Tel:-(0570) 470216
Closed Xmas-New Year
B&B £10-£12
EM £4.50-£5
Sleeps 6

18th Century farmhouse mansion of charm & character in the Vale of Aeron. Holds the BTA Commended & WTB Farmhouse Award. This ancestral home with its antiques, is centrally heated and has both canopy and 4-poster beds, shower room ensuite. Tea/coffee making facilities. Private fishing, shooting. Fresh country food whenever possible. Licensed dining room. Car essential. OS Ref SN 563955

FH LLWYNWERMOD FARM Maenygroes, Nr New Quay, Dyfed, SA45 9JR

Sheila Larsson
Tel:-(0545) 560083
Closed Xmas
B&B £8-£10
EM From £4.50
Red'n for children.
Sleeps 6

Situated 1m from New Quay. Ideal for anglers, walkers, (NT coastal path), bird watchers, or those who just choose to relax. The lounge has colour TV and log fire. Bedrooms are comfortably furnished with H/C, tea/coffee facilities, central heating. Some rooms have shower/toilet. We offer wholesome food home/locally grown fruit & veg. Ample car-parking. Baby sitting. OS Ref 376582

Ceredigion Dyfed WALES

(CH) MINYLLAN Llanwemog, Llanybydder, Dyfed, SA40 9UT

Mair Davies
Tel:-(0570) 480378
Open Easter-Sep
B&B   £9-£9.50
EM   From £6
CH   Sleeps 4

(5)

Welcome to Minyllan, a country house with panoramic views overlooking the Teifi Valley, near the historic Llanwenog church, 7m from Lampeter. Riding, fishing, walking nearby with the coast 13m. Spacious lounge has colour TV. Double & twin bedrooms have washbasins and tea/coffee facilities. Homely atmosphere where guests can enjoy traditional meals with a taste of Wales. OS Ref SN 455 493

(FH) BRYNCASTELL FARM BUNGALOW Bryncastell Farm, Llanfair Road, Lampeter, Dyfed, SA48 8JY

E.A. Beti Davies
Tel:-(0570) 422447
Open all year
B&B   £8.50-£9
EM   From £4
       Sleeps 4 + cot

Spacious bungalow on 140 acre farm. Commanding panoramic views over the Teifi Valley. All modern facilities with unrivalled hospitality and excellent cuisine. Access to farm facilities, invigorating hillside walks, or gentle strolls along river bank in an area of unspoilt beauty. Wonderful opportunity for a relaxing rural break. 1m, delightful market town of Lampeter. OS Ref SN 591484

(FH) BRYNOG MANSION FARMHOUSE Felinfach, Lampeter, Dyfed, SA48 8AQ

Nell Davies
Tel:-(0570) 470266
Closed Xmas and New Year
B&B   £9.50-£10.50
EM   £4.50
       Sleeps 12

Enjoy a holiday in the friendly atmosphere of a 200 yr old mansion. A 200 acre farm in the Vale of Aeron between Lampeter & Aberaeron, 10 mins drive. The house is approached by a ¾m rhododendron lined drive off the A482 road. 1 en-suite family bedroom, others with H/C, shaving points, CH, tea making facilities. Home cooking. Rough shooting, birdwatching, fishing. WTB Farmhouse Award. Car essential. OS Ref SN 529573

(FH) ERWBARFE FARMHOUSE Devil's Bridge, Aberystwyth, Dyfed, SY23 3JR

Elaine Lewis
Tel:-(097085) 251
Open Easter-Oct
B&B   £9-£11
EM   £5-£6
       Sleeps 4

400 acre mixed farm, set in beautiful countryside on the A4126 between Ponterwyd and Devil's Bridge. Famous for its falls and steam railway. Ideal fishing facilities are available at nearby reservoirs. Ideal centre for touring. A warm welcome at this peaceful and comfortable farmhouse with 2 double rooms with washbasins. Tea/coffee making facilities. Good home cooking. Rural Tourism Award. OS Ref SN 754784

(SC) ABERMEURIG MANSION Lampeter, Dyfed, SA48 8PP

Mallo Rogers-Lewis
Tel:-(0570) 470216
Open all year
SC   £100-£160   Approved
       Sleeps 6

Self catering cottage-wing of imposing mansion. The property is spacious and comfortable and of great character. Upstairs, 2 double bedrooms, bathroom and toilet, airing cupboard with immersion heater. Downstairs, large dining/sitting room overlooking mansion lawns. Comfortably furnished with colour TV, electric fires, fully equipped kitchen, central heating, metered electricity. Private fishing and shooting. Coast 8 miles. OS Ref SN 563565

(SC) CASTELL FARMHOUSE Bryncastell Farm, Llanfair Rd, Lampeter, Dyfed, SA48 8JY

E A Beti Davies
Tel:-(0570) 422447
Open all year
SC   £115-£150   4 Dragons
       Sleeps 9 + cot

140 acre mixed farm with this charming farmhouse, full of atmosphere. Spacious lounge, beamed ceilings, fully fitted kitchen, ample parking. ¾m fishing, rough shooting. Situated amid lush meadows of the Teifi Valley. Minutes away from Lampeter. Ideal for persons seeking serenity without isolation. Warm welcome assured. OS Ref SN 592484

(sc) **LLWYN GRAWYS FARM COTTAGES** Dyffryn, Llangoedmore, Cardigan, Dyfed, SA43 2LS

Lynette George
Tel:-(023987) 227
Open May-Oct
SC   £95-£335   5 Dragons
     Sleeps 2/8

Charming cottages on 600 acre farm tastefully converted and furnished combining tradition with modern conveniences. Sandy beaches, riding, fishing, golf, boating nearby. Children's play area, indoor playroom, laundry room, linen provided, colour TV. OS Ref SN 465 215

GWENT

GWENT

To the north of the county are the Black Mountains and the Brecon Beacons with majestic peaks and deep sheltered valleys. This area is part of the Brecon Beacons National Park which provides opportunities for pony-trekking, walking and many other outdoor activities.

Eastern Gwent is very different — the countryside is pastoral, with undulating, wooded hills and the river valleys of the Usk and Wye. Ancient market towns and picturesque villages are dotted throughout this part of the county. This is the area of the Welsh Marches and there are a number of strategically placed castles, including Raglan and Chepstow, reminders of less peaceful times. Tintern Abbey, immortalised by Wordsworth, shows a more tranquil face of the county.

Western Gwent can boast bracing, beautiful mountainsides, spectacular views and lovely walking country. It also has a rich industrial heritage with a wealth of attractions for those fascinated by the way we used to live.

Apart from its own attractions Gwent is an ideal base from which to explore Cardiff, the South Wales Valleys, the Gower Peninsula, the Black Mountains, the Brecon Beacons National Park, the Forest of Dean, the Mendip Hills, the Cotswolds, Bristol and Bath . . . all within 60 miles of its borders.

GROUP CONTACT:
Jean Arnett (02913) 2878

(FH) PENTWYN FARM   Little Mill, Pontypool, Gwent, NP4 0HQ

Ann Bradley
Tel:-(049 528) 249
Open Feb-Nov
B&B £10
EM £5.50
Sleeps 6

Pentwyn, a 125 acre working farm, is the home of Stuart & Ann Bradley and their three daughters. Set in the beautiful hills of Gwent, the 16th Century farmhouse stands in a ½ acre garden with its own swimming pool. A warm welcome & high standard of farmhouse cooking is assured. AA Best Family Establishment 1984-Wales. WTB Farmhouse Award. Restaurant Licence. Attractive self-catering stable cottages available. OS Ref SO 325035

(FH) TY-GWYN FARM   Gwehelog, Usk, Gwent, NP2 1RG

Jean Arnett
Tel:-(02913) 2878
Open Apr-Oct & New Year
B&B £9.50-£10
EM £6.50
Sleeps 4
Van £2.50

Ty-Gwyn is a large modernised farmhouse. Easily accessible from M4. Leave at junction 24, take A449 and A472 to Usk. Follow Gwehelog sign for 3m. Fishing, golf, and pony trekking nearby. Tea making facilities in bedrooms. High standard and generous meals made with mostly home grown produce. AA Listed and WTB Farmhouse Award. OS Ref OS 386045

(FH) THE WENALLT FARM   Gilwern, Nr Abergavenny, Gwent, NP7 0HP

Janice Harris
Tel:-(0873) 830694
Open all year
B&B £10-£13
EM £6.50
Sleeps 16

Situated in the Brecon Beacons National Park this 16th Century comfortable Welsh longhouse with oak beams and inglenook fireplace has commanding views over the Usk Valley. Seven bedrooms (five en-suite) all with tea making facilities, drawing room, TV lounge and dining room with restaurant licence where good home cooking is served. Ideally situated to explore the unspoilt countryside or visit local market towns. OS Ref SO 245138

(FH) LITTLE TREADAM   Llantilio Crossenny, Abergavenny, Gwent, NP7 8TA

Beryl Ford
Tel:-(060085) 326
Open all year
B&B £10-£12
EM £6.50
Sleeps 6
Tent £1-£2
Van £2-£5

35 acre mixed farm with delightful old character farmhouse, surrounded by secluded gardens. Good home cooking using a high proportion of home grown produce. Perfectly located near Welsh/English border meaning variety in every direction. On B4233 within walking distance of White Castle, Offa's Dyke path. Whether walking, touring, relaxing we are sure you will return home with pleasant memories. Reduced weekly rates. OS Ref SO 376159

(CH) PARSONS GROVE   Earlswood, Nr Chepstow, Gwent, S Wales, NP6 6RD

Mrs. Gloria Powell
Tel:-(02917) 382
Open Jan-Nov
B&B £10-£12
SC £60-£135   3 Dragons
Max guests 4/5 + baby in flat   5 Dragons

Set in 17 acres of pastureland, with panoramic views. Heated swimming pool, childrens' adventure playground and newly planted vineyard, bordered by trout stream. Self-contained wing of country house and 2 semi-detached single storey cottages, all furnished to high standard. Fully carpeted, colour television. Wales Tourist Board Graded. Electricity metered. All linen included. Bed and breakfast also available. WTB, BB Farmhouse Award. AA recommended. OS Ref ST 452943

(CH) CLAWDD FARM   Bullmore Road, Caerleon, nr Newport, Gwent

Janet Hughes
Tel:-(0633) 423250
Open all year
B&B £10-£12.50   Listed
EM From £5.50
Sleeps 12
SC £50-£120
Sleeps 2

On former farm, now peaceful woodland, secluded yet only minutes from M4 Junction 25/25, close to historical Roman village of Isca (Caerleon). Relax in the friendly atmosphere of an early Edwardian house full of odd objects and eat Janet's professionally produced food (all tastes adjusted to). Enjoy the small licences leisure centre opposite & all the other activities Gwent offers. Reductions for children. OS Ref ST 180330

BRECON ß RADNOR
Powys

57

BRECON & RADNOR, POWYS

Mid Wales makes the ideal touring centre, the dramatic mountains of the north are less than two hours drive away through some beautiful countryside, and the coastline of south west Wales almost takes your breath away.

There's plenty to do in mid-Wales, Langorse Lake has excellent facilities for dinghy sailors, and for the more adventurous — the mid and south west mountain ranges may not be as famous as those in the north for rock climbing, but both the Brecon Beacons and the Black Mountains offer exhilarating walks and scrambles for the enthusiast. One of the most famous salmon rivers — the Wye — runs through this region but for the more modest fisherman, there is a wealth of small trout rivers, streams, lakes and reservoirs within easy reach and with easy access.

The British and Monmouth Canal cuts through this region and provides enjoyment for canal enthusiasts, canoeists and walkers. Whether you are a serious walker or a once a year type, the hillsides and forest trails, rivers and canals entice you out of your cars for a gentle stroll or a full day's walk.

The National Park Information Centres have a wealth of information on walks of all types within the area including the Offa's Dyke and Glyndwr Way.

GROUP CONTACT:
Mrs. M. Adams (0874) 82505

(FH) BRYNFEDWEB FARM Trallong Common, Sennybridge, Brecon, Powys, LD3 8HW

Mrs Mary Adams
Tel:-(087 482) 505
Open Apr-Oct
B&B £10
EM £5
Sleeps 6
TV £2

Brynfedwen, situated between Brecon & Sennybridge is 118 acre livestock farm, with lovely views over Brecon & Usk Valley. Excellent facilities for all country pursuits or touring & exploring. Modernised stone centrally heated farmhouse, TV lounge with log fire. 2 family bedrooms, share bathroom. 1 twin-bedded room (en suite), equipped for disabled. Personal attention and good home cooking. OS Ref SN 310955

(FH) UPPER TREWALKIN Pengenfford, Talgarth, Brecon, Powys, LD3 0HA

Meudwen Stephens
Tel:-(0874) 711349
Open Apr-Oct
B&B £11
EM £6.50
Sleeps 6

(4)

Upper Trewalkin is a family run sheep and cattle farm. Built in the 1600s, the farmstead commands panoramic views of the Black Mountains, part of the Brecon Beacons National Park. An excellent centre for touring mid-Wales, and for participating in the many outdoor pursuits of the Welsh countryside. Recipient of a farmhouse award given by the Welsh Tourist Board. OS Ref SO 158300

(FH) TREWALTER FARM Llangorse, Brecon, Powys, LD3 0PS

Mary Eckley
Tel:-(087484) 662
Open Feb-Nov
B&B £10-£11
EM From £6
Sleeps 9

Trewalter Farm is set amidst glorious scenery, 1 mile from Llangorse Lake where water sports can be enjoyed. The farm covers 230 acres supporting cattle & sheep, while during the summer pick your own fruit is available. Cosy family home with good traditional farmhouse cooking. Visitors' lounge, dining room, 2 bathrooms and 4 WC's. Open fire. Babysitting can be arranged. OS Ref SO 128298

(FH) TREHENRY FARM Felin-Fach, Brecon, Powys, LD3 0UN

Theresa Jones
Tel:-(0874 85) 312
Open Easter-Nov
B&B £10-£12
EM £6
Sleeps 7

Trehenry Farm situated east of Brecon off A470. Farmhouse has outstanding views of surrounding countryside. Cattle, sheep, cereals are main enterprises on 200 acres. Brecon, Hay-on-Wye, Builth Wells close by are friendly market towns with many interesting places. Trehenry is ideal base, centrally situated, for visits around Mid South, West Wales. Traditional farmhouse food, warm welcome. Farmhouse Award Winner.

(SC) GROVESIDE COTTAGE Glencoe, Glasbury-on-Wye, (nr Hay on Wye), Herefs

Mrs Claudia Smith
Tel:-(049 74) 246
Open all year
SC £90-£140
Sleeps 5

Applied

A renovated stone cottage in a small hamlet, overlooking and with access to the lovely River Wye, where there is swimming, fishing, canoeing and bird watching. Shops and friendly pub with children's games room nearby. Pony trekking in the Black Mountains 2 miles, Hay-on-Wye, town of books 4 miles. Three bedrooms, 1 double, 1 twin (2' 6" beds), 1 single. OS Ref SO 175392

(SC) GWERNALWYE Penrheol, Clyro, (nr Hay on Wye), Hereford, HR3 5JH

Virginia Phillips
Tel:-(04975) 669
Open all year
SC £80-£150
Sleeps 4

(8)

Approved

Comfortable stone farmhouse near Hay-on-Wye (4 miles), situated on edge of 3000 acres of open hill offering wonderful walking, riding and birdwatching. Local fishing. Two bedrooms, one twin, one with large bunk beds. Sitting room/kitchenette, large bathroom. Colour TV, payphone, linen provided plus logs for open fire. Central heating. Stabling available. OS Ref SO 438 183

Brecon & Radnor WALES

(sc) **THE OLD STABLES   Trefeinon Farm, Llangorse, Brecon, Powys, LD3 OPS**

Pete & Liz Sheppard
Tel:-(087484) 607
Open all year
SC   £75-£180   Approved
      Sleeps 2-7

Six luxury self contained apartments in stone built converted barn on 200 acre working farm in the Brecon Beacons National Park. Cosy woodburning stoves make winter breaks our speciality. One or 2 bedrooms, sleep 2/4 or 4/7 with bedsettees in the lounge. All with colour TV, full size cooker and fridge. Two miles from Llangorse Lake. AA listed. OS Ref SO 136299

(sc) **RHIWLAS   Craig End, The Bank, Talgarth, Powys, LD3 OBN**

Megan Price
Tel:-(087484) 648
Open Easter-New Year
SC   £80-£150   Approved
      Sleeps 2-7

Rhiwlas is an attractive 16th century character farmhouse, with many oak-beamed ceilings, inglenook etc. Recently renovated to a high standard. Situated in lovely countryside between Black Mountains, Brecon Beacons. Ideal for walking with pony trekking, gliding, boating 1-2m or touring Mid-South Wales. 4 bedrooms, kitchen, living, dining room, lounge, bathroom. Storage heaters, TV, bed linen provided.

(sc) **GWRLODDE   Whitelow Farm, Talgarth, Brecon, Powys, LD3 OEY**

Mary Evans
Tel:-(0874) 711291
Open Apr-Nov
SC   £80-£150   Approved
      Sleeps 8

Unwind in the peace and quiet of our tastefully renovated cottage, set in unspoilt countryside, ideal for walking, bird-watching, pony trekking and gliding close by. Sleeps 1-8 people, bed linen provided, cot available. Bathroom, shower, 2 toilets, sitting room, kitchen/dining room with electric cooker, refrigerator, heating by storage heaters. Electricity extra. OS Ref SO 164305

FOLLOW THE COUNTRY CODE

Countryside COMMISSION

TAKE CARE OF THE COUNTRY

Enjoy the countryside and
respect its life and work.
Guard against all risk of fire.
Fasten all gates.
Keep your dogs under close control.
Keep to public paths across farmland.
Use gates and stiles to cross fences,
hedges and walls.
Leave livestock, crops and machinery alone.
Take your litter home.
Help to keep all water clean.
Protect wildlife, plants and trees.
Take special care on country roads.
Make no unnecessary noise.

58 HILLS & VALES OF MID WALES, Powys

HILLS & VALES OF MID WALES, POWYS

We can offer practically every sport or pastime that requires an outdoor or country environment, also craft work holds an important place in our community life.

Pony trekking, of course, for which the area is pre-eminently famous, fishing, including salmon and trout, hill walking, bird watching, nature study, canoeing, foot hounds, photography and art. Golfers, tennis and bowls players are also catered for.

If, however, you want the less active and more varied type of holiday, then you will soon discover that there is so much to see and do. The area is steeped in history and we are within easy reach of Roman encampments, castles, caves, old mine workings, old churches and monuments, the coast, miniature railways and, of course, most famous of all, the Elan Valley Lakes.

Most people find that the bracing hill air makes the evening a time for relaxation and quiet. Perhaps a meal at one of the many inns, restaurants or hotels in the area, followed by a gentle return to your farmhouse is all you will want.

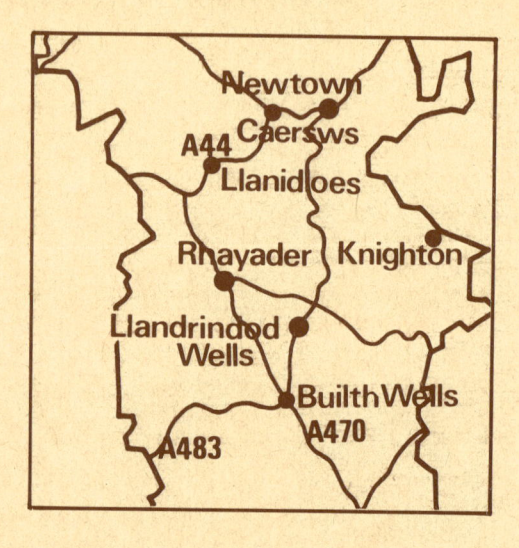

If you seek entertainment of a more positive kind, then you will probably find something to suit your taste in one of the nearby towns such as Builth Wells, Llandrindod Wells, Llanidloes, Newtown or Aberystwyth.

GROUP CONTACT:
Yvonne Riley (0597) 810240

Hills & Vales of Mid Wales WALES

(FH) DOWNFIELD FARM   Rhayader, Powys, LD6 5PA

Glenys Price
Tel:-(0597) 810394
Open Mar-Nov
B&B   £8-£8.50   Listed
          Sleeps 6

Downfield Farm is a mixed farm, situated 1 mile east of Rhayader, set back off the A44, Crossgates Road, with good clean access, private parking space. Surrounded by hills and lakes, fishing, pony trekking and good walking country nearby. We extend a warm welcome to all our guests. Three double bedrooms, all with hot and cold water and tea making facilities. OS Ref SN 988685

(FH) TYNPISTYLL   Rhayader, Powys, LD6 5EY

Violet Lewis
Tel:-(0597) 810398
Open May-Oct
B&B   £8.50-£9   Listed
          Sleeps 5

Originally a traditional Radnorshire long house, Tynpistyll still retains its oak beams & inglenook fireplace, & is furnished in keeping with its character. Only ½m from Rhayader and 3m from the beautiful Elan valley - a working farm with cattle and sheep, offering peace and tranquility in a friendly atmosphere. Excellent base for pony trekking, fishing, walking and bird watching. One double and 1 twin bedded room. OS Ref SO 994698

(FH) GIGRIN FARM   Rhayader, Powys, LD6 5BL

Lena Mary Powell
Tel:-(0597) 810243
Open Easter-Nov
B&B   £8.50-£9   Listed
EM   £5
          Sleeps 4

"Gigrin" is a 17th Century Welsh long house retaining original oak beams and homely atmosphere. Situated ½ mile south of Rhayader, overlooking Wye Valley and surrounding hills. 2 double bedrooms with washbasins. Bathroom with shower. Traditional farmhouse cooking. The 200 acre stock rearing farm offers a "farm trail" to residents or anyone visiting the area. A friendly welcome awaits you. OS Ref SO 980677

(FH) GWYSTRE FARM   Gwystre, Llandrindod Wells, Powys

Cissie Drew
Tel:-(0597 87) 316
Open Mar-Oct
B&B   £7.50-£8   Listed
EM   From £5
          Sleeps 4

Gwystre is a 200 acre beef and sheep farm with ponies, situated 50 yards off the main A44 road and only 100 yards from village inn. Surrounded by hills and lakes its nearest town is Llandrindod Wells, which offers swimming, golf, tennis and bowling. At Gwystre a warm welcome awaits, with 1 twin bedded room, 1 double room, tea making facilities, TV, electric radiators. OS Ref SO 066656

(CH) DOLIFOR   Llanwrthwl, (Rhayader), Llandrindod Wells, LD1 6NU

Chippy Riley
Tel:-(0597) 810240
Open Easter-Oct
B&B   £7.50-£9   Listed
EM   £5.50
CH   Sleeps 5

Stone-built oak beamed farmhouse in quiet situation in beautiful Elan Valley. The house is centrally heated and guests have their own shower room, sitting room with TV. Tea/coffee facilities. 1 single, 1 double, 1 twin room. Special diets are catered for. An RSPB reserve adjoins the property which overlooks the River Elan. OS Ref SN 958657

(FH) PENBRYNCENNAU FARM   Abbeycwmhir, Llandrindod Wells, Powys, LD1 6PT

Janet Rees
Tel:-(059783) 246
Open Apr-Oct
B&B   £8-£9   Listed
EM   From £5
          Sleeps 6

Our 280 acre hill farm is situated in beautiful scenic and peaceful countryside. Traditional stone built farmhouse. Children are very welcome, we specialise in catering for families. Tea making facilities provided. Farm trail and childrens play area. Family and double rooms. OS Ref 052745

FH BEILI NEUADD Rhayader, Powys, LD6 5NS

Ann Edwards
Tel:-(0597) 810211
Closed Xmas
B&B   £8.50-£9.50
EM   From £6.50
Sleeps 6

An attractive 16th Century, stone-built farmhouse set amidst beautiful countryside in a quiet secluded position approx 2 miles from small market town of Rhayader. Guests are assured of every comfort with central heating, log fires and spacious accommodation in single, double and twin-bedded rooms, shower and bathrooms. WTB Farmhouse Award winner. Centre for most countryside pursuits. Pets by arrangement. OS Ref SO 994698

FH DYFFRYN FARM Llanwrthwl, Nr Llandrindod Wells, Powys, Wales, LD1 6NU

Frederika Duffell
Tel:-(0597) 811017
Closed Xmas and New Year
B&B   £8.50-£10
EM   £5.50
Sleeps 4

A delightful old stonebuilt farmhouse superbly situated high in the Cambrian mountains above the River Wye and an ideal base for exploring "Wild Wales", birdwatching, pony trekking or just relaxing. Very comfortable and attractive rooms with panoramic views, log fires, hundreds of books, dried flowers (some for sale), colour TV, Laundry, wholefoods and mostly home produce. Many animals, from ponies to peacocks. OS Ref SN 972 645

HEART OF WALES
Powys

59

HEART OF WALES, POWYS

The Heart of Wales has unspoilt villages, bustling little towns, and marvellous scenery — hills and mountains, sparkling streams, superb woodlands, tranquil lakes and reservoirs.

It is also surprisingly compact, with plenty to do and see without travelling far from your base. Roads are usually uncluttered (none of the properties is much more than one hour's drive from the sandy beaches and rugged cliffs of the coast); there are plenty of country pubs for a lunchtime snack; and the food we serve is largely fresh local produce, often from our own gardens.

English is understood everywhere, but you will hear Welsh spoken, particularly in the north and west. You will soon become accustomed to the seemingly difficult sounds of our places and personal names (we are all used to advising guests on pronunciation!) We also make a point of having information in our houses about events and places of interest, to help you enjoy your stay.

We have castles and battlefields, reminders of border struggles years ago; and the 8th century rampart built by King Offa is now a 170-mile public footpath. Among other man-made attractions, our area is renowned for its unique black-and-white buildings, including cruck houses, box-framed houses and their many variations.

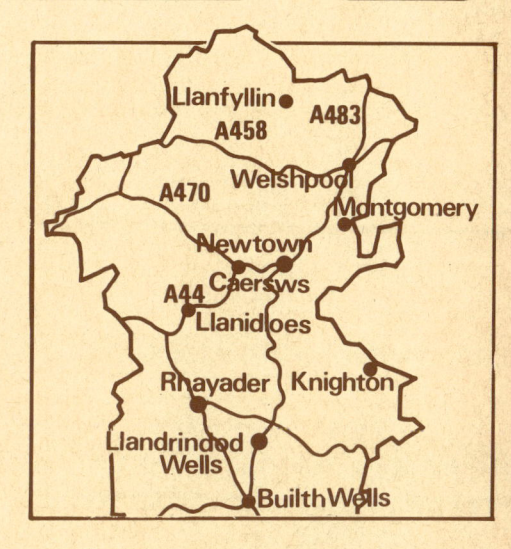

VACANCY SECRETARY:
Freda Emberton (0938) 3175

(FH) LOWER GWESTYDD FARMHOUSE Llanllwchaiarn, Newtown, Powys, SY16 3AY

Iris Jarman
Tel:-(0686) 26718
Open Mar-Dec
B&B   £10-£10.50
EM   £4.50
Sleeps 6

Nestling in quiet hillside with superb views this 17th Century farmhouse with 200 acres, has tea-making facilities, washbasins, shaving points. Centrally heated, shower room, dining and lounge with TV Large garden providing fresh fruit and veg for the table. Miniature railways, castles, mountains, lakes, golden beaches all within easy day trips, sports centre and theatre close by. WTB Farmhouse Award. OS Ref SO 126936

(FH) THE DREWIN FARM Churchstoke, Montgomery, Powys, Wales, SY15 6TW

Ceinwen Richards
Tel:-(05885) 325
Open Easter-Oct
B&B   £8.50-£10
EM   £4.50
Sleeps 6

17thC border farmhouse, inglenook fireplace & a wealth of oak beams. Panoramic views over beautiful countryside. Games room with snooker table available. Good home cooking & a warm welcome is given at the Drewin which is a mixed farm of sheep, cattle and corn. Ideal base for exploring Mid Wales & the border counties. Offa's Dyke footpath runs through the farm. OS Ref OS 905261

(FH) DOL-LLYS FARM Llanidloes, Powys, SY18 6JA

Olwen Evans
Tel:-(05512) 2694
Open Easter-Oct
B&B   £9-£10
EM   £5
Sleeps 6
TV   £3-£3.50

Dol-llys is a 17th Century farmhouse, intriguing because it has so many levels & small staircases. On the banks of River Severn 1m from Llanidloes. We have mixed farm of cattle, sheep, poultry & a child's pony. Ideal centre for the scenic walks & lakes of Mid-Wales. Every effort made to give you comfort & freedom. Fishing & shooting available on the farm. WTB Farmhouse Award. OS Ref 961857

(FH) LITTLE BROMPTON FARM Montgomery, Powys, Mid-Wales, SY15 6HY

Gaynor Bright
Tel:-(068681) 371
Open all year
B&B   £9-£10
EM   £4-£5

A delightful 17C farmhouse in glorious peaceful countryside, our family home for the last 50 years. Situated 2m from Georgian town of Montgomery. We offer delicious cooking & a family atmosphere. Personal attention with value for money are our priorities. The comfort of today with the charm & character of by-gone days. Offas Dyke runs through the 100 acre farm. WTB award. OS Ref SO 244941

(FH) TYNLLWYN FARM Welshpool, Powys, SY21 9BW

Freda Emberton
Tel:-(0938) 3175
Open all year
B&B   £10.50
EM   £5.50
Sleeps 12

AA, RAC, WTB Farmhouse Award. Licensed. Mixed/dairy farm, 1m from Welshpool with beautiful views, and a warm welcome, CH, wash units, colour TV, tea/coffee facilities in all bedrooms. Modernised bathroom & shower room. High standard. Home cooking & generous meals, ideal touring centre for the beautiful lakes, mountains, coasts. Nearby pony trekking, canal trips, Powys Castle & the little steam railway. Pets by arrangement. OS Ref SJ 091221

(FH) CYFIE FARM Llanfihangel Yng Ngwynfa, Llanfyllin, Powys, SY22 5JE

George & Lynn Jenkins
Tel:-(069184) 451
Closed Xmas
B&B   £10.50-£11.50
EM   £6
Sleeps 6

George and Lynn offer a warm welcome to their 17th Century farmhouse set high above a beautiful Welsh Valley. Beamed rooms, open log fires and superb traditional cooking. Holder of British Tourist Authority Commended Award and Wales Tourist Board Farmhouse Award. Ideal for touring the historic beauty spots of Mid-Wales. OS Ref SJ 085147

Heart of Wales WALES

(FH) HIGHGATE FARM Newtown, Powys, SY16 3LF

Linda Whitticase
Tel:-(0686) 25981
Open Mar-Oct
B&B   £10.50
EM   From £5.50
Sleeps 6

Superbly sited half-timbered farmhouse. Lovely views, scenic walks. All rooms centrally heated with H/C plus showers. Farm provides fishing, shooting, riding, waterfowl. Farmhouse cooking with home produced meat and vegetables plus own family supervision. Ideally located in mid Wales for castles, railways, theatre and sports centre. One hour from beaches. WTB award, AA listed. Licensed bar. OS Ref SN 280280

(FH) GUNGROG HOUSE Rhallt, Welshpool, Powys, SY21 9HS

Eira Jones
Tel:-(0938) 3381
Open Apr-Oct
B&B   £10.50
EM   £5.50
Sleeps 6

Gungrog House is set in 21 acres. The 300 year old farm house commands superb views of the Severn Valley. The tiny hamlet of Rhallt is 1½m from Welshpool. The historic towns of Shrewsbury and Chester are within driving distance and for the more energetic there is Offa's Dyke. Good home cooking is our speciality. Bedrooms have shower and toilet ensuite.

(FH) MOAT FARM Welshpool, Powys, SY21 8SE

Wyn & Gwyneth Jones
Tel:-(0938) 3179
Closed Xmas
B&B   £10-£11
EM   From £5
Sleeps 16

Moat Farm in beautiful Severn Valley has 250 acres, we rear all our own calves, milk 140 cows, night & morning. Farmhouse dates from 17th Century, offering warm, comfortable accommodation. Guests have their own TV lounge, fine timbered dining room with log fire in canopied stone firegrate. Tennis lawn, spacious garden, games room. Quiet pony, friendly dog, plenty of kittens to see. WTB Farmhouse Award. OS Ref SJ 214 042

(FH) GROFFTYDD FARM Carno, Newtown, Powys, SY17 5JR

Prue Lewis
Tel:-(0686) 420274
Open all year
B&B   From £9
EM   From £4.50
Sleeps 6

Grofftydd Farm, the home of Glynne and Prue Lewis is pleasantly situated near the village of Carno among the rolling hills of Mid Wales. The 180 acre family farm produces beef, sheep and crops. Mountains, miniature railways, beaches, castles and lakes are within easy reach. Pony trekking, fishing, hill walking and clay pigeon shooting. Home cooking and warm hospitality awaits you.

(SC) LLWYN Red House, Trefeglwys, Nr Caersws, Powys, SY17 5PN

Gwyneth Williams
Tel:-(05516) 285
Open all year
SC   £60-£150   2 Dragons
Sleeps 7 + cot

Two miles from Caersws, it stands in an elevated area of beauty overlooking the Trannon Valley and within easy reach of many mid-Wales attractions. This highly furnished property has games room, fully equipped kitchen, with open fire and TV in the lounge. Heating in all rooms. Guests can also enjoy walks on our stock rearing farm. WTB s/c award. OS Ref SJ 992899

(SC) RED HOUSE Trefeglwys, Nr Caersws, Powys, SY17 5PN

Gwyneth Williams
Tel:-(05516) 285
Closed Xmas-New Year
SC   £60-£100   3 Dragons
Sleeps 5 + cot

A self contained part of the owners farmhouse, it overlooks the idyllic Trannon Valley. The kitchen is compact and fully equipped with dining facilities. The spacious lounge is fully carpeted and can also be used as a diner. The property accommodates 5 plus cot. Come to Red House, meet the family, explore and go for walks on the farm. OS Ref SJ 992899

(sc) **GUNGROG COTTAGE** Gungrog House, Rhallt, Welshpool, Powys, SY21 9HS

Fira Jones
Tel:-(0938) 3381
Open all year
SC   £60-£100   Approved

This award winning property has been tastefully converted into a well appointed cottage, retaining much of its original charm and character. Set in 21 acres, it is ideally situated 1½m from Welshpool. The historic towns of Shrewsbury and Chester and the coast are within easy driving distance. Large garden with barbecue.

TANAT VALLEY POWYS/CLWYD

GO

TANAT VALLEY, POWYS/CLWYD

The Tanat Valley is one of the lesser known but one of the most beautiful areas of Wales. It is conveniently situated for both Oswestry and Welshpool, and is easily accessible from the A5.

The area offers lakes, hills, forests and mountains, together with one of the finest waterfalls in Wales, and a rural charm which is enjoyed by walkers, cyclists, motorists and the casual visitor alike. For the more energetic, windsurfing, canoeing and pony trekking are just a few of the many activities within easy reach.

This is hill farming country with flocks of sheep being worked by sheepdogs on almost every hillside, hedgerows full of wild flowers and a paradise for bird watchers.

The valley was the route of the historic Tanat Valley Railway, servicing the workings of Lead and Slate Mines into the second half of the century, many of which are still visible. The forestry trails of the Lake Vyrnwy estate offer an ideal opportunity to get off the beaten track — yet the valley is within easy reach of Welshpool, Bala and Oswestry.

Many visitors return again and again, once having found the valley which provides all the elements for a perfect holiday in a compact area — or perhaps it is the friendliness of the valley people, always pleased to welcome old and new visitors alike; a friendliness echoed in the welcome you will receive from all our Members.

PLACES TO VISIT

Chwarel Wynne Slate Mine, Glyn Ceiriog
Chirk Castle
Bala Lake and Farm Trail
Centre for Alternative Technology Machynlleth
Llangedwyn Mill and Craft Centre
The Painted Room — Llanfyllin
Challenge Centre — Outdoor Pursuits, Llanfyllin
R.S.P.B. Visitor Centre — Lake Vyrnwy
Erddig Hall Wrexham
Llangollen
Museum of Early Childhood — Oswestry
The Leisure Centre Oswestry
Old Racecourse and part of Offas Dyke Oswestry
Butterfly Farm
Snowdonia National Park
Sycharth Ancient Hill Fort

GROUP CONTACT:
Lorraine Paschen (069189) 521

(FH) **BWLCH-Y-RHIW FARM** Llansilin, Oswestry, Shropshire, SY10 7PT

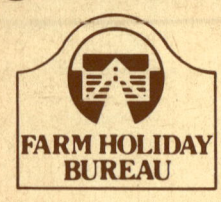

Brenda M Jones
Tel:-(069170) 261
Open Easter-Oct
B&B   £10
       Sleeps 6

Bwlch-y-Rhiw meaning the pass in the hill is an 18th Century limestone farmhouse having splendid views of the Tanat Valley. A warm welcome awaits you here. Three spacious bedrooms have bathroom ensuite and tea making facilities. The character-filled dining room has an inglenook fireplace & old oak furniture. Comfortable lounge with colour TV. Ideal spot for all country pursuits. Offa's Dyke nearby. OS Ref SJ 303225

(CH) **BRON HEULOG** Waterfall St, Llanrhaeadr-ym-Mochnant, Nr Oswestry, Shrops, SY10 0JX

Lorraine Pashen
Tel:-(069189) 521
Open all year
B&B   £8
EM   £5
       Sleeps 6

Situated in picturesque Tanat Valley noted for its bird life, historical and conservation areas with Pistyll Rhaeadr Waterfall one of the seven wonders of Wales, 4 miles away. This Victorian home set in its own large garden is tastefully furnished with antique furniture, open fire and CH. Family's rare breeds farm is ¼m from main house. A warm welcome awaits. OS Ref SJ 123263

(SC) **ARLLEN FAWR** Pen-y-Bont Fawr, Oswestry, Shrops, SY10 0BH

Ann Jones
Tel:-(0691 74) 209
Open all year
SC   £50-£85
      Sleeps 9

Delightful part farmhouse in 210 acres, at the base of Berwyn mountains. Fishing on farm. Llanrhaeard Waterfall 6m, pony trekking. ½m from Peny-Bont Fawr with pub, off licence, village store & chip shop. House has 2 bedrooms, living room, kitchen, open fires or electric fires available.

ALL BED AND BREAKFAST PROPERTIES IN THIS GUIDE HAVE BEEN PERSONALLY INSPECTED.

ENGLISH TOURIST BOARD

WALES TOURIST BOARD

In England and Wales, the properties have been inspected and classified as 'Listed,' or '1, 2, 3 or 4 Crowns' by the English or Wales Tourist Boards. (See Introduction for details). The higher classification does not indicate that one property is better than another, but that it provides a greater range of facilities.

CLWYD

CLWYD

Clywd — its northern boundary strung with seaside resorts — comes up with some surprising contrasts; from the sandcastle and holiday atmosphere of the coast to the fortresses left behind by mediaeval construction teams. It's a splendid area of Wales, which away from that necklace of sea towns is relatively unvisited.

St. Asaph, at the head of the Vale of Clwyd, might be just a village, but it's also a cathedral city — even if the cathedral is the smallest in the country and one of the oldest in Wales. It dates back to the 15th century and houses treasures like William Morgan's Welsh translation of the Bible.

Further into the country lies Ruthin, a mediaeval market town famous for its curfew bell, rung every night at 8pm since the 11th century. Ruthin also boasts a castle, where you can enjoy a mediaeval banquet, and the Maen Huail stone where King Arthur is said to have beheaded his rival in love, the unfortunate Huail. The craft centre in Ruthin is worth a visit, as are the ones at Nannerch and Llanesa.

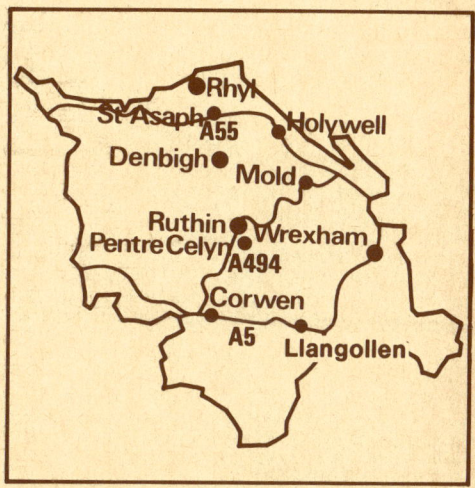

Crafts of a different nature are found in Llangollen, where horse-drawn barges glide along the Shropshire Union Canal. For a faster pace, what about a trip along the restored section of the Great Western Railway from Llangollen to Fford Junction?

To the west is Llyn Brenig, a fishing and sailing centre, with nearby forests full of inviting trails and picnic sites.

VACANCY SECRETARY:
Beryl Jones (08242) 2481

RHEWL FARM Waen, St. Asaph, Clwyd, N. Wales, LL17 ODT

Mrs. Eirlys Jones
Tel:-(0745) 582287
Open Mar-Nov
B&B   £8
       Sleeps 6

A warm welcome awaits you at our 180 acre farm, conveniently situated ½ m from A55, in a peaceful setting with excellent scenery. Double bedroom with en-suite facilities. Twin and family bedrooms with washbasins. Spacious lounge with exposed beams and original inglenook fireplace. Excellent breakfast using fresh eggs from farm. Reductions for children. Games room. Ideal touring centre. Coast 6 miles. OS Ref SJ 054743

LLAINWEN UCHA Pentre Celyn, Ruthin, Clwyd, LL15 2HL

Elizabeth Parry
Tel:-(097888) 253
Closed Xmas-New Year
B&B   £8-£9   Listed
EM   £4.50
       Sleeps 4

A very pleasant modern house where you can be assured of a warm welcome. We offer 2 pleasant rooms with modern amenities, an ideal base for touring this lovely region of North Wales. Overlooking the beautiful Vale of Clwyd and in easy reach of Snowdonia and coast. Local fishing and pony riding school. Cot provided.

COLLEGE FARM Peniel, Denbigh, Clwyd, LL16 4TT

Helen Parry
Tel:-(074570) 276
Open Apr-Nov
B&B   £8-£9
EM   £5
       Sleeps 6

"Croeso cynnes i chwi". College is a 140 acre mixed farm with cattle, sheep & arable crops. Easily reached from Denbigh (2½m) (B4501) with its ancient castle in the beautiful Vale of Clwyd. Good centre for touring with walking, fishing & sailing facilities in the vicinity (5m) at Brenig Reservoir. You are assured of a warm Welsh welcome by the bi-lingual Parry family. OS Ref SJ 035632

CAE MADOC FARM Llandegla, Wrexham, Clwyd, LL11 3BD

David & Del Crossley
Tel:-(097888) 270
Open Easter-Dec
B&B   £8.50-£10   Listed
EM   From £5
       Sleeps 6
Tent   40p-60p; Max 10
Van   £2-£2.50; Max 5

Cae Madoc is a working farm with sheep & cattle. The stone & slate house is 200 yrs old, has beams & large garden. Central heating. Accommodates 6 guests. Situated 22 miles from Chester on route to Dolgellau, nestling in hills betwixt Llangollen/Ruthin. Car essential unless walking or riding. Offa's Dyke nearby. Stabling & grazing available. Childrens playroom. OS Ref SJ 181495

BRYN AWEL FARM Bontuchel, Ruthin, Clwyd, LL15 2DE

Beryl Jones
Tel:-(082 42) 2481
Closed Xmas
B&B   £7-£9   Listed
EM   as requested
       Sleeps 6

Farmhouse on a 35 acre working farm on the outskirts of the picturesque market town of Ruthin. Convenient for Chester, North Wales coast, Snowdonia. Both English & Welsh spoken & a traditional Welsh welcome awaits you. Planned routes available for motoring and country walks, ½m private fishing available & arrangements can be made for Mediaeval banquets, horse riding & sailing. WTB & AA approved. Vegetarian diets provided.

TY COCH FARM Llangynhafal, Denbigh, Clwyd, LL16 4LN

A. Lloyd Richards
Tel:-(08244) 423
Closed Xmas and New Year
B&B   £8.50-£9   Listed
EM   £4.50-£5
       Sleeps 6

Working dairy/sheep farm at foot of Clwydian range looking down on the picturesque Vale of Clwyd - one of the most beautiful vales in the country. Fluent Welsh speaking family, we offer a homely welcome together with the legendary Welsh hospitality and good home cooking. Central for touring and have pleasant walks, including Offa's Dyke - a section of which passes over our mountain.

Clwyd WALES

(FH) BACH-Y-GRAIG   Tremeirchion, St. Asaph, Clwyd, N. Wales, LL17 OUH

Anwen Roberts
Tel:-(074 574) 627
Open Mar-Nov
B&B £8-£10
EM £5
Red'n for children
Sleeps 6

Bach-y-Graig is a 200 acre mixed farm in the beautiful Vale of Clwyd. A 16th Century farmhouse, recently modernised, but still retaining its old charm. The comfort of our guests is our priority, log-fires, CH, colour TV, good food, family bedroom has bathroom ensuite, twin & double H/C & Tea/Coffee making facilities. Lovely walks, central for coastal resorts, Snowdonia mountains & Chester. Games room. Families welcome. OS Ref SJ 075713

(CH) PEN-Y-BONT FAWR   Cynwyd, Corwen, Clwyd, LL21 OET

Mrs Kay Culhane
Tel:-(0490) 2226
Open all year
B&B £10-£12
EM £5.50
CH Sleeps 10
(4)

Come and stay in our comfortable guesthouse in a beautifully converted 300 year old stone barn. We are right in the country and all rooms have lovely views over fields and hills. Ideal location for exploring North Wales. Wholefood and/or vegetarian cooking a speciality. We also arrange guided walking and cycling holidays - brochure available. OS Ref SJ 051411

(FH) BODANGHARAD   Llanfwrog, Ruthin, Clwyd, LL15 2AH

Mrs Enid Jones
Tel:-(08242) 2370
Open Easter-Oct
B&B £8.50-£9
EM £5.50
Sleeps 6
Listed

Bodangharad is a 100 acre dairy/sheep farm in unspoilt countryside with a wealth of wild flowers and hedgerows. Panoramic views of the Vale of Clywd. A few mins drive from Ruthin market town. Easy access to Chester, coast & Snowdonia. Interesting interior, with exposed beams and spacious rooms for guests. It offers peace and tranquility and plenty of farmhouse fresh food. OS Ref SJ 578910

(FH) BODLYWYDD FAWR   LLanelidan, Ruthin, Clwyd, LL15 2LA

Jennifer Rogers
Tel:-(08245) 383
Open Mar-Oct
B&B £8.50-£10
EM From £4.50
Sleeps 5
Listed

A warm welcome awaits you at Bodlywydd Fawr, a smallholding in the beautiful Vale of Clwyd, 5 miles from mediaeval Ruthin. The farmhouse is traditionally built with thick stone walls, oak beams and diamond paned windows. Guests own lounge and dining room. 2 bedrooms. Good farmhouse cooking using local produce. Ideal touring and walking centre. Families welcome with child reductions. OS Ref SJ 135507

(FH) SAITH DARAN FARM   Llandegla, Wrexham, Clwyd, N. Wales, LL11 3BA

Pat Thompson
Tel:-(097 888) 685
Closed Xmas and New Year
B&B £7.50-£10
EM £4
Sleeps 5
TV £1.50

We run an 85 acre mixed farm producing milk, potatoes and beef, beautifully situated near the top of the Horseshoe Pass at the junction of A5104 and A542,near Llangollen and ideal for touring N. Wales coast, Snowdonia and Chester. Bedrooms have showers, washbasins, electric blankets, tea and coffee facilities and shaver points. Home cooking from local produce. Reductions for children. OS Ref SJ188512

(SC) TYDDYN ISAF   Rhewl, Ruthin, Clwyd, LL15 1UH

Elsie Jones
Tel:-(08242) 3367
Open all year
SC £60-£100
Sleeps 6 + cot
Approved

A warm welcome awaits you at this spacious self-contained part of the farmhouse on this 80 acre working farm, convenient for visiting Snowdonia, Llangollen, Bala & the coast. Sleeps 6 in double & family rooms. Bathroom with separate toilet, lounge/diner with oak beams, TV, radio, high chair. Kitchen, electric cooker, fridge, washing & ironing facilities. CH winter months.

(SC) **GARDEN COTTAGE** Bathafarn Hall, Llanbeds, Ruthin, Clwyd, LL15 2UU

Jane & Wyn Smith
Tel:-(08242) 2187
Open all year
SC £60-£120
Sleeps 7
Van Max 5

The cottage is situated in the tranquil grounds of a dairy farm in the beautiful Clwyd Vale. The mediaeval town of Ruthin is a little over a mile away. The cottage has a pretty living room, 3 bedrooms which sleep 7 in total, bathroom and kitchen, games room, lounge, play area, tennis, a stocked lake. Nearby there is pony trekking, golf etc. OS Ref SJ 152 580

SNOWDONIA & ANGLESEY, Gwynedd

SNOWDONIA & ANGLESEY, GWYNEDD

In Snowdonia you have a wealth of sightseeing from the early Welsh 12th century fortresses at Dolbardarn and Dolwyddelan to the magnificent castles of Edward 1st at Caernarfon, Beaumaris, Harlech and Conwy. The National Trust's historic houses include Plas Newydd on Anglesey and Penrhyn Castle near Bangor. Segontium Fort at Caernarfon is witness to the four hundred years of Roman occupation and there is an interesting museum nearby.

A boat trip along the Menai Straits, a ride on a steam train into the mountains with Talyllyn or Ffestiniog Railways or by Llanberis Lake or even up Snowdon itself, a visit to the heart of a Welsh slate quarry, a trip to the theatre at Bangor or Harlech, or seeing craftsmen a their work are some of the many choices available. Add to this the Sports Council's excellent centres near Caernarfon and Capel Curig, heated swimming baths at Caernarfon, Bangor and Harlech, golf at one of the many courses with superb sea views, some really excellent restaurants and pubs and walks in the mountains or forests, often a week is all too short a time to stay with us.

Most of us are Welsh speaking as Snowdonia is the heartland of the Welsh language, and we will be very happy to teach you a few Welsh greetings or tell you more about our ancient language.

GROUP CONTACT:
Carol Mills (0286) 830091

(FH) TYDDYN PARTHLE Bontnewydd, Caernarfon, Gwynedd, LL54 7YE

Carol Mills
Tel:-(0286) 830091
Closed Xmas-New Year
B&B   £9.50-£10.50
EM   £5
Sleeps 6

Friendly farmhouse offers antiques, gleaming brasses, masses of books, log fire. Jersey cow, sheep, lambs, calves, milking goats, poultry, all kindly treated on organic smallholding. Good, honest food with wholefood/vegetarian dishes if liked. "Exclusive Use" holiday for one family 4-6 persons each week during high season, economy rates for couples in low season. Near sandy beaches, Snowdonia National Park. OS Ref SH 593492

(FH) TRER-DDOL FARM Llanerchymedd, Anglesey, Gwynedd, LL71 7AR

Ann Astley
Tel:-(0248) 470278
Open Jan-Nov
B&B   £9-£10
EM   £5.50
Sleeps 8

A true Welsh welcome assured at this former historic 17th Century manor house. Centrally situated. 200 acres of freedom with panoramic views of Snowdonia. Riding and participation in farm activities which include preparing cattle for "shows". Spacious bedrooms, H/C etc. Cosy lounge, log fires, separate tables in dining room. Homely atmosphere with emphasis on traditional farmhouse fare and cleanliness. W.T.B. Farmhouse Award. OS Ref OS 392812

(FH) PENGWERN Saron, Llanwnda, Caernarfon, Gwynedd, LL54 5UH

Jane Lloyd Rowlands
Tel:-(0286) 830717
Open Easter-Oct
B&B   £9-£10
EM   £5-£6
Sleeps 6

Pengwern is a 130 acre cattle/sheep farm situated in quiet location with views of Snowdonia. The land runs down to the sea and is noted for its bird life. Conveniently situated 3m from historic town of Caernarfon and 3m from Dinas Dinlle beach. Farmhouse food including home produced beef and lamb is served in the dining room. WTB farmhouse award. OS Ref SH 459587

(FH) CAE'R EFAIL Llanfaglan, Caernarfon, Gwynedd, North Wales, LL54 5RE

Mari Williams
Tel:-(0286) 76226
Open Easter-Sep
B&B   £9
EM   £5.50
Sleeps 6

In its grounds of 20 acres enjoying perfect peace, seclusion & magnificent views of Snowdonia & Anglesey. A trip on one of the great little trains is not to be missed. Built at turn of the century, recently modernised, Cae'r Efail offers comfortable, tastefully furnished accommodation. Good food is of prime importance, using home/local produce. 2 doubles, 1 twin. Reduced rates for children. OS Ref SH 464602

(FH) PLAS TIRION FARM Llanrug, Caernarfon, Gwynedd, North Wales, LL55 4PY

Cerid Mackinnon
Tel:-(0286) 3190
Open Easter-Oct
B&B   £8-£12
Sleeps 12

A warm Welsh welcome awaits you at Plas Tirion, situated 4 miles from Caernarfon and Llanberis. Guests are offered warm and comfortable accommodation with hospitality to match. Central heating throughout, all bedrooms have washbasins and tea making facilities. Fire certificate, residential licence. Two bathrooms, AA listed, WTB farmhouse award. Les Routiers recommended. Special diets on request. Rough shooting. OS Ref SH 524626

(FH) PLAS TREFARTHEN Brynsiencyn, Anglesey, Gwynedd, N. Wales

Marian Roberts
Tel:-(0248) 73379
Closed Xmas
B&B   £11-£12
EM   £5
Sleeps 10
SC   £100-£190   4 Dragons
(7) Sleeps 6

Plas Trefarthen stands in 200 acres of land overlooking Snowdonia on the shore of the beautiful Menai Straits. All bedrooms have bathrooms en-suite, plus tea-making facilities. There is a full size snooker table, table tennis and fishing. Close to Plas Newydd National Trust House. Home produced meat & vegetables served. Warm Welsh Welcome. High class self catering available, sleeps 6. WTB Farmhouse Award. OS Ref SH 486496

Snowdonia & Anglesey, Gwynedd WALES

FH TY'N RHOS Seion, Llanddeiniolen, Caernarfon, Gwynedd, LL55 3AE

Lynda Kettle
Tel:-(0248) 670489
Closed Xmas-New Year
B&B £13-£16
EM £6.50-£7.50
Sleeps 17

Situated between Snowdonia & Anglesey. Although a working farm with friendly animals it offers superb accomodation & comfort. The high standards of furnishing, decor & ensuite bathrooms are equivalent to the finest hotels. Our own & local produce is used in imaginative cooking. (Home produced Cheddar cheese a speciality.) WTB award. AA recommended, featured on the "Holiday Programme", Taste magazine, Womens Realm & In Britain. Licensed. OS Ref SH 545667

CH LLYS BENNAR Dyffryn Ardudwy, Gwynedd, Wales, LL44 2RX

Catrin Rutherford
Tel:-(03417) 316
Open Feb-Oct
B&B £9.50
EM From £6
CH Sleeps 6

Lovely 18th Century converted farm buildings in courtyard setting surrounded by farmland and small stream. In Snowdonia National Park between castle town of Harlech & resort of Barmouth. Ten minutes from village and broad sandy beach. Colour television in guest lounge. Attractive bedrooms with private bathrooms, tea making facilities. Superb home cooking, friendly and welcoming service. Pets by arrangement. WTB Award. OS Ref SH 581225

FH TYDDYN PERTHI FARM Tan-y-Maes, Port Dinorwic, Gwynedd, LL56 4UQ

Barbara Lewis
Tel:-(0248 670) 336
Closed Xmas-New Year
B&B £9-£10
EM £5.50
Sleeps 6

Tyddyn Perthi, 50 acre working dairy farm, situated between Caernarfon and Bangor (A487), is ideal to visit Snowdonia, Lleyn Peninsula and Anglesey. 2 letting bedrooms, with washbasins, 1 double, 1 family room which assures our guests they will be "well looked after". Home made yoghurt, bread and good wholesome food are served in the dining room. A warm welcome awaits you. OS Ref SH 667526

SC BODAFONWYN Tynllan, Tregaian, Llangefni, Anglesey, Gwynedd, LL77 7UW

Eleanor Jones
Tel:-0248 750248
Open all year
SC £80-£150
Sleeps 6
+ cot

Approved

Exceptionally attractive period farmhouse, traditionally furnished surrounded by 200 acre cattle and sheep breeding farm. The accommodation comprises spacious and comfortable lounge, dining room, compact modern kitchen, 3 bedrooms, sleeps 6 + cot, bathroom. Ample parking within court yard, large garden. Conveniently situated for visiting historic places, lovely beaches, birdwatching, fishing and relaxing.

SC PEN-Y-BRYN Chwilog, Pwllheli, Gwynedd, LL53 6SX

(Mrs) Sulwen Edwards
Tel:-0766 810 208
Open all year
SC £75-£295
Sleeps 8

5 Dragons

Tastefully restored farmhouse wing, luxury holidays for the connoisseur. Superbly equipped and luxurious to make your holiday relaxed and memorable, dishwasher, washing machine, tumble dryer, colour TV, teasmades, linen. Breathtaking views. Shooting on 120 acre dairy farm. Private picnic tables on banks of River Dwyfach for that tranquil afternoon, towns and beaches within easy reach. Personal supervision ensures highest standards. OS Ref SH 457 388

SC LLYS BENNAR Dyffryn Ardudwy, Gwynedd, Wales, LL44 2RX

Catrin Rutherford
Tel:-(03417) 316
Open all year
SC £80-£190
Sleeps 4-8

5 Dragons

Lovely 18th Century stone farm buildings converted into 2 high standard cottages in courtyard setting. The smaller, sleeping 4, has attractive oak beams, inglenook fireplace. The larger, with oak beams, converted from the granary to sleep 7. Both have storage heating and lawned garden. Ten minutes walk to village or broad sandy beach. In Snowdonia National Park. Pets by arrangement. OS Ref SH 581225

265

(SC) **BRYN BEDDAU** Bontnewydd, Caernarfon, Gwynedd, Wales

Eleri Carrog
Tel:-(0286) 830117
Open May-Sept
SC £60-£275
    Sleeps 4/9

4 Dragons

Delightful stone-built farmhouse with spacious light rooms. Modernised but characterful, beamed ceilings, inglenook log fireplace. Central heating, ceramic hob, microwave, fridge & freezer. Large garden, climbing frame, barbecue. Central to Snowdonia, touring, walking and beaches. Caernarfon town 3m, indoor pools, watersports, riding, trout fishing all nearby. Sleeps 8/9 plus cot, highchair. Farmhouse available May-Sept. Also Stable Cottage sleeping 4, open Oct-Apr. [Also (0286) 3795] OS Ref SH 492593

TALYLLYN RAILWAY

Tywyn, on the Mid Wales Coast

Historic narrow gauge steam trains through Welsh hill scenery. Train services Easter to October inclusive and during Christmas and New Year holiday. Forest walks, waterfalls. Narrow Gauge Railway Museum, shops and refreshments.

Timetables and Information:
WHARF STATION, TYWYN, GWYNEDD, LL36 9EY.
Tel: Tywyn (0654) 710472

LLEYN PENINSULA
Gwynedd

63

LLYN PENINSULA, GWYNEDD

With more than 70 miles of coastline, backed by the blue mountains of Snowdonia, this is an area of outstanding natural beauty where the warm waters of the Gulf Stream give a mild climate all year round.

The Welsh language and way of life still flourish here and while you struggle with the seemingly impossible Celtic names, you'll appreciate the very Welshness of it all.

It is also an area compact enough to travel around and get to know — and one that you'll want to come back to time and time again.

No-one comes to this part of Wales without setting foot on the mighty mountain, Snowdon; and even if you only clamber for a relatively short distance you will be rewarded with views the like of which you never have seen before. And you could always walk one way and take the famous narrow gauge railway the other!

Right at the foot of the Peninsula lies Bardsey Island — a bird sanctuary, place of pilgrimage and the legendary resting place of 20,000 saints.

And almost in the mouth of the Llyn you will find Portmeirion, the Italian extravaganza created by the late Sir Clough Williams Ellis, full of delightful surprises in the shape of statues, follies and typically Italianate buildings.

VACANCY SECRETARY:
Mrs. M. Evans (0758) 612260

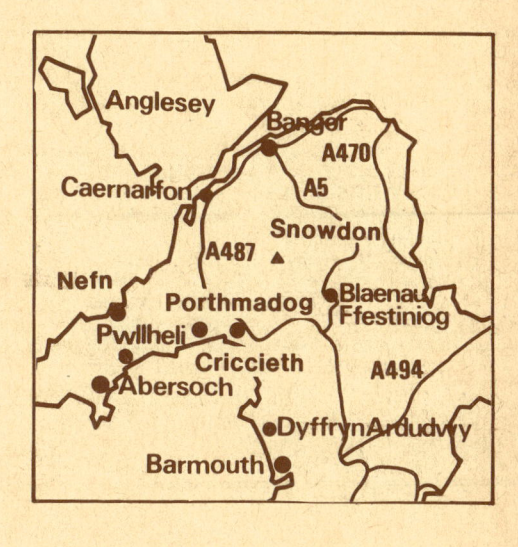

(FH) GRAEANFRYN Morfa Nefyn, Nr Pwllheli, Gwynedd, LL53 6YQ

Ellen Llewelyn
Tel:-(0758) 720455
Open May-Sep
B&B £8-£10 Listed
Sleeps 6
SC £60-£150 2 Dragons

Attractive farmhouse situated 1½ miles Nefyn, Morfa Nefyn beaches and golf links. Comfortable, spacious rooms, 1 single, 2 double and 1 family bedrooms with washbasins. Bathroom/shower/shaving points. We specialise in good home cooking. Also self catering bungalow (open all year) 10 minutes walk to sandy beach at Towyn, Tudweiliog. Fully modernised, colour TV. OS Ref 3829

(FH) YOKE HOUSE FARM Pwllheli, Gwynedd, LL53 5TY

Annwen Hughes
Tel:-(0758) 612621
Open Mar-Oct
£8.50-£9.50
Sleeps 6

A beautiful wooded drive welcomes you to this Georgian farmhouse on a 290 acre working farm, where guests are invited to watch the milking, calf feeding etc. Accommodation, given the Wales Tourist Board "Farmhouse Dragon Award", consists of 1 double, 1 family and 1 twin bedded rooms, all with washbasins and shaver points. BB or optional evening meal. OS Ref 3737

(FH) MATHAN UCHAF FARM Boduan, Pwllheli, Gwynedd, LL53 8TU

Jean Coker
Tel:-(0758) 720 487
Open May-Sep
B&B £9-£10 Listed
EM £6
Sleeps 6

A 190 acre dairy farm peacefully situated off the main road and centrally positioned for the northern/southern beaches of the Peninsula. Guests can participate in farm activities and a large garden provides a safe play area. 1 double room, 1 family room with washbasins and 1 twin bedded room. Dining/sitting room with colour TV. Good food and a friendly atmosphere are our aim. OS Ref 3136

(SC) GWYNFRYN FARM Pwllheli, Gwynedd, LL53 5UF

Mrs S E Ellis
Tel:-(0758) 612536
Closed Nov
B&B £8-£10 Listed
EM £5.50
SC £46-£230 3 Dragons
Tent £2-£5
Van £3-£5

An organic dairy farm 1½ miles from beaches. Self contained units sleeping 4/8, one with open fire. Free storage heating and colour TV. There is a launderette, play area and play room on site. Elec. 50p meter. Cooked dishes/meals to order. Pets by arrangement. Join in farm activities. Colour brochure. All units AA listed. 1 unit with WTB Award. Also BB in farmhouse.

(SC) TYN DON HOLIDAY COTTAGES Tyn Don, Llanengan, Pwllheli, Gwynedd, LL53 7LG

Kathleen Thomas
Tel:-(075 881) 2688
Closed Jan, Feb and Dec
SC £65-£260 3 Dragons
Sleeps 5/8

Heritage Coast. Peaceful and relaxing self-contained cottages and bungalows, sleeping 5/8 people. 200 yds from and overlooking the beautiful unspoilt sandy beach of Porth Neigwl, with private access. Furnished and equipped to a high standard. Heaters in all rooms, also storage heaters. Elec. 50p meters. Children's play area. Launderette. Pay-phone. Small dogs by arrangement in two of the cottages. WTB Grade 3. Brochure. OS Ref 2827

(SC) NYTH-Y-DRYW Llwyn Helyg, Llangybi, Pwllheli, Gwynedd, LL53 6TB

Enid Rees-Roberts
Tel:-(076688) 394
Open all year
SC £65-£180 5 Dragons
Sleeps 6

Nyth-Y-Dryw - bungalow. WTB Award. Both positioned in own grounds, private parking on a peaceful mixed farm. Central to beaches and mountains. Criccieth 5 miles. Both have modern facilities, open fires, storage/wall heaters and colour TV. Bed linen provided. No pets. SAE brochure. OS Ref 4542

Lleyn Peninsula/Gwynedd WALES

(SC) PUNT GWYNEDD   Towyn, Llanengan, Abersoch, Gwynedd, LL53 7LS

Jane Owen
Tel:-(075881) 2302
Open all year
SC   £65-£200
      Sleeps 6

Approved

The house, on an arable and livestock farm, consists of 2 double bedrooms and 1 twin bedded + cot, bathroom/toilet, sitting room, dining room, sun lounge and well equipped kitchen. Safe play area for children, 5 minutes walk from beach. Colour TV. Linen provided. Electricity 50p meter. Ideally situated for a quiet family holiday. OS Ref 2828

(SC) TOWYN FARM   Tudweiliog, Pwllheli, Gwynedd, LL53 8PD

Iona Wyn Owen
Tel:-(075887) 230
Open Easter-Sep
SC   £60-£180
      Sleeps 8 +
      cot

4 Dragons

A mixed farm situated in area of outstanding natural beauty, 200 yards from renowned Towyn beach. Large 300 year old farmhouse, fully modernised, carpeted throughout, colour TV, 4 bedrooms sleeping 8 with continental quilts. Lawn garden with barbecue and furniture. Elec. meter reading. Free baby sitting. Also ground level cottage same standard sleeping 8, suitable for handicapped persons. OS Ref 2338

(SC) LLAWRDREF FARM   Llangian, Abersoch, Pwllheli, Gwynedd, LL53 7LT

Annie Owen
Tel:-(075 881) 2570
Open May-Oct
SC   £60-£180
      Sleeps 6
Van   Takes 5
      c'vans

Approved

Llawdref - a beef, sheep and arable farm with a comfortable and well maintained farmhouse situated in the peace and tranquility of the countryside with a safe play area for children. Nearest beach 1m. Sitting/dining room, kitchen, 2 double, 1 twin bedded rooms + cot, bathroom/toilet, furnished and equipped to a high standard. Heaters in all rooms and storage heaters. Linen optional. Electricity meter. No Pets. OS Ref 2829

(SC) RHYDOLION   Llangian, Abersoch, Pwllheli, Gwynedd, LL53 7LR

Catherine Llewelyn Morris
Tel:-(075881) 2342
Open May-Sep
SC   £70-£160
      Sleeps 6 +
      cot

Approved

This late 16th Century farmhouse is situated 3m from Abersoch and only ¾m from Hell's Mouth beach, shops, pub 1½m. Accommodation - 2 double bedrooms & 1 with bunk beds, bathroom/separate toilet, sitting room, colour TV, dining hall, fully equipped kitchen, washing machine & fridge freezer, garden over looking large yard with furniture and back garden, safety play area. Free linen. Pets by arrangements. OS Ref 282274

(SC) TYNEWYDD COTTAGE   Sarn Bach, Abersoch, Pwllheli, Gwynedd, LL53 7LE

Mrs Janno Jones
Tel:-(075881) 2446
Open all year
SC   £60-£150
      Sleeps 5

3 Dragons

A working dairy farm 1m from many sandy beaches, overlooking Abersoch and Hell's Mouth beach. Accommodation - modern farm cottage sleeping 5 in 1 double, 1 single and bunk beds. Well equipped kitchen, sitting/dining room with TV, bathroom with flush toilet, electric fires, CH in Winter, patio for sunbathing. No pets. Also a modern 6 berth caravan with all mod. cons. on our small quiet site. OS Ref 2927

(SC) BRON PHILIP   Trefaes Fawr, Sarn, Pwllheli, Gwynedd, LL53 8RH

Dilys Jones
Tel:-(075883) 675
Open all year
SC   £60-£160
      Sleeps 6

Approved

Bron Philip is situated on the outskirts of this attractive village with open views of the bay to Hell's Mouth, with ample parking and playing areas. The comfortable accommodation sleeps 6 + cot in 2 twin bedded and 1 twin bunk bedded rooms, with bathroom, lounge with open views, diner/kitchenette with elec. cooker and fridge, immersion heater and high chair. Pets welcome. Elec. meter. OS Ref 2533

CRUGAN FARM Llanbedrog, Pwllheli, Gwynedd, LL53 7LN

Catrin Jones
Tel:-(0758) 740873
Open Easter-Oct
SC £90-£185
Sleeps 6 + cot

Approved

A modernised farmhouse, pleasantly furnished, yet retaining a lot of 'olde-worlde' charm. Large enclosed garden and patio for safe playing. Llanbedrog beach less than 2 minutes walk along a private path. Shops/pubs at Llanbedrog ½ mile away. Two doubles, two single rooms sleep 6 + cot. Lounge, colour TV, kitchen, dining room and bathroom. Bed linen and high chair free. Electricity extra. OS Ref 3333

TY'N CAE Barrach Fawr, Llangian, Pwllheli, Gwynedd, LL53 7LP

Margaret Griffith
Tel:-(075881) 2212
Open all year
SC £50-£170
Sleeps 7

Approved

Ty'n Cae, a 17th Century farmhouse, is situated near the river Soch on the outskirts of Llangian 2m from Abersoch and 1½m from Hell's Mouth. Accommodation for 7 comprises 1 double, 1 twin and 1 family rooms, bathroom, spacious lounge with inglenook fireplace, oak beams, secret stairs and French windows to the garden. Modern kitchen. No linen. No pets. Payphone. Elec. meter. OS Ref 2929

PENLLECHOG FARM Llanaelhaearn, Caernarfon, Gwynedd, LL54 5BH

S Pierce Ellis
Tel:-(075885) 232
Open May-Sep
SC £90
Sleeps 6

3 Dragons

A 380 acre beef and sheep farm nestling at the foot of Gyrn Ddu. Panoramic views across to Cardigan Bay, a tranquil base for exploring the Peninsula, Anglesey, Caernarfon, Snowdonia etc. Farmhouse comprises of 3 double bedrooms and 1 bunk bedroom + cot, upstairs bathroom. Spacious sitting room with colour TV and kitchen/dining area. Fitted carpets throughout and traditional furniture. Safe play area for children. Electricity extra. OS Ref 4539

MIN-Y-MYNYDD Carnguwch, Llithfaen, Nr Pwllheli, Gwynedd

Bethan Ellis
Tel:-(075 885) 247
Open Easter-Oct
SC £55-£180
Sleeps 4

Approved

Traditional Welsh Cottage, situated in an area designated of outstanding natural beauty. Visitors are welcome to roam the farm, with its own mountain, an old church, and small river providing excellent trout fishing. We accommodate up to 6 in 2 cosy bedrooms, 1 double and 1 double & bunk. Lounge with exposed beams, colour TV, kitchen/diner, bathroom with shaver point. Colour brochure on request.

CARROG Ty Mawr Farm, Sarn, Pwllheli, Gwynedd, LL53 8EF

Mrs Gladys Thomas
Tel:-(075883) 670
Open all year
SC £60-£200
Sleeps 6/10

Approved

Carrog Farm sleeping 10 persons in 5 bedrooms, is a beef and sheep farm, with a southerly aspect and within 5 mins of nearest beach. Bathroom & shower room. Also well equipped kitchen - freezer & washing machine. Bronllwyd Fawr, sleeps 6 persons in 3 bedrooms. Both have sitting room with colour TV, well equipped kitchen, bathroom/toilet and central heating in Autumn/Winter. Pets welcome. OS Ref 2133

SCOTLAND

The Scottish Highlands and Islands — the last great wide-open space in Europe, is a unique land of beauty and splendour where you can experience a feeling of freedom, fresh air like you've never 'tasted' it before, and unrivalled scenery. Choose, if you can, from Skye, Orkney, Arran, Lewis — or leave time to visit them all.

You can stay near such historic towns as Inverness, the Highland Capital, Fort William at the foot of Ben Nevis, Britain's highest peak; or take a short cruise on Loch Ness, you never know what you might see!

The North East is farming and fishing country, with fertile farmland and small fishing villages along the craggy coast. It is also a land of castles — Craigievar, Crathes, Broadie and Fraser.

Winding roads lead you to quiet villages and only the bustle of Aberdeen reminds you of the prosperity that North Sea oil has brought to this part of Scotland.

Central Scotland brings you Glasgow and Edinburgh with shops, museums, theatres and restaurants. There are also the smaller towns to wander around, Callender and Stirling, Lanark and Biggar. To the west is Loch Lomond, where the 'Countess Fiona' offers you a trip on this most beautiful of lochs. Here you can also explore the Trossachs and marvel at the Museums of Scottish Tartans at Comrie.

The Scottish Borders is a land of rolling hills and wooded river valleys, where its turbulent past is evident from the hilltop ruins of castles and keeps — while the Border abbeys of Melrose, Jedburgh and Kelso are reminders of more peaceful days. Ideal walking country, the Border Walkway — stretching across the Cheviot Hills — offers a challenge to the long distance walker.

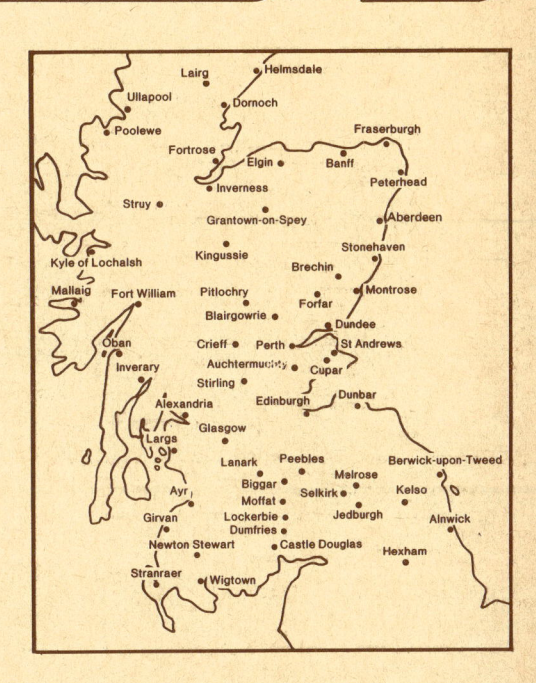

Tucked into the South West corner in Scotland is Dumfries and Galloway — the 'Quiet Country' — a haven for those seeking peace and solitude. To the north is Ayrshire — Burns Country; the Burns Heritage Trail provides a theme for touring the area with sites at Ayr, Irvine, Dumfries and many other places.

(FH) CANDY FARM Glenfarg, Perth, PH2 9QL

Mrs Wilma Lawrie
Tel:-(05773) 217
Open Easter-Oct
B&B £10-£11
EM £6
Sleeps 6

Commended 🌷🌷

Situated in the peaceful Perthshire Hills 4 miles from M90. 6m from Kinross, 11m Perth A520. Hill farm carries 400 ewes and 150 suckler cows. A comfortable centrally heated farmhouse with 1 double and 2 twin rooms all with washbasins, shaver points and tea/coffee making facilities electric blankets, splendid views. Golf, fishing and riding nearby. Sorry no pets. SAE Brochure. OS Ref NT 098119

(FH) NETHER BORELAND Boreland, Lockerbie, Dumfriesshire, DG11 2LL

Marjorie Rae
Tel:-(05766) 248
Open Apr-Oct
B&B £8-£9
EM £6
Sleeps 6

Approved
Listed

A warm welcome awaits you at this 200 acre sheep and suckler cow farm in the picturesque Dryfe Valley. Three bedrooms, family, double and single. Information and directions are willingly given to find the many places of interest including castles, beaches, shops and scenic day drives. OS Ref NY 169 911

(FH) AUCHENLECK FARM Minnigaff, Newton Stewart, Wigtownshire, DG8 7AA

Margaret Hewitson
Tel:-(0671) 2035
Open Easter-Oct
B&B £9-£10
EM £5
Sleeps 6

Approved 🌷🌷

Auchenleck Farm (103 acres beef/black-faced sheep) in Kirroughtree Forest, part of Glentrool National Park, where red, roe & fallow deer abound. Ideal centre for hill climbing & forest walking, plenty to interest naturalists; river, loch & sea fishing nearby. Large turreted farmhouse, built by Earl of Galloway as a shooting lodge, offers a high standard of accommodation with guests returning year after year.

(CH) CAMBO ESTATE Kingsbarns, St. Andrews, Fife, KY16 8QD

Peter Erskine
Tel:-(0333) 50313
Closed Xmas and New Year
B&B £20-£30/person
CH Sleeps 2

Applied

A rare opportunity to stay in style in a four poster bed in a large fully operational Victorian Mansion. The house is the hub of a wooded, coastal, lowland estate where the family have lived for 300 yrs. Parts of the mainly arable farm grow organic crops. There is one room available for guests (with private facilities). Pre booking essential. OS Ref NO 604116

(FH) BELFORD-ON-BOWMONT Yetholm, Kelso, Roxburghshire, TD5 8PY

Alison Johnson
Tel:-(057382) 362
Open Apr-Oct
B&B £8.50-£9.00
EM £4.50
Sleeps 6

Commended 🌷🌷

A 19th Century farmhouse with central heating and open fire on 1350 acre sheep farm in the foothills of the Cheviots. Shooting on farm also fishing on the farm and locally. There is a craft shop on the farm selling locally made products. Come and spend a holiday with our 2,000 ewes and their lambs and 3 thoroughbred mares and their foals. OS Ref NT 814209

(FH) CLUGSTON FARM Wigtown, Wigtownshire, DG8 9BH

Janet Adams
Tel:-(067183) 338
Open May-Oct
B&B £7.50-£8
EM £3.50
Sleeps 6

Commended
Listed

Clugston Farm is about 2½ miles from Kirkcowan on a B class road. Two double rooms one with washbasin, one twin. Sitting room with colour TV. A varied menu of home cooking includes roast beef/lamb. Home made soup and sweets. Car is essential (parking). Near the sea, hill walking, golf etc. Reduced rates for families. OS Ref NX 354 574

SCOTLAND

(FH) LOCHEND FARM   Denny, Stirling, FK6 5JJ

Jean Morton
Tel:-(0324) 822778
Open all year
B&B   £9-£10
EM   From £6
Sleeps 6

Commended 🌷🌷

(3)

An upland sheep farm beautifully situated beside Loch Coulter - lovely views all around 18th Century farmhouse, modernised, well furnished with central heating, washbasins in bedrooms plus tea/coffee making facilities. The Trossachs, Loch Lomond, Edinburgh, St Andrews and Glasgow with its famous Burrell collection all within easy reach by car. Stirling 6m, 5m from junction 9 of M80/M9. OS Ref E 86 87

(FH) BALLAGAN FARM   Culloden Moor, Inverness Shire, IV1 2TY

Phyllis Alexander
Tel:-(0463) 790213
Open Apr-Sep
B&B   £9-£10
EM   £4-£5
Sleeps 5

Applied

(1)

A comfortable farmhouse. Set in quiet peaceful countryside with Culloden Battlefield close by, central for touring Highlands. 1 family and 1 twin bedroom. Guests sitting room with open fire and colour TV. Warm welcome awaits visitors, with good cooking and baking. This small working farm of 90 acres has cattle, with crops for winter feed.

(CH) COLLIN HOUSE   Auchencairn, Castle Douglas, Kirkcudbrightshire, DG7 1QN

Frances Cannon
Tel:-(055 664) 242
Open Mar-Oct
B&B   £10-£11.50
EM   £5-£6
CH   Sleeps 6

Commended 🌷🌷

Spend a relaxing holiday in a historical Georgian farmhouse in bonnie Galloway with panoramic views over Auchencairn Bay. Walking, fishing, golfing etc are within easy reach and driving is a pleasure on quiet country roads with many places of scenic beauty and historical interest to visit. 3 bedrooms, 1 en suite. Tea making facilities. Well laid out garden of ½ acre. OS Ref NX 524 794

(FH) BURNFOOT FARM   Colmonell, Girvan, Ayrshire, KA26 0SQ

David & Grace Shankland
Tel:-(046588) 220/265
Open Apr-Oct
B&B   £9-£10
EM   £5
Sleeps 6
W'kly b'king/
Children redn

Commended 🌷🌷

A warm welcome awaits you at Burnfoot a family run dairy/beef unit, nestled in the beautiful Stinchar Valley, enjoy the clear fresh country air of this now industrial river famous for Salmon fishing. An ideal base for touring Ayrshire coast, Burns Country and Galloway Hills, with many interesting places to visit. Home cooking and baking a speciality with fresh fruit and vegetables from the garden. OS Ref NX 16 86

(FH) ARDCHOILLE FARMHOUSE   Woodmill Farm, Dunshalt, Auchtermuchty, Fife, KY14 7ER

Isobel & Donald Steven
Tel:-(0337) 28414
Open Jan-Oct
B&B   £15-£17
EM   £10
Sleeps 6
SC   £100

Commended 🌷🌷🌷

A warm welcome awaits you at Ardchoille, a modern centrally heated farmhouse in the midst of golfing country. (St. Andrews 30 mins., Gleneagles 40 mins.). 1 Double, 1 twin, 1 family rooms, 2 with ensuite facilities. H/C; colour TV; electric blankets; radio; hairdryer; tea makers (home made shortbread provided). Superb breakfast with free range eggs; Jersey milk, home made bread and preserves.

(FH) BLIBBERHILL   Brechin, Angus, DD9 6TH

Margaret Stewart
Tel:-(030 783) 225
Closed Xmas-New Year
B&B   £9
EM   From £5
Sleeps 6

Commended 🌷🌷

Blibberhill is an 18th Century farmhouse, spacious, well appointed and in peaceful surroundings. Situated between coast and Glens, near Glamis Castle. All bedrooms have washbasins, 1 with private bathroom. Good home cooking, all home cooking and baking served. OS Ref NO 5657

273

FH DAVIOT MAINS FARM — Daviot, Inverness, IV1 2ER

Margaret & Alex Hutcheson
Tel:-(046385) 215
Open all year
B&B £9–£10
EM £6
Sleeps 8–10
Weekly terms available

Commended

Our stock rearing farm is 6m south of Inverness near Culloden Moor. Ideal for touring the Highlands. Cawdor Castle, Nairn Beach & Loch Ness within easy reach. After your day out return home to a Taste of Scotland dinner, then relax in front of a log fire. You'll have a lovely time when your comfort is our pleasure. Recommended by Elizabeth Grundey's "Staying Off The Beaten Track."

FH BORLUM FARMHOUSE — Drumnadrochit, Inverness, IV3 6XN

Duncan & Vanessa Macdonald-Haig
Tel:-(045 62) 358
Open Easter-Nov
B&B £10.50–£15
EM £9
Sleeps 18
SC £95–£205
TV £3–£5.50

Commended

This outstanding traditional farmhouse commands a spectacular view overlooking Loch Ness. Each year visitors world wide are delighted with the beautiful fresh rooms, good food, and warm friendly atmosphere. Borlum is a working hill farm, stocking sheep and suckler cows, and also has its own BHS approved riding centre, making it the ideal place for an inclusive riding holiday.

FH WOOD OF AULDBAR FARM — Aberlemno By Brechin, Angus, Scotland, DD9 6SZ

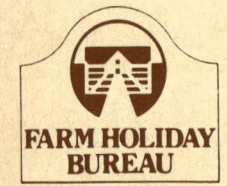

Jean Stewart
Tel:-(030783) 218
Open all year
B&B £9–£9.50
EM £4.50
Sleeps 6

Commended
Listed

Spacious farmhouse set in beautiful countryside. 1 single, 1 double, 1 family bedrooms available. Guests' own dining room and lounge with TV. Central heating throughout. All home cooking and baking provided. Near to many castles, glens and historical buildings, golf courses and fishing. AA Recommended.

FH EASTER DALZIEL FARM — Dalcross, Inverness, IV1 2JL

Bob and Margaret Pottie
Tel:-(0667) 62213
Open Easter-Oct
B&B £9–£10.50
EM £5
Sleeps 6

Commended

A warm welcome and family atmosphere await the visitor to this beautiful old stonebuilt farmhouse. 3 comfortable bedrooms all with washbasins. Choice of delicious breakfasts, homebaking and evening tea/coffee included in price, 210 acre stock rearing and arable farm. Sometimes pet lambs and chicks to feed. Culloden Moor, Cawdor Castle, Fort George and Loch Ness, all within easy reach. OS Ref 509 756

FH LINNE MHUIRICH — Unapool Croft Road, Kylesku by Lairg, Sutherland, IV27 4HW

Mrs Fiona MacAulay
Tel:-(0971) 2227
Open May-Dec
B&B £9–£10
EM £6
Sleeps 9

Commended

A Highland welcome awaits you at our superbly situated croft Guest House, heated throughout. "Taste of Scotland" recommended menus include local fish and seafood, unusual salads, delicious desserts. Choices at meals. Ideal for walkers, wildlife-lovers and for exploring northwest Scotland. Residents' lounge, 2 bathrooms/showers. Accommodation 1 double, 1 twin, 1 family, 1 single, all with washbasins & tea/coffee trays. Fire certificate. Brochure available. OS Ref NC 236 333

SC MOUNTQUHANIE HOLIDAY HOMES — Mountquhanie Farms, Cupar, Fife, KY15 4QJ

Felicity & Andrew Wedderburn
Tel:-(082624) 252
Open all year
SC £55–£250
Sleeps 4–13

Approved
Highly Comm

Cosy cottages or family farmhouse or spacious self contained flat in elegant Georgian mansion on working farm. Quiet hideaway for visitors of all ages and their pets who appreciate rural tranquility. Farm trail, tennis, fishing, walking, discovering Scotland. Great opportunity to experience farming, forestry, conservation in harmony. Quality properties. AA approved, STB 4 crowns, up to highly commended. OS Ref NO 348 212

SCOTLAND

(sc) COACHMANS HOUSE & COTTAGES Dalreoch, Dunning, Perth, Scotland, PH2 0QJ

Mrs Wilma Marshall
Tel:-(0764 84) 368
Open Easter-Oct
SC £95-£120
    £195-£295
Sleeps 2-8

Well appointed coachhouse in delightful rural setting, close to Dunning village. Accommodation for 8 provides linen, towels, colour TV, washing and drying facilities. Wet weather games facilities in our chapel. 9 hole golf course and tennis courts at Dunning. Gleneagles Hotel Golf Courses 7 miles. Oak Tree Cottage and Gean Tree Cottage both sleep 4. Ask for our brochure. OS Ref 148008

(sc) CARMICHAEL ESTATE COTTAGES Carmichael Estate Office, BY Biggar, Scotland, ML12 6PG

Richard Carmichael
Tel:-(08993) 336
Open all year
SC £100-£150
Sleeps 4

Commended

Two, two double bedroomed, 200 year old listed cottages on 700 year old historic border estate with woods, red deer, highland cows, plus sheep cattle and crops. One hour from everywhere: England, Highlands, Edinburgh, Ayrshire, Glasgow, Stirling. Quality fully equipped serviced 4 person cottages, cosy, quiet rest or walk Tinto and Border hills. Everyone welcome. Plenty to see and do. OS Ref NS 392 937

FARM HOLIDAY BUREAU

(sc) TORWOOD CROFT Poolewe, Ross-Shire, IV22 2JY

Alex Urquhart
Tel:-(044586) 268
Open all year
SC £70-£245
Sleeps 11

Approved

Traditional Highland home for your carefree self catering holiday, superb accommodation, suitable for large or small parties, secluded situation on the croft. Excellent views of river, Loch Maree and mountains. 5 bedrooms, 2 public rooms, kitchen & bathroom. Poolewe a quiet village with the Inverewe tropical gardens, great centre for touring, climbing and birdwatching. Close by golf, fishing, sailing, swimming pool and sandy beaches.

(sc) ARDBLAIR CASTLE STABLES Ardblair Castle, Blairgowrie, Perthshire, PH10 6SA

Jenny Blair Oliphant
Tel:-(0250) 3155
Open all year
SC £150-£230
Sleeps 5/9

Highly Comm
to

Surrounded by 800 acres of mixed farmland, Ardblair Castle Stables are situated in the grounds of historic Ardblair Castle. The accommodation is of the highest standard, and there are plenty of walks and trails to explore in the area. The Highland cattle by the Stables are a popular attraction, and in spring there are often lambs which guests may help to feed! OS Ref NO 164 446

(sc) BARNCROSH FARM Castle Douglas, Kirkcudbrightshire, DG7 1TX

Liz & Ronnie Ball
Tel:-(055668) 216/315
Open all year
SC £45-£225
Sleeps 2/6

Approved
to
Commended

Situated amongst rolling Galloway countryside on working farm of 500 acres are 3 modernised houses and 6 self-contained flats converted from the old Stable Block. We offer peace and quiet for that "get-away" holiday. An ideal touring base for historic South West Scotland within easy reach of the M6. Forestry and moorland walks with abundant wild-life and bird-watching. Open for short breaks in the off-season. OS Ref NX 7259

(sc) EASTER DEANS & GLENRATH Glenrath Farm, Kirkton Manor, Peebles, EH45 9JW

Catherine Campbell
Tel:-(07214) 221
Open all year
SC £69-£287
Sleeps 8

to
Commended

We have five very attractive properties ranging from a luxury farmhouse to a 2 bedroom cottage. All centrally heated. Situated on working hill farm in the county of Tweeddale. The farmhouse is only 25 mins from Edinburgh and the town of Peebles is only 15 mins from any of the properties. Course fishing and hill walking. Pets welcome. Ideal for children.

275

GAGIE HOUSE FARM Gagie House, By Dundee, Angus, DD4 0PR

Mrs Clare Smoor
Tel:-(082621) 207
Open July-Sept
SC £95-£145
Sleeps 5/10

Gagie House is the centre of a working fruit/sheep farm, 5m from Dundee, in a delightful wooded setting. An interesting flat in the historic mansion house (sleeps 5) and a charming cottage in its own garden in the grounds (sleeps 10), both well equipped and with TV. Many varieties of soft fruit for you to pick. Excellent base for touring hills, golfing or beach. OS Ref NO 737344

WHITMUIR ESTATE Whitmuir, Selkirk, Selkirkshire, TD7 4PZ

Hilary Dunlop
Tel:-(0750) 21728
Open all year
SC £92-£230
Sleeps 2/6

Commended

Country House apartments and coach house court cottages for 2/6 people at the centre of our large private estate. Extensive gardens private loch fishing with boats, games room, sauna, laundry, linen, colour TV. Open all year. Small animals welcome. Suitable for the disabled. Good centre for touring and sightseeing. OS Ref NT 348 626

GLENGENNET COTTAGE Barr, Girvan, Ayrshire, KA26 9TY

Vera Dunlop
Tel:-(046586) 220
Open Apr-Nov
SC £60-£135
Sleeps 6

Commended

Situated in the River Stinchar Valley 1½ miles from Barr, Glengennet Cottage, a self contained wing of farmhouse offers spacious, comfortably furnished accommodation for 6 plus baby. Three double bedrooms, one with twin beds, lounge/dining room, colour TV and well equipped kitchen one bedroom and bathroom on ground floor all electric with storage heaters. Linen supplied. AA listed. BB also available. OS Ref NX 288959

THE HOLMES St. Boswells, Melrose, Roxburghshire, Scotland

Rosemary Joy Dale
Tel:-(0835) 22356
Open all year
SC £65-£150
Sleeps 4/6

Commended to

Stay on private estate (180 acres) beside River Tweed overlooking park with donkeys, geese & rare breeds of sheep - perfect for families, with safe garden & woods to play in. Two flats situated within the original servants' quarters: The Butler's Flat (sleeps 6) & The Cook's Flat (sleeps 4), which includes the original 'Upstairs, Downstairs' kitchen. Also Stable Cottage (sleeps 5). Trout fishing included in rental.

CULLIGRAN COTTAGES Glen Strathfarrar, Struy, Nr Beauly, Inverness-Shire, IV4 7JX

Frank & Juliet Spencer Nairn
Tel:-(046376) 285
Open Easter-Oct
SC £89-£229
Sleeps 5-7

Commended to
Highly Comm

Regulars come back year after year to this very special secluded glen, in part a nature reserve. Superior accommodation. Guided tours of the deer farm, river fishing, abundant wildlife, bikes for hire and much more. Nearby hotel and inn. Payphone and deep freeze on site. Situated 20m west of Inverness. Spectacular Autumn colours. Send for brochure/price list without obligation. OS Ref NH 384408

CAMBO HOUSE Nr St. Andrews, Fife, KY16 8QD

Peter Erskine
Tel:-(0333) 50313
Open Jun-Sept
SC £65-175
Sleeps 2/8

Approved to
Commended

Even if you never visit the enchanting fishing villages, historic houses, abundant beaches and golf courses and many other varied attractions of the area, there is plenty for everyone just on this picturesque lowland estate and working farm with some organic crops, play areas, woodland walks, golden sands, tennis, lawn games. Flats in vast Victorian Mansion and cottages. OS Ref NO 604116

SCOTLAND

(SC) FLOWERBURN HOUSE HOLIDAY HOMES Rosemarkie, Fortrose, Ross-Shire, IV10 8SL

Alisdair Fraser
Tel:-(0381) 21069
Open all year
SC £100-£225
Sleeps 4-6
Commended
🌷🌷🌷

Our A frame chalets are situated in private grounds on a working farm on the Black Isle. Each comprises 2 bedrooms, bathroom, open plan kitchen/lounge area with balcony. Full size cooker, fridge and TV are provided. At an altitude of 700ft yet only 1m from the sea, the location provides excellent views over the Moray Firth. Colour brochure available on request.

(SC) SHEMORE COTTAGE Shemore Farm, Luss, Alexandria, Dunbartonshire, G83 8RH

Mrs Ailsa Lennox
Tel:-(038 985) 239
Open May-Oct
SC £95-£135
Sleeps 4
Commended
🌷🌷🌷

Attractive cottage on extensive sheep farm with beautiful views over the southern end of Loch Lomond. 3m south of the picturesque village of Luss and ½m from the A82 with tarmac access road. Conveniently situated for visiting many of Scotlands attractions. Ideal for hill walking and with numerous viewpoints and places to explore on the farm. OS Ref NS 884345

(SC) EASTER DALZIEL COTTAGES Dalcross, Inverness, IV1 2JL

Bob and Margaret Pottie
Tel:-(0667) 62213
Open Easter-Oct
SC £90-£170
Sleeps 4/6
Commended
🌷🌷🌷

These traditional stonebuilt cottages are comfortably furnished and set amid farmland, situated 7 miles east of Inverness between the A96 and B9039. Ideally placed for visits to Culloden Moor, Cawdor Castle, Fort George, and Loch Ness. Also central for scenic day trips to Deeside, Ullapool and John O' Groats. 210 Acre Easter Dalziel rears beef cattle and grows oats and barley. OS Ref 510 757

A TASTE OF SCOTLAND

When eating out, be discerning and select a TASTE OF SCOTLAND establishment.

Taste of Scotland members are carefully checked and regularly inspected. They promise you a warm welcome and a memorable meal.

Scotland has probably Europe's finest supply of beef, lamb, fish, shellfish and game, and it has the chefs and cooks to prepare the produce with care and imagination and present them invitingly.

The range of Scottish dishes is extensive so make a point of enjoying a truly Scottish experience.

In the current Taste of Scotland brochure you will find listed some 300 hotels and restaurants offering the best of local fare.

For information on how to obtain a copy of the brochure — which is usually available at Scottish Tourist Board Information Centres — please enquire of:

Taste of Scotland Scheme Ltd. 23 Ravelston Terrace, Edinburgh EH4 3EU. Telephone: 031-332 9798

SCOTTISH FARMHOUSE HOLIDAYS

North of the Border, the system for booking a farmhouse holiday is different. Scottish Farmhouse Holidays — established five years ago by a farmer's wife, Jane Buchanan — enables you to choose and book your holiday with the minimum of effort. Often, just one telephone or letter is all that is needed, Scottish Farmhouse Holidays will arrange the rest.

The details in this section will give you a taste of what is on offer. The map shows the locations of the different farms, but if you would like more detailed information, send to Scottish Farmhouse Holidays for this free detailed brochure.

Your Farmhouse Holiday

Each farm and croft house has been inspected by Jane Buchanan of Scottish Farmhouse Holidays; all are homely and comfortable with heating in every bedroom; each one has adequate bathroom and toilet facilities, and many have showers. They are all family homes to which you are warmly welcomed.

All farms and crofts are being worked full or part-time by the family you stay with. This means that you can see what is going on, you can talk with the farmer and see farm activities close at hand, but you must pay heed to the farmer as farm machinery can be dangerous. Some farms have hens and ducks, ponies or pet lambs, and on some you may actually be able to lend a hand. But other farms are more specialised and, for example, concentrate on growing wheat or barley, so there is relatively little to see and do. Crofts are smaller and the crofter will usually have a full-time occupation, returning to his croft to do his farming in the evening and at weekends.

Home from home

All the farms offer bed and breakfast or bed, full Scottish breakfast and evening meal, and a cup of tea later on. The evening meal will usually be dinner or the more traditional high tea — a main course accompanied by plates piled high with bread, scones, oatcakes, bannocks and followed by cakes and biscuits. And, if you're going off for the day, the farmer's wife may be able to provide a packed lunch — but at extra cost and with prior notice.

Free brochure

The entries list the characteristics of each farm and will help you make up your mind. Please tell Jane Buchanan if you have any special requirements as she will be making all your arrangements, e.g. diets, dogs.

Centred and Touring

You can choose either a Centred or a Touring Holiday. On a Centred Holiday you stay at one farmhouse or croft all the time; on a Touring Holiday you move around.

Scottish Farmhouse Holidays can be booked only through Jane Buchanan at Scottish Farmhouse Holidays.

The price of your holiday

Evening meal, bed and breakfast — all prices inclusive of VAT at 15%.

£15 per person per night
*£9 for child 12 years and under
*£5 for child 5 years and under
Babies under 1 year free

* Reductions where sharing bedroom with one or more persons paying adult rate.

OR

Bed and Breakfast
£10 per person per night with reductions for children.

There are no supplements for high season or single room occupancy. Most farms are open all the year round.

Scottish Farmhouse Holidays can be booked only through:
Jane Buchanan,
Scottish Farmhouse Holidays
19 Drumtenant, Ladybank KY7 7UG
Fife, Scotland
Telephone (0337) 30451.
Telex 76284 Judge G.

Write — or better still — telephone for details

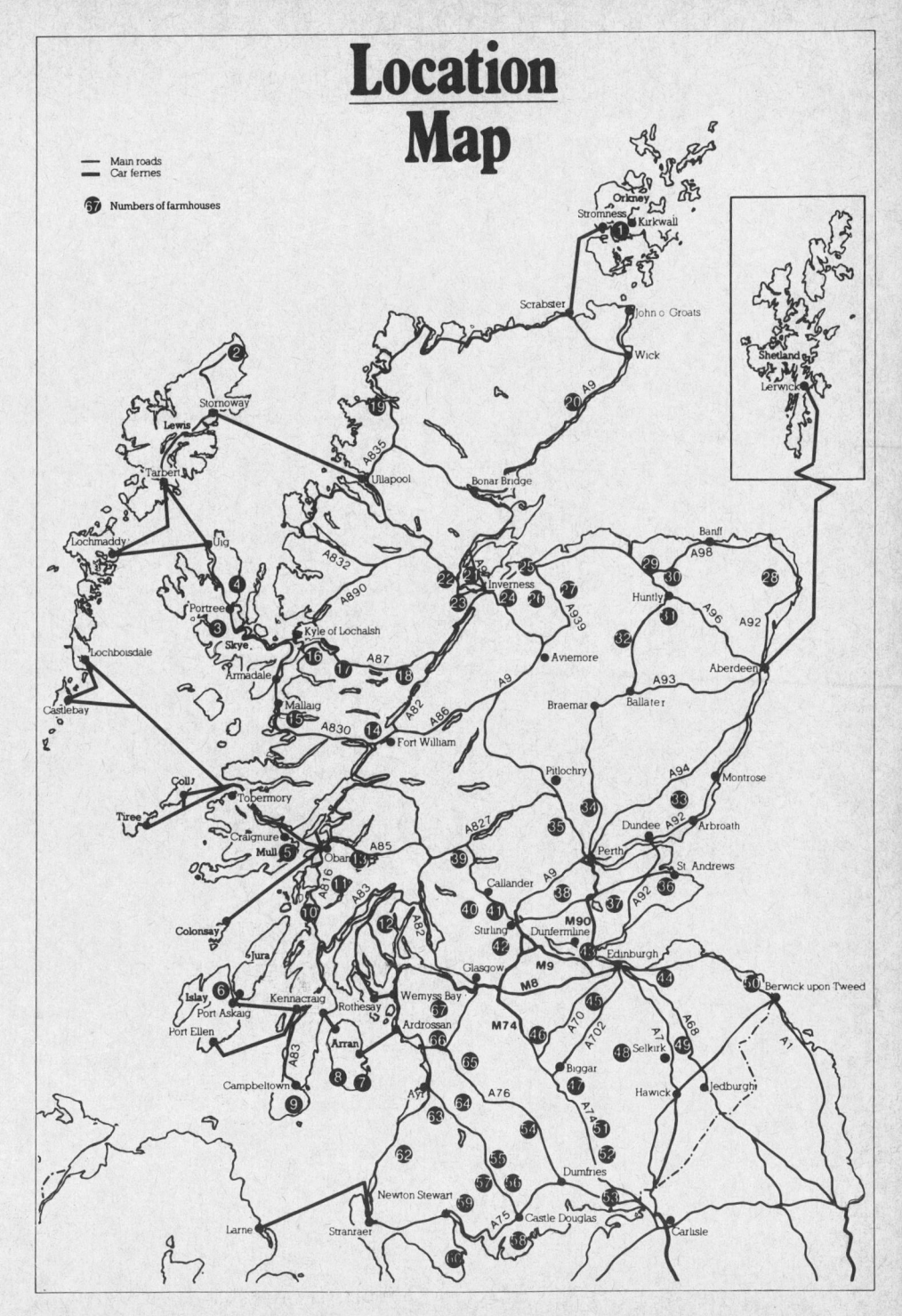

SCOTLAND

Location Map

65 DOWN

DOWN

The populous dormitory fringe along Belfast Lough (don't miss the Folk Museum at Cultra) and the ancient shrines of St. Patrick's Country round the cathedral hill of Downpatrick; the flat golden beaches of the Ards Peninsula and the mountainous Kingdom of Mourne; lively Newcastle with its seaside festival, and stately homes like Mount Stewart and Castle Ward open to visitors. Horse riding, sailing, angling, golf are everywhere within reach, also motor racing at Kirkistown and sea angling in Strangford Lough.

GROUP CONTACTS:
North Down
—Joan McKee (0247) 817526
South Down
—Cissie Annett (03967) 22740

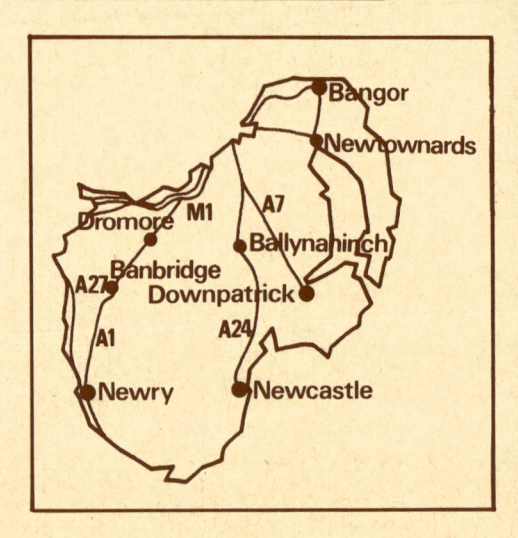

Down N. IRELAND

(FH) "ORANA" 62 Carr Road, Boardmills, Lisburn, Co. Down, BT27 6YG

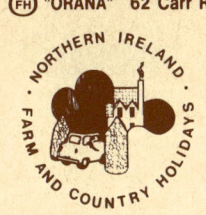

Mrs Jean Foreman
Tel:-(0232) 812584
Open Jan-Nov
B&B £9.50-£10.50   Approved
EM   £5
     Sleeps 4

Modern centrally heated bungalow on 15 acre farm, with a panoramic view of the Mourne Mountains. Homely atmosphere and cooking a speciality. 2 double bedrooms. 6 miles from Lisburn on B6 and 6 miles south of Belfast off A24 on Belfast/Ballynahinch Road. 2 miles past Carryduff, second road on right and first lane on left. Dogs allowed (outside). OS Ref J 335362

(CH) ABBEY FARM 17 Ballywalter Road, Greyabbey, Newtownards, BT22 2RF

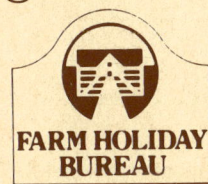

Mabel Hall
Tel:-(024 774) 207
Closed Xmas-New Year
B&B £9-£10   Approved
EM   £5-£6.50
CH   Sleeps 6

Farmhouse on 50 acre mixed farm convenient to sea-fishing, sailing horse-riding, golf. Mountstewart and Castleward - Rowallane (National Trust properties), Kirkistown Racing Circuit. 2 family rooms (both H/C). Babysitter. From Greyabbey take B5 Ballywalter Road. Ballywalter beach 1½m, Greyabbey 1½m, Newtownards 8 miles, Bangor 12m, Portaferry/Strangford Ferry 12m. Dogs by arrangement. OS Ref 361369

(CH) THE MAGGIMINN 11 Bishops Well Road, Dromore, Co. Down, BT25 1ST

Rhoda & Wilson Mark
Tel:-(0846) 693520
Open all year
B&B £10-£12   Approved
EM   £4-£6
CH   Sleeps 6

New countryhouse in quiet lane with panoramic views of Dromara Hills and Mourne Mountains. 30 mins drive from Belfast. 1 double, 1 family bedroom with ensuite, 1 twin-bedded. From A1, heading north, take Milebush Road on your left, then Maypole Road immediately left. Bishop's Well Road is second right. Lane to house immediately over disused railway bridge. Hillsborough historic village 4 miles. Dogs allowed (outside). OS Ref J 322354

(FH) IONA FARMHOUSE 161 Newcastle Road, Kilkeel, Co. Down, BT34 4NN

Maura Fitzpatrick
Tel:-(06937) 62586
Open Apr-Oct
B&B From £8.50   Approved
     Sleeps 6

Georgian farmhouse with spacious gardens. 1 single, 2 double, 1 family room, 1 ground floor bedroom. Pony on farm. Close to Mournes, fishing, golf, pony trekking, swimming. Babysitter available. Kilkeel 1 mile. Annalong 4 miles. Newcastle 11 miles. Off A2. Dogs allowed (outside). OS Ref J 333316

(FH) THE MOOR LODGE 20 Ballynafern Road, Annaclone, Banbridge, Co. Down, BT32 5AE

Brigid & Jim McClory
Tel:-(082067) 516
Open all year
B&B £8   Approved
EM   £5
     Sleeps 9

Chalet bungalow (central heating) situated near the renowned Bronte Glen. Excellent fishing, golf and country walks. 3 doubles, 1 twin (all H/C). ½ mile off Banbridge/Rathfriland Road (B10) midway between these towns. Dogs by arrangement. OS Ref J316341

(CH) GREENACRES 5 Manse Road, Newtownards, Co. Down, BT23 4TP

Dorothy Long
Tel:-(0247) 816193
Closed Xmas-New Year
B&B £10-£12   Approved
EM   £6
CH   Sleeps 8

Country house (central heating). Stone built situated near Ards Shopping Centre and the centre of Newtownards and National Trust properties. Landscaped gardens front and rear. Golf, fishing and the flying club convenient. 2 double, 1 twin and 1 family room all with hot and cold water. Electric blankets when needed. Take Blair Mayne Road off dual carriageway, turn left into Manse Road. OS Ref J347373

281

(CH) RATHGLEN VILLA 7 Hilltown Road, Rathfriland, Co. Down, BT34 5NA

Madge Maginn	
Tel:-(0206) 38090	
Closed Xmas-New Year	
B&B £10	Grade A
EM £7	
CH Sleeps 8	

Grade A country house on elevated site, with beautiful views of the Mourne Mountains. Close to forest parks and beach. Horse riding. Fishing on the River Bann. Golf. 2 doubles, 2 twin-bedded and 1 family room. All ground floor with hot and cold water and central heating. Babysitter available. OS Ref J 319334

(CH) GRASMERE 16 Marguerite Park, Bryansford Road, Newcastle, Co. Down, BT33 OPE

Jean N Hart	
Tel:-(039 67) 22450	
Open Mar-Oct	
B&B £10-£12	Approved
CH Sleeps 5	
(10)	

Detached bungalow (central heating) in landscaped gardens overlooking the mountains of Mourne. 1 double and 1 twin-bedded room. Hot and cold water. Close to golf course and forest parks. Ulster Way nearby. Beach 10 minutes walk. Off B180 Newcastle to Bryansford Road. OS Ref J 336334

(FH) SHARON FARM HOUSE 6 Ballykeel Road, Ballymartin, Co. Down, BT34 4PL

Margaret E Bingham	
Tel:-(06937) 62521	
Closed Xmas-New Year	
B&B £8.50-£9	Approved
EM £5	
Sleeps 7	

Modern farm bungalow, 2 double & one family room. H/C water & central heating. The farm house is situated in the centre of the Mourne area designated as an Area of Outstanding Natural Beauty & an Environmentally Sensitive Area. Convenient for mountain walking & 10 minutes walk from beach. A warm & homely atmosphere. Wholesome home cooking is our speciality. OS Ref J 336 165

(FH) CARGINAGH LODGE 195 Carginagh Road, Silent Valley, Kilkeel, Co. Down, BT34 4QA

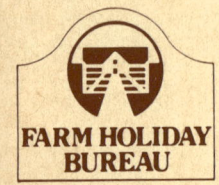

Stella Stronge	
Tel:-(06937) 62085	
Closed Xmas-New Year	
B&B £7.50	Approved
EM £4	
CH Sleeps 4	

Bungalow (central heating) in Mournes with sea view. Fishing, tennis, golf, bowls nearby. 2 double rooms (H/C) both ground floor. Babysitter. Dogs allowed (outside). 3 miles off Newcastle - Kilkeel Road (A2) on Carginagh Road, Silent Valley 5 minutes walk. Kilkeel 3½ miles. Spelga Dam 4 miles. Newcastle 13 miles. Rostrevor 11 miles. Home baking & electric blankets. OS Ref J 332322

(FH) "ERNSDALE" 120 Mountstewart Road, Carrowdore, Newtownards, Co. Down, BT22 2ES

Dot McCullagh	
Tel:-(0247) 861208	
Open Jan-Nov	
B&B £8.50-£9	Approved
EM £5	
Sleeps 6	

Farmhouse (CH). 1 double room, 1 twin-bedded room, 1 family room (2 H/C). 2 ground floor all with electric blankets. Convenient to Ballywalter, Bangor, Millisle, Donaghadee, Newtownards and National Trust properties. Babysitting available. Dogs by arrangement. OS Ref J 358373

(FH) GLENSIDE FARMHOUSE 136 Tullybrannigan Road, Newcastle, Co. Down, BT33 OPW

Mary Murray	
Tel:-(03967) 22628	
Closed Xmas and New Year	
B&B £6-£8.50	Approved
EM From £4	
Sleeps 6	
SC £80-£100	

Farmhouse 1½m from Newcastle on 30 acre sheep farm set in magnificent sea and mountain scenery. Riding, fishing and golf convenient. 1 double (H/C), 2 family rooms. CH. From Newcastle sign on Bryansford Road take Tullibrannigan Road on left, farm ¼m. Self-catering caravan also available. OS Ref J 336333

Down N. IRELAND

(CH) "WYNCREST" 30 Main Road, Ballymartin, Kilkeel, Co. Down, BT34 4NV

Irene Adair
Tel:-(06937) 63012
Open Apr-Oct
B&B £10-£12   Grade A
EM £6-£8
CH Sleeps 6
Redn for
w'kly b'kings

Modern centrally heated guesthouse on mixed farm in view of sea and Mourne Mountains. Home cooking specialising in traditional wholesome food. A warm welcome assured. Ideal for touring Co. Down coast. 3 double and 2 twin-bedded rooms, 2 with ensuite, (all H/C), electric blankets. On main Newcastle-Kilkeel road (A2). Kilkeel 3 miles. Newcastle 10 miles. BHS & UDTA Award Winner 1985, BTA Commended 1987. OS Ref J 335316

(FH) BRESSA FARM 55 Bresagh Road, Boardmills, Lisburn, Co. Antrim, BT27 6TU

Elsie Girvin
Tel:-(0846) 638316
Open all year
B&B £10   Approved
Sleeps 4

(12)

Modern farmhouse on 60 acre mixed farm. Home cooking a speciality. Near Rowallane Gardens (National Trust). Water skiing on Lough Henney. 2 double bedrooms. Hot and cold water and central heating. 10 miles south of Belfast on A24. Lisburn 7 miles, Ballynahinch 4 miles. Saintfield 3 miles. OS Ref J 335359

(FH) BROOK LODGE 79 Old Ballynahinch Road, Lisburn, Co. Antrim, BT27 6TH

Dulcibel Moore
Tel:-(0846) 638454
Open all year
B&B £10   Approved
EM £5
Sleeps 8

(6mths)

Farmhouse (central heating) on 65-acre mixed farm. View of Dromara hills and Mournes. Hillsborough Forest 6m, golf 7m, water-skiing at Lough Henney (3m). 2 doubles, 1 twin, 2 single rooms, all ground floor (H/C). Babysitter. Dogs allowed (outside). M1 Exit 6, B6 1½m; old Ballynahinch road 1½m, lane on left past crossroads, Lisburn 5m. Hillsborough 4m. OS Ref J 316604

(FH) BEECHHILL FARM GUESTHOUSE 10 Loughries Road, Newtownards, Co. Down, BT23 3RN

Joan McKee
Tel:-(0247) 817526
Closed Xmas-New Year
B&B £10   Grade B
EM £7
Sleeps 6

Farmhouse pleasantly situated in the Ards Peninsula on a working farm. 3 double and 1 family room. Hot and cold water and central heating. Golf 4 miles, flying 3 miles. Claybird shooting and fishing by arrangement. Babysitter available. Dogs by arrangement only. OS Ref J 353372

(FH) HAVINE FARM GUEST HOUSE 51 Ballydonnell Road, Downpatrick, Tyrella, Co. Down, BT30 8EP

Mrs Myrtle Macauley
Tel:-(039685) 242
Closed Xmas
B&B £8.50-£9.50   Grade B
EM £4.50-£5.50
Sleeps 6

Situated in heart of St. Patrick's country, amidst his first church, healing wells and burial ground. We are mixed farming, suckling herd, beef and sheep. The house is Georgian, modernised. Central heating etc, part over 300 years old. With a river at the bottom of the gardens meandering its way to the sea and Tyrella shores. Home cooking a speciality & a very warm welcome. OS Ref J346338

(CH) CARRIG-GORM 27 Bridge Road, Helen's Bay, Bangor, Co. Down, BT19 1TS

Mrs Elizabeth Eves
Tel:-(0247) 853680
Closed Easter, Xmas
B&B £7.50-£12   Approved
CH Sleeps 5

Spacious Victorian residence, part 18th Century, in secluded garden ½ mile from the sea. Folk and transport museum 3 miles. Six golf courses within 5 miles. Coastal walks and fishing. Central heating. 1 twin-bedded and 1 family bedroom. Dogs by arrangement only. OS Ref J 348382

283

(FH) MORNE ABBEY GUEST HOUSE 16 Greencastle Road, Kilkeel, Co. Down, BT34 4DE

Annabel Shannon
Tel:-(06937) 62426
Open Apr-Sep
B&B £9-£12
EM £5.95
Sleeps 13

Grade B

New farmhouse on mixed farm in magnificent setting, ½ mile from Kilkeel. A warm welcome assured, home cooking a speciality. Fishing, riding, tennis, bowls and golf nearby. Sea 1 mile distance, Silent Valley 4 miles. Babysitter available. 1 single, 2 double, 2 twin bedded rooms. All H/C. OS Ref J 330315

(CH) WIN-STAFF 45 Banbridge Road, Dromore, Co. Down, BT25 1NE

Esther Erwin
Tel:-(0846) 692252
Open all year
B&B £10.50-£12
EM £5
CH Sleeps 8

Approved

Country house in spacious gardens. Central heating. Homely atmosphere and cooking. 1 single, 1 double and 2 twin-bedded rooms. Babysitter available. Close to golf, fishing, hillwalking and parks. First Dromore turn-off from Banbridge dual carriageway, ¼ mile on right. Dogs allowed (outside). OS Ref J 319553

(CH) CUAN CHALET 41 Mile Cross Road, Newtownards, Co. Down, BT23 4SR

Winifred Cochrane
Tel:-(0247) 812302
Open all year
B&B £10
EM £6
CH Sleeps 5

Approved

Bungalow (CH) in landscaped garden. Squash, golf, sailing and flying nearby. 1 family and 1 twin bedded room. Parking. Opposite Dickson's Nursery off A20 dual carriageway west of town. OS Ref J 348374

(CH) THE COTTAGE 377 Comber Road, Dundonald, Belfast, BT16 0XB

Elizabeth Muldoon
Tel:-(0247) 878189
Open all year
B&B £10.50-£12
CH Sleeps 5

Approved

Carefully restored 200 year old cottage with oak beams. CH in all rooms. All bedrooms with wash basins (H/C water). 2 double, 1 single bedrooms, (1 double with toilet). 2 miles from Dundonald on main A22 to Comber. OS Ref J 345372

(FH) HEATH HALL 160 Moyadd Road, Kilkeel, Co. Down, BT34 4HJ

Marie McGlue
Tel:-(06937) 62612
Open Apr-Oct
B&B £8-£9
EM £4-£5.50
Redn for under 12's
Sleeps 8

Approved

Stone built farmhouse (central heating) with spacious gardens. Panoramic view of Mourne Mountains and sea. Fishing, swimming, golf and bowls nearby. Silent Valley 3 miles. Babysitting and snooker room available. Dogs allowed (outside). 1 single, 1 double, 1 family room. On main Kilkeel - Hilltown Road (B27). Kilkeel 1½ miles. OS Ref J 328316

(CH) BRACKNEY HOUSE 2 Green Road, Conlig, Newtownards, Co. Down, BT23 3PZ

Ann Thompson
Tel:-(0247) 461423
Closed Xmas
B&B £11
CH Sleeps 8

Approved

Country house (CH) with large garden and panoramic views. Good base for golf (Clandeboye), horse riding, beaches, National Trust properties, Ulster Folk and Transport Museum. Convenient to some of the best shopping areas in Northern Ireland, Bangor 1 mile, Newtownards 3 miles and Belfast 12 miles. 2 family rooms, one twin bedded room (all H/C), electric blankets, babysitter. Spacious guest lounge. Off A21 dual carriageway. OS Ref J 351377

Down N. IRELAND

(CH) "ROCKDENE" 4 Springvale Road, Ballywalter, Newtownards, Co. Down, BT22 2PE

Frances Dickson
Tel:-(02477) 58205
Closed Xmas and New Year
B&B   £9.50   Approved
CH   Sleeps 4

Modern bungalow (central heating and TV) on sea front on main coast road from Donaghadee to Portaferry. Convenient to Mount Stewart Gardens, Kirkistown. Racing circuit, golf, sea fishing, birdwatching, tennis courts and children's playground nearby. Strangford Ferry 13 miles, Newtownards 11 miles. 2 doubles and 1 family room. OS Ref J 363371

(FH) OLD TOWN FARM 25 Corrigs Road, Newcastle, Co. Down, BT33 OJZ

Cissie Annett
Tel:-(03967) 22740
Open Apr-Sep
B&B   £8.50-£9   Approved
      Sleeps 6

Modern farmhouse on 88 acre dairy farm in quiet surroundings with panoramic view of Mourne 1½ miles from Newcastle, near forest parks. Golf, fishing, pony-trekking. 2 double rooms, 1 family room. From Newcastle take A50 (Castlewellan road). First road on right past caravan site and first lane on right along Corrigs Road. 1 bedroom has its own private bathroom. OS Ref J 337333

(CH) GLENDALE HOUSE Flagstaff Road, Newry, Co Down, BT35 8QU

Eileen Poucher
Tel:-(0693) 4137
Open Mar-Nov
B&B   £9.50-£10.50   Approved
CH   Sleeps 6

Modern country bungalow (CH) in the picturesque area of Flagstaff Newry, near to one of Ireland's most beautiful views - Carlingford Lough & the Mourne Mountains. Golf, fishing & pony riding ½ mile radius. Wind surfing, water skiing & sea fishing nearby. 5 mins drive from Arts Centre, indoor pool and Sports Centre. Country walks & scenic drives. Babysitting facilities. 2 double, 1 twin, 1 single, all H/C. OS Ref 308326

(CH) LAUREL HOUSE 99 Carryduff Road, Temple, Lisburn, Co. Antrim, BT27 6YL

Evelyn Stewart
Tel:-(0846) 638422
Open all year
B&B   £12-£14   Grade A
EM   £5.50-£8.50
CH   Sleeps 16

Grade A country guesthouse (CH) situated on main Belfast - Newcastle road 9 miles from Belfast. Bus stops at door and shops are 100 yards away. 3 doubles, 2 twin, 2 family rooms with shower. Licensed restaurant. Home baking, traditional cooking. Convenient to National Trust properties and good shopping towns. Dogs allowed (outside). OS Ref J 337367

(FH) GREENLEA FARM 48 Dunover Road, Ballywalter, Newtownards, Co. Down, BT22 2LE

Evelyn McIvor
Tel:-(02477) 58218
Open all year
B&B   £7.50-£9   Approved
EM   From £5
      Sleeps 8

Modernised farmhouse. 120 acres overlooking sea. ½m village, churches & A2. Covenient to National Trust properties, Folk Museum, antique shops, pottery, bowling green, tennis courts etc. Central heating, H/C in all bedrooms, 1 double, 2 twin, 1 family. Sun lounge. Porta and Strangford ferries 12m, Newtownards 10m, Bangor 11m, Belfast 20m. First farm on left on Dunover Road after speed limit sign. OS Ref J 363370

(FH) CORNERHOUSE 182 Dunmore Road, Ballynahinch, Co. Down, BT24 8QQ

Mary Rogan
Tel:-(0238) 562670
Open June-Sep
B&B   £9   Approved
      Sleeps 6

Modernised farmhouse on 30 acre farm in a rural setting near Mournes. Forest parks, fishing and golf. One single, one double and one family room. (1 H/C). Babysitter available. Off A24 near Spa. Ballnahinch 5 miles. Castlewellan 5 miles. OS Ref J 336348

FH LARAGH HOUSE 24 Ballyvalley Road, Mayobridge, Newry, Co. Down, BT34 2RS

Jim & Therese Rooney
Tel:-(069 385) 311
Open all year
B&B   £9   Approved

Farmhouse (CH) on 25 acre mixed farm with river. Mountain views. Fishing 2m. Golf, riding, water skiing, windsurfing. French/German Spoken. 1 double, 1 twin-bedded and 1 family bedroom (1 with ensuite bathroom). Babysitter Dogs allowed. B8 from Newry, turn right opposite Gorman's Bar, house ½m on left. Newry 5m. Newcastle 13 miles. OS Ref J 316327

CH BURNSIDE 26 Ballyblack Road, Newtownards, Co. Down, BT22 2AP

Jean Bartholomew
Tel:-(0247) 812920
Open all year
B&B   £9   Approved
CH   Sleeps 5

Bungalow (CH, TV lounge) with spacious garden, situated in quiet countryside near National Trust properties. Strangford Lough. 1 single, 1 double and 1 twin-bedded rooms. All ground floor. (2 with H/C). Babysitter available. Dogs allowed (outside). A20 (Portaferry direction) from Newtownards left at Millisle signpost. 1½m. Newtownards 3½m. OS Ref J 352373

FH BALLYCASTLE HOUSE 20 Mountstewart Road, Newtownards, Co. Down, BT22 2AL

Margaret Deering
Tel:-(024774) 357
Open all year
B&B   £10.50   Approved

Farmhouse (CH) on 35 acre farm. Vintage engine collection. Beside Mount Stewart (N.T.) overlooking lough. Fishing, sailing, golfing, flying club. 3 double bedrooms (1 with ensuite bathroom), 1 ground floor (3 with H/C). Dogs allowed (outside). A20 south from Newtownards, 4m left at Ballywalter signpost, farmhouse ⅔m on left. OS Ref J 354371

FH WHITESPOTS FARM 296 Bangor Road, Newtownards, Co Down, BT23 3PA

Moyra and Declan Graham
Tel:-(0247) 814210
Open all year
B&B   £7-£9   Approved
EM   £5-£10
25% redn for children & OAPs
Sleeps 4

Red brick farmhouse, garden to front, farmyard to side. Views over countryside. Convenient for golf, fishing, shooting, sailing, flying, sports centre, National Trust properties and Ards Peninsula. 1 double, 1 family room, lounge with TV. Baby sitting. Pony riding. Vegetarian cuisine our speciality plus traditional cooking with local or home grown produce. Bus stop convenient. OS Ref J 350375

FH GORDONALL 93 Newtownards Rd, Greyabbey, Newtownards, Co Down, BT22 2QJ

Billy & Angela Martin
Tel:-(024774) 325
Open Apr-Oct
B&B   £10   Approved
Sleeps 5

Centrally heated farmhouse on 160 acre mixed farm overlooking Strangford Lough and Mourne Mts. Birdwatching, fishing, golf, flying club. 1 single bedded room, 1 family room. On A20 first farm on left after Mount Stewart (N.T.), Newtownards 6m, Greyabbey 1m. Dogs allowed outside. OS Ref J 356368

FH MILLVIEW FARM 8 Abbacy Road, Ardkeen, Newtownards, Co Down, BT22 1HH

John and Rachel Birch
Tel:-(02477) 28030
Open Easter-Sep
B&B   £9-£10   Approved
EM   £5
Sleeps 2 + child

Farmhouse - family room with toilet and handbasin, facilities for morning tea. Dining room with colour TV. Sun porch. Situated on shores of Strangford Lough. OS Ref J 360357

Down N. IRELAND

(FH) ROSEVALE FARM 76 Cootehall Road, Crawfornburn, Bangor, Co Down, BT19 1UW

Ann Irwin
Tel:-(0247) 852880
Closed Easter, Xmas & New Year   Approved
B&B £12
Sleeps 2 adults
2 children + cot

One large family room, H/C, electric blanket and kettle in room. Room at rear of house overlooking countryside and Belfast Lough. Rare breed farm animals. OS Ref J 474 807

(FH) TRENCH FARM 35 Ringcreevy Road, Comber, BT23 5JR

Maureen Hamilton
Tel:-(0247) 872558
Open all year
B&B £10   Approved
Sleeps 5

Farmhouse on 100 acres horticulture. Mount Stewart (N.T.), Golf. Driving ponies kept as hobby. 1 double, 1 single both with H/C. Electric blankets. A21 Newtownards Road from Comber first road on right. Comber 1½m, Newtownards 2½m, Belfast 10m. No vouchers accepted. OS Ref J347370

(CH) HOMESYDE 7 Shandon Drive, Kilkeel, BT34 4DT

Eleanor Haugh
Tel:-(06937) 62676
Open all year
B&B £9.50   Approved
Sleeps 4

Bungalow with central heating situated in a quiet cul de sac 5 mins walk from Kilkeel centre. Local beach sports amenities 10 mins walk. Babysitting available. 2 double rooms (1 H/C), both on ground floor. OS Ref J331315

FARM HOLIDAY BUREAU

TAKE CARE OF THE COUNTRY

FOLLOW THE COUNTRY CODE — Countryside COMMISSION

Enjoy the countryside and respect its life and work.
Guard against all risk of fire.
Fasten all gates.
Keep your dogs under close control.
Keep to public paths across farmland.
Use gates and stiles to cross fences, hedges and walls.
Leave livestock, crops and machinery alone.
Take your litter home.
Help to keep all water clean.
Protect wildlife, plants and trees.
Take special care on country roads.
Make no unnecessary noise.

GG ANTRIM

ANTRIM

To the south-east of the county, Belfast provides six-day shopping and city entertainment; to the north-west lies the Causeway Coast, a playground of holiday resorts, with the Giant's Causeway itself the dominant feature. Between lie the nine Glens of Antrim and their quaint waterfoot villages, the spectacular coast road, Carrickfergus Castle, and inland towns like Antrim with its ancient round tower and splendid park. There's a lakeside steam railway at Shane's Castle, pony trekking near Ballycastle, golf at Royal Portrush, besides bathing, boating and fishing along its hundred miles of shore.

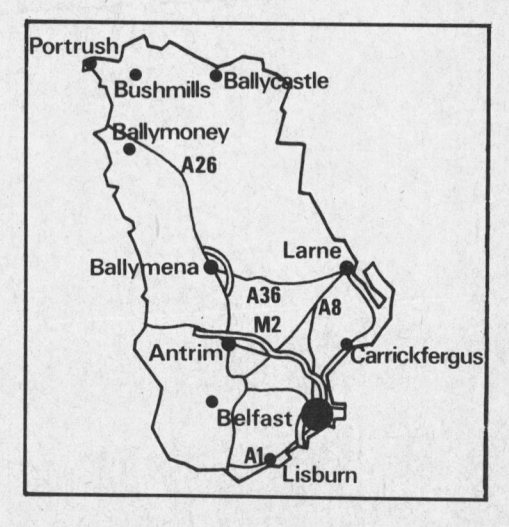

GROUP CONTACTS:
North Antrim
—Elsie Rankin (0265) 823407
South Antrim
—Eileen Duncan (08494) 52768

Antrim N. IRELAND

(FH) MADDYBENNY FARMHOUSE 18 Maddybenny Park, Off Loguestown Road, Portrush, Co. Antrim, BT52 2PT

Rosemary White
Tel:-(0265) 823394
Closed Xmas-New Year
B&B £9-£10 Approved
EM £10
Sleeps 8

Spacious countryhouse set in 1½ acres of mature gardens. Comfortably furnished in fine antiques. Convenient to golf courses, sea angling, and water sports. 10 minutes from Giant's Causeway & Safari Park. 2m from Portrush, Portstewart Strands and "Water World". Salmon, trout fishing permits available locally. Snooker, TV room. 6 rooms including 2 'family suites' (2 rooms per family). Babysitting. Cordon Bleu cook. Off A29. OS Ref C 285439

(CH) DANESCROFT 171 Whitepark Road, Bushmills, Nr Portbradden, BT57 8SS

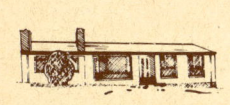

Olga Rutherford
Tel:-(02657) 31586
Closed Xmas
B&B £11-£12 Approved
EM £6.50-£7
CH Sleeps 5

Modern bungalow on A2 coast road 4½ miles from Bushmills overlooking Whitepark Bay and Rathlin Island. Full central heating. Home baking. 1 double, 1 twin bedrooms, both with private bathrooms and 1 single bedroom. Dogs by arrangement. OS Ref C 298443

(CH) "ARDNAREE" 105 Dunluce Road, White Rocks, Portrush, Co. Antrim, BT56 8NB

Elsie Rankin
Tel:-(0265) 823407
Closed Xmas and New Year
B&B £9-£10.50 Approved
CH Sleeps 6

Chalet bungalow, full central heating, double glazing and TV lounge on Coast Road (A2). Panoramic views. 3 mins from beach and Royal Portrush golf course. 5 miles from Giant's Causeway, 3 miles from Bushmills Distillery. 1 single, 1 double on ground floor. 1 double and 1 family room ensuite on first floor. Dogs allowed (outside). OS Ref C288 442

(CH) ASHDENE 60 Ballymacvea Road, Shankbridge, Ballymena, Co. Antrim, BT42 2LT

Jean Tennant
Tel:-(0266) 898100
Open Jan-Nov
B&B £9-£10 Approved
CH Sleeps 5
(4)

Georgian bungalow (central heating) with view of open countryside with secluded gardens. Bedrooms with radio and TV. Home cooking. Convenient to Antrim and Ballymena Sports Complex. Angling, golf and boating in area. Ideal for touring Glens of Antrim. Midway on Antrim - Ballymena Road (A26) turn right into Ballymacvea Road and Ashdene is third bungalow on right (200 yards). Belfast International Airport 10m. OS Ref D 314795

(CH) WHITE GABLES 83 Dunluce Road, Bushmills, Co. Antrim, BT57 8SJ

Ria Johnston
Tel:-(02657) 31611
Open Easter-Oct
B&B £12.50-£15 Grade B
EM £7.50
CH Sleeps 8
(10)

Modern villa (CH) on A2 coast road, near Dunluce Castle, Bushmills Distillery and Giants Causeway. Panoramic views of North Antrim coast. All bedrooms H/C, tea/coffee making facilities. 2 with private showers and WC. Large, comfortable guests lounge with colour TV etc. Ample car parking space. OS Ref C 293 443

(FH) BEECHGROVE 412 Upper Road, Troopers Lane, Carrickfergus, Co. Antrim, BT38 8PW

Mr. & Mrs. John Barron
Tel:-(09603) 63304
Open all year
B&B From £9 Approved
EM £4.50
Sleeps 9

Farmhouse (central heating) on a 16 acre mixed farm near the sea. Fishing, golf, riding, Knochagh Monument, Belfast Zoo, leisure centre nearby. Lounge, colour TV, H/C water in all bedrooms. OS Ref J 340386

289

(FH) LOGUESTOWN FARM 59 Magheraboy Road, Portrush, Co. Antrim, BT56 8NY

Mary Adams
Tel:-(0265) 822742
Closed Dec, Xmas and New Year
B&B £9-£10
EM From £3
Sleeps 14
Approved

Modernised farmhouse (CH) on 28 acre dairy farm close to amenities of the triangle area: Portrush 1 mile, Portstewart 3 miles, Coleraine 4 miles off A29. 4 double and 3 family rooms (6 with H/C), 3 ground floor rooms. Babysitter available. Separate dining tables. Home baking. OS Ref C 285439

(FH) BRYNHEDD 122 Newbridge Road, Ballymoney, Co. Antrim, BT53 6QN

Bertha Boyce
Tel:-(02656) 63097
Open Jan-Nov
B&B £8.50-£9
Sleeps 9
Approved

Bungalow (central heating) set in 1 acre lawns. Panoramic views. Close to Antrim coast, fishing, sailing, golf, leisure centre. 2 doubles, 1 twin, 1 family room with shower and toilet, all ground floor, all H/C. Babysitter. TV lounge. Dogs allowed (outside). On A26, 1m North of Ballymoney roundabout. Ballymoney 1½ miles, Coleraine 5 miles, Safari Park 4 miles. OS Ref C 295427

(FH) COUNTRY GUEST HOUSE 41 Kirk Road, Ballymoney, Co. Antrim, BT51 8HB

Dorothy Brown
Tel:-(02656) 62620
Closed Xmas-New Year
B&B £7.50-£8
Sleeps 8
Grade B

Modern bungalow (central heating) in 1 acre of alpine and rare plants, near Antrim Glens. Recreation centre 1 mile. 3 double & 1 family all rooms have private shower, toilet etc. Supper available at no extra charge. Babysitter available. Safari park 3m. Giant's Causeway 10m. From Ballymoney by-pass (A26), 50 yards along B147. Ballymoney 1m. Lounge with colour TV for guests. OS Ref C 296428

(CH) ASHMORE 10 Quarterland Road, Dundrod, Crumlin, Co. Antrim, BT29 4TU

Moira McClure
Tel:-(023125) 307
Open all year
B&B £8-£9
CH Sleeps 6
Approved

Modern country house (central heating and open fire) in 2½ acres situated on the Ulster Grand Prix circuit. Rural setting. Convenient to Lough Neagh and Antrim Forum sports centre and fishing. 1 single, 1 double, 1 family room. Babysitter available. B101 from Belfast International Airport to Dundrod. B154 for 1 mile Antrim, Lisburn 8, airport 4. OS Ref J322477

(FH) 46 CASTLECATT ROAD Bushmills, Co. Antrim, BT57 8TN

Kathleen Richmond
Tel:-(02657) 31359
Open Easter-Sep
B&B £9-£9.50
EM £5.50
Sleeps 6
Approved

Modern farmhouse (CH), TV lounge with garden. Home baking, fresh farm produce. Seaside resorts, golf, river fishing nearby. One double, one family room (both H/C). Babysitter available. One mile from Bushmills on Dervock Road (B66). Giant's Causeway 3m. Portrush 6m. Safari Wonderland 4m. OS Ref C296438

(CH) BALLYWATT 174 Ballybogey Road, Coleraine, BT52 2LP

Jean Brown
Tel:-(02657) 31627
Closed Xmas and New Year
B&B £10-£12
EM £6
CH Sleeps 15
Approved

Bungalow (CH) with spacious lawns. Homely atmosphere and home baking. On Ballymoney-Portrush Road (B62). 4 double rooms, 1 twin-bedded and 1 family (4 ground floor). Central for touring North Antrim coast. OS Ref C 291435

Antrim N. IRELAND

(FH) MONTALTO GUEST HOUSE 5 Craigaboney Road, Bushmills, Co. Antrim, BT57 8XD

Dorothy Taggart
Tel:-(02657) 31257
Open Mar-Oct
B&B £10-£12   Grade B
EM   £6
Sleeps 6

Large 19th Century farmhouse on 73 acre mixed farm (CH, TV) with lawns affording splendid views of countryside and sea. Golf and salmon fishing nearby. Giant's Causeway 2m, Old Bushmills Distillery 1 mile, Dunluce Castle 2m. 2 single, 2 double, (all H/C). Babysitter available. Off Bushmills - Coleraine Road (B17) beside Dunluce Manse. Dogs allowed (outside). OS Ref C 292438

(CH) ISLAY - VIEW 36 Leeke Road, Ballymagarry, Portrush, BT56 8NH

Eileen Smith
Tel:-(0265) 823220
Open Easter-Sep
B&B From £9.50   Approved
EM   From £4
CH   Sleeps 6

Farm bungalow on 60 acre mixed farm (CH), near White Rocks with view of Giant's Causeway. Home baking, fresh farm produce. Donkey for children. 1 double, 2 family rooms, all ground floor (all H/C). Electric fires, electric blankets as required. Wheelchair ramp. Babysitter. Dogs allowed (outside). Off Ballymagarry road, off Ballymoney-Portrush road (B62), Portrush 2½m, Coleraine 6m. OS Ref C290428

(FH) CRAIGS FARM 90 Hillhead Road, Ballycarry, Carrickfergus, Co. Antrim, BT38 9JF

Jean Craig
Tel:-(09603) 72769
Open all year
B&B £9   Approved
EM   £4
Sleeps 6

Modernised farmhouse (CH) on 70 acre farm. Convenient to Carrickfergus (7m), sailing, golf, fishing. 1 double, 1 twin-bedded, 1 family room, lounge for visitors. Babysitter available. A2 from Larne, right at sign for Ballycarry, 3m along Ballypollard Road. Larne 6m. Whitehead 3m. Ballycarry ¾ mile. Dogs allowed (outside). OS Ref NI1044986

(FH) "HILLVALE FARM" GUEST HOUSE 11 Largy Road, Crumlin, Co. Antrim, BT29 4AH

Eileen Duncan
Tel:-(08494) 22768
Open all year
B&B £8.50-£10   Approved
Sleeps 6

Modernised farmhouse (central heating) with sun porch and large gardens overlooking Crumlin Glen, beside river and close to Lough Neagh (128 acre dairy farm with pedigree Ayrshire herd). Convenient to Antrim Forum Sports Centre. 1 single, 1 double, 1 family room, all H/C. 1 mile Crumlin village, 7 miles Antrim and 3 miles Belfast International Airport. Touring caravans available on site on farm or can be hired for towing. OS Ref J 314 376

(CH) LISSANDUFF HOUSE Lissanduff Avenue, Portballintrae, Co. Antrim, BT57 8RU

Mrs. E. Adjey
Tel:-(02657) 32096
Open Easter-Oct
B&B From £9   Approved
EM   From £6
CH   Sleeps 8

Country house in 10 acres overlooking beaches and coastline. Views of Scotland and Donegal. Giant's Causeway nearby, also fishing, golf, tennis, water sports, children's play park close to house. All rooms H/C. 2 doubles, 2 twin-bedded, 1 family room. Bushmills 1 mile, Portrush 5 miles. OS Ref C 294442

(FH) DRUMADOON HOUSE 236 Frocess Road, Cloughmills, Ballymena, BT44 9PX

Kathleen Allen
Tel:-(026 563) 221
Open Jan-Nov
B&B £10   Approved
Sleeps 6

Spacious 18th Century coaching-inn on 105 acre farm. CH. Fishing on Maine and Bush Rivers, walking, scenic drives. 2 single rooms, 1 double room and 1 family room, all (HC). 10 miles from Ballymena, 8 miles to Ballymoney, Portrush 20 miles. Safari Park 10 miles, Glens of Antrim 12 miles. OS Ref D 306417

291

(CH) AUBERGE DE SENEIRL 28 Ballyclough Road, Bushmills, Co. Antrim, BT57 8UZ

Barbara Defres
Tel:-(02657) 41536
Open all year
B&B   £14.50-£18.50   Approved
EM   £8-£15
CH   Sleeps 10

Converted 19th Century country school (CH). Licenced Restaurant. Near Bush River, 5 mins from Antrim coast. 3 doubles, 2 twins, 1 family room, 3 ground floor (all private services). All rooms have colour TV & clock radio. Indoor swimming pool. Babysitter available. Dogs allowed (outside). Giant's Causeway 5m. Safari Park 2m. Portrush 6m. 1m off B62 Ballymoney-Portrush Road. OS Ref C 293433

(FH) CAIRNVIEW 69 Irish Hill Road, Ballyclare, Co. Antrim, BT39 9NJ

Norman & Jenny Bradford
Tel:-(096 03) 22607
Open all year
B&B   £9   Approved
Sleeps 8

Farmhouse set in 17 acres of pasture. Horse riding, golf, fishing, leisure centre all nearby. 1 single, 1 double, 1 twin, 1 family room. Baby sitter. Off Larne - Belfast Road A8. Ballyclare 3 miles, Larne 11 miles, Carrickfergus 5 miles, Straid 1½ miles. OS Ref J 329391

(FH) WOODFORD FARM 30 Woodburn Road, Carrickfergus, Co. Antrim, BT38 8PX

Marion Graham
Tel:-(09603) 64602
Open all year
B&B   £9   Approved
Sleeps 4

Modernised farmhouse (central heating) with private fishing facilities. Convenient to shops, transport etc. 1 mile from town centre, Carrickfergus Castle, Leisure Centre, Golf Club, bowling green nearby. Dogs allowed (outside). OS Ref J 388341

(FH) THE VILLA 185 Torr Road, Cushendun, Co. Antrim, BT44 0PU

Catherine Scally
Tel:-(026674) 252
Open Apr-Nov
B&B   £9.50   Approved
Sleeps 9

Tudor style 19th Century 2 storey farmhouse (central heating) on Ulster Way with views of the Nine Glens of Antrim. Excellent cuisine. Dining room open to non-residents. Local fishing, sailing, golf and pony trekking. 2 double, 1 twin-bedded, 1 family room (all H/C). Babysitter available. Cushendun Village 1m. Ballycastle 13m. OS Ref D 326434

(FH) CROSSROADS 1 Largy Road, Crumlin, Co. Antrim, BT29 4AH

William & Vanessa Lorrimer
Tel:-(08494) 52259
Open all year
B&B   £10   Approved
Sleeps 8

Countryhouse furnished in traditional manner (central heating, open fires) in 1 acre garden. 1 single, 1 double, 1 twin-bedded, 1 family room (all H/C). Horse available for guests. Small licensed restaurant in grounds. Guest lounge, dining room, pool room. Fishing, golf, boating. Belfast International Airport 3m. Belfast 14m. On first crossroads on Crumlin to Antrim Road from Crumlin. OS Ref J 315376

(CH) HILLCREST HOUSE 306 Whitepark Road, Bushmills, Co. Antrim, BT57 8SN

Edith Dinsmore
Tel:-(02657) 31577
Open all year
B&B   From £11.50   Approved
CH   Sleeps 8

Family run, modernised country house set in landscaped garden overlooking sea and country. One single, 2 double and 1 family room. Central heating, (H/C) 2 with ensuite facilities. Morning coffee, afternoon tea, home baking, meals for non-residents, Bushmills Distillery, fishing, golf and watersports all nearby. OS Ref C 300444

Antrim N. IRELAND

(FH) CARNSIDE GUEST HOUSE   23 Causeway Road, Giant's Causeway, Bushmills, Co. Antrim, BT57 8SU

Frances Lynch
Tel:-(02657) 31337
Open Mar-Oct
B&B   £10   Approved

Farmhouse (CH) on 200 acre dairy farm. Coastal view. Fishing, golf, water sports. Old Bushmills Distillery (2m) has weekday tours. 1 single, 4 doubles, 1 twin, 2 family rooms, 2 ground floor (all H/C). Babysitter. Dogs allowed (outside). Bushmills 2m. Ballycastle 12m. OS Ref C 294444

(FH) 200 BALLYBOGEY ROAD   Bushmills, Co. Antrim, BT57 8UH

Rosa Rankin
Tel:-(02657) 31352
Open Mar-Oct
B&B   £9.50   Approved
      Sleeps 6

Farmhouse (CH) with over 100 acres mixed farming. TV lounge. Beaches, golf, fishing nearby. 1 double bedroom, 1 family room, both with hot and cold water. Babysitter. Dogs allowed (outside). On Ballymoney - Portrush road (B62). Portrush 3 miles. OS Ref C290438

(CH) THE CARA   114 Duneaney Road, Rasharkin, Co. Antrim, BT44 8SR

Mary McDonnell
Tel:-(026653) 318
Open Easter-Sept
B&B   £10   Grade A

Country grade A guesthouse (central heating) in 10-acre grounds. Lounge with TV and stereo). Guests collected from airport/ferry. Fishing, sailing, (River Bann), riding, golf, hill walking, birdwatching, 1 double, 3 twin, 1 family room (all H/C and private facilities). Babysitter. Dogs allowed (outside). Take B64 from Rasharkin for ¼m. 3rd lane on right (white pillars). Ballymena 10m. Ballymoney 7m. Portrush 16m. OS Ref C298413

(FH) THE OLD SCHOOL HOUSE   106 Ballyrobin Road, Muckamore, Co Antrim, BT41 4TJ

Jim & Margaret Kelly
Tel:-(08494) 63209
Closed Xmas
CH   Sleeps 8   Approved
B&B   £11
EM   £5-£7.50

Century old converted schoolhouse set in an acre of mature wooded garden situated a few minutes from Belfast International Airport. All bedrooms centrally heated with private facilities. Attractive lounge with panoramic views of surrounding countryside and Lough Neagh.

BOOKING TIPS

NO VACANCIES? If you have any difficulty finding a vacancy in this area, contact the Vacancy Secretary or Group Contact whose name appears at the beginning of this section.

FARM HOLIDAY BUREAU

67 LONDONDERRY

LONDONDERRY

This is a fertile agricultural county, with small farms scattered across the broad sweeping land, and long Atlantic beaches. The city of Londonderry is best known for its massive ring of fortified walls and singing pubs. In the county's north-east corner is Coleraine (with one of the main campuses of the University of Ulster), conveniently close to the seaside resorts of Portsteward and Castlerock for sea angling, golf and children's amusements. For rewarding scenic drives the Sperrin Mountains are best approached from Limavady and the beautiful Roe Valley Country Park. The Bann river is noted for trout and salmon.

GROUP CONTACT:
Margaret Moore (026585) 229

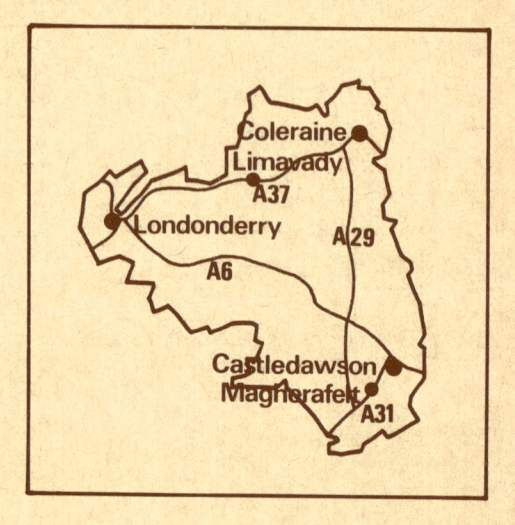

Londonderry N. IRELAND

(FH) KILLENAN HOUSE — 40 Killenan Road, Drumahoe, Co. Londonderry, BT47 3NG

Averil Campbell
Tel:-(050487) 710
Closed Xmas-New Year
B&B £7-£7.50   Approved
EM £3
Sleeps 6

Modern farmhouse (central heating) on 170 acre farm in rural setting close to historic city, north coast, Donegal, airport. Fishing, golf, flying club nearby. 1 double, 2 twin, 1 family room (all H/C). Babysitter available. Dogs allowed (outside). From Londonderry take Claudy Road (A6), after 5 miles turn left for Eglinton (B118) 1½ miles, left at Killenan Road, first road on right. OS Ref C 250415

(CH) CAMUS HOUSE — 27 Curragh Road, Coleraine, Co. Londonderry, BT51 3RY

Josephine King
Tel:-(0265) 2982
Open all year
B&B £10   Approved
EM £7
CH Sleeps 6
(11)

Spacious countryhouse built 1685, listed. Comfortably furnished with TV. Tea/coffee making in all bedrooms, mixed farming, overlooking one of the most scenic spots of the River Bann, close to Salmonleap. Salmon & trout fishing (permit available locally) convenient to golf courses & Giants Causeway. 8 miles (approx) from Castlerock, Portstewart & Portrush Strands 3 miles from Coleraine on A54. OS Ref C 288 426

(FH) GREENHILL HOUSE — 24 Greenhill Road, Aghadowey, Coleraine, Co. Londonderry, BT51 4EU

Mrs Elizabeth Hegarty
Tel:-(026585) 241
Open Mar-Oct
B&B £10.50-£12.50   Grade A
EM £8
Sleeps 14/17

Grade A, B.T.A. commended country guest house (Georgian with central heating). Good views across wooded countryside to the Bann Valley and the Antrim hills. Convenient to North coast. Fishing nearby. 2 double, 3 twin-bedded and 2 family rooms (all H & C, 2 with shower and w.c. - 1 with shower). Garvagh 3m, Coleraine 7m. 11km on A29 from Coleraine and then B66 (Ballymoney). OS Ref C 2099 8487

(CH) "THE POPLARS" — 352 Seacoast Road, Limavady, Co. Londonderry, BT49 OLA

Mrs. Helen McCracken
Tel:-(05047) 50360
Open all year
B&B £8.50   Approved
EM £7
CH Sleeps 10

Farm bungalow in gardens, views of Binevenagh, Donegal hills. Fishing ¼ mile, golf 6 miles, Roe Valley Country Park 7 miles. Ulster Gliding Club ½ mile. 3 double, 1 twin-bedded and 2 family rooms. All ground floor. Babysitter available. Limavady 6½ miles. Coleraine 10 miles. Londonderry 24 miles. OS Ref 267430

(FH) BALLYCARTON FARM — Bellarena, Limavady, Co. Londonderry, BT49 OHZ

Emma Craig
Tel:-(05047) 50216
Open all year
B&B From £8.50   Approved
EM £5
Sleeps 6

Modern farmhouse on 50 acre farm amid spectacular coastal and mountain scenery. Sandy beaches. Gliding, mountain climbing and fishing. One single, 1 double, 1 twin-bedded and 2 family rooms. Babysitter available. On coast road. Coleraine 14 miles. Limavady 5 miles. OS Ref C 268429

(FH) KILLEAGUE HOUSE — 156 Drumcroon Road, Blackhill, Coleraine, Co. Londonderry, BT51 4HJ

Margaret Moore
Tel:-(026585) 229
Open Jan-Dec
B&B £9   Approved
EM £6
Sleeps 6

Large three-storey Georgian farmhouse on 130 acre dairy farm. Colour television. Outdoor riding arena. Fishing in river running through farm. 1 double and 1 family bedroom. Babysitter available. Hot and cold water and central heating. On A29. Garvagh 5 miles. Coleraine 6½ miles. OS Ref C 283424

(FH) CARNEETY HOUSE 120 Mussenden Road, Castlerock, BT51 4TX

Carol Henry
Tel:-848640
Closed Xmas and New Year
B&B £9-£10   Approved
EM   £6
     Sleeps 6

🐎 (6) 🐎

Large centrally heated farmhouse, central for shopping, swimming, scenic drives, pony trekking, fishing, golfing, forest walks, hang gliding and beaches. Dogs by arrangement.

(CH) MOYOLA LODGE Castledawson, Magherafelt, Co. Londonderry, BT45 8ER

Margaret & Lawson Swinerton
Tel:-(0648) 68224
Open all year
B&B £12.50   Approved

🐎

Georgian country house (CH) in 10 acres with licesed restaurant. Salmon and trout fishing. 18 hole golf (5 mins) Ballyronan Marina 6 miles. 2 twin-bedded and 1 double room. (All H/C) Babysitter. Castledawson ¾ mile. Magherafelt 3 miles. Dogs allowed (outside). OS Ref C 293393

(FH) FOYLEVIEW FARM Gortgar, Greysteel, Eglinton, Co. Londonderry

Marie McGinnis
Tel:-(0504) 811186
Open Mar-Oct
B&B £10   Grade A
     Sleeps 8

🐎 🐎 ♿

Farm guesthouse with views of Lough Foyle near north coast, Donegal, flying fishing. 2 doubles, 2 twins. All ground floor with H/C, one with bathroom. Babysitter. Off A2 (Londonderry-Limavady) opposite Nicholl's filling station, in Greysteel village, ¼m turn right, Londonderry 10m, Limvady 8m. Eglinton airport 2m. OS Ref C 258422

(CH) 14 EXORNA LANE Castlerock, Coleraine, BT51 4UA

Mrs Mary Henry
Tel:-(0265) 848033
Open Easter-Sep
B&B £9   Approved
EM   £4
CH   Sleeps 4

🐎 (10) ♿

Modern centrally heated bungalow, set in ¼ acre of garden with scenic views. Convenient for golf course, sandy beaches and Trust Properties. 1 double and 1 twin bedded rooms both with H/C.

(CH) 118 STATION ROAD Portstewart, Co Londonderry, BT55 7PU

Mrs Vi Anderson
Tel:-(026583) 2826
Open all year
B&B £12.00   Grade A
     Sleeps 10

Modern country bungalow. 1 double, 1 twin both with H/C, 1 double (with ensuite bath & WC), 1 family (with ensuite shower & WC). On B185. Follow the Portstewart signs on Coleraine ring road, at end turn right and travel approx. 2m (alongside railway line), 1st house on left at 40mph speed limit sign. Coleraine 3m, Portstewart ½m. Dogs allowed outside. Vouchers not accepted. OS Ref C 438283

(FH) INCHADOGHILL HOUSE 196 Agivey Road, Aghadowey, Coleraine, BT51 4AL

Mamie & Ann McIlroy
Tel:-(026585) 250
Open all year
B&B £9   Approved
     Sleeps 5

🐎

Georgian farmhouse with central heating situated on a 150 acre mixed farm. Colour TV. Home cooking. River fishing on farm. Golf nearby. 2 double rooms, 1 single room all with H/C. Babysitting available. Dogs allowed outside. Off A54 Coleraine 9m, Ballymoney 6m, Kilrea 5m. OS Ref C421289

TYRONE

TYRONE

Between the Sperrins in the north and the green Clogher Valley with its village cathedral in the south lies the region of great historical interest. The county's associations with the USA are recalled at the Ulster-American Folk park near Omagh and Gray's old printing shop at Strabane still contains its 18th-century presses. A mysterious ceremonial site of stone circles and cairns near Davagh Forest has recently been uncovered, and there are other Stone Age and Bronze Age remains in the area. There are forest parks, Gortin Glen and Drum Manor, for driving or rambling, excellent trout and salmon waters near Newtownstewart, market towns for shopping and recreation. Dungannon is notable for its fine glassware, Tyrone Crystal.

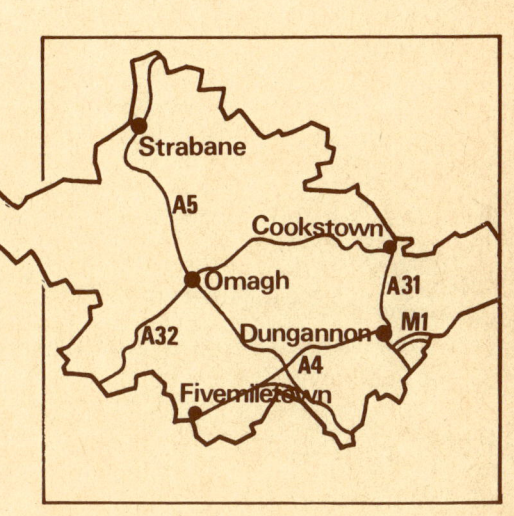

GROUP CONTACT:
Frances Reid (0662) 841325

(FH) THE BEECHES 25 Creevagh Road, Killycurragh, Cookstown, Co. Tyrone, BT80 9LR

Rachel Tomb
Tel:-(064 87) 51327
Open all year
B&B £9   Approved
EM £4.50
    Sleeps 6

Renovated farmhouse (central heating) on 50-acre hill farm. Beautiful views. Home produce, baking. Private lake stocked with brown trout. Golf, swimming & National Trust properties nearby. 1 single, 1 double, 1 family room. Babysitter available. Dogs allowed (outside). From Cookstown take A53 (Orritor Road), 3m, take Killycurragh road. At crossroads turn right, 2nd lane on right. Springhill, Moneymore 9m. OS Ref H 756823

(CH) THE GRANGE 15 Grange Road, Ballygawley, Co. Tyrone, BT70 2HD

Ella Lyttle
Tel:-(066 253) 8053
Open Apr-Oct
B&B £9.50   Approved
CH   Sleeps 7

Cottage built 1720 (central heating) convenient for fishing and scenic drives, the Parkanaur Forest and U.S. President Grant's ancestral home. 1 twin, 1 family and 1 ground floor bedroom (all with hot and cold water). Babysitter. Just off Ballygawley roundabout, midway between Dungannon and Omagh (A4/A5 intersection). OS Ref H 263 358

(FH) GREENMOUNT LODGE 58 Greenmount Road, Gortaclare, Omagh, Co. Tyrone, BT79 0YE

Frances Reid
Tel:-(0662) 841325
Open all year
B&B £9-£10   Approved
EM £5.50-£8
    Sleeps 12

Farm guest house on 150 acre farm. Superb accommodation, excellent cuisine. Central for sightseeing. Fermanagh Lakeland, The Sperrin Mountains. A5 from Ballygawley to Omagh, left before Traveller's Inn at Fintona sign 1 mile. OS Ref H252464

(CH) MULEANY HOUSE 86 Gorestown Road, Moy, Dungannon, Co. Tyrone, BT71 7EX

Mary Mullen
Tel:-(08687) 84183
Closed Xmas and New Year
B&B £8.50-£10   Grade A
EM £4.50
CH Sleeps 20

Country house set in 10 acres of grazing and horticultural land ½m from fishing on Blackwater river. Horse riding and game shooting can be arranged. Central for visits to the historical City of Armagh (8 miles) and Dungannon 4 miles. 2 single, 2 double, 2 twin-bedded, 1 family and 1 ground floor bedrooms. OS Ref H285356

(CH) THE PIPER'S CAVE 38 Cady Road, Cookstown, Co. Tyrone, BT80 9BD

Jean Warnock
Tel:-(064 87) 63615
Open all year
B&B £8.50   Approved
EM £7
CH Sleeps 10

Modern bungalow with souvenir shop. Fishing, horse riding, golf at Cookstown. 3 twin-bedded & 3 single rooms. Hot & cold water & central heating. On A29. Cookstown 4 miles. Dungannon 6 miles. OS Ref H 282376

(CH) CREEVAGH LODGE Carland, Dungannon, Co. Tyrone, BT70 3LQ

Gillmor & Elizabeth Nelson
Tel:-(08687) 61342
Open all year
B&B £9.50-£10.50 Approved
EM £4.50
CH Sleeps 14

Country house located on hilltop in typical Co. Tyrone rolling countryside. 400 yards West off A26 on Dungannon side of Carland village. House double glazed and centrally heated throughout. Electric blankets and H/C in all bedrooms. 3 double rooms ensuite with colour TV and teasmades, 2 double rooms and 4 single rooms. OS Ref H661786

Tyrone N. IRELAND

(FH) GLENELLY ROAD   254 Glenelly Road, Cranagh, Plumbridge, Omagh, Co. Tyrone BT79 8LS

Mr & Mrs Bennie Conway
Tel:-(066 26) 48334
Open all year
B&B   £8-£9   Approved
EM   £3.50-£5
Sleeps 8

New chalet farmhouse (central heating) on 22 acre mixed farm, in heart of Sperrin Mountains overlooking Glenelly River, noted for trout. Walking and climbing country. 1 double, 2 family rooms and 2 ground floor rooms. Babysitter available. Dogs allowed (outside). On B47, 8 miles east of Plumbridge, 13 miles west of Draperstown. OS Ref H 257393

(CH) GRANGE LODGE   7 Grange Road, Dungannon, Co. Tyrone, BT71 7EJ

Norah Brown
Tel:-(086 87) 84212
Closed Xmas and New Year
B&B   £12   Approved
EM   £9.95
CH   Sleeps 6

Georgian countryhouse on 20 acres in spacious grounds, mature trees and tennis court near River Blackwater, 17th Century Quaker Meeting House, National Trust properties. Snooker, darts and table tennis available. 3 doubles with TV, electric blankets. On main A29 between Dungannon and Moy. 1m from M1 intersection signposted Grange Meeting House, immediately turn in right, 1st house on right. Dogs allowed (outside). OS Ref H 283359

(FH) FARM BUNGALOW   Cohannon, 225 Ballynakelly Road, Dungannon, BT71 6HJ

Jean Currie
Tel:-(08687) 23156
Open all year
B&B   £10   Approved
Sleeps 4

Farm bungaalow, 15 acres of grazing/horticulture. Fishing in Blackwater (½m).National Trust Properties. Home produce, baking. 1 double, 1 twin both on ground floor, both with H/C. Babysitter. Dogs allowed (outside). From M1 exit 14 onto A45, 400 yds, turn left, 100 yds BB sign. Dungannon 4m. Moy 3m. Armagh 8m. OS Ref H 286362

(CH) 38 LECKPATRICK ROAD   Artigarvan, Strabane, Co. Tyrone, BT82 OHB

Jean Ballantine
Tel:-(0504) 882714.
Open Jun-Sep
B&B   £9   Approved

Countryhouse (central heating) with views of Foyle and Donegal. Central for walled city, Ulster-American Folk Park (15m). Fishing at Moorlough. 1 single, 2 double (all H & C). Babysitter. Dogs allowed (outside). Turn off B49 opposite Leckpatrick Dairy, 1st on right. Strabane 3m. Londonderry 10m. OS Ref H 401238

(FH) TANNAGHLANE HOUSE   Caledon, Co. Tyrone, BT68 4XU

Mrs N J Ella Reid
Tel:-(0861) 568247
Open all year
B&B   £12-£18   Approved
EM   £7-£10
sleeps 2

Georgian farmhouse on large farm in open countryside. Fishing, boating at 5 different lakes within ⅔ miles. Wildlife, shooting on 5 acres of plantation. 1 double with hot and cold water and private shower/W.C. Babysitter available. Dogs allowed (outside). From Caledon take Dungannon (B45) road. After 2 miles turn left. 1st house on right. Dungannon 10 miles. Armagh 10. Aughnacloy 8 miles. OS Ref 276346

69 FERMANAGH

FERMANAGH

Ulster's Lakeland spreads its web of waterways, islands, forest and glen, castles and abbey ruins, right across the county. Enniskillen, county town and shopping centre, strides the narrows between Upper and Lower Lough Erne. From there pleasure boats run daily cruises in summer. Golf, sailing, water-skiing and even pleasure flying are available nearby. Fishermen need no reminder that these are the waters where record catches are made. Two of Ulster's finest houses in National Trust care, Florence Court and Castle Coole, are in Fermanagh, too. Visitors to the old pottery at Belleek can watch craftsmen at work on fine porcelain.

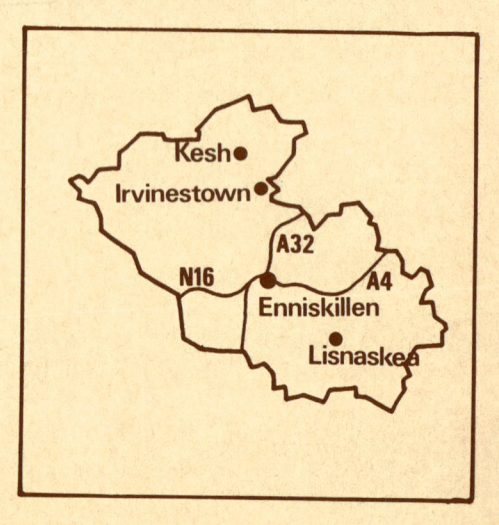

GROUP CONTACT:
Vera Gilmore (03655) 21298

Fermanagh N. IRELAND

(FH) RIVERSIDE FARM Gortadrehid, Culkey P.O, Enniskillen, Co. Fermanagh

Mollie Fawcett
Tel:-(0365) 22725
Open all year
B&B £10-£12   Approved
EM   £6
     Sleeps 14
SC   £200-£230
     Sleeps 5/6

Modernised farmhouse (central heating) on 65 acre beef rearing farm, in sheltered surroundings with river running through grounds. This river is the Sillies River, which holds the World Record for coarse fishing. Near to Marble Arch caves and Florencecourt, National Trust properties, scenic drives, golfing nearby. 1 double, 2 twin, 2 family rooms all with H/C. OS Ref 223338

(FH) BAYVIEW GUEST HOUSE Tully, Churchill, Enniskillen, Co. Fermanagh, BT74 7BW

Dorothy Hassard
Tel:-(036564) 250
Open Easter-Oct
B&B £8-£10.50   Grade B
EM   £5
     Redn children
     Sleeps 9

Spacious modern farmhouse (central heating) on 60 acre dairy farm overlooking Tully Bay, Lough Erne. Home baking, fresh vegetables. Central for fishing, boating, touring Lough Navar Forest, National Trust properties. 2 doubles, 2 family rooms. 1 ground floor (all H/C). Babysitter. Situated 11m from Enniskillen on A46 Belleek Road. Derrygonnelly 3 miles. OS Ref H 218351

(FH) TULLYHONA FARM GUESTHOUSE Marble Arch Road, Florencecourt, Co Fermanagh

Rosemary Armstrong
Tel:-(036582) 452
Open all year
B&B £8.50-£9.50   Approved
EM   £5.90
     Sleeps 9

450 acre beef & sheep farm situated 1½ miles from Marble Arch caves. 300yds from N.T. property. All home cooking & baking choice of menu, flexible meal times. Friendly atmosphere, central for watersports, sports complex, fishing, golf. Baby sitting & cot available. Colour TV. Central heating. All rooms H/C, 1 ensuite. Snacks & meals served to non-residents in peak months. OS Ref H 219335

(FH) LACKABOY FARM GUEST HOUSE Tempo Road, Enniskillen, Co. Fermanagh, BT74 6HR

Elma Noble
Tel:-(0365) 22488
Closed Xmas
B&B £10   Grade A
EM   £6
     Sleeps 18

Grade A farm guest house on 60 acre dairy farm. Adjacent to Castle Coole National Trust estate. Central for lakes, golf and scenic drives. 3 singles, 5 doubles, 2 family bedrooms (4 ensuite). Hot and cold water and central heating. Babysitter available. OS Ref H 226345

(FH) LAKEVIEW FARM GUEST HOUSE Drumcrow, Blaney P.O, Enniskillen, Co. Fermanagh

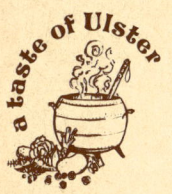

Mrs Jason W D Hassard
Tel:-(036564) 263
Closed Xmas
B&B £9-£9.50   Grade A
     Sleeps 10

Grade A guest house quietly situated overlooking and adjoining one of the most panoramic parts of Lower Lough Erne, famous for fishing and cruising, near Marble Arch caves and places of historical interest. Central for touring Donegal and Yeats country, Sligo and Belleek Pottery. 4 bedrooms, central heating, H/C. Separate tables, home cooking. 10 miles from Enniskillen on A46 road to Belleek. OS Ref H 217352

(CH) BRINDLEY GUEST HOUSE Tully, Killadeas, Enniskillen, Co. Fermanagh

Olive Flood
Tel:-(03656) 28065
Closed Xmas
B&B £10.50-£11.50   Grade A
EM   £6-£7
CH   Sleeps 14

New country guest house overlooking Lough Erne on B82 road. 2 twins, 2 doubles, 2 family rooms all ensuite. 3 ground floor rooms. H/C water, CH, new fire regulations. NITB Grade A and British Airways Certificate. Near Castle Archdale Country Park and Forest. Scenic routes and Devenish Island by ferry. Fishing nearby. Dogs allowed (outside). OS Ref H 223358

MALLARD HOUSE Mallard House, Drumany, Lisnaskea, Co. Fermanagh

Jean McVitty
Tel:-(03657) 21491
Open Mar-Nov
B&B £8.50-£9
EM £4-£5
Sleeps 8
(5)

Grade A

Grade A farm guest house situated on 100 acre dairy farm, 2m from Lisnaskea, yet in the heart of Fermanagh's lakeland. Excellent scenery of Lough Erne & the lakes. Privately owned coarse fishing, (1½m) internationally known as 'McVitty's Mile', birdwatching & wildtowling in a designated area for wildlife. With 4 guest bedrooms and traditional farmhouse fare, this combines to be a very homely atmosphere & welcome. Personal supervision. OS Ref H 235 335

"AL-DI-GWYN" LODGE Al-Di-Gwyn Lodge, 103 Clabby Road, Fivemiletown, Co. Fermanagh, BT75 OQY

Vera Gilmore
Tel:-(03655) 21298
Open Jan-Dec
B&B £10-£12
EM £7
CH Sleeps 25
Van £3-£5
(6)

Grade A

Grade A guesthouse close to Clogher Valley and mountain scenery. National Trust properties, ancient monuments nearby. Excellent fishing. Home baking, Colour TV, CH, Seven double, 3 twin-bedded and 2 family bedrooms, 4 ground floor. Babysitter and cot available. 2½ miles from Fivemiletown on B107. Marble Arch Caves 20m. Dogs allowed (outside). OS Ref H 244349

AGHNACARRA HOUSE Carrybridge, Lisbellaw, Co Fermanagh

Norma Ensor
Tel:-(0365) 87077
Open all year
CH Sleeps 17
B&B £10-£15
EM £5
(5)

Grade B

Purpose built luxury chalet style guesthouse. Fully CH, double glazed. Guest lounge with TV. Separate dining room. Scenic views. 4 triple bedrooms ground floor. 1 triple & 1 family room 1st floor. All H/C. Bath & shower rooms. All facilities for the angler, bait shed, tackle room, drying room, bait stockist. Run by English Match Angler Dave Ensor. Good fishing/boating 500 yds. Carrybridge 10 mins to Enniskillen. Belfast-Dublin. OS Ref H 29 38

DUNROVIN Skea, Arney, Enniskillen, Co. Fermanagh

Catherine Harron
Tel:-(036 582) 354
Open all year
B&B £8.50-£10
EM £5-£6
Sleeps 9

Approved

Country house on 1 acre built in 1981. Near lakes, rivers and caves and National Trust properties. 2 single and 2 family rooms. Babysitter available. Boat and engine available on Lough Erne. Dogs allowed (outside). From Enniskillen take A4 Sligo Road for 2½ miles. A32 for Swalinbar 2¼ miles. At junction turn left for Arney. First house on left. Enniskillen 5 miles. OS Ref H 221338

BROADMEADOWS GUEST HOUSE Cleenish Island Road, Bellanaleck, Enniskillen, Co. Fermanagh

Liliann McKibbin
Tel:-(036582) 395
Open all year
B&B £9

Approved

Bungalow (CH) close to Lough Erne. Angling, sailing near Florencecourt, National Trust. 1 single, 2 double, 1 twin bedrooms, all ground floor. 3 H/C, 1 with ensuite bathroom. Babysitter. Suitable for elderly and disabled visitors. Personal attention (owner a qualified nurse). Dogs allowed (outdoors). 1½ miles east of Bellanaleck on road to Cleenish Island. Enniskillen 6 miles. OS Ref H 223339

COLORADO HOUSE 102 Lisnagole Road, Lisnaskea

John & Eileen Scott
Tel:-(03657) 21486
Open all year
B&B £9
Sleeps 16

Grade A

Grade A country house (central heating). Fishing and water sports, ancient monuments, leisure centre. 20mins drive Marble Arch caves. Babysitter. Dogs allowed outside. 3 double, 3 twin, 2 family rooms all with H/C. 1 with ensuite shower and WC. 2 reception rooms with TV. First left at Maguiresbridge, 1m from Lisnaskea on A34 main road to Dublin. Enniskillen 12m. OS Ref H 235337

INDEX OF ♿ DISABLED WELCOME ESTABLISHMENTS

Ch 1 CORNWALL
FH	LONGSTONE FARM	10
SC	TREVALGAN FARM	14
SC	PENNANCE MILL FARM	15
SC	KEEPERS COTTAGE	16
SC	MORLAND COTTAGES	14
SC	GRANARY STEPS AND THE HAYLOFT	14

Ch 2 UPPER TAMAR
SC	THORNE MANOR	18

Ch 4 NORTH DEVON
SC	NORTHCOTT BARTON FARM	25
SC	WILLESLEIGH FARM COTTAGE	25

Ch 7 CREAM OF DEVON
FH	HELE FARM	33
FH	WEEK FARM	33

Ch 8 DARTMOOR AND SOUTH DEVON
FH	NEW COTT FARM	36
FH	LOWER SOUTHWAY FARM	38
SC	WOODER FARM	39

Ch 9 MOOR TO SHORE
SC	FLEAR FARM COTTAGES	42
SC	HOPE BARTON FARM COTTAGES	43

Ch 10 EAST DEVON
CH	THE BULSTONE	45

Ch 11 EXMOOR
CH	FOLLY	50
SC	EMMETTS GRANGE FARMHOUSE	51

Ch 13 NORTH SOMERSET & AVON
CH	WAYSIDE BUNGALOW	58

Ch 14 WILTSHIRE
FH	LONG WATER	62
FH	SEVINGTON FARM	62

Ch 15 DORSET
FH	PINE TREES FARM	66
FH	MANOR FARMHOUSE	65
FH	DOWNWOOD VINEYARD	66
FH	HALE FARM	65
FH	HOLEBROOK FARM	65
SC	MANOR FARM COTTAGE	67
SC	YEW HOUSE COTTAGES	67

Ch 16 HEART OF DORSET
SC	NEWMANS DROVE	70

Ch 17 ISLE OF WIGHT
CH	BARWICK	73
FH	ASHENGROVE FARM	74

CH 18 HAMPSHIRE
FH	BROCKLANDS FARM	78
SC	WOODSIDE FARM	78

Ch 19 SUSSEX AND SURREY
FH	MILL HOUSE FARM	82
SC	BROWNINGS FARM HOLIDAY COTTAGES	82
SC	HOLLY & HONEYSUCKLE COTTAGES	82

Ch 20 KENT
CH	BEACHBOROUGH PARK	85
SC	THE CLYDESDALE/SUFFOLK PUNCH	86
SC	SPRING GROVE OAST	88
SC	BRATTLE FARM	87
SC	GOLDING HOP FARM COTTAGE	87

Ch 21 ESSEX
FH	ROCKELLS FARM	90

FH	NEWHOUSE FARM	90
FH	BONNYDOWNS FARM	91
SC	THE HOLIDAY COTTAGES	91

Ch 22 SUFFOLK & NORFOLK
CH	MONK SOHAM HALL	95
FH	HILLVIEW FARM	94
FH	OLD HALL FARM	95
SC	STABLE COTTAGES	96
SC	WHISPERING WILLOWS BUNGALOW	100

Ch 26 THAMES VALLEY
CH	THE ELMS COUNTRY HOUSE	103
FH	MANOR FARM	102
FH	HAWTHORN FARM	104
SC	HILL GROVE COTTAGE	104

Ch 27 COTSWOLD & FOREST OF DEAN
FH	DOWN BARN FARMHOUSE	104
FH	GILBERTS	107
FH	KILMORIE	111
SC	WESTLEY FARM	112
SC	FOLLY FARM COTTAGES	112
SC	SUNSHINE	112

Ch 28 HEREFORDSHIRE
FH	CHADWYNS FARM	116
SC	HIGH HOUSE FARMHOUSE	117

Ch 29 WORCESTERSHIRE
SC	OLD YATES COTTAGES	125

Ch 30 WARWICKSHIRE
FH	NOLANDS FARM	129
SC	EDSTONE COTTAGES	133

Ch 31 SOUTH SHROPSHIRE
FH	RECTORY FARM	136
SC	EUDON BURNELL COTTAGES	137

Ch 32 NORTH SHROPSHIRE
FH	THE SETT VILLAGE FARM	141
FH	CHURCH FARM	140
FH	LONGLEY FARM	140
FH	LOWER HUNTINGTON FARM	142
FH	LOWER HUNTINGTON FARM	143

Ch 33 VALE OF TRENT
FH	FISHERS PIT FARM	147
SC	FISHERS PIT FARM	151

Ch 34 PEAK AND MOORLANDS
CH	FOURWAYS DINER MOTEL	154
CH	HENMORE GRANGE FARM	153
FH	BANK END FARM MOTEL	157
FH	PEAR TREE FARM	155
SC	MEADOWFOLD	161
SC	THE OLD STABLES	161
SC	SHATTON HALL FARM	158
SC	GLENWOOD HOUSE FARM	158
SC	BEECHENHILL COTTAGE	158
SC	PEAR TREE FARM	161

Ch 35 DOVEDALE
FH	HOME FARM	164
FH	NEW PARK FARM	165
FH	CHEVIN GREEN FARM	165
SC	HAYES FARM SELF CATERING	166
SC	NEW BUNGALOW, SHIRLEY	166
SC	ROSE COTTAGE	166

303

Ch 36 NORTHAMPTONSHIRE

FH	DAIRY FARM	169
FH	BARWELL FIELDS	169
FH	OLD WHARF FARM	169
SC	PAPLEY FARM COTTAGES	170

Ch 37 LEICESTERSHIRE

FH	THE GREENWAY, KNAPTOFT HOUSE FARM	172
FH	THREE WAYS FARM	172
FH	THE OLD RECTORY	172

Ch 38 SHERWOOD FOREST

SC	NO. 3 FRANDERGROUND BUNGALOW	176
SC	WOLDS FARM	176

Ch 39 LINCOLNSHIRE

FH	MIDDLE FARM	178
SC	PENFOLD FARM	179

Ch 40 CHESHIRE

FH	GREEN FARM	182
FH	BEECHWOOD HOUSE	182
FH	SPROSTON HILL FARM	184

Ch 41 RIBBLE VALLEY

CH	MYTTON FOLD FARM HOTEL	187
FH	WYTHA FARM	188
FH	FALICON FARM	188

Ch 42 VALE OF LUNE

SC	KEEPERS COTTAGE	191

Ch 43 SOUTH PENNINES

FH	UPLANDS FARM	193
FH	SHIRE COTTAGE	193

Ch 44 YORKSHIRE DALES

FH	CRAVEN HEIFER FARM	196
SC	SEAT HOUSE FARM	197
SC	WESTFIELD FARM COTTAGES	197
SC	CAWDER HALL	197

Ch 45 HERRIOT COUNTRY

CH	NURSERY COTTAGE	200
FH	BAXBY MANOR	200
SC	BRIDGE COTTAGE AND THE LODGE	201
SC	DALES FARMHOUSE AND COTTAGES	201
SC	THE LODGE	202
SC	HARDSTYLES COTTAGE	202
SC	STANHOW FARM BUNGALOW	201
SC	GREEN GABLES	201

Ch 47 YORKSHIRE COAST

FH	ACRES	208
SC	MANOR FARM COTTAGE	210

Ch 48 SOUTH LAKELAND

CH	FIELD END	212
SC	GRAYGABLES COTTAGE	215
SC	HORNSBARROW NEW END	216

Ch 49 EDEN VALLEY AND ALSTON MOOR

CH	ASHLEY BANK	218
SC	CROSSFIELD FARM AND FISHERY	219
SC	SKIRWITH HALL COTTAGE	219
SC	GREEN VIEW LODGES	220
SC	HOWHILL COTTAGE	221

Ch 50 HADRIANS WALL

FH	WHITE CRAIG FARM	223
FH	NEW PALLYARDS	223

Ch 52 NORTHUMBERLAND

SC	BRACKENSIDE BUNGALOW	232
SC	DOXFORD FARM COTTAGES	232
CH	THE COACH HOUSE	232

Ch 53 PEMBROKESHIRE

FH	UPPER VANLEY FARM	235
FH	TORBANT FARM GUEST HOUSE	235
FH	LITTLE NEWTON FARM	235
FH	TREVACCOON FARM	236
FH	PENRALLT MEREDITH	237

FH	HIGHLAND GRANGE FARM GUEST HOUSE	237
SC	TORBANT FARM GUEST HOUSE	237

Ch 54 DYFED COAST AND COUNTRY

FH	CWMDWYFRAN FARM	239
FH	TY HEN FARM	240
FH	GLANGRAIG FARM	240

Ch 55 CEREDIGION

FH	BRYNCASTELL FARM BUNGALOW	243
SC	CASTELL FARMHOUSE	243
SC	LLWYN GRAWYS FARM COTTAGES	239

Ch 56 GWENT

CH	PARSONS GROVE	246
FH	THE WENALLT FARM	246

Ch 57 BRECON AND RADNOR

FH	BRYNFEDWEB FARM	

Ch 58 HILLS AND VALES OF MID WALES

Ch 61 CLWYD

CH	PEN-Y-BONT FAWR	261
FH	COLLEGE FARM	260
SC	GARDEN COTTAGE	260

Ch 62 SNOWDONIA AND ANGLESEY

CH	LLYS BENNAR	265
FH	TRER-DOOL FARM	264
FH	TY'N RHOS	265
SC	LLYS BENNAR	265
SC	BRYN BEDDAU	265

Ch 63 LLEYN PENINSULA

FH	GRAEANFRYN	268
SC	TYN DON HOLIDAY COTTAGES	268
SC	NYTH-Y-DRYW	268
SC	TYNEWYDD COTTAGE	269
SC	GWYNFRYN FARM	268

Ch 64 SCOTLAND

FH	BORLUM FARMHOUSE	274
SC	MOUNTQUHANIE HOLIDAY HOMES	274
SC	COACHMANS HOUSE AND COTTAGES	275
SC	CARMICHAEL ESTATE COTTAGES	275
SC	TORWOOD CROFT	275
SC	ARDBLAIR CASTLE STABLES	275
SC	BARNCROSH FARM	275
SC	GAGIE HOUSE FARM	276
SC	WHITMUIR ESTATE	276
SC	GLENGENNET COTTAGE	276
SC	EASTER DEANS AND GLENRATH	275

Ch 65 DOWN

CH	THE MAGGIMINN	281
CH	BRACKNEY HOUSE	284
FH	SHARON FARM HOUSE	282
FH	BALLYCASTLE HOUSE	286

Ch 66 ANTRIM

CH	ISLAY - VIEW	291
CH	BALLYWATT	290
CH	AUBERGE DE SENEIRL	292
FH	CARNSIDE GUEST HOUSE	293
FH	THE OLD SCHOOL HOUSE	293

Ch 67 LONDONDERRY

CH	14 EXORNA LANE	296
FH	FOYLEVIEW FARM	296

Ch 68 TYRONE

CH	THE PIPERS CAVE	298
CH	GLENELLY ROAD	299

Ch 69 FERMANAGH

CH	BRINDLEY GUEST HOUSE	301
CH	AL-DI-GWYN LODGE	302
CH	BROADMEADOWS GUEST HOUSE	302
CH	AGHNACARRA HOUSE	302
FH	RIVERSIDE FARM	301